Chugworth Academy, the most prestigious educational establishment in New Bumpshire. Are you rich? Are you successful? Do you have an Hispanic servant whose name you don't know, so you just call him "Amigo"? Then Chugworth Academy is the ONLY place to send your little ones! A world famous institute of unrivaled learning, Chugworth Academy's fine faculty of pretentious professors will make sure your children are equipped for everything the world won't throw at them!

Seven Seas

Chugworth Academy

First published online at http://chugworth.com/

Publisher: Seven Seas Entertainment
Visit us online at www.gomanga.com

ISBN: **1-933164-17-4**

Printed in Canada
First printing: May, 2006

10 9 8 7 6 5 4 3 2 1

Seven Seas

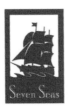

Contents

FOREWORD
BY FRED GALLAGHER (THAT MEGATOKYO THING GUY)

I'm not about to admit which Chugworth Academy strip made me chuckle enough to finally bookmark it. I don't *read* sites that have "you must at least pretend to be old enough to read this" landing pages.
So what am I doing here?

The cast of Chugworth do stuff i'd never let anyone see my own characters do. I've learned things reading Chugworth Academy that I really don't think i needed to know. I've read Chugworth comics that have made me cringe, run in terror, quickly close Firefox and reboot my computer. Why do I torture myself so?

I think it's the girls. In fact, I'm pretty sure of it. The girls of Chugworth fascinate me. They aren't just wonderful eye candy (Dave's skill at rendering the female cast is more than admirable (I wish I could draw waists like that)). These young women have attitude, character and curious personalities. Dave is somehow able to infuse them with more than enough of these traits to counter the vast array of behavioral problems they seem to suffer from. It's like there is a real counterpoint between the hearty warmth of the girls and the almost surrealistic nihilism that permeates their temporal existence. Whatever that means.

Oh, and in case you didn't already know this -- it's all about bunny girl. She's the real brains behind it all. If you keep that in mind, Chugworth Academy suddenly makes a whole lot more sense.

Fred "Piro" Gallagher
April 13, 2006

Bring on the Random.

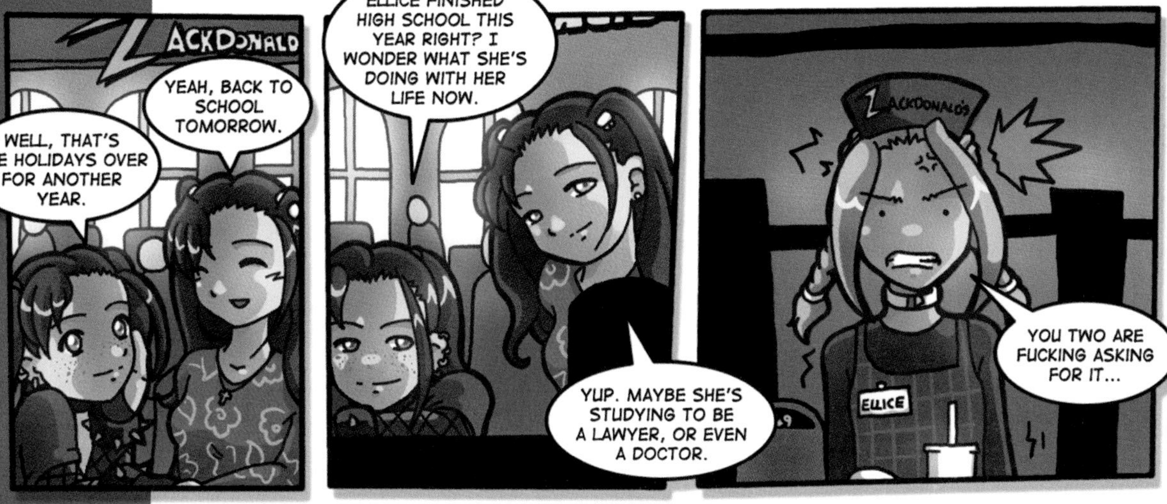
ACKDONALD
WELL, THAT'S THE HOLIDAYS OVER FOR ANOTHER YEAR.
YEAH, BACK TO SCHOOL TOMORROW.
ELLICE FINISHED HIGH SCHOOL THIS YEAR RIGHT? I WONDER WHAT SHE'S DOING WITH HER LIFE NOW.
YUP. MAYBE SHE'S STUDYING TO BE A LAWYER, OR EVEN A DOCTOR.
ACKDONALD'S
ELLICE
YOU TWO ARE FUCKING ASKING FOR IT...

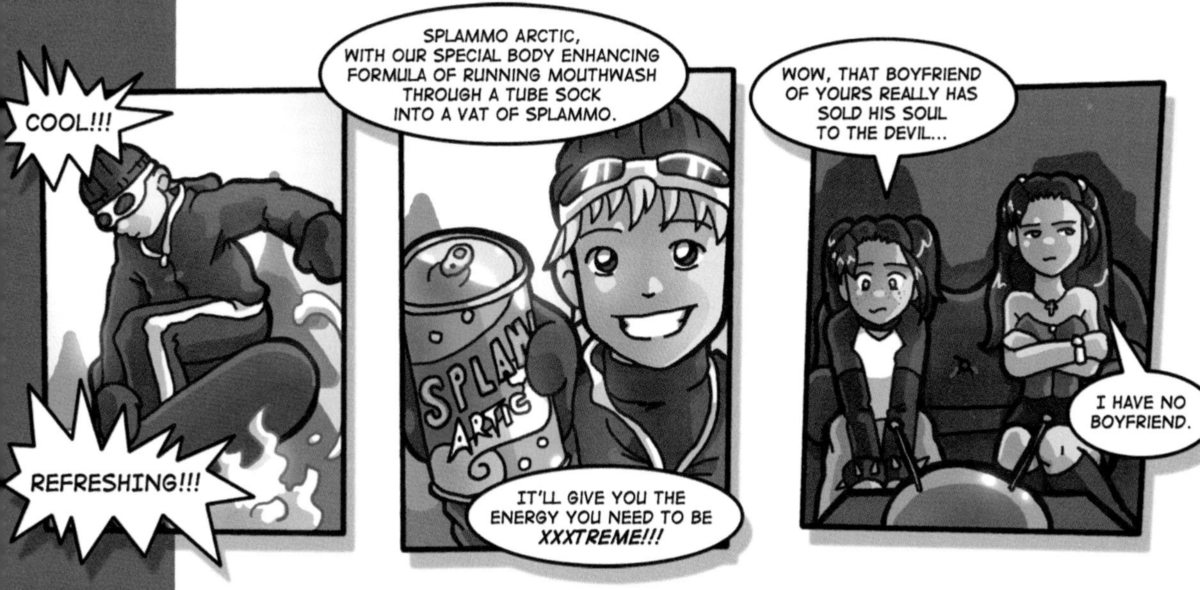
COOL!!!
REFRESHING!!!
SPLAMMO ARCTIC, WITH OUR SPECIAL BODY ENHANCING FORMULA OF RUNNING MOUTHWASH THROUGH A TUBE SOCK INTO A VAT OF SPLAMMO.
SPLAM
ARTIC
IT'LL GIVE YOU THE ENERGY YOU NEED TO BE XXXTREME!!!
WOW, THAT BOYFRIEND OF YOURS REALLY HAS SOLD HIS SOUL TO THE DEVIL...
I HAVE NO BOYFRIEND.

#5

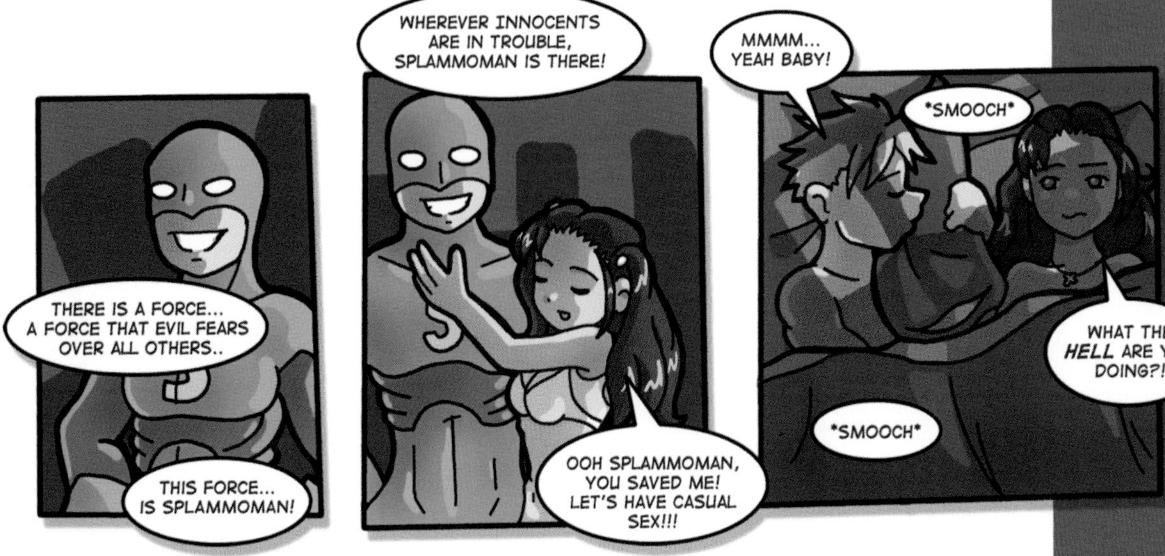
THERE IS A FORCE... A FORCE THAT EVIL FEARS OVER ALL OTHERS..
THIS FORCE... IS SPLAMMOMAN!
WHEREVER INNOCENTS ARE IN TROUBLE, SPLAMMOMAN IS THERE!
OOH SPLAMMOMAN, YOU SAVED ME! LET'S HAVE CASUAL SEX!!!
MMMM... YEAH BABY!
SMOOCH
WHAT THE ***HELL*** ARE YOU DOING?!
SMOOCH

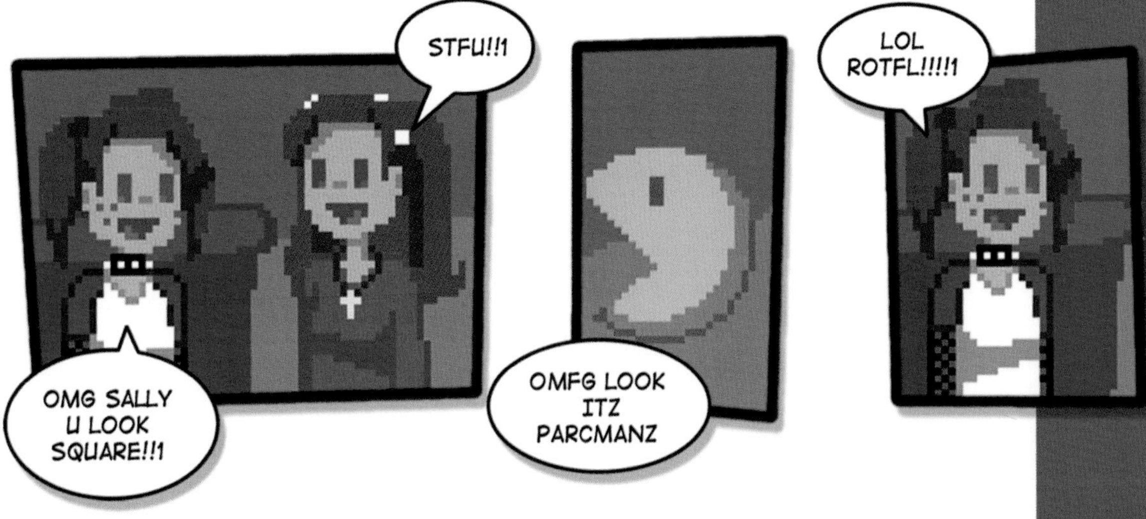
OMG SALLY U LOOK SQUARE!!1
STFU!!1
OMFG LOOK ITZ PARCMANZ
LOL ROTFL!!!!1

#6

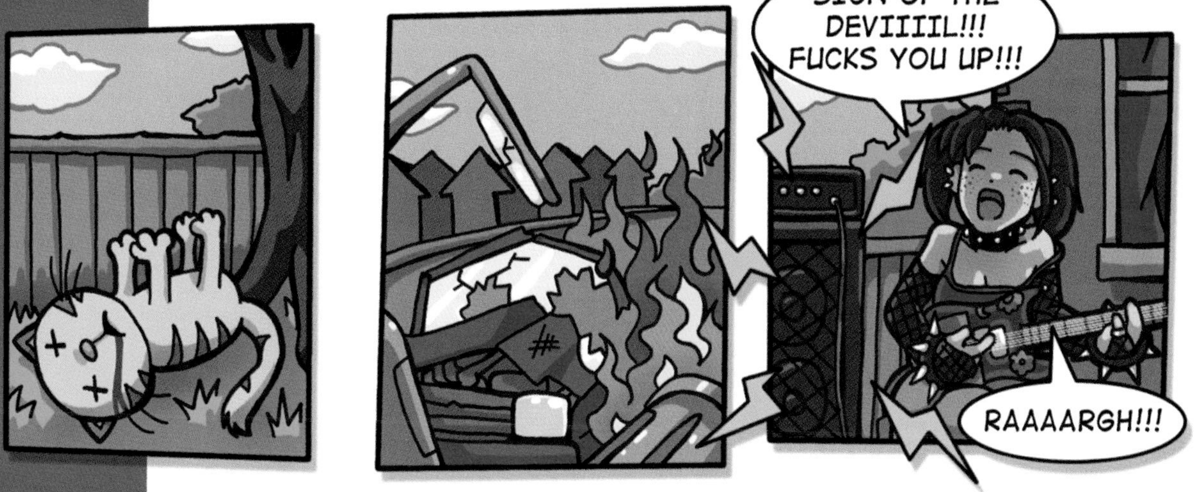
SIGN OF THE DEVIIIIL!!! FUCKS YOU UP!!!
RAAAARGH!!!

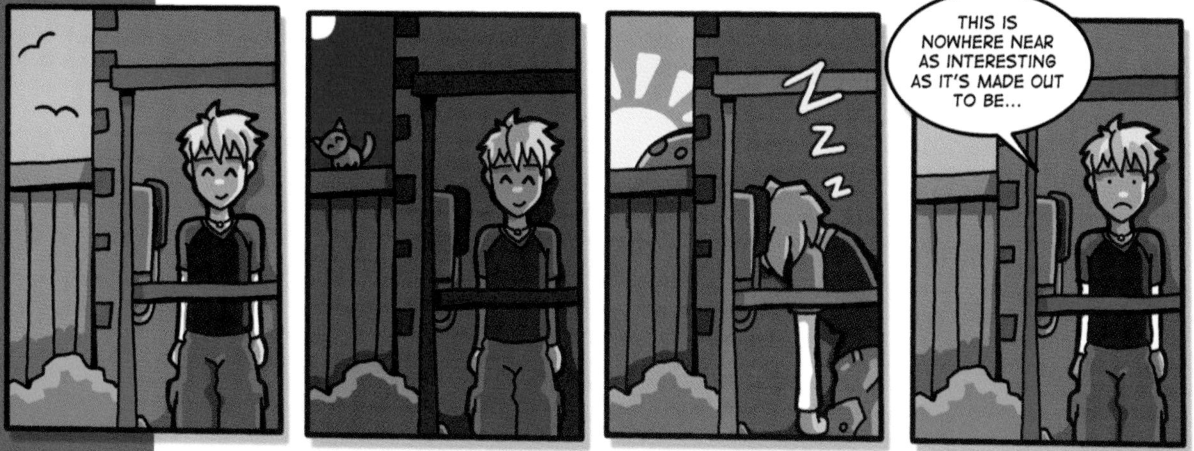
THIS IS NOWHERE NEAR AS INTERESTING AS IT'S MADE OUT TO BE...

I STILL CAN'T BELIEVE THEY FIRED ME!
UH HUH.
IT'S AN OUTRAGE I TELL YOU! I MEAN, SERIOUSLY!
SURE.
WHAT DID THEY FIRE YOU FOR ANYWAY?
SOME GUY'S BEEN PISSING IN THE FRIES, AND I GOT THE BLAME.
...

GUESS WHAT!
GUESS WHAT!
I LANDED A JOB ON A *T.V SHOW*!
WHO DID YOU HAVE TO SLEEP WITH TO SCORE *THAT*?
NOBODY...
GOOD JOB!
I'M PROUD OF YOU.
IT LOOKS LIKE YOU'RE FINALLY BEGINNING TO RESPECT YOURSEL...
HEY BABY! HURRY UP! DADDY WANTS TO DO MORE SPANKING!!!
WHO WAS THAT?
THE PRODUCER...

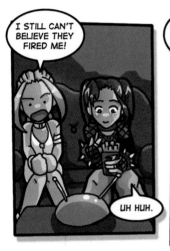

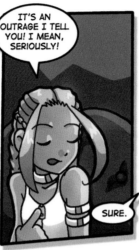

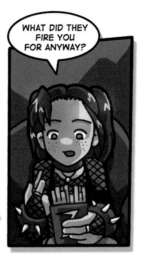

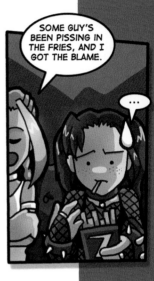

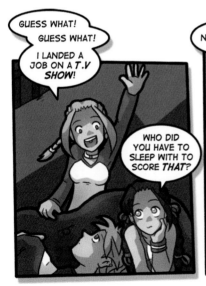

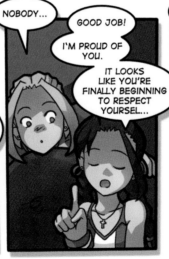

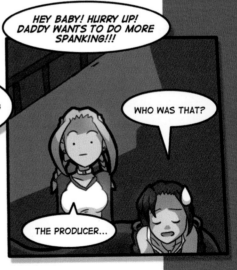

#8

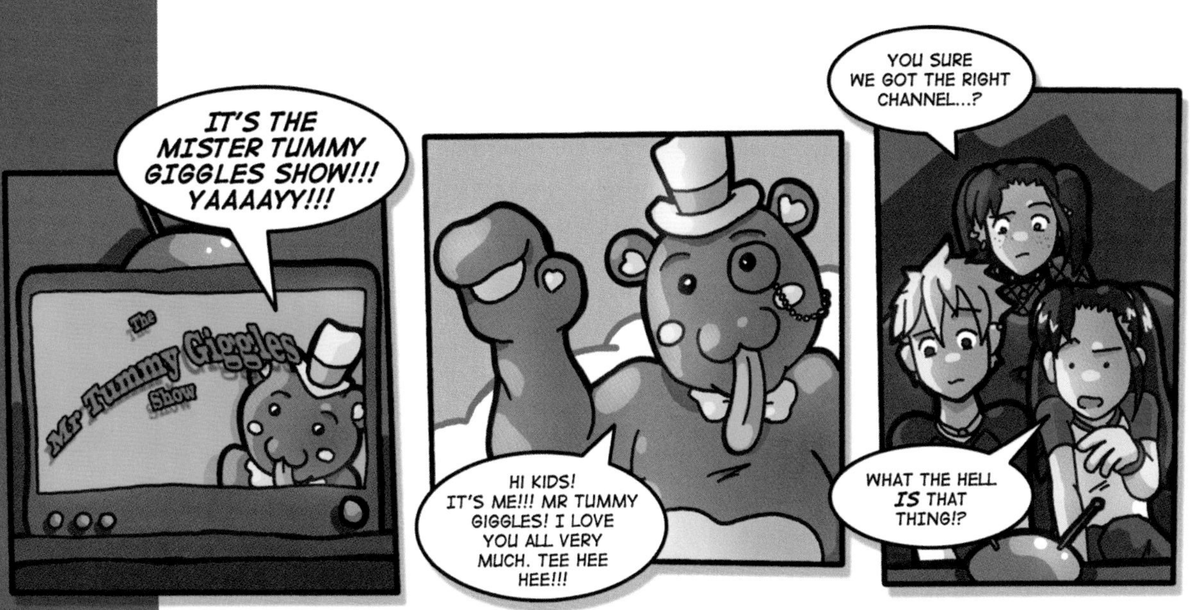
IT'S THE MISTER TUMMY GIGGLES SHOW!!! YAAAAYY!!!
The Mr Tummy Giggles Show
HI KIDS! IT'S ME!!! MR TUMMY GIGGLES! I LOVE YOU ALL VERY MUCH. TEE HEE HEE!!!
YOU SURE WE GOT THE RIGHT CHANNEL...?
WHAT THE HELL IS THAT THING!?

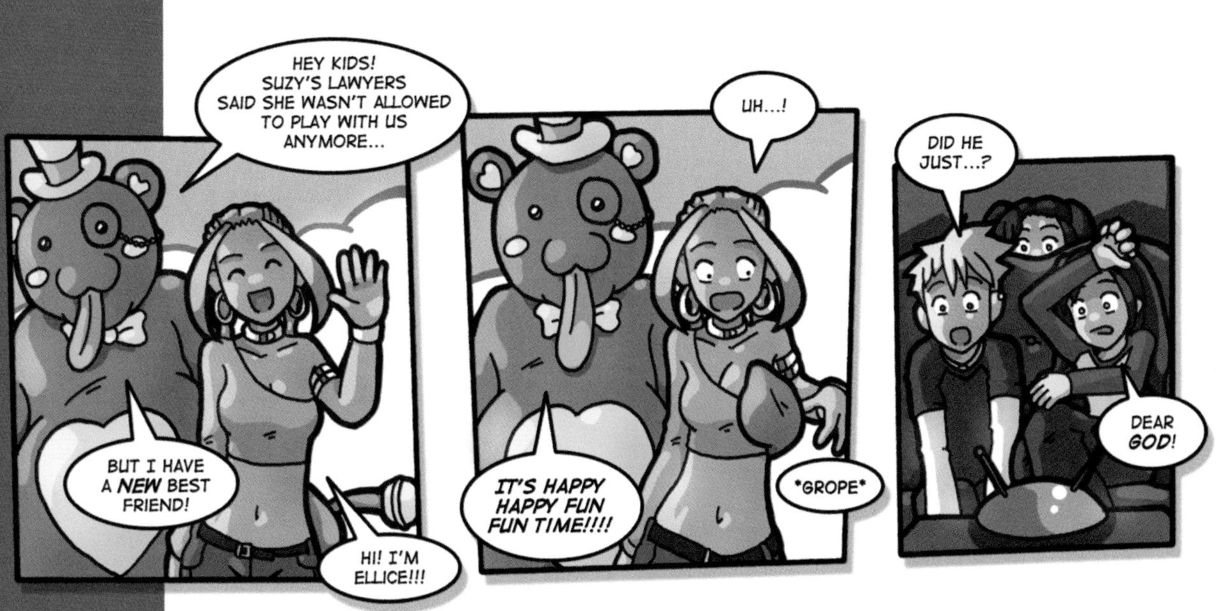
HEY KIDS! SUZY'S LAWYERS SAID SHE WASN'T ALLOWED TO PLAY WITH US ANYMORE...
BUT I HAVE A NEW BEST FRIEND!
HI! I'M ELLICE!!!
UH...!
IT'S HAPPY HAPPY FUN FUN TIME!!!!
GROPE
DID HE JUST...?
DEAR GOD!

Ahoy Matey!

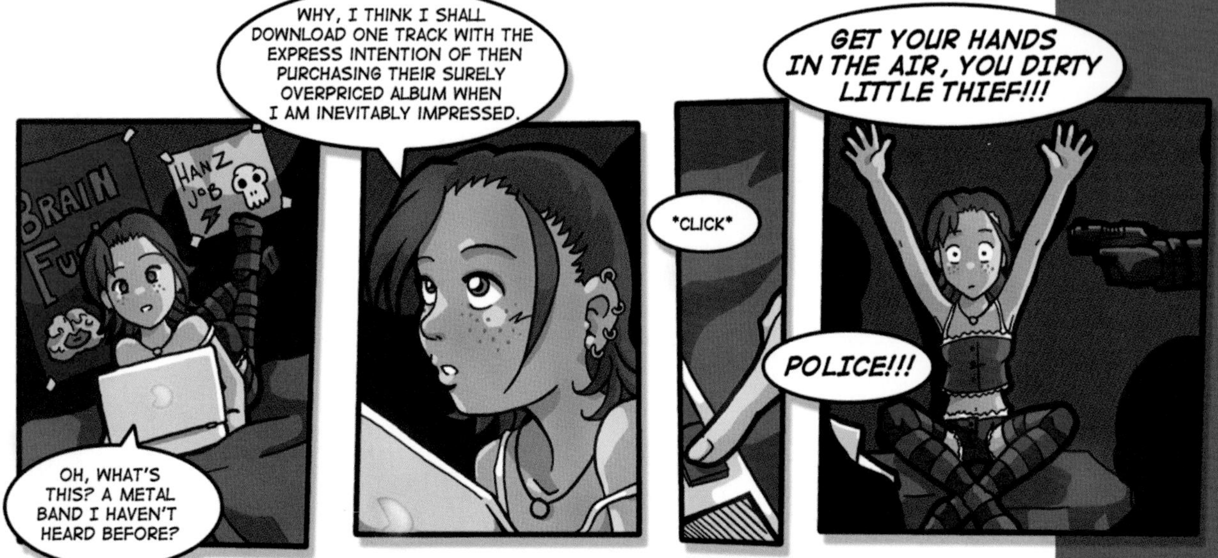
OH, WHAT'S THIS? A METAL BAND I HAVEN'T HEARD BEFORE?
WHY, I THINK I SHALL DOWNLOAD ONE TRACK WITH THE EXPRESS INTENTION OF THEN PURCHASING THEIR SURELY OVERPRICED ALBUM WHEN I AM INEVITABLY IMPRESSED.
CLICK
GET YOUR HANDS IN THE AIR, YOU DIRTY LITTLE THIEF!!!
POLICE!!!

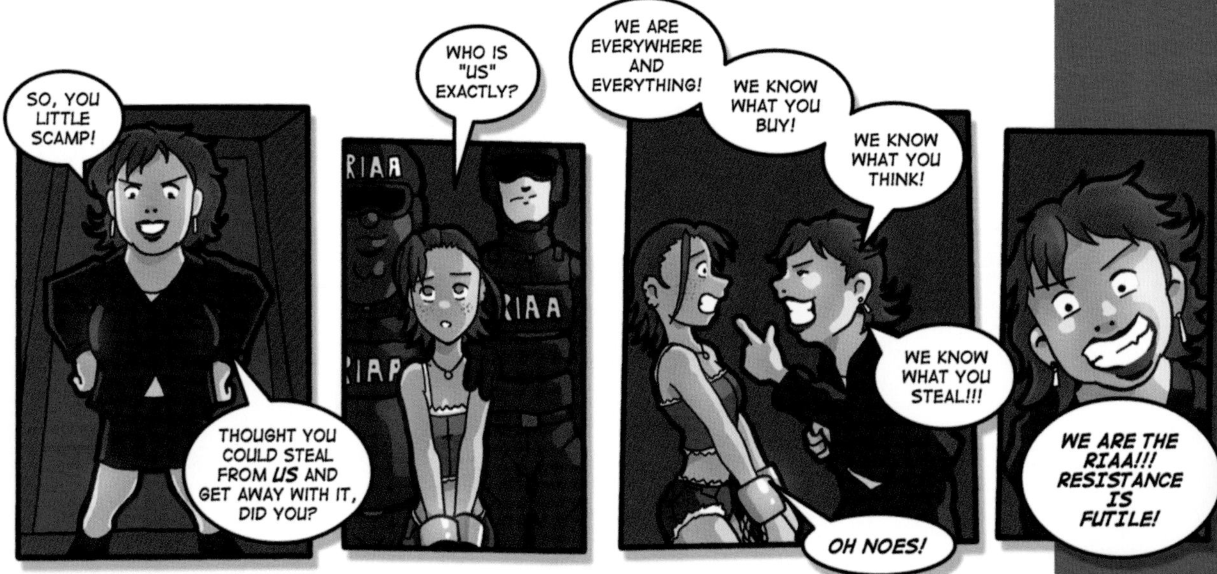
SO, YOU LITTLE SCAMP!
THOUGHT YOU COULD STEAL FROM *US* AND GET AWAY WITH IT, DID YOU?
WHO IS "US" EXACTLY?
WE ARE EVERYWHERE AND EVERYTHING!
WE KNOW WHAT YOU BUY!
WE KNOW WHAT YOU THINK!
WE KNOW WHAT YOU STEAL!!!
OH NOES!
WE ARE THE RIAA!!! RESISTANCE IS FUTILE!

#10

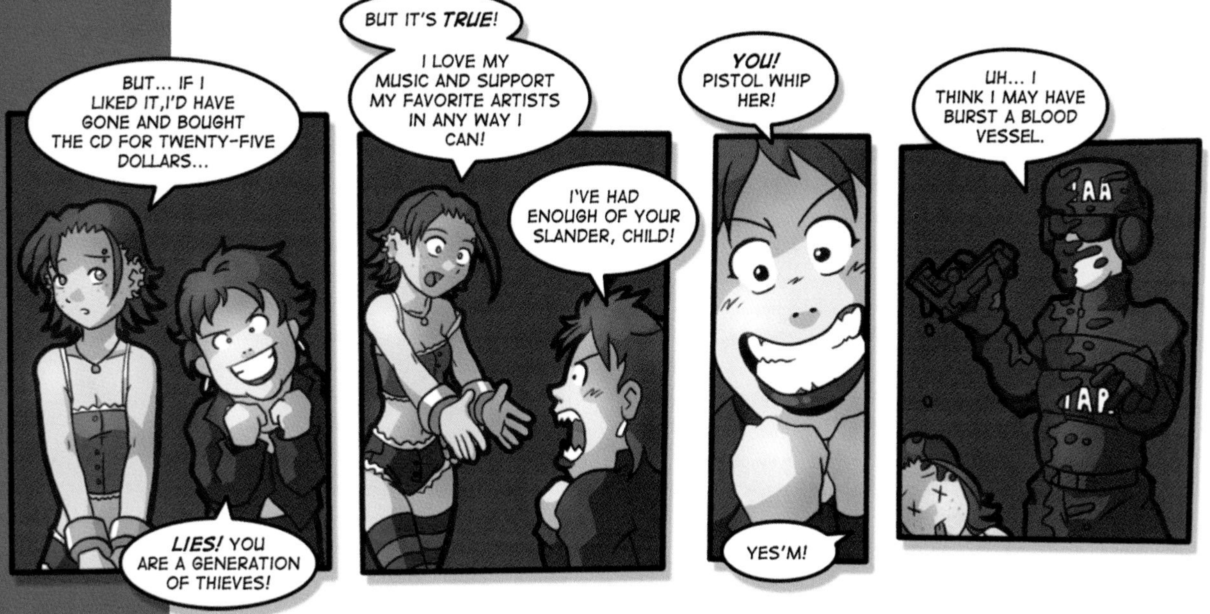
BUT... IF I LIKED IT,I'D HAVE GONE AND BOUGHT THE CD FOR TWENTY-FIVE DOLLARS...
LIES! YOU ARE A GENERATION OF THIEVES!
BUT IT'S TRUE!
I LOVE MY MUSIC AND SUPPORT MY FAVORITE ARTISTS IN ANY WAY I CAN!
I'VE HAD ENOUGH OF YOUR SLANDER, CHILD!
YOU! PISTOL WHIP HER!
YES'M!
UH... I THINK I MAY HAVE BURST A BLOOD VESSEL.

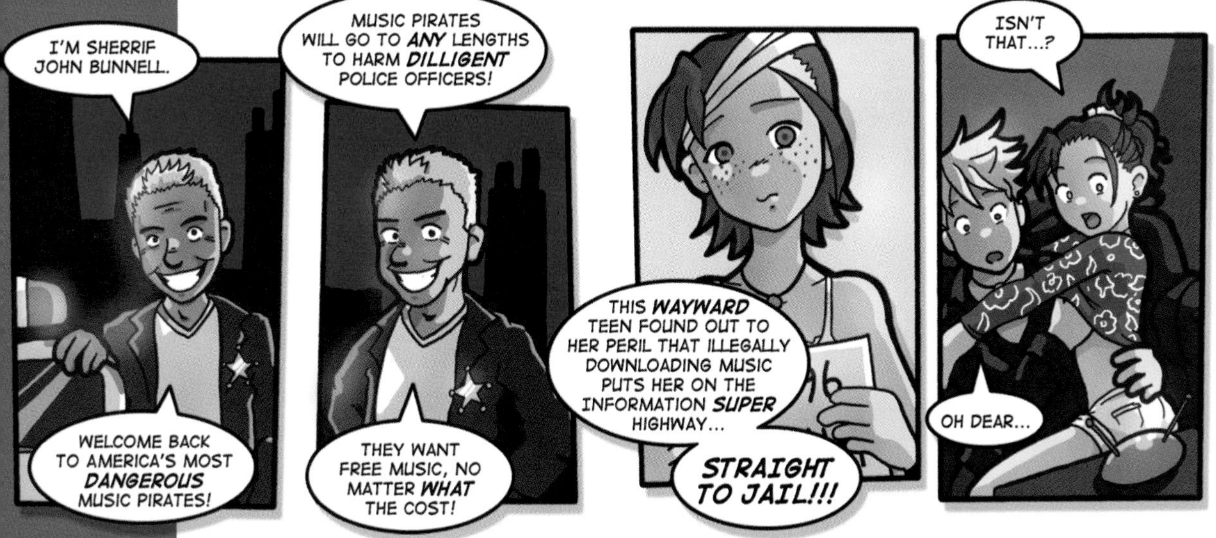
I'M SHERRIF JOHN BUNNELL.
WELCOME BACK TO AMERICA'S MOST DANGEROUS MUSIC PIRATES!
MUSIC PIRATES WILL GO TO ANY LENGTHS TO HARM DILLIGENT POLICE OFFICERS!
THEY WANT FREE MUSIC, NO MATTER WHAT THE COST!
THIS WAYWARD TEEN FOUND OUT TO HER PERIL THAT ILLEGALLY DOWNLOADING MUSIC PUTS HER ON THE INFORMATION SUPER HIGHWAY...
STRAIGHT TO JAIL!!!
ISN'T THAT...?
OH DEAR...

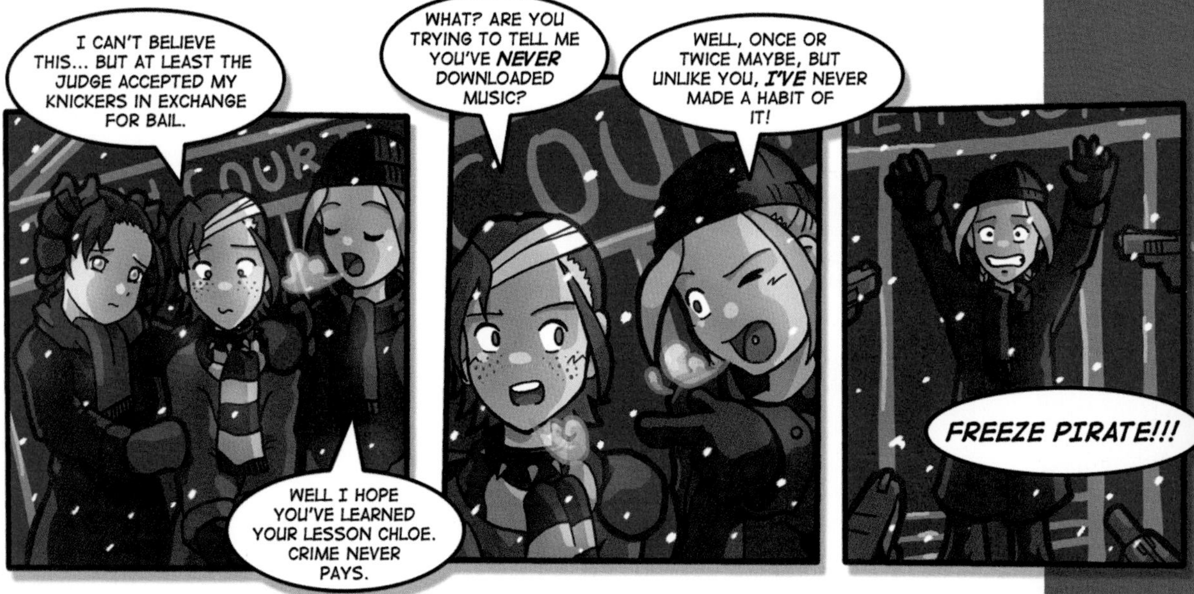
I CAN'T BELIEVE THIS... BUT AT LEAST THE JUDGE ACCEPTED MY KNICKERS IN EXCHANGE FOR BAIL.
WELL I HOPE YOU'VE LEARNED YOUR LESSON CHLOE. CRIME NEVER PAYS.
WHAT? ARE YOU TRYING TO TELL ME YOU'VE ***NEVER*** DOWNLOADED MUSIC?
WELL, ONCE OR TWICE MAYBE, BUT UNLIKE YOU, ***I'VE*** NEVER MADE A HABIT OF IT!
FREEZE PIRATE!!!

#12

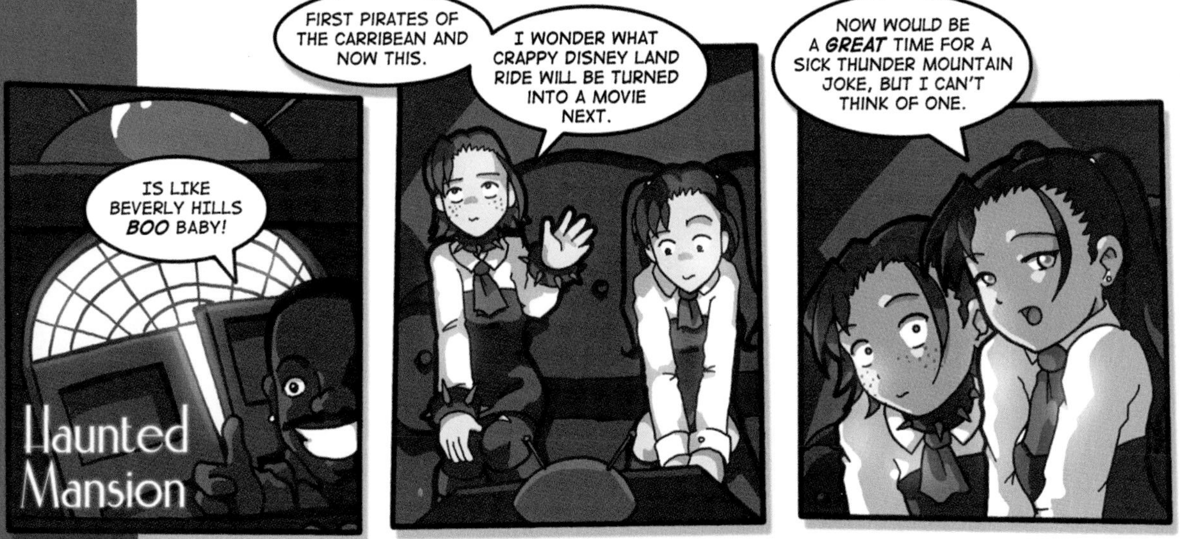
IS LIKE BEVERLY HILLS BOO BABY!
Haunted Mansion
FIRST PIRATES OF THE CARRIBEAN AND NOW THIS.
I WONDER WHAT CRAPPY DISNEY LAND RIDE WILL BE TURNED INTO A MOVIE NEXT.
NOW WOULD BE A GREAT TIME FOR A SICK THUNDER MOUNTAIN JOKE, BUT I CAN'T THINK OF ONE.

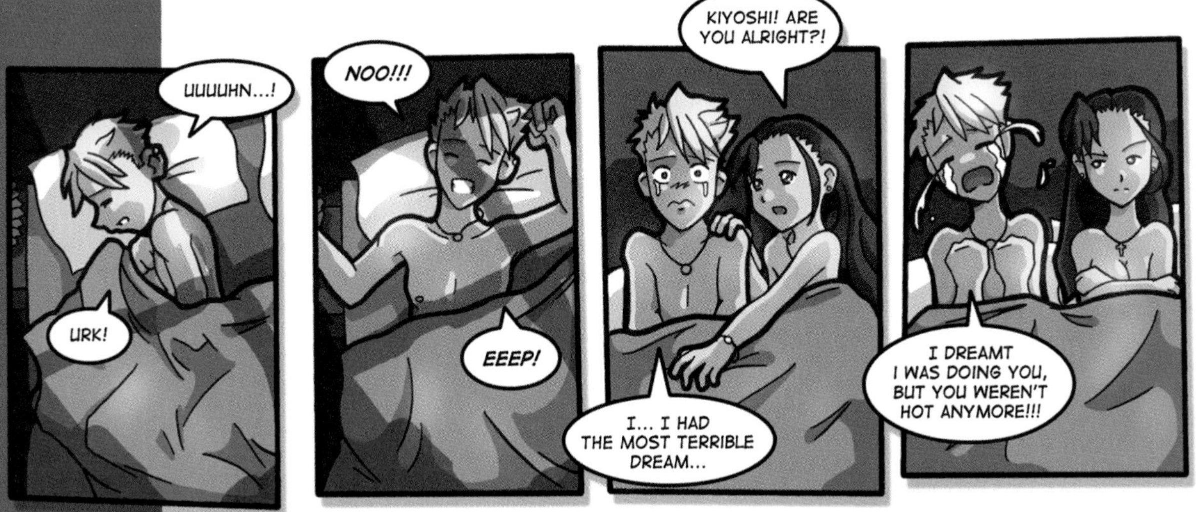
UUUUHN...!
URK!
NOO!!!
EEEP!
KIYOSHI! ARE YOU ALRIGHT?!
I... I HAD THE MOST TERRIBLE DREAM...
I DREAMT I WAS DOING YOU, BUT YOU WEREN'T HOT ANYMORE!!!

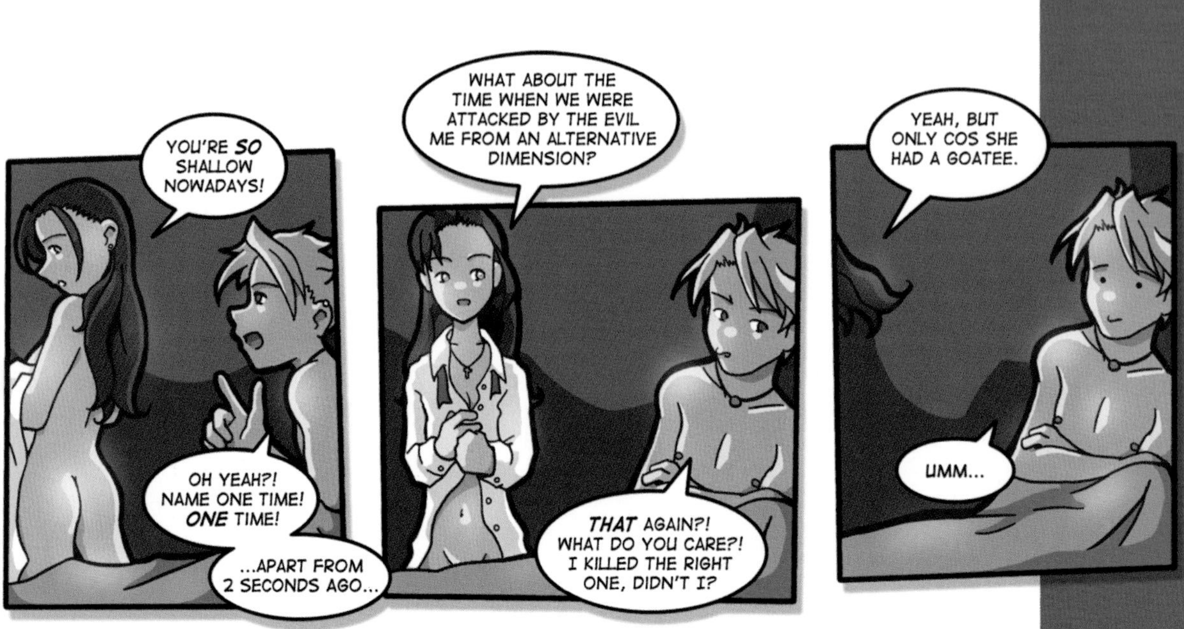
YOU'RE **SO** SHALLOW NOWADAYS!
OH YEAH?! NAME ONE TIME! **ONE** TIME!
...APART FROM 2 SECONDS AGO...
WHAT ABOUT THE TIME WHEN WE WERE ATTACKED BY THE EVIL ME FROM AN ALTERNATIVE DIMENSION?
THAT AGAIN?! WHAT DO YOU CARE?! I KILLED THE RIGHT ONE, DIDN'T I?
YEAH, BUT ONLY COS SHE HAD A GOATEE.
UMM...

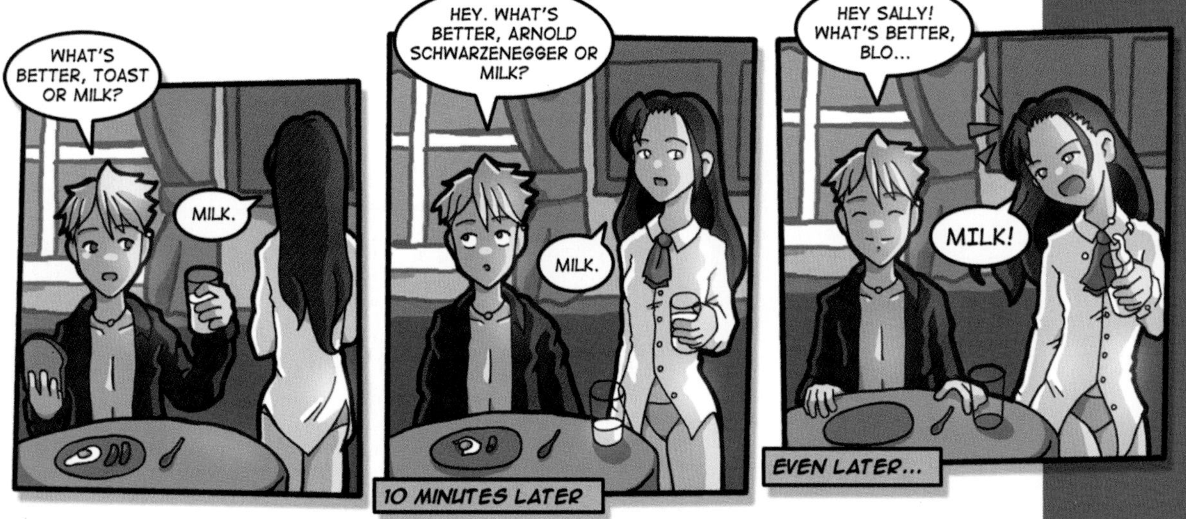
WHAT'S BETTER, TOAST OR MILK?
MILK.
10 MINUTES LATER
HEY. WHAT'S BETTER, ARNOLD SCHWARZENEGGER OR MILK?
MILK.
EVEN LATER...
HEY SALLY! WHAT'S BETTER, BLO...
MILK!

#14

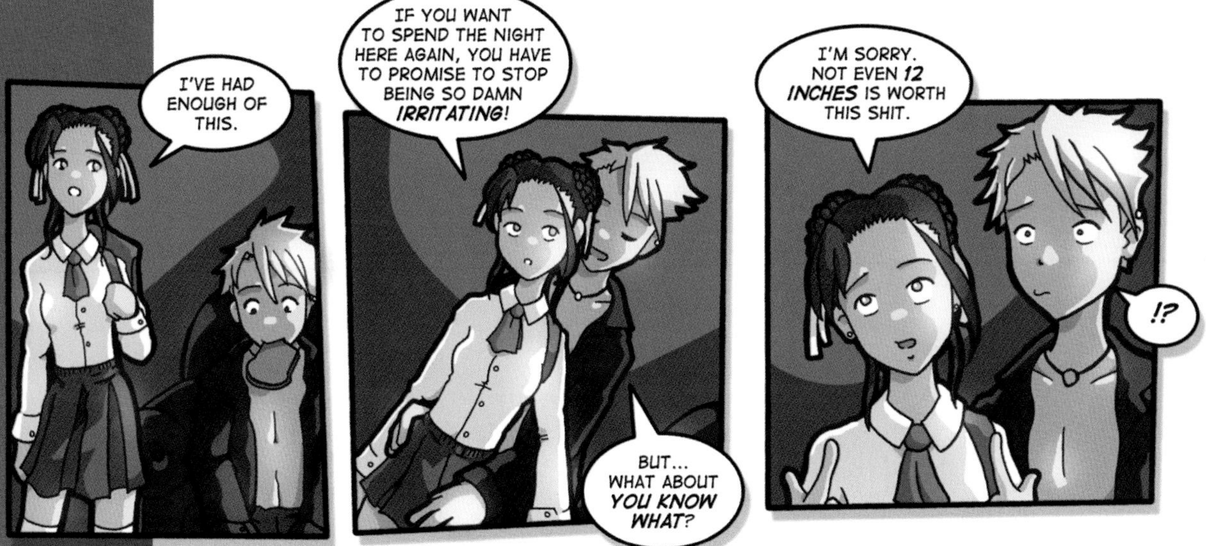
I'VE HAD ENOUGH OF THIS.
IF YOU WANT TO SPEND THE NIGHT HERE AGAIN, YOU HAVE TO PROMISE TO STOP BEING SO DAMN *IRRITATING*!
BUT... WHAT ABOUT *YOU KNOW WHAT*?
I'M SORRY. NOT EVEN *12 INCHES* IS WORTH THIS SHIT.
!?

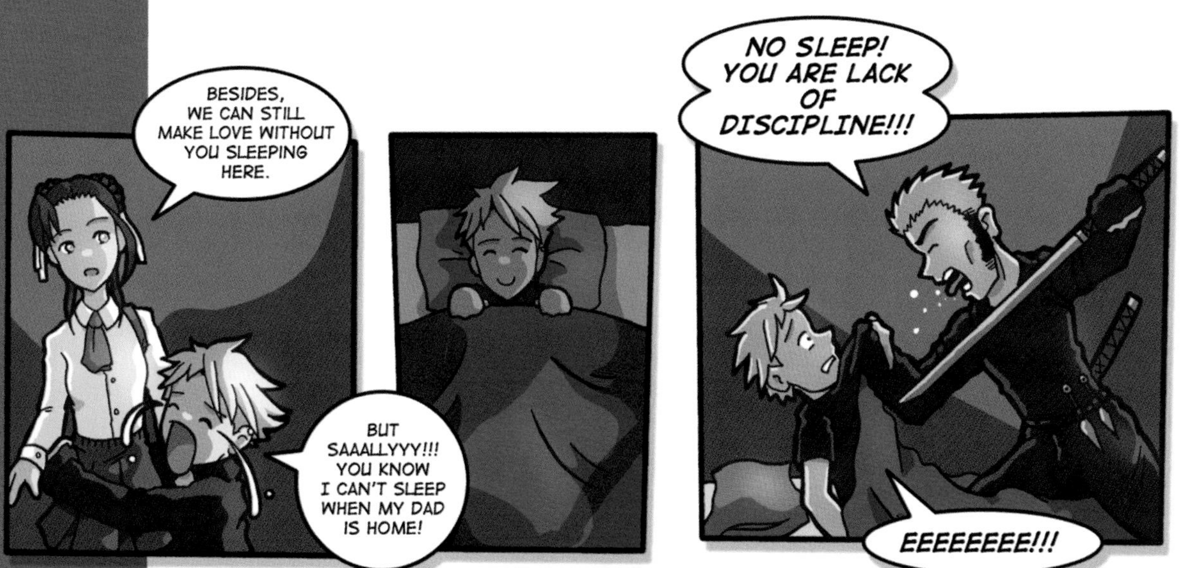
BESIDES, WE CAN STILL MAKE LOVE WITHOUT YOU SLEEPING HERE.
BUT SAAALLYYY!!! YOU KNOW I CAN'T SLEEP WHEN MY DAD IS HOME!
NO SLEEP! YOU ARE LACK OF DISCIPLINE!!!
EEEEEEEE!!!

Get a Room!

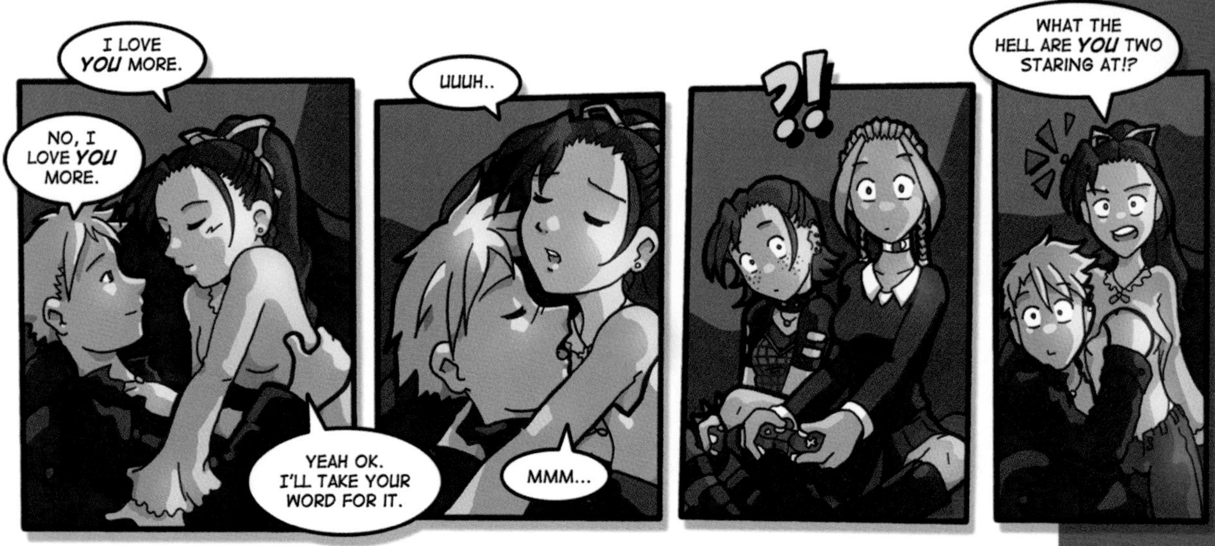
I LOVE *YOU* MORE.
NO, I LOVE *YOU* MORE.
YEAH OK. I'LL TAKE YOUR WORD FOR IT.
UUUH..
MMM...
?!
WHAT THE HELL ARE *YOU* TWO STARING AT!?

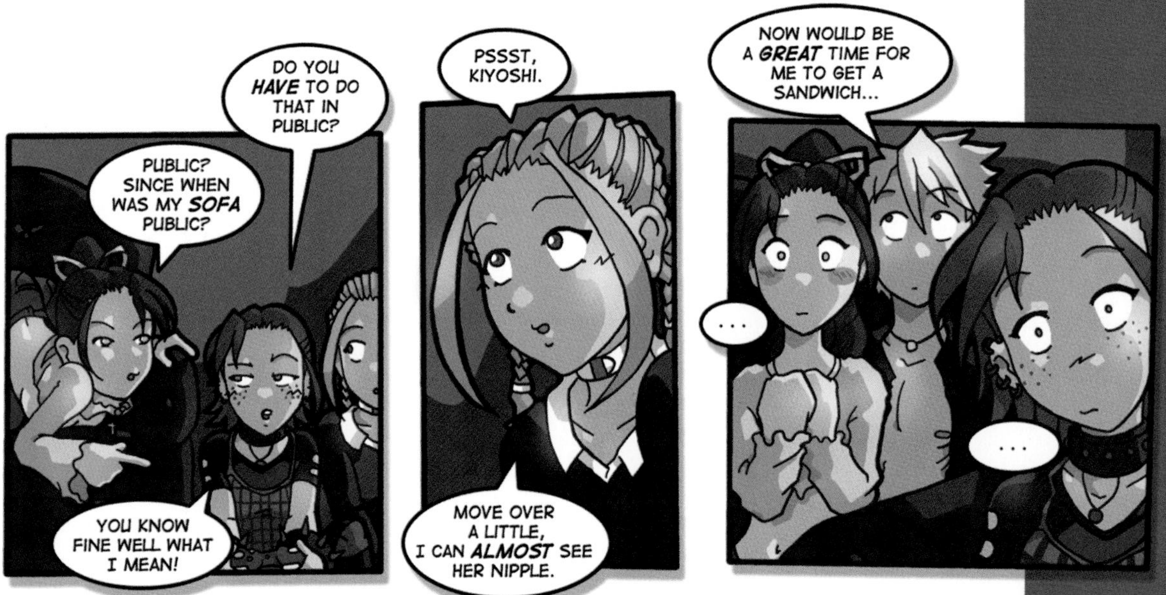
DO YOU *HAVE* TO DO THAT IN PUBLIC?
PUBLIC? SINCE WHEN WAS MY *SOFA* PUBLIC?
YOU KNOW FINE WELL WHAT I MEAN!
PSSST, KIYOSHI.
MOVE OVER A LITTLE, I CAN *ALMOST* SEE HER NIPPLE.
NOW WOULD BE A *GREAT* TIME FOR ME TO GET A SANDWICH...
...
...

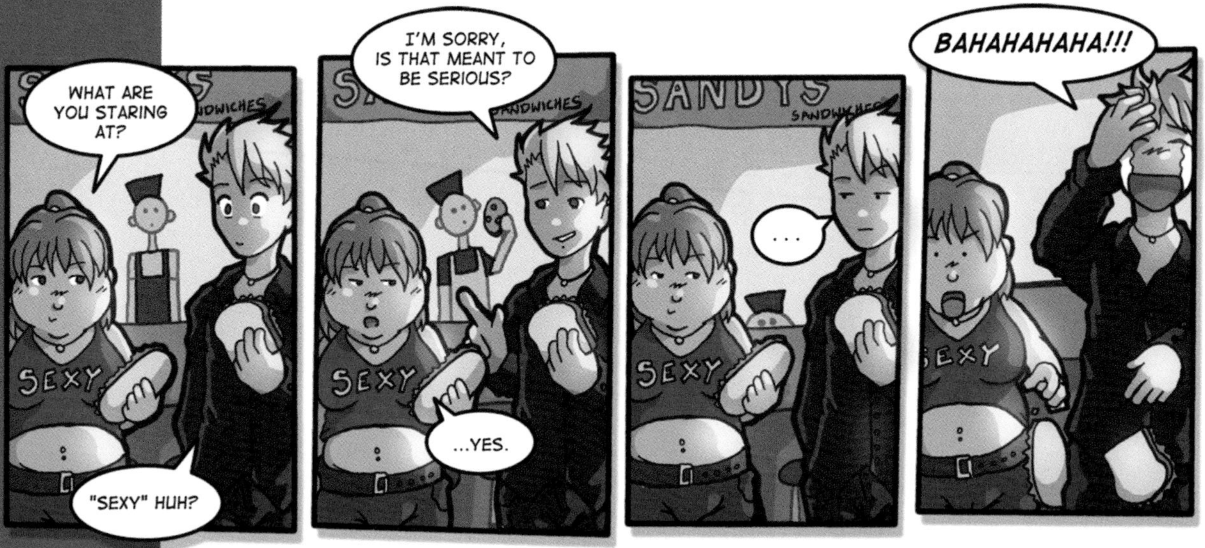
WHAT ARE YOU STARING AT?
"SEXY" HUH?
I'M SORRY, IS THAT MEANT TO BE SERIOUS?
...YES.
SANDYS
...
BAHAHAHAHA!!!

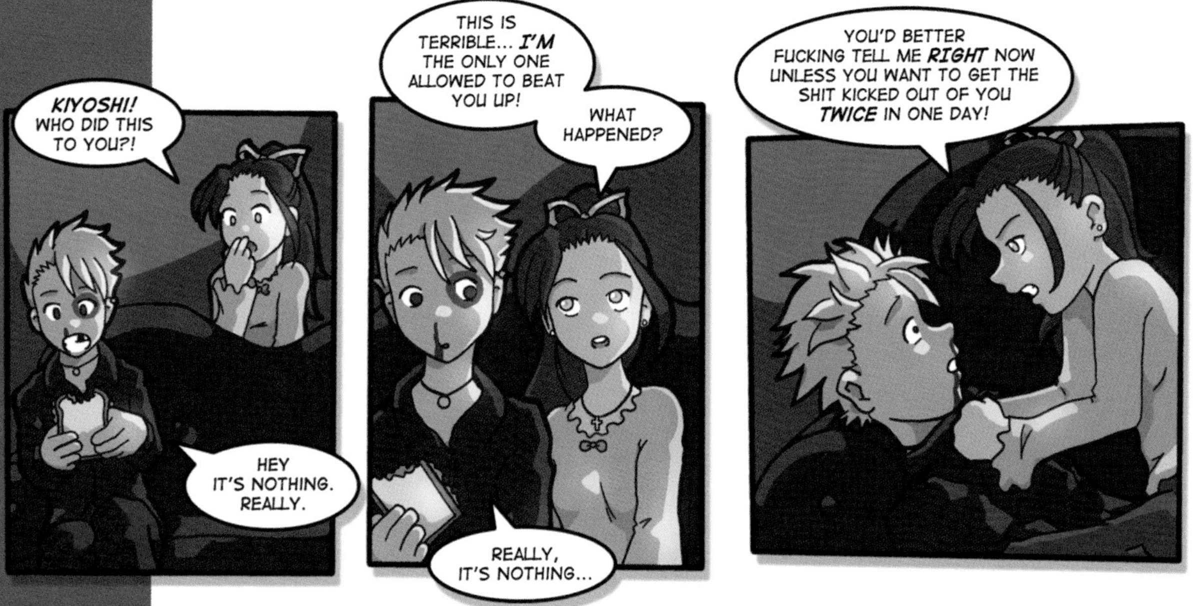
KIYOSHI! WHO DID THIS TO YOU?!
HEY IT'S NOTHING. REALLY.
THIS IS TERRIBLE... *I'M* THE ONLY ONE ALLOWED TO BEAT YOU UP!
WHAT HAPPENED?
REALLY, IT'S NOTHING...
YOU'D BETTER FUCKING TELL ME *RIGHT* NOW UNLESS YOU WANT TO GET THE SHIT KICKED OUT OF YOU *TWICE* IN ONE DAY!

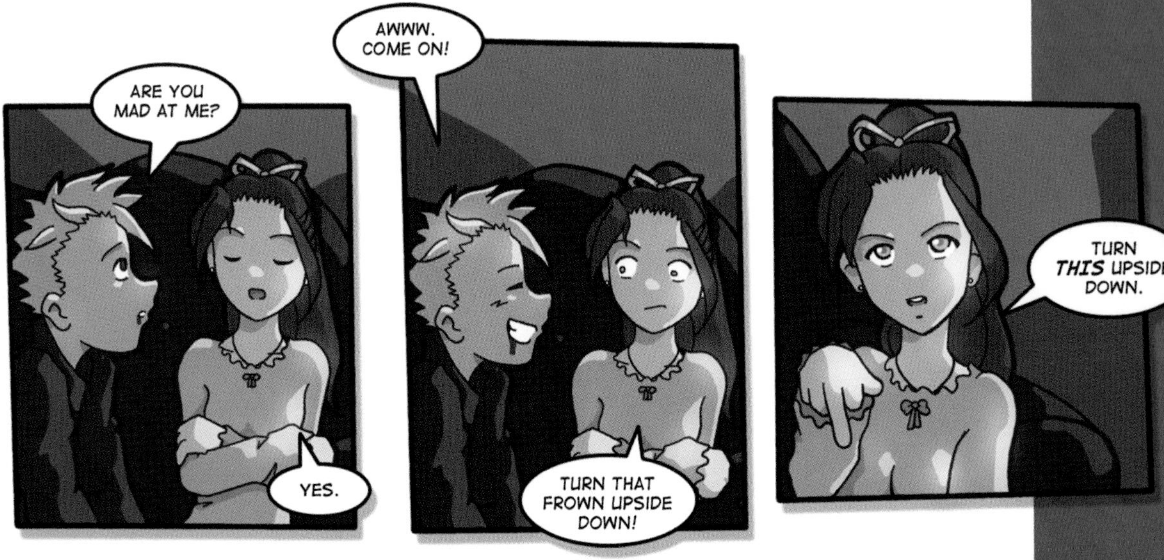
ARE YOU MAD AT ME?
YES.
AWWW. COME ON!
TURN THAT FROWN UPSIDE DOWN!
TURN **THIS** UPSIDE DOWN.

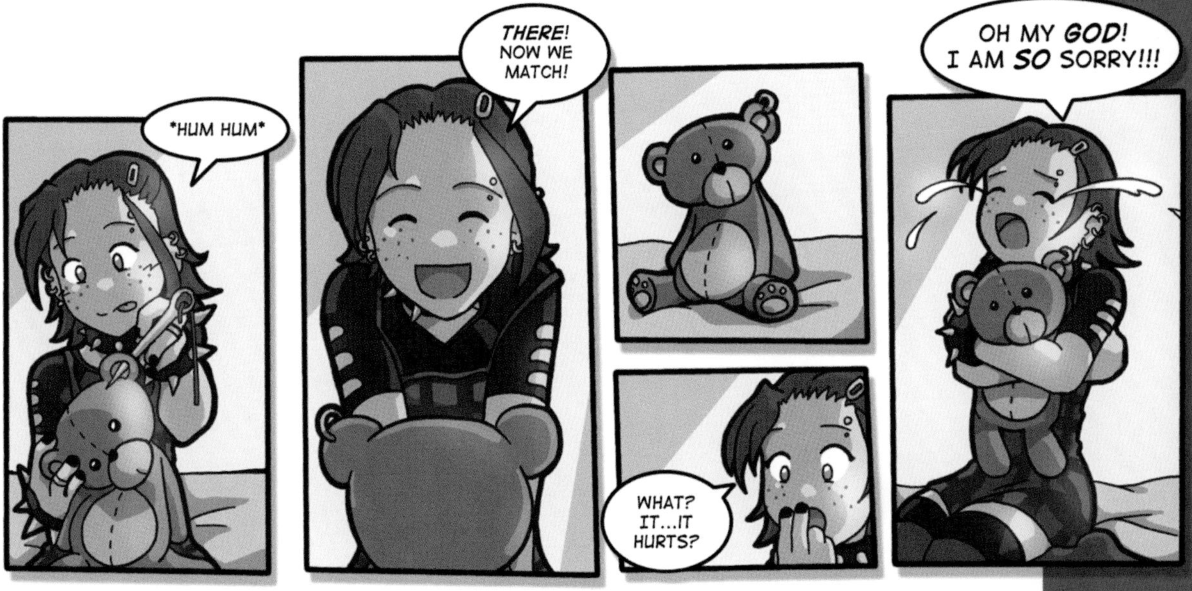
HUM HUM
THERE! NOW WE MATCH!
WHAT? IT...IT HURTS?
OH MY **GOD**! I AM **SO** SORRY!!!

#18

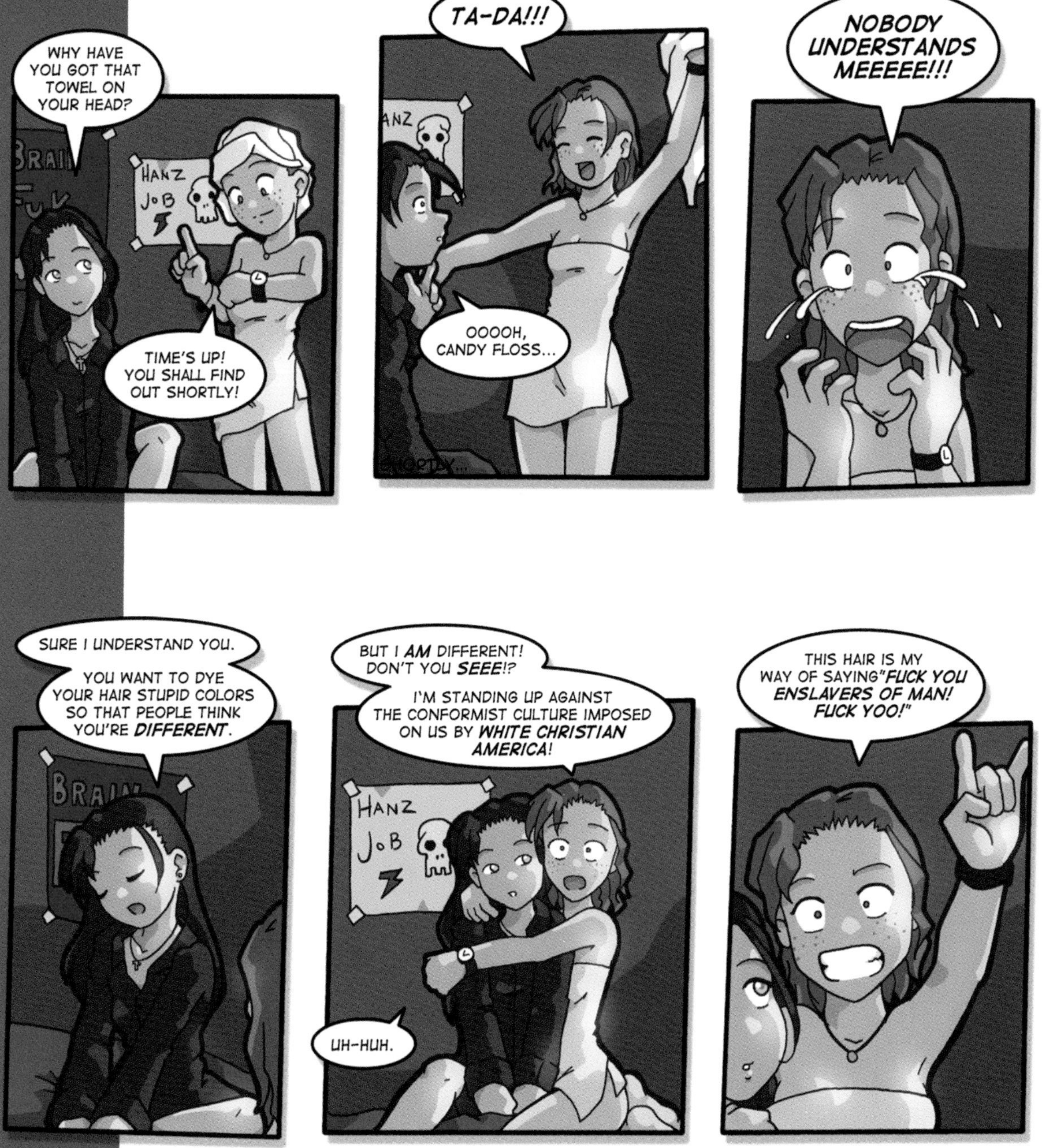
WHY HAVE YOU GOT THAT TOWEL ON YOUR HEAD?
TIME'S UP! YOU SHALL FIND OUT SHORTLY!
TA-DA!!!
OOOOH, CANDY FLOSS...
SHORTLY...
NOBODY UNDERSTANDS MEEEEE!!!
SURE I UNDERSTAND YOU.
YOU WANT TO DYE YOUR HAIR STUPID COLORS SO THAT PEOPLE THINK YOU'RE DIFFERENT.
BUT I AM DIFFERENT! DON'T YOU SEEE!?
I'M STANDING UP AGAINST THE CONFORMIST CULTURE IMPOSED ON US BY WHITE CHRISTIAN AMERICA!
UH-HUH.
THIS HAIR IS MY WAY OF SAYING "FUCK YOU ENSLAVERS OF MAN! FUCK YOO!"

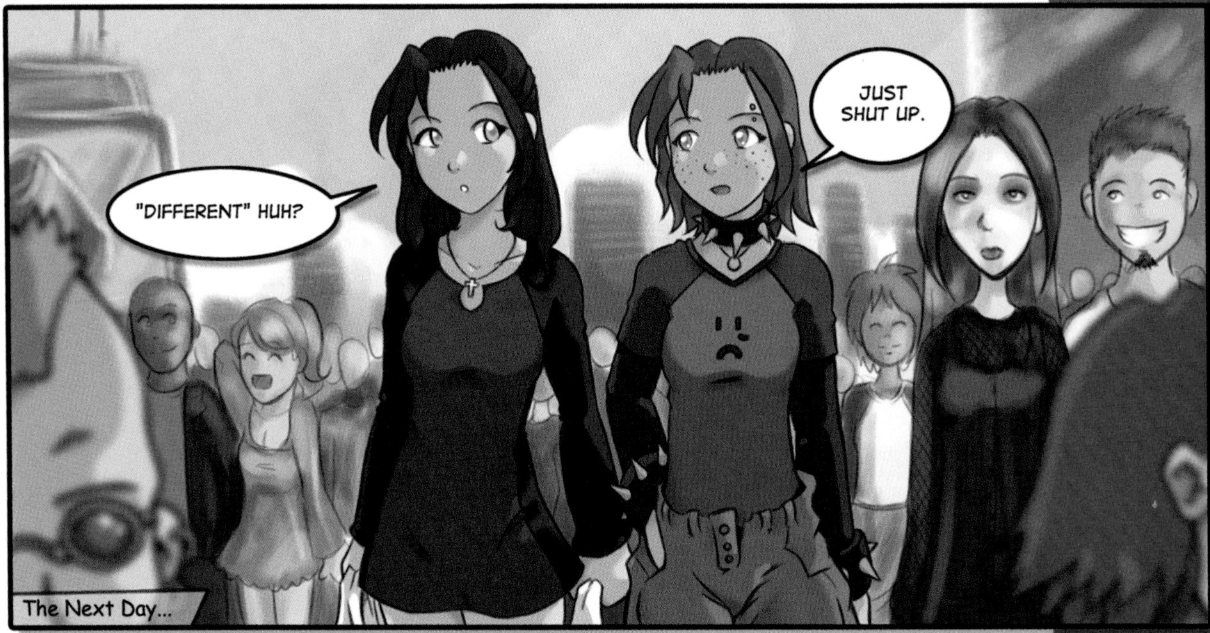
"DIFFERENT" HUH?
JUST SHUT UP.
The Next Day...

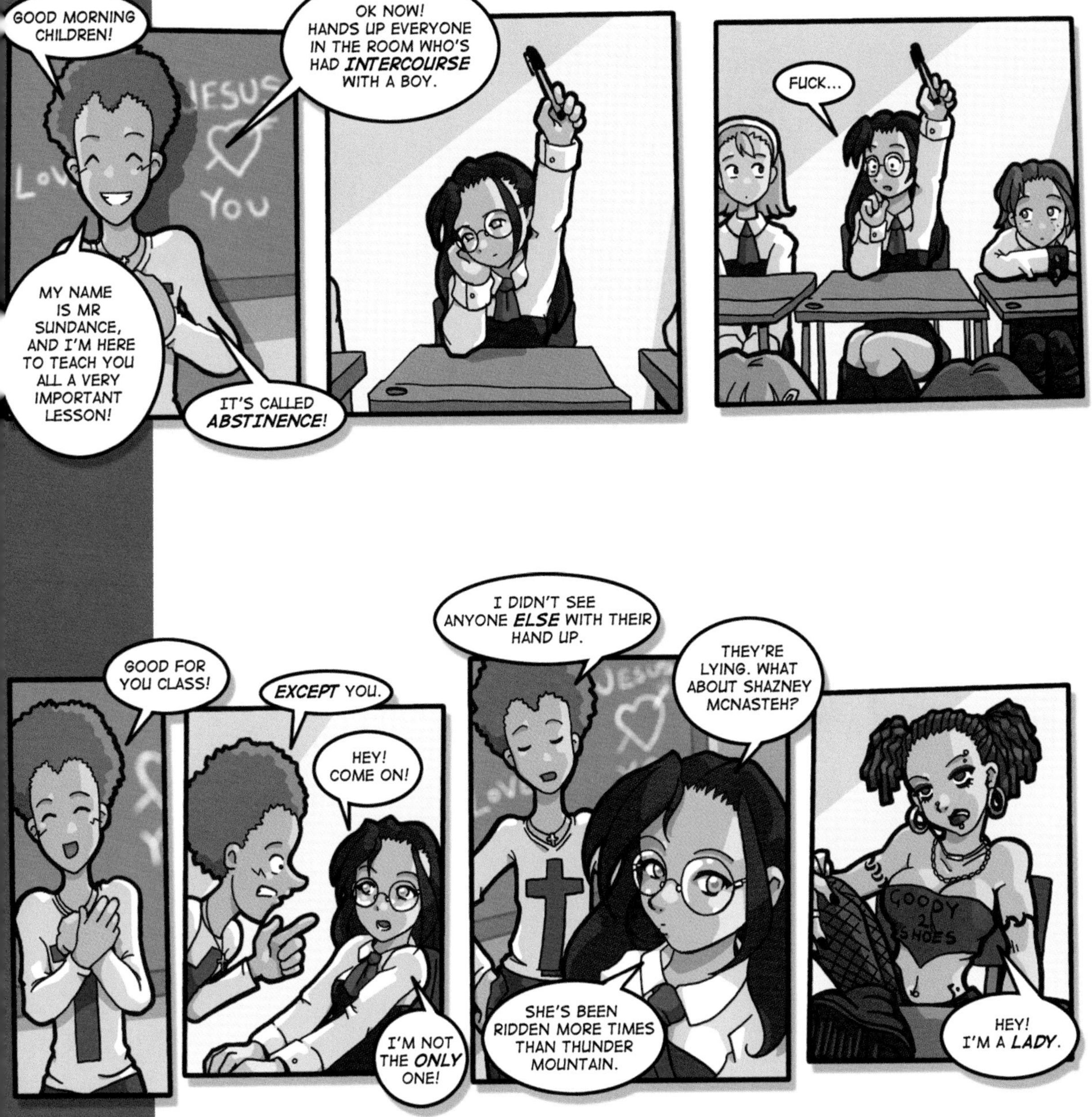
GOOD MORNING CHILDREN!
MY NAME IS MR SUNDANCE, AND I'M HERE TO TEACH YOU ALL A VERY IMPORTANT LESSON!
IT'S CALLED ***ABSTINENCE!***
OK NOW! HANDS UP EVERYONE IN THE ROOM WHO'S HAD ***INTERCOURSE*** WITH A BOY.
FUCK...
GOOD FOR YOU CLASS!
EXCEPT YOU.
HEY! COME ON!
I'M NOT THE ***ONLY*** ONE!
I DIDN'T SEE ANYONE ***ELSE*** WITH THEIR HAND UP.
THEY'RE LYING. WHAT ABOUT SHAZNEY MCNASTEH?
SHE'S BEEN RIDDEN MORE TIMES THAN THUNDER MOUNTAIN.
GOODY 2 SHOES
HEY! I'M A ***LADY***.

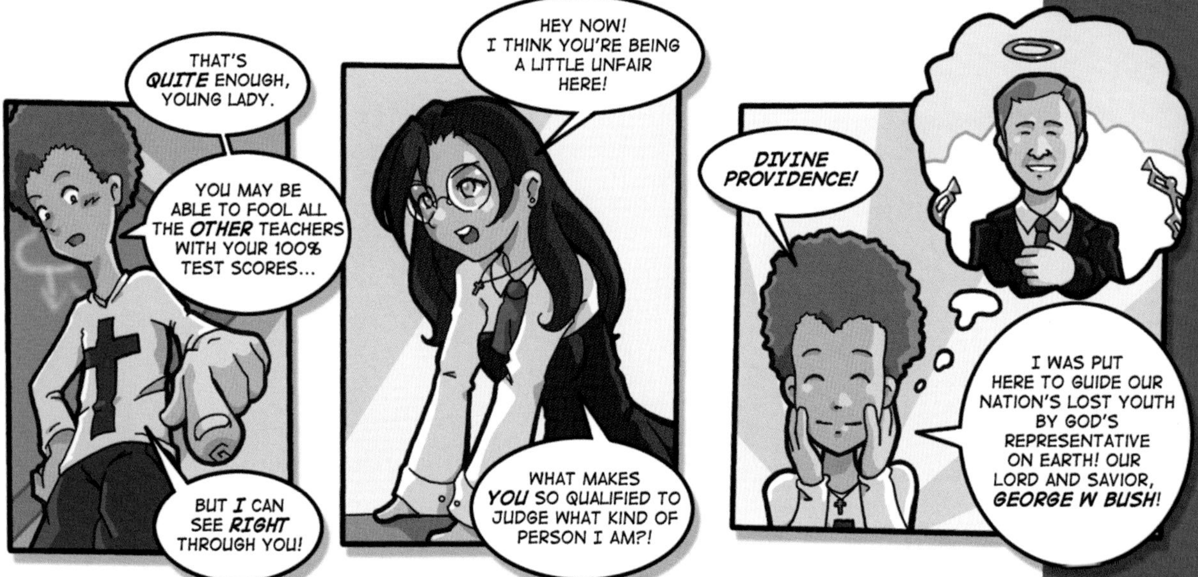
THAT'S QUITE ENOUGH, YOUNG LADY.
YOU MAY BE ABLE TO FOOL ALL THE OTHER TEACHERS WITH YOUR 100% TEST SCORES...
BUT I CAN SEE RIGHT THROUGH YOU!
HEY NOW! I THINK YOU'RE BEING A LITTLE UNFAIR HERE!
WHAT MAKES YOU SO QUALIFIED TO JUDGE WHAT KIND OF PERSON I AM?!
DIVINE PROVIDENCE!
I WAS PUT HERE TO GUIDE OUR NATION'S LOST YOUTH BY GOD'S REPRESENTATIVE ON EARTH! OUR LORD AND SAVIOR, GEORGE W BUSH!

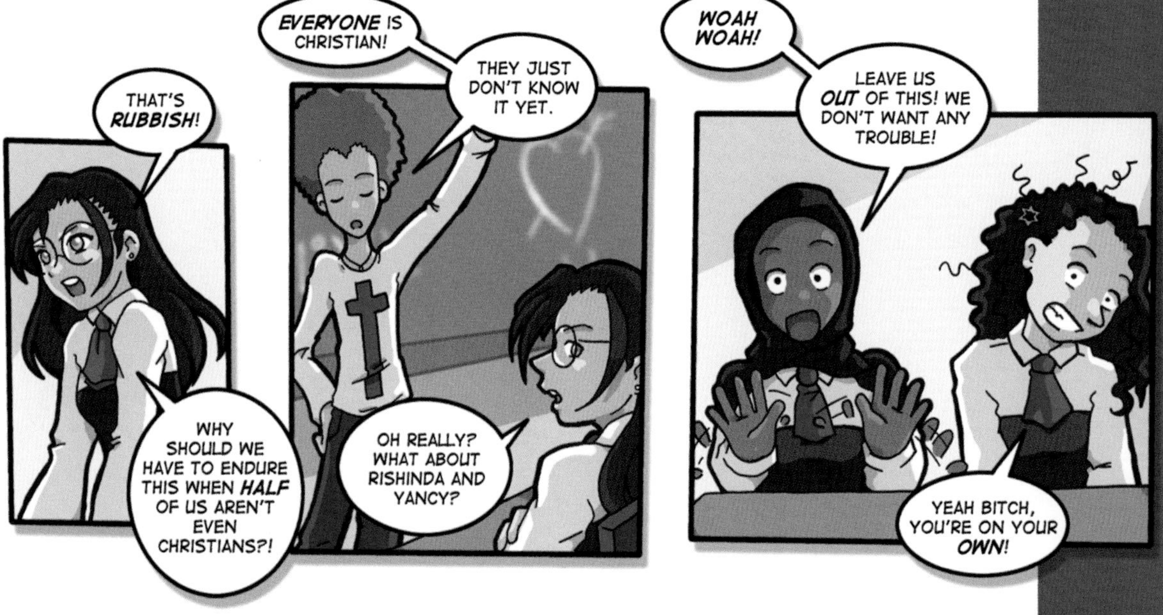
THAT'S RUBBISH!
WHY SHOULD WE HAVE TO ENDURE THIS WHEN HALF OF US AREN'T EVEN CHRISTIANS?!
EVERYONE IS CHRISTIAN!
THEY JUST DON'T KNOW IT YET.
OH REALLY? WHAT ABOUT RISHINDA AND YANCY?
WOAH WOAH!
LEAVE US OUT OF THIS! WE DON'T WANT ANY TROUBLE!
YEAH BITCH, YOU'RE ON YOUR OWN!

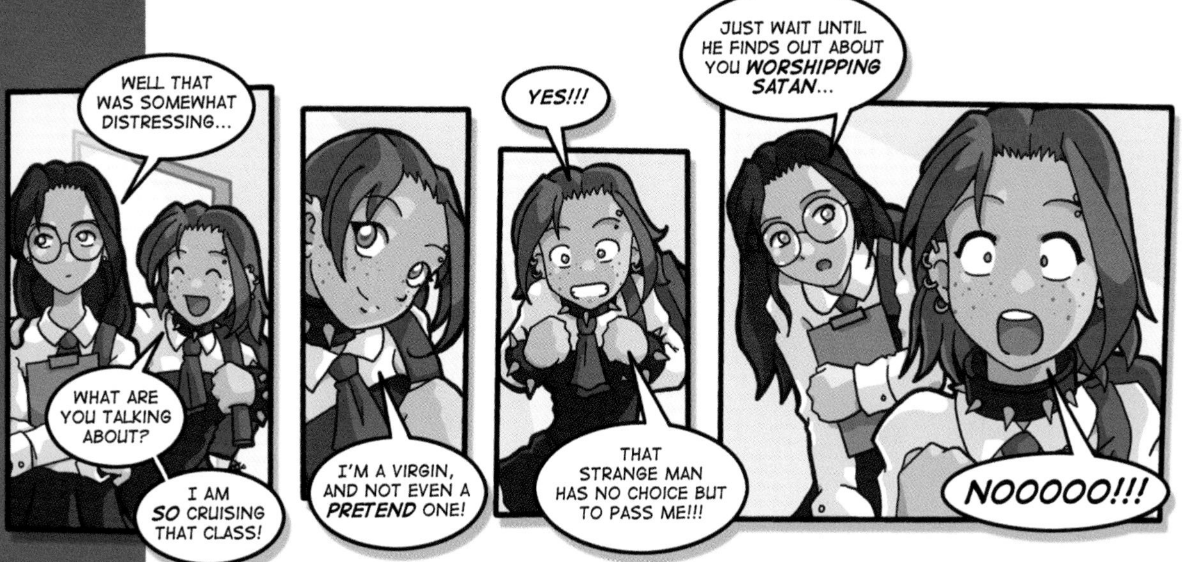
WELL THAT WAS SOMEWHAT DISTRESSING...
WHAT ARE YOU TALKING ABOUT?
I AM *SO* CRUISING THAT CLASS!
I'M A VIRGIN, AND NOT EVEN A *PRETEND* ONE!
YES!!!
THAT STRANGE MAN HAS NO CHOICE BUT TO PASS ME!!!
JUST WAIT UNTIL HE FINDS OUT ABOUT YOU *WORSHIPPING SATAN*...
NOOOOO!!!

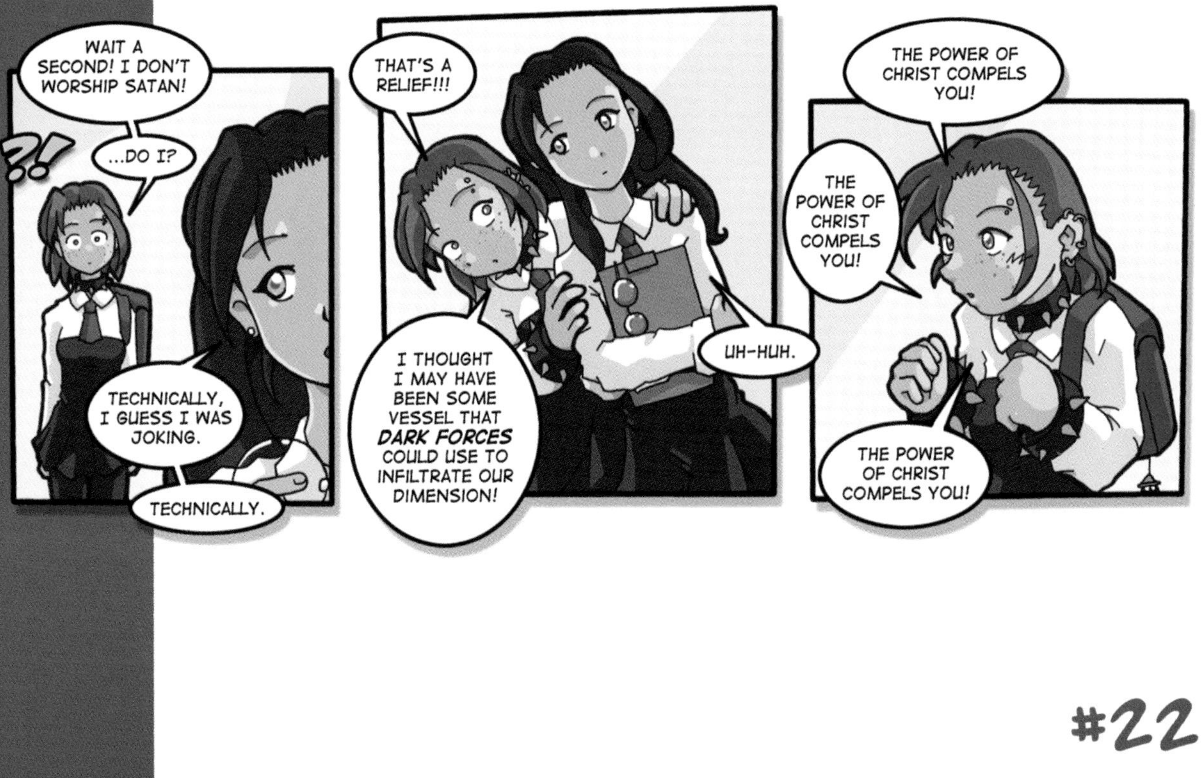
WAIT A SECOND! I DON'T WORSHIP SATAN!
?!
...DO I?
TECHNICALLY, I GUESS I WAS JOKING.
TECHNICALLY.
THAT'S A RELIEF!!!
I THOUGHT I MAY HAVE BEEN SOME VESSEL THAT *DARK FORCES* COULD USE TO INFILTRATE OUR DIMENSION!
UH-HUH.
THE POWER OF CHRIST COMPELS YOU!
THE POWER OF CHRIST COMPELS YOU!
THE POWER OF CHRIST COMPELS YOU!

#22

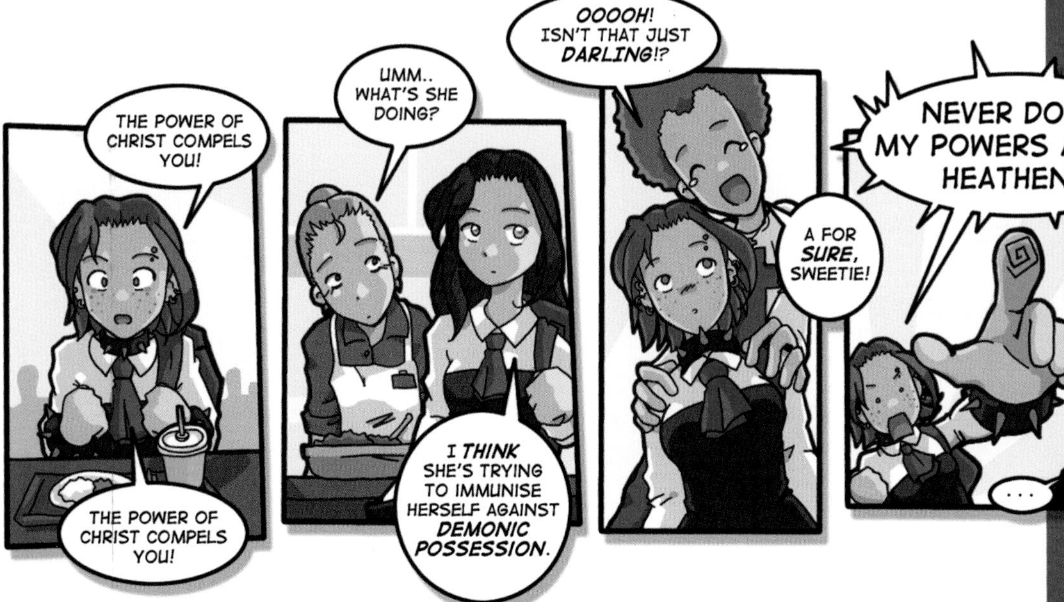
THE POWER OF CHRIST COMPELS YOU!
THE POWER OF CHRIST COMPELS YOU!
UMM.. WHAT'S SHE DOING?
I *THINK* SHE'S TRYING TO IMMUNISE HERSELF AGAINST *DEMONIC POSSESSION*.
OOOOH! ISN'T THAT JUST *DARLING*!?
A FOR *SURE*, SWEETIE!
NEVER DOUBT MY POWERS AGAIN, HEATHEN!!!
...

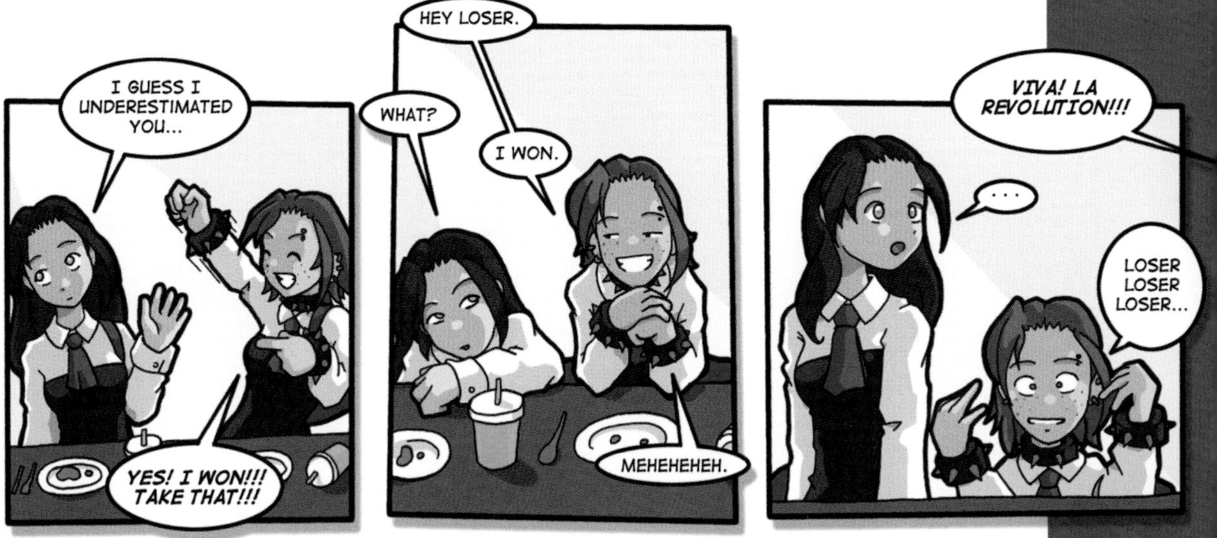
I GUESS I UNDERESTIMATED YOU...
YES! I WON!!! TAKE THAT!!!
HEY LOSER.
WHAT?
I WON.
MEHEHEHEH.
VIVA! LA REVOLUTION!!!
...
LOSER LOSER LOSER...

#24

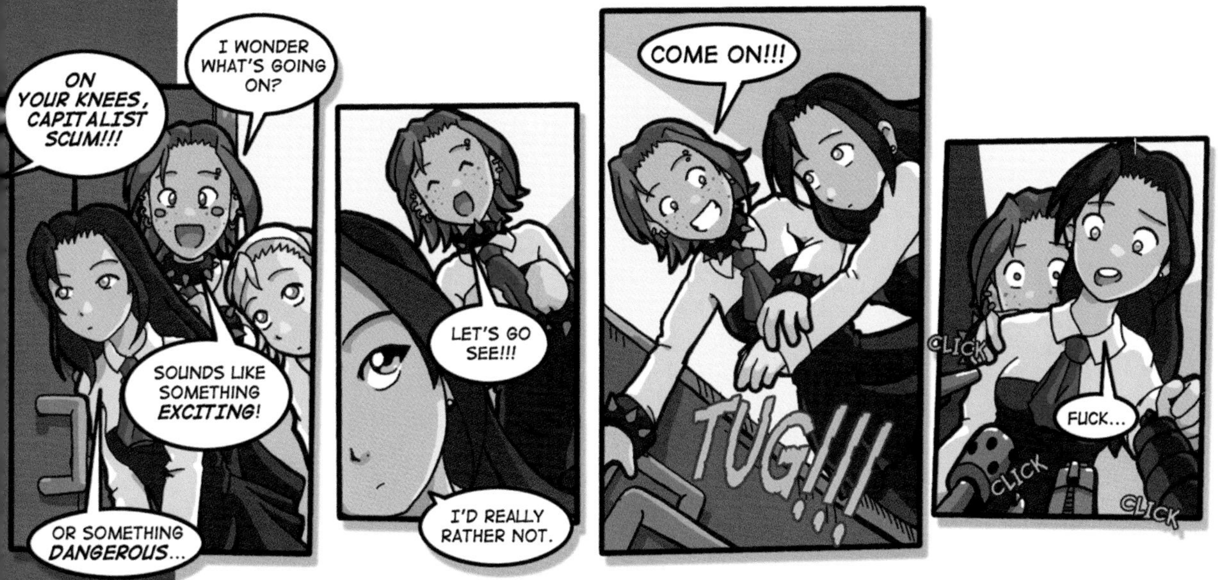
ON YOUR KNEES, CAPITALIST SCUM!!!
I WONDER WHAT'S GOING ON?
SOUNDS LIKE SOMETHING *EXCITING*!
OR SOMETHING *DANGEROUS*...
LET'S GO SEE!!!
I'D REALLY RATHER NOT.
COME ON!!!
TUG!!!
CLICK
FUCK...
CLICK
CLICK

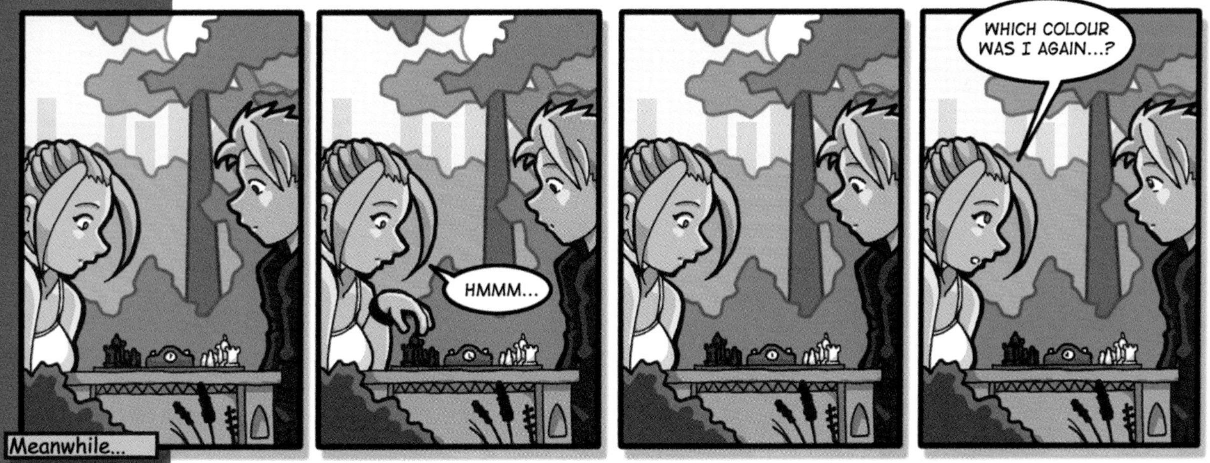
Meanwhile...
HMMM...
WHICH COLOUR WAS I AGAIN...?

#25

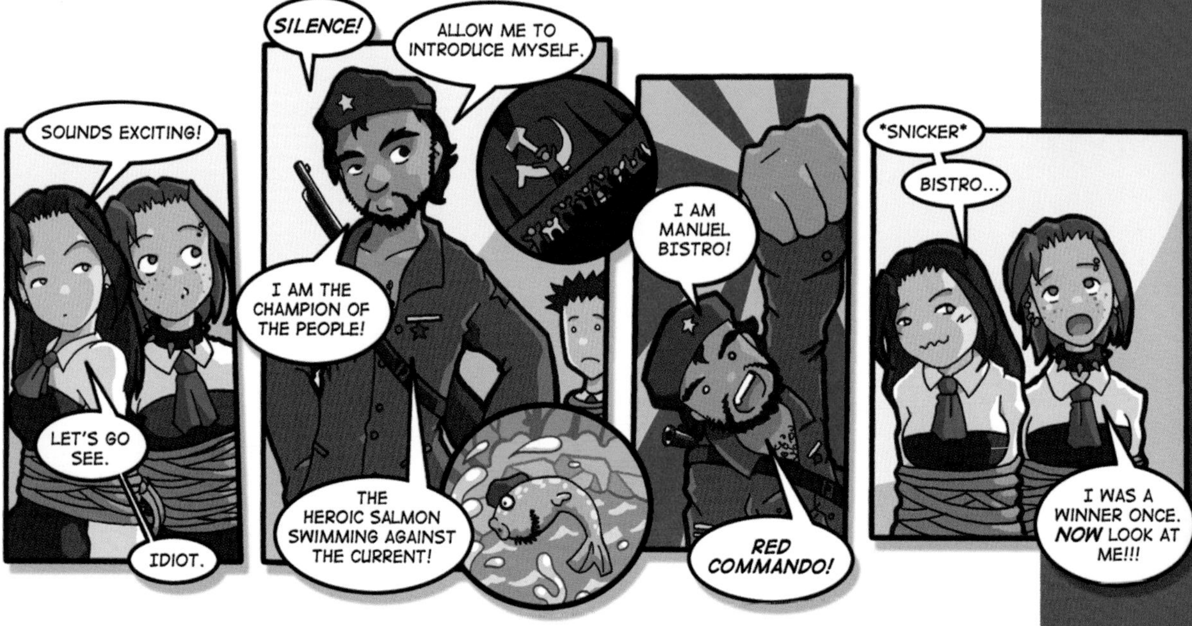
SOUNDS EXCITING!
LET'S GO SEE.
IDIOT.
SILENCE!
ALLOW ME TO INTRODUCE MYSELF.
I AM THE CHAMPION OF THE PEOPLE!
THE HEROIC SALMON SWIMMING AGAINST THE CURRENT!
I AM MANUEL BISTRO!
RED COMMANDO!
SNICKER
BISTRO...
I WAS A WINNER ONCE. NOW LOOK AT ME!!!

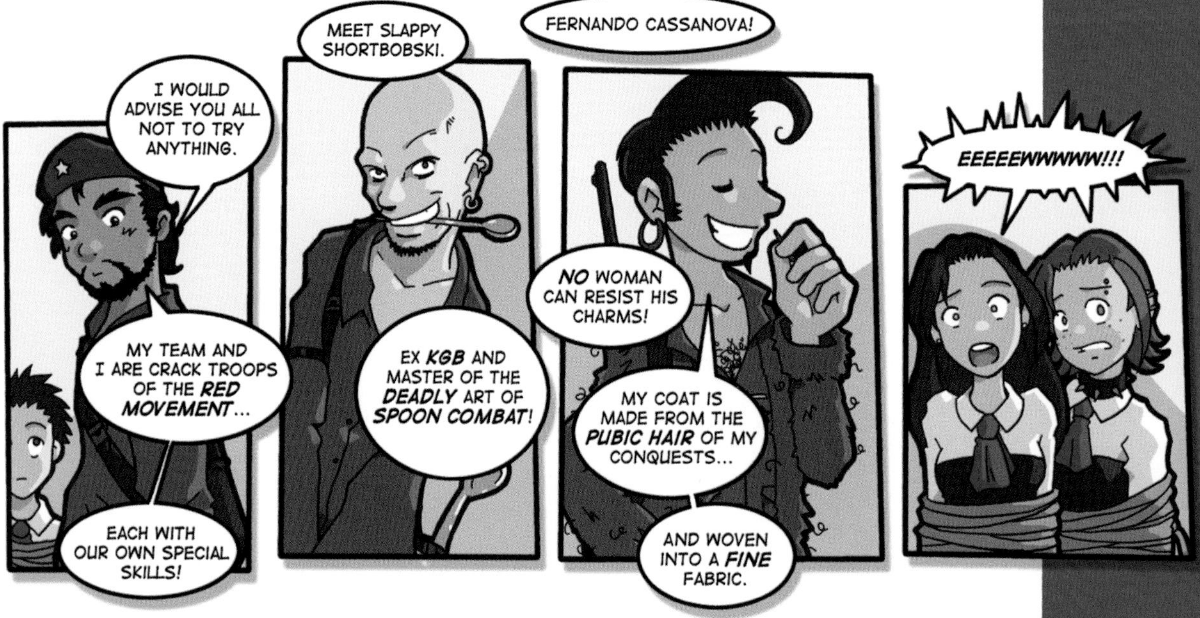
I WOULD ADVISE YOU ALL NOT TO TRY ANYTHING.
MY TEAM AND I ARE CRACK TROOPS OF THE RED MOVEMENT...
EACH WITH OUR OWN SPECIAL SKILLS!
MEET SLAPPY SHORTBOBSKI.
EX KGB AND MASTER OF THE DEADLY ART OF SPOON COMBAT!
FERNANDO CASSANOVA!
NO WOMAN CAN RESIST HIS CHARMS!
MY COAT IS MADE FROM THE PUBIC HAIR OF MY CONQUESTS...
AND WOVEN INTO A FINE FABRIC.
EEEEEWWWWW!!!

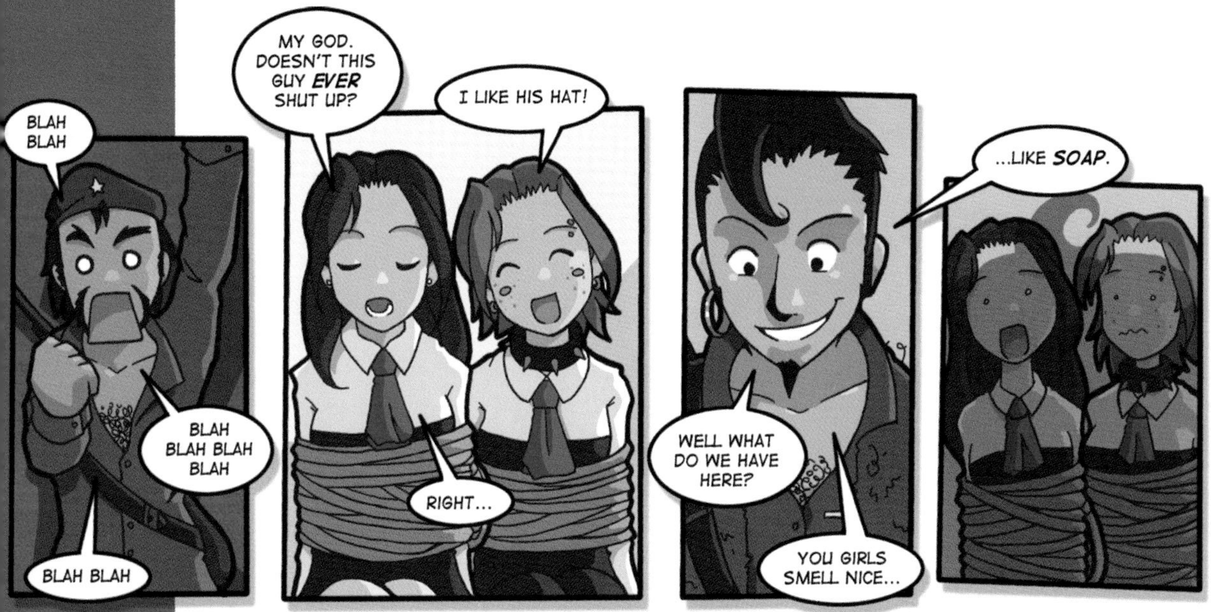
BLAH BLAH
BLAH BLAH BLAH BLAH
BLAH BLAH
MY GOD. DOESN'T THIS GUY ***EVER*** SHUT UP?
I LIKE HIS HAT!
RIGHT...
WELL WHAT DO WE HAVE HERE?
YOU GIRLS SMELL NICE...
...LIKE ***SOAP***.

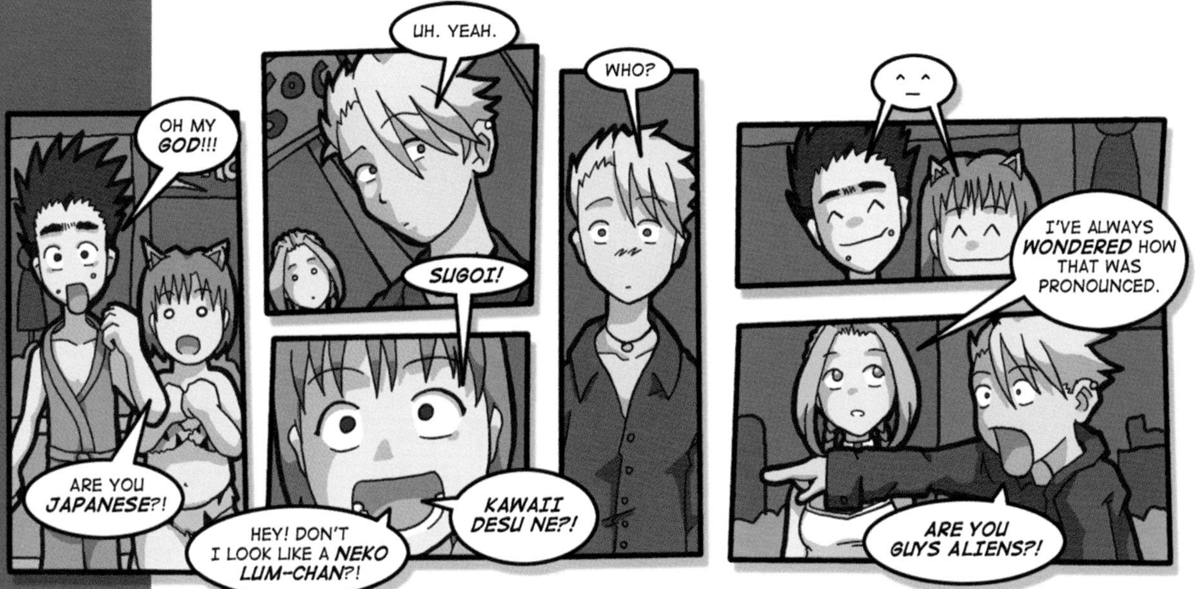
OH MY ***GOD***!!!
ARE YOU ***JAPANESE***?!
UH. YEAH.
SUGOI!
HEY! DON'T I LOOK LIKE A ***NEKO LUM-CHAN***?!
KAWAII DESU NE?!
WHO?
I'VE ALWAYS ***WONDERED*** HOW THAT WAS PRONOUNCED.
ARE YOU GUYS ALIENS?!

#27

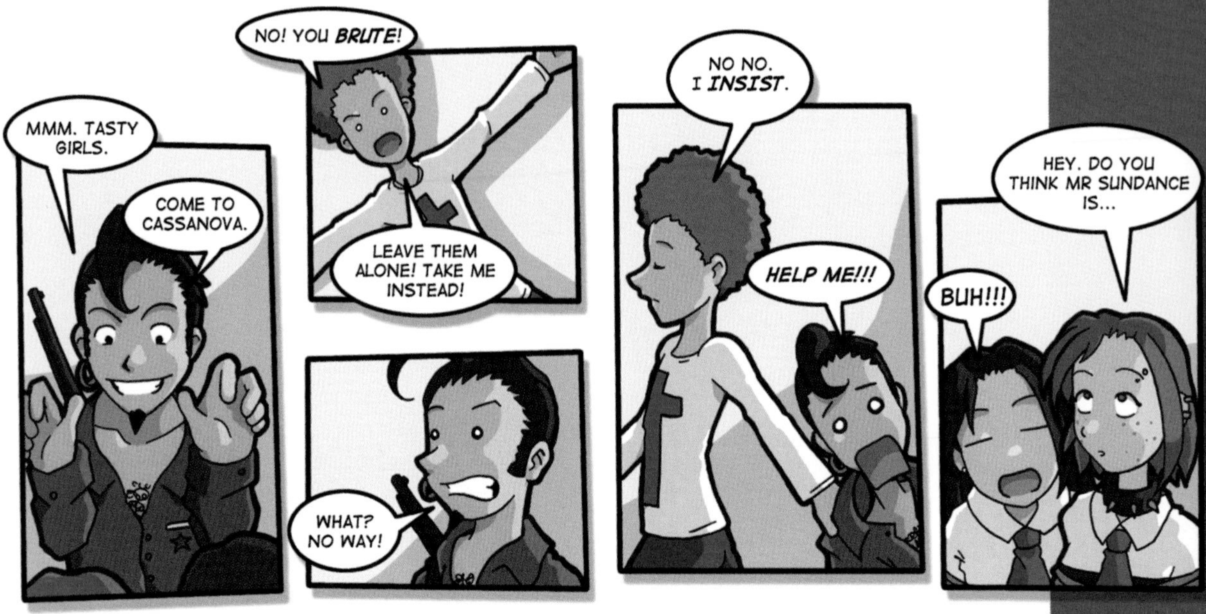
MMM. TASTY GIRLS.
COME TO CASSANOVA.
NO! YOU **BRUTE**!
LEAVE THEM ALONE! TAKE ME INSTEAD!
WHAT? NO WAY!
NO NO. I **INSIST**.
HELP ME!!!
HEY. DO YOU THINK MR SUNDANCE IS...
BUH!!!

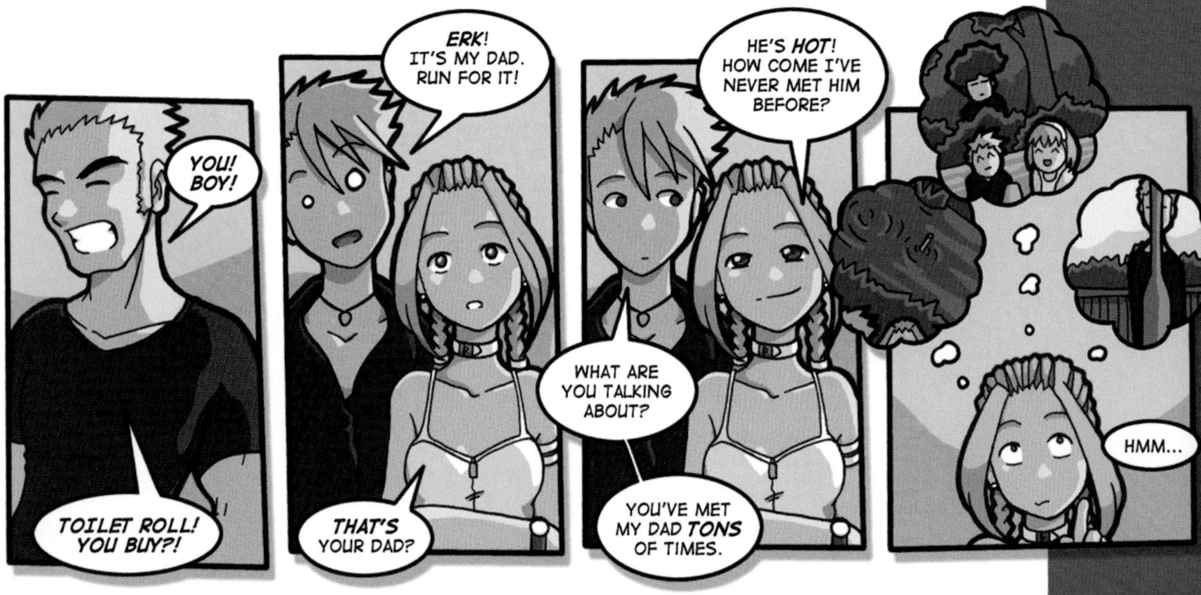
YOU! BOY!
TOILET ROLL! YOU BUY?!
ERK! IT'S MY DAD. RUN FOR IT!
THAT'S YOUR DAD?
HE'S **HOT**! HOW COME I'VE NEVER MET HIM BEFORE?
WHAT ARE YOU TALKING ABOUT?
YOU'VE MET MY DAD **TONS** OF TIMES.
HMM...

#28

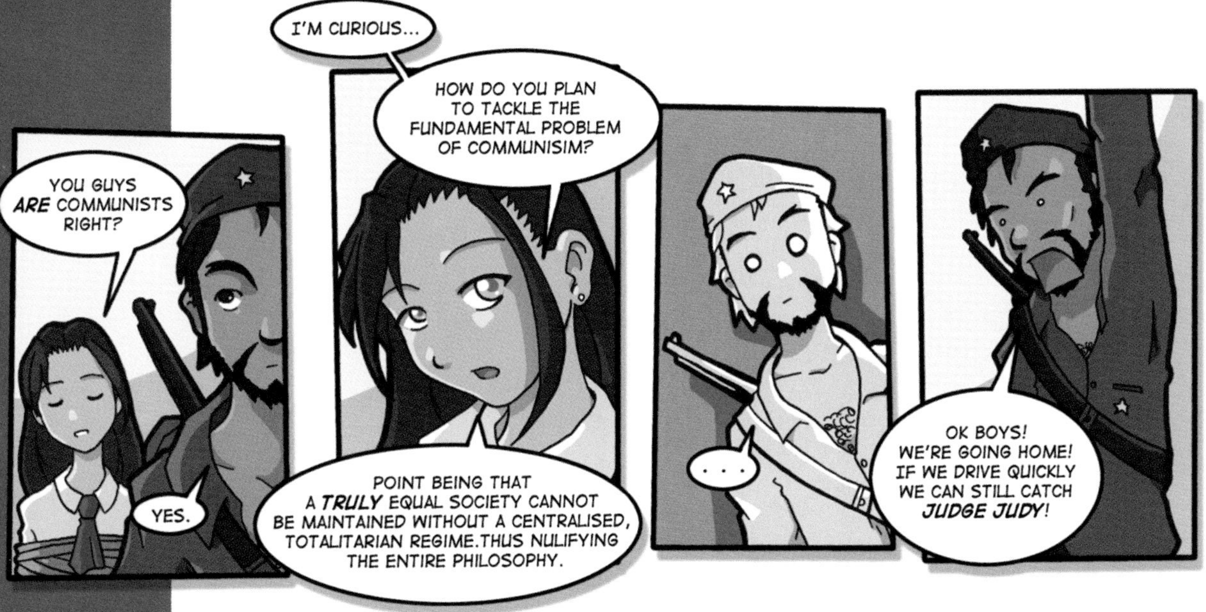
YOU GUYS **ARE** COMMUNISTS RIGHT?
YES.
I'M CURIOUS...
HOW DO YOU PLAN TO TACKLE THE FUNDAMENTAL PROBLEM OF COMMUNISIM?
POINT BEING THAT A ***TRULY*** EQUAL SOCIETY CANNOT BE MAINTAINED WITHOUT A CENTRALISED, TOTALITARIAN REGIME.THUS NULIFYING THE ENTIRE PHILOSOPHY.
...
OK BOYS! WE'RE GOING HOME! IF WE DRIVE QUICKLY WE CAN STILL CATCH ***JUDGE JUDY***!

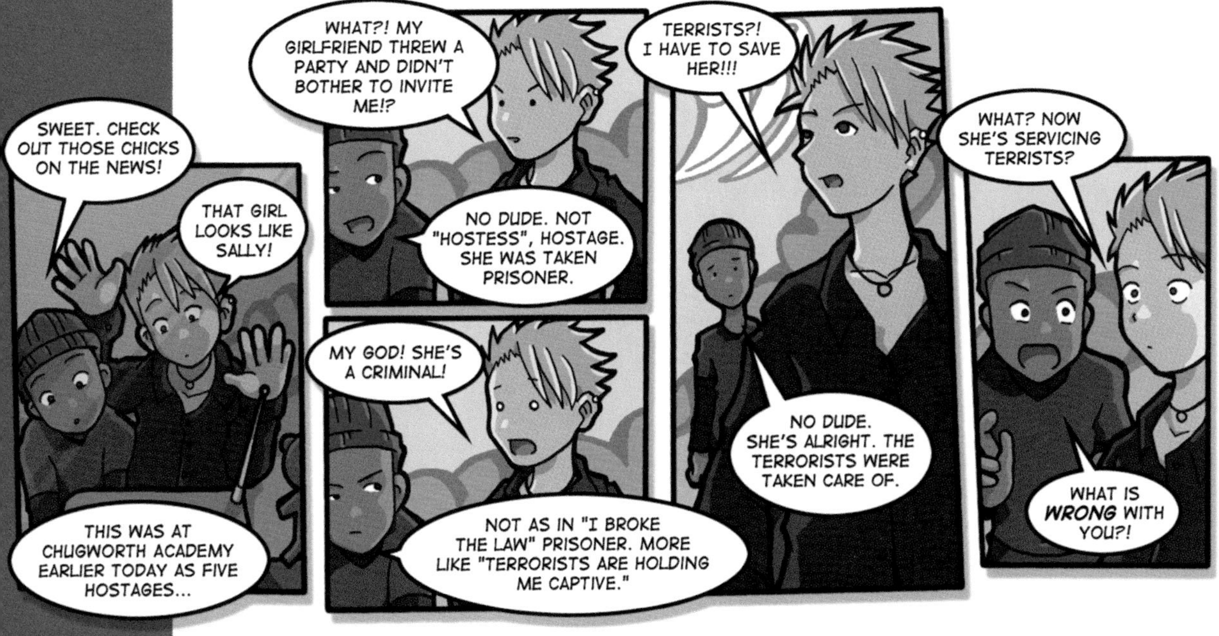
SWEET. CHECK OUT THOSE CHICKS ON THE NEWS!
THAT GIRL LOOKS LIKE SALLY!
THIS WAS AT CHUGWORTH ACADEMY EARLIER TODAY AS FIVE HOSTAGES...
WHAT?! MY GIRLFRIEND THREW A PARTY AND DIDN'T BOTHER TO INVITE ME!?
NO DUDE. NOT "HOSTESS", HOSTAGE. SHE WAS TAKEN PRISONER.
MY GOD! SHE'S A CRIMINAL!
NOT AS IN "I BROKE THE LAW" PRISONER. MORE LIKE "TERRORISTS ARE HOLDING ME CAPTIVE."
TERRISTS?! I HAVE TO SAVE HER!!!
NO DUDE. SHE'S ALRIGHT. THE TERRORISTS WERE TAKEN CARE OF.
WHAT? NOW SHE'S SERVICING TERRISTS?
WHAT IS **WRONG** WITH YOU?!

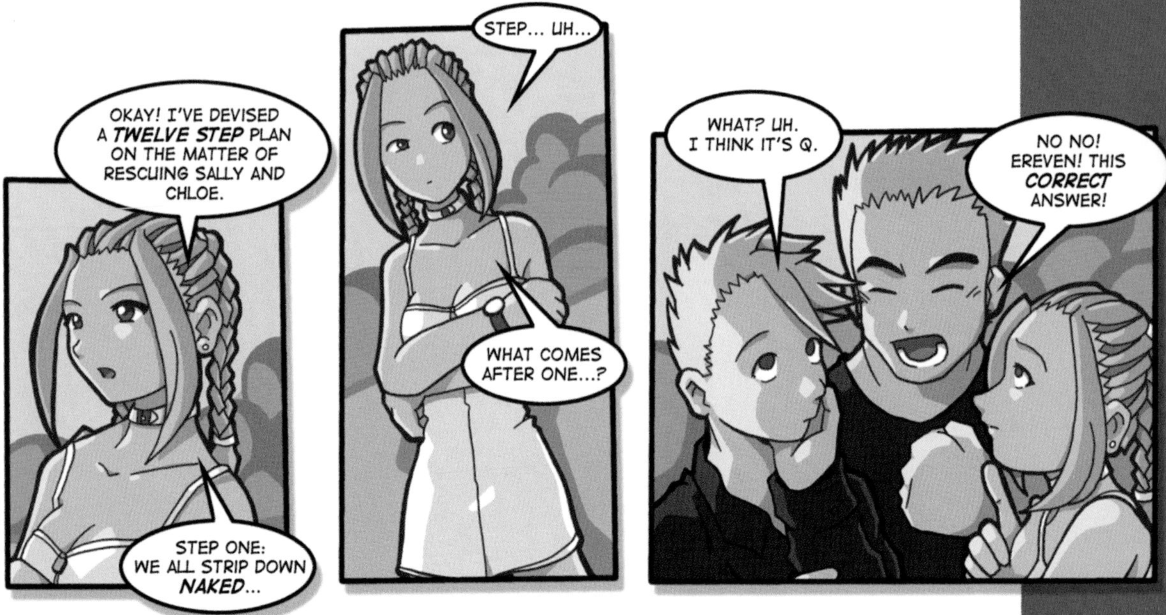
OKAY! I'VE DEVISED A **TWELVE STEP** PLAN ON THE MATTER OF RESCUING SALLY AND CHLOE.
STEP ONE: WE ALL STRIP DOWN **NAKED**...
STEP... UH...
WHAT COMES AFTER ONE...?
WHAT? UH. I THINK IT'S Q.
NO NO! EREVEN! THIS **CORRECT** ANSWER!

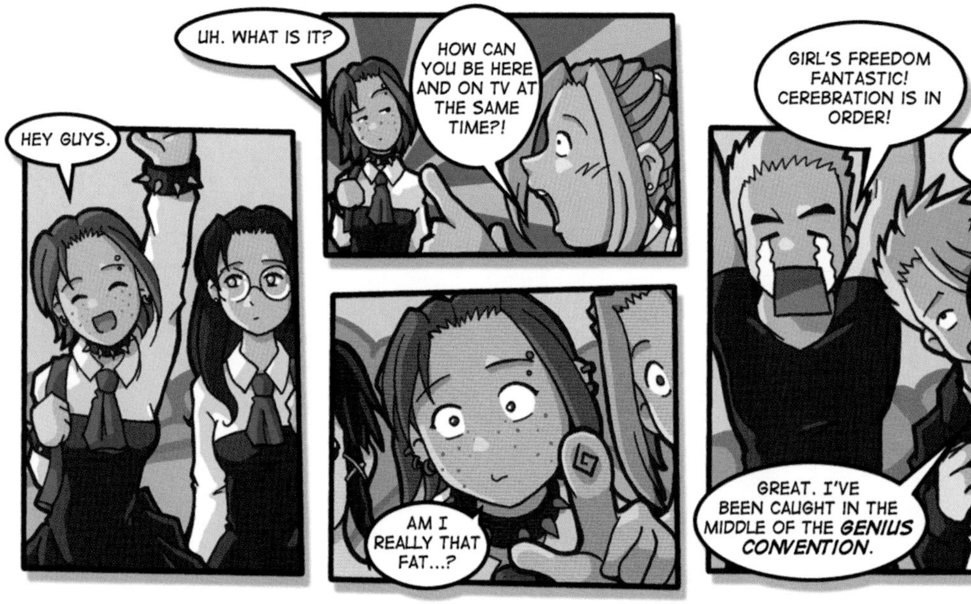
HEY GUYS.
UH. WHAT IS IT?
HOW CAN YOU BE HERE AND ON TV AT THE SAME TIME?!
AM I REALLY THAT FAT...?
GIRL'S FREEDOM FANTASTIC! CEREBRATION IS IN ORDER!
WELL IF IT ISN'T MY TERRORIST **WHORE** OF A GIRLFRIEND!
GREAT. I'VE BEEN CAUGHT IN THE MIDDLE OF THE ***GENIUS CONVENTION***.

#30

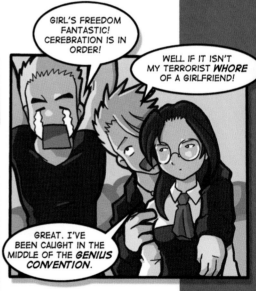

Splammo: The Movie!

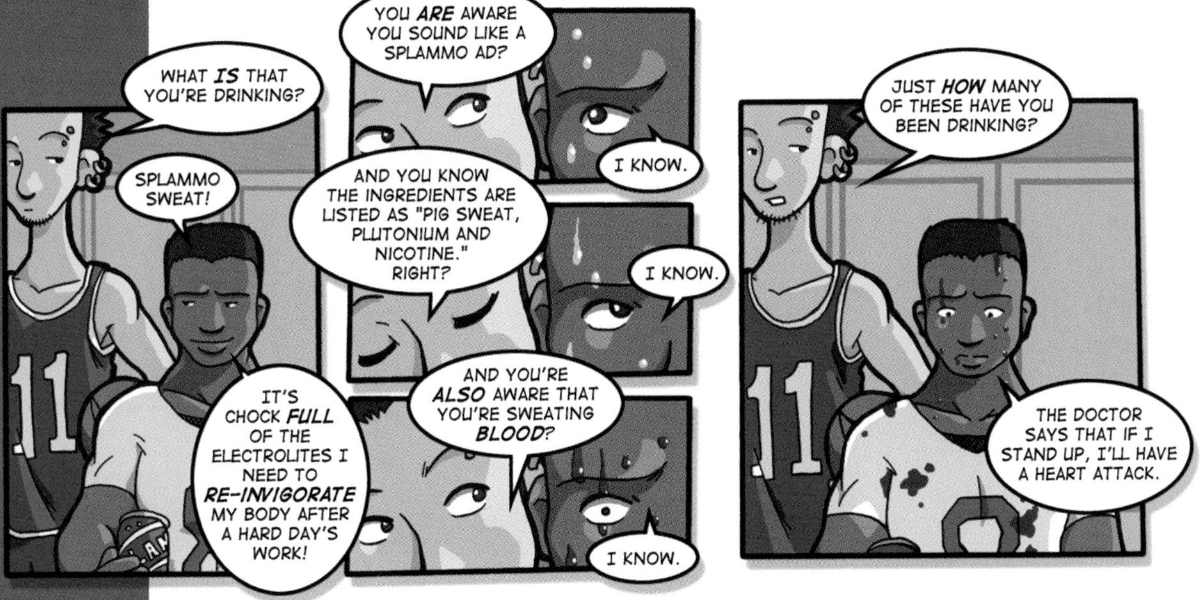
WHAT *IS* THAT YOU'RE DRINKING?
SPLAMMO SWEAT!
IT'S CHOCK *FULL* OF THE ELECTROLITES I NEED TO *RE-INVIGORATE* MY BODY AFTER A HARD DAY'S WORK!
YOU *ARE* AWARE YOU SOUND LIKE A SPLAMMO AD?
I KNOW.
AND YOU KNOW THE INGREDIENTS ARE LISTED AS "PIG SWEAT, PLUTONIUM AND NICOTINE." RIGHT?
I KNOW.
AND YOU'RE *ALSO* AWARE THAT YOU'RE SWEATING *BLOOD*?
I KNOW.
JUST *HOW* MANY OF THESE HAVE YOU BEEN DRINKING?
THE DOCTOR SAYS THAT IF I STAND UP, I'LL HAVE A HEART ATTACK.

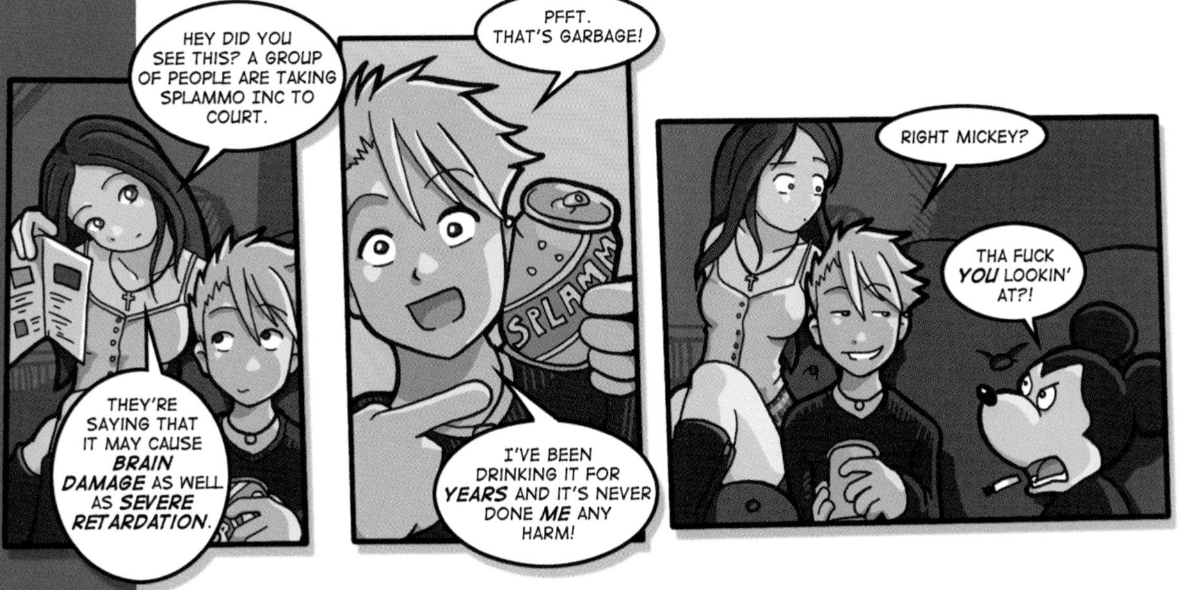
HEY DID YOU SEE THIS? A GROUP OF PEOPLE ARE TAKING SPLAMMO INC TO COURT.
THEY'RE SAYING THAT IT MAY CAUSE *BRAIN DAMAGE* AS WELL AS *SEVERE RETARDATION*.
PFFT. THAT'S GARBAGE!
I'VE BEEN DRINKING IT FOR *YEARS* AND IT'S NEVER DONE *ME* ANY HARM!
RIGHT MICKEY?
THA FUCK *YOU* LOOKIN' AT?!

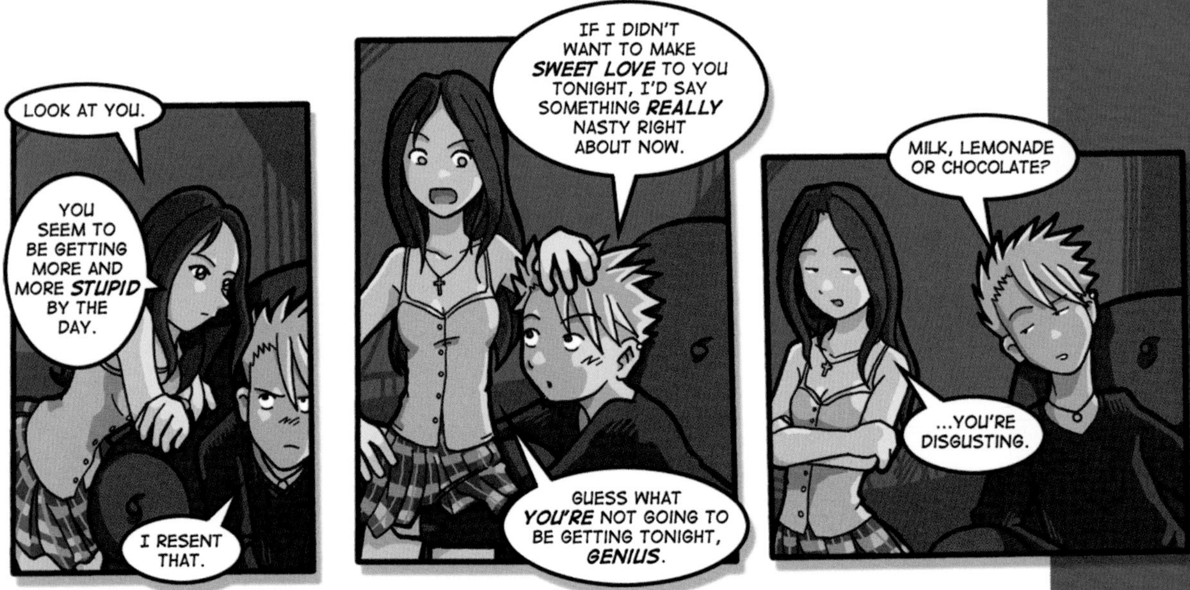
LOOK AT YOU.
YOU SEEM TO BE GETTING MORE AND MORE STUPID BY THE DAY.
I RESENT THAT.
IF I DIDN'T WANT TO MAKE SWEET LOVE TO YOU TONIGHT, I'D SAY SOMETHING REALLY NASTY RIGHT ABOUT NOW.
GUESS WHAT YOU'RE NOT GOING TO BE GETTING TONIGHT, GENIUS.
MILK, LEMONADE OR CHOCOLATE?
...YOU'RE DISGUSTING.

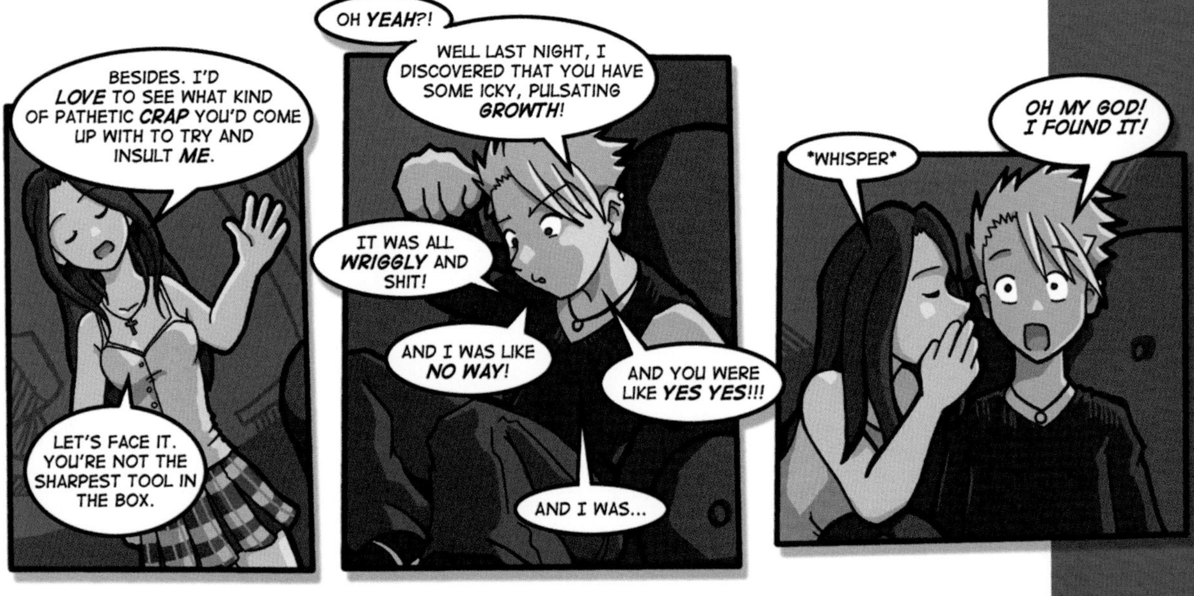
BESIDES. I'D LOVE TO SEE WHAT KIND OF PATHETIC CRAP YOU'D COME UP WITH TO TRY AND INSULT ME.
LET'S FACE IT. YOU'RE NOT THE SHARPEST TOOL IN THE BOX.
OH YEAH?!
WELL LAST NIGHT, I DISCOVERED THAT YOU HAVE SOME ICKY, PULSATING GROWTH!
IT WAS ALL WRIGGLY AND SHIT!
AND I WAS LIKE NO WAY!
AND YOU WERE LIKE YES YES!!!
AND I WAS...
WHISPER
OH MY GOD! I FOUND IT!

#32

I THINK YOU SHOULD GET A NEW JOB.
WHY?
WELL THINK ABOUT IT.
THE BACKLASH FROM ALL THIS IS GOING AFFECT *YOU* MORE THAN YOUR BOSSES.
WHY?
COS YOU'RE THE GUY IN THE ADS.
WHY?
BECAUSE THEY HIRED YOU?
WHY?
WHY?
BECAUSE!
KRUGE KILLED KIRK'S SON. HIS *SON* FOR FUCK'S SAKE!
AAAAAH...
I STILL DON'T GET IT...
GRRR...

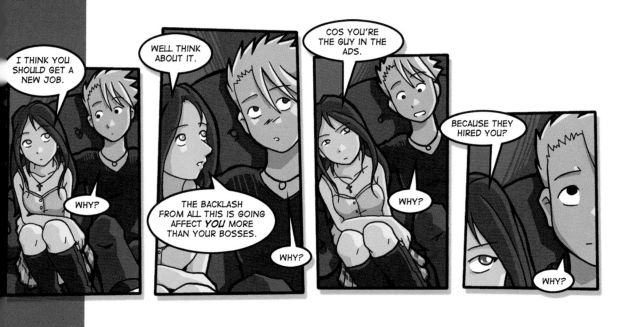

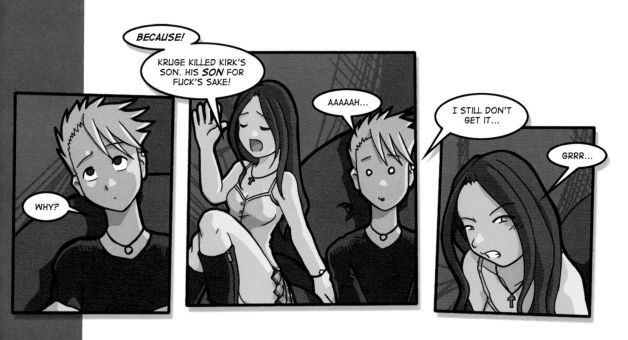

#33

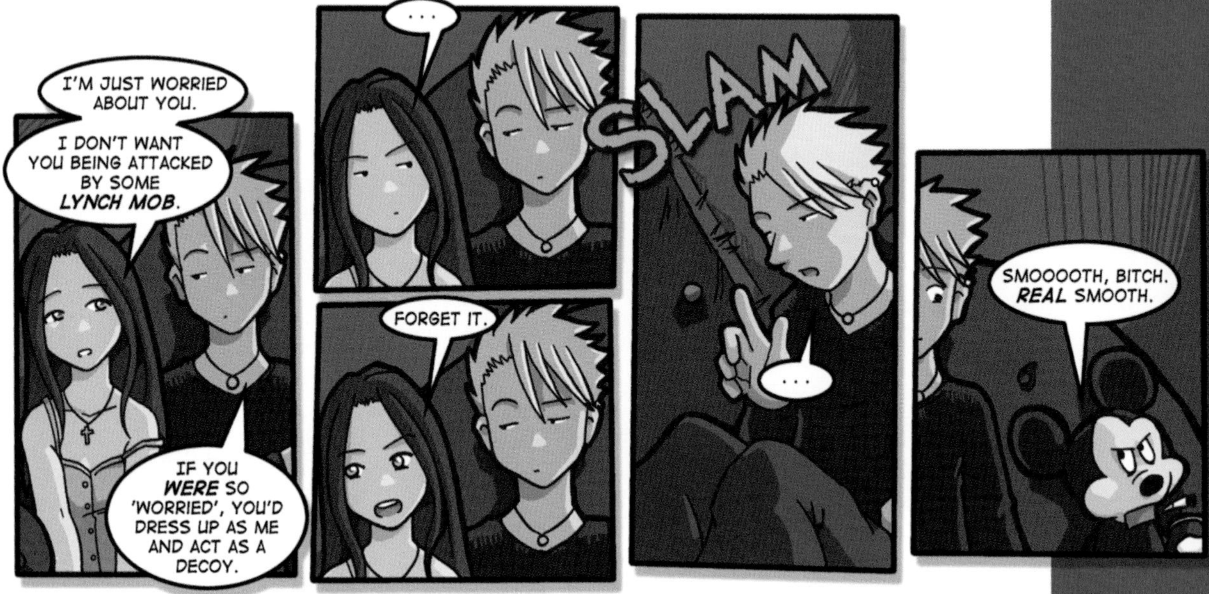
I'M JUST WORRIED ABOUT YOU.
I DON'T WANT YOU BEING ATTACKED BY SOME LYNCH MOB.
IF YOU WERE SO 'WORRIED', YOU'D DRESS UP AS ME AND ACT AS A DECOY.
. . .
FORGET IT.
SLAM
. . .
SMOOOOTH, BITCH. REAL SMOOTH.

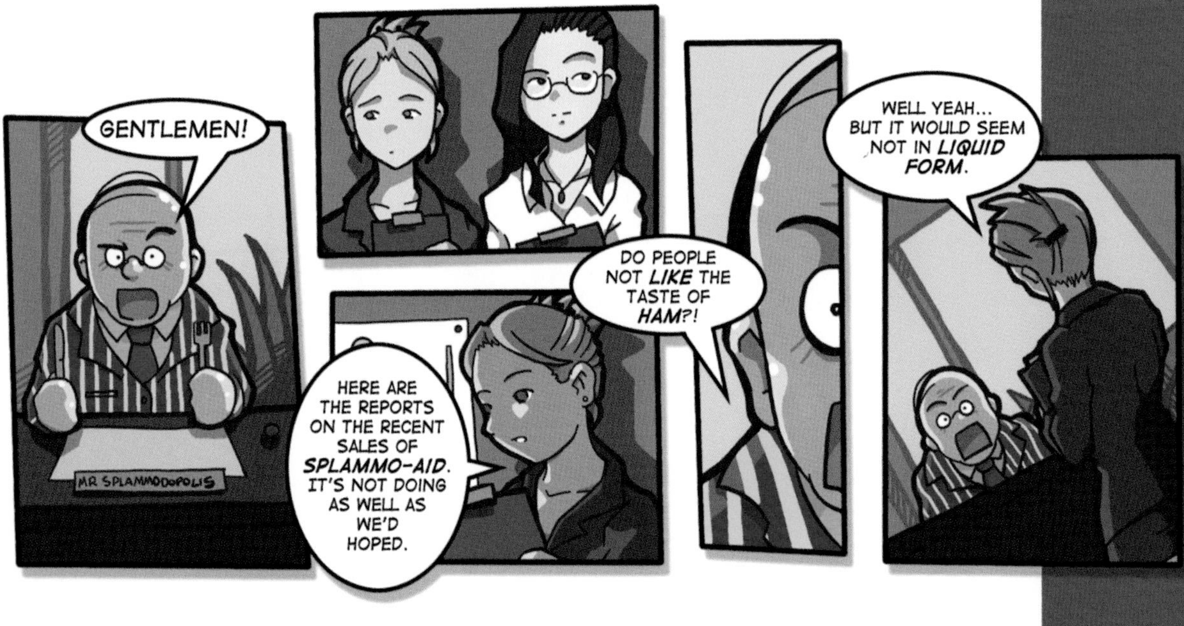
GENTLEMEN!
HERE ARE THE REPORTS ON THE RECENT SALES OF SPLAMMO-AID. IT'S NOT DOING AS WELL AS WE'D HOPED.
MR SPLAMMODOPOLIS
DO PEOPLE NOT LIKE THE TASTE OF HAM?!
WELL YEAH... BUT IT WOULD SEEM NOT IN LIQUID FORM.

#34

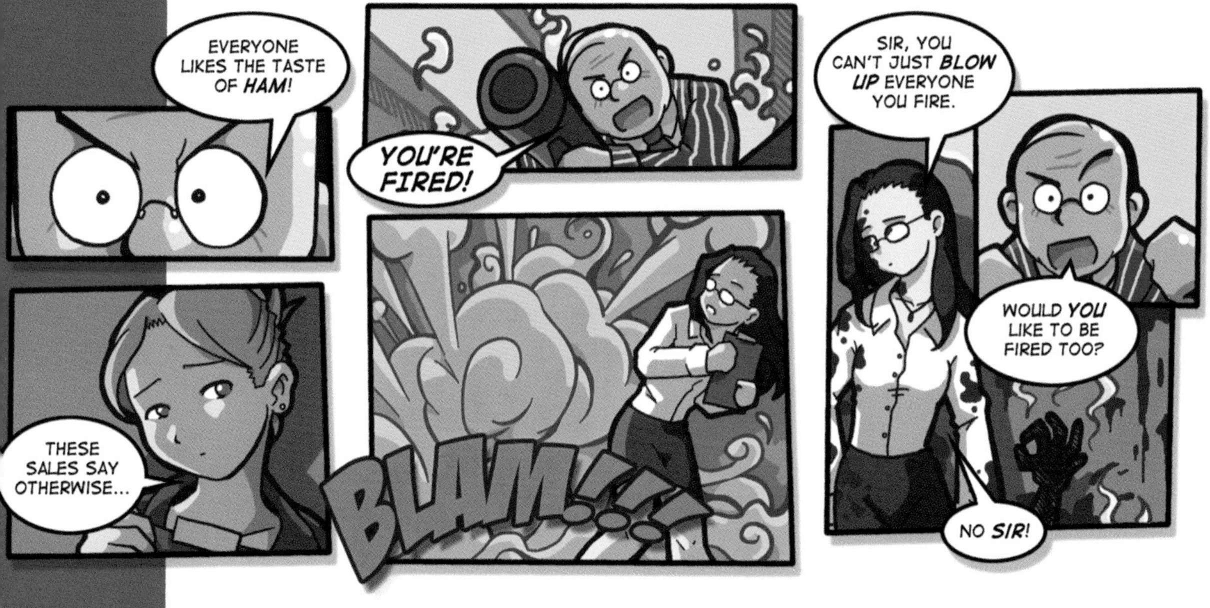
EVERYONE LIKES THE TASTE OF **HAM**!
THESE SALES SAY OTHERWISE...
YOU'RE FIRED!
BLAM...!
SIR, YOU CAN'T JUST **BLOW UP** EVERYONE YOU FIRE.
WOULD **YOU** LIKE TO BE FIRED TOO?
NO **SIR**!

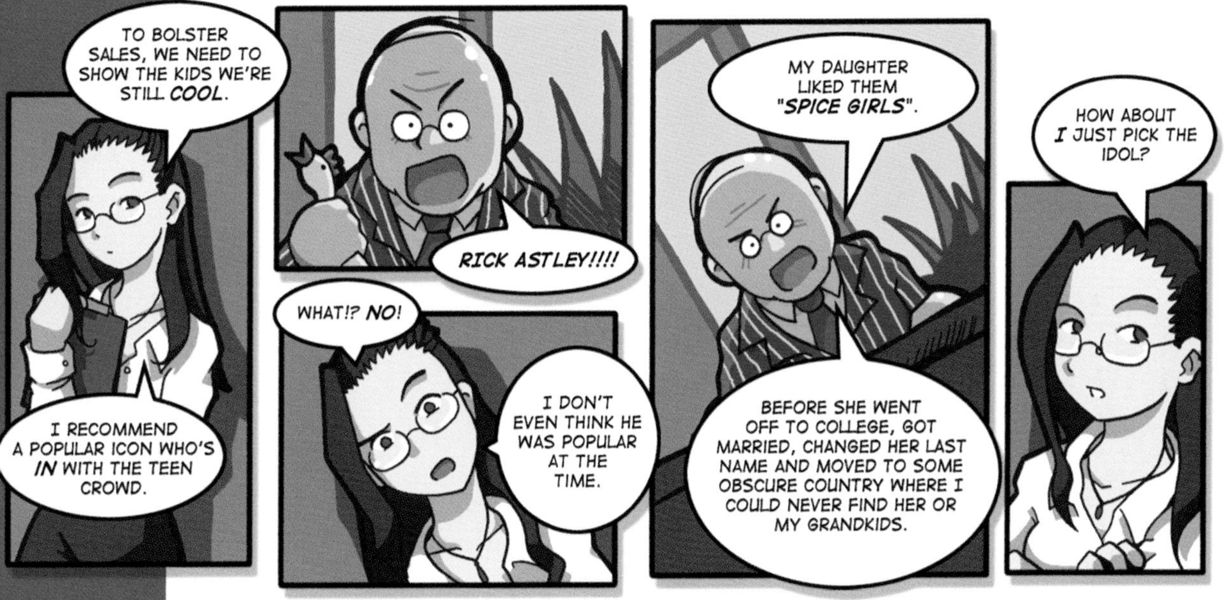
TO BOLSTER SALES, WE NEED TO SHOW THE KIDS WE'RE STILL **COOL**.
I RECOMMEND A POPULAR ICON WHO'S **IN** WITH THE TEEN CROWD.
RICK ASTLEY!!!!
WHAT!? **NO**!
I DON'T EVEN THINK HE WAS POPULAR AT THE TIME.
MY DAUGHTER LIKED THEM "**SPICE GIRLS**".
BEFORE SHE WENT OFF TO COLLEGE, GOT MARRIED, CHANGED HER LAST NAME AND MOVED TO SOME OBSCURE COUNTRY WHERE I COULD NEVER FIND HER OR MY GRANDKIDS.
HOW ABOUT **I** JUST PICK THE IDOL?

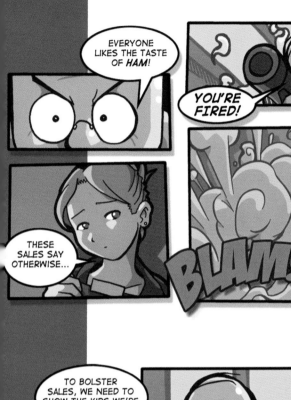

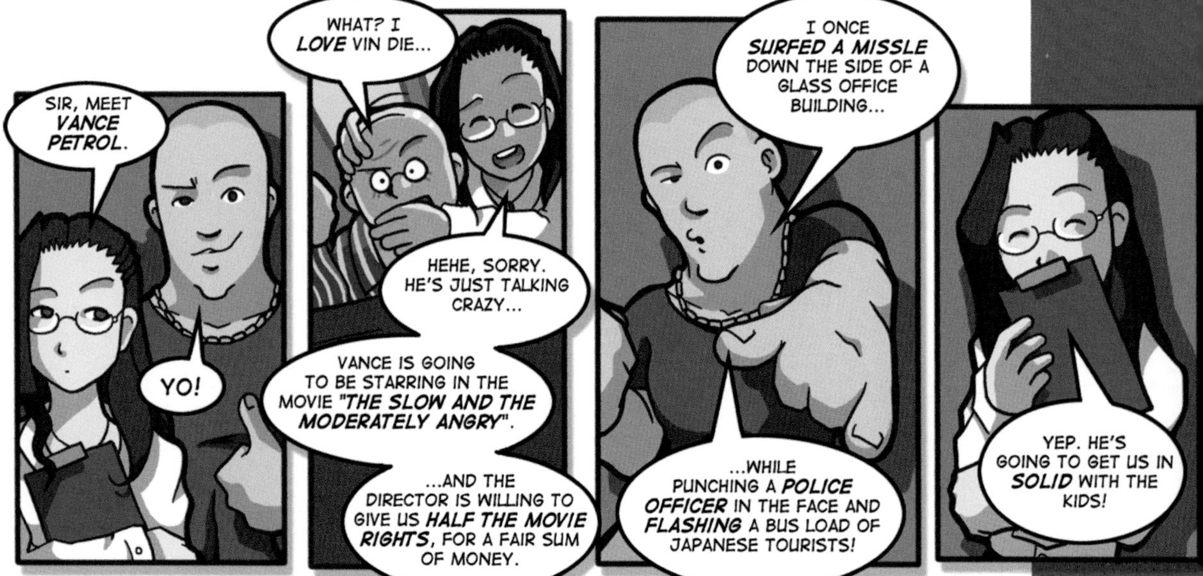
SIR, MEET VANCE PETROL.
YO!
WHAT? I LOVE VIN DIE...
HEHE, SORRY. HE'S JUST TALKING CRAZY...
VANCE IS GOING TO BE STARRING IN THE MOVIE "THE SLOW AND THE MODERATELY ANGRY".
...AND THE DIRECTOR IS WILLING TO GIVE US HALF THE MOVIE RIGHTS, FOR A FAIR SUM OF MONEY.
I ONCE SURFED A MISSLE DOWN THE SIDE OF A GLASS OFFICE BUILDING...
...WHILE PUNCHING A POLICE OFFICER IN THE FACE AND FLASHING A BUS LOAD OF JAPANESE TOURISTS!
YEP. HE'S GOING TO GET US IN SOLID WITH THE KIDS!

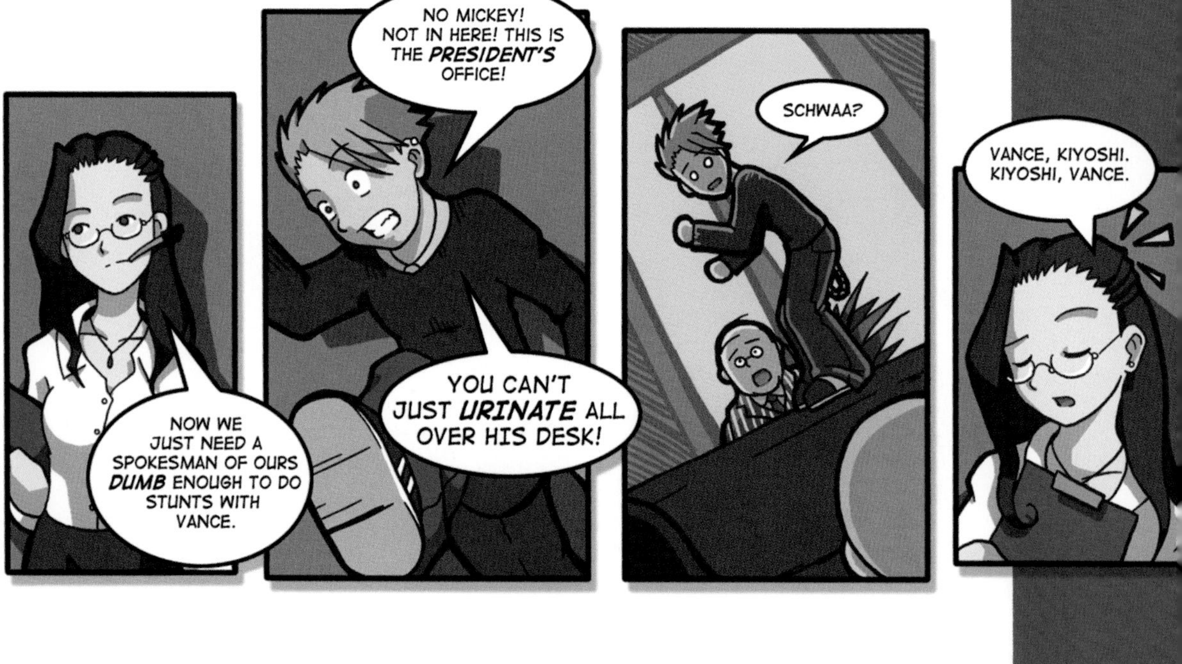
NOW WE JUST NEED A SPOKESMAN OF OURS DUMB ENOUGH TO DO STUNTS WITH VANCE.
NO MICKEY! NOT IN HERE! THIS IS THE PRESIDENT'S OFFICE!
YOU CAN'T JUST URINATE ALL OVER HIS DESK!
SCHWAA?
VANCE, KIYOSHI. KIYOSHI, VANCE.

#36

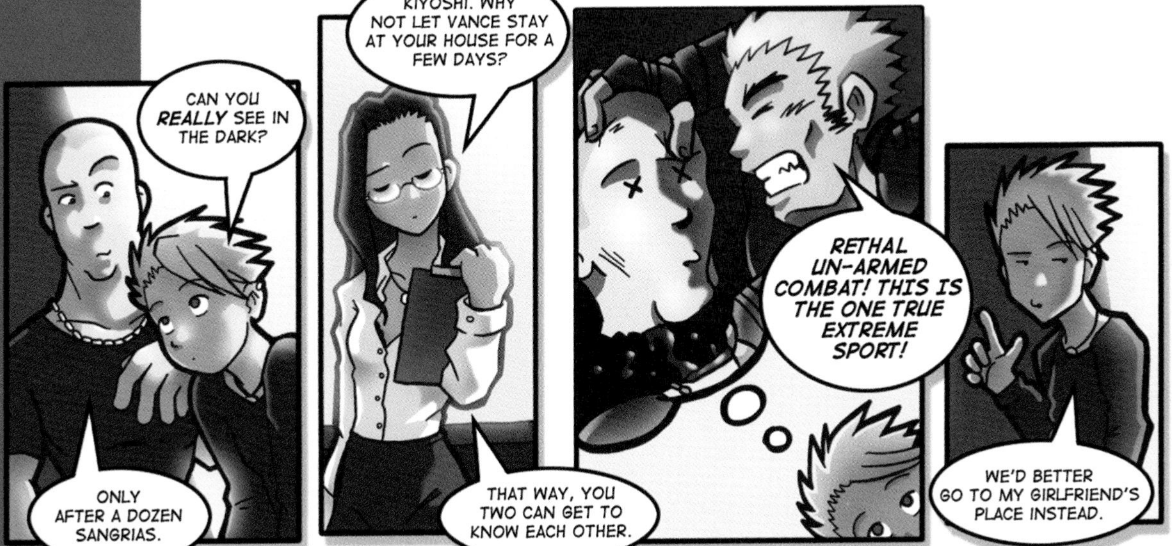
CAN YOU REALLY SEE IN THE DARK?
ONLY AFTER A DOZEN SANGRIAS.
KIYOSHI. WHY NOT LET VANCE STAY AT YOUR HOUSE FOR A FEW DAYS?
THAT WAY, YOU TWO CAN GET TO KNOW EACH OTHER.
RETHAL UN-ARMED COMBAT! THIS IS THE ONE TRUE EXTREME SPORT!
WE'D BETTER GO TO MY GIRLFRIEND'S PLACE INSTEAD.

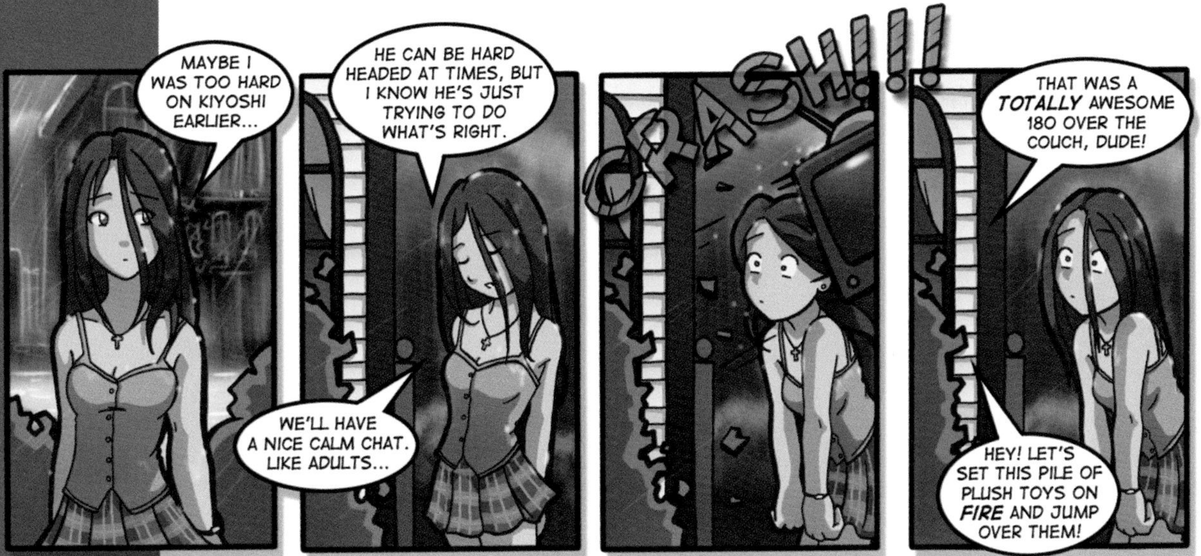
MAYBE I WAS TOO HARD ON KIYOSHI EARLIER...
HE CAN BE HARD HEADED AT TIMES, BUT I KNOW HE'S JUST TRYING TO DO WHAT'S RIGHT.
WE'LL HAVE A NICE CALM CHAT. LIKE ADULTS...
CRASH!!!
THAT WAS A TOTALLY AWESOME 180 OVER THE COUCH, DUDE!
HEY! LET'S SET THIS PILE OF PLUSH TOYS ON FIRE AND JUMP OVER THEM!

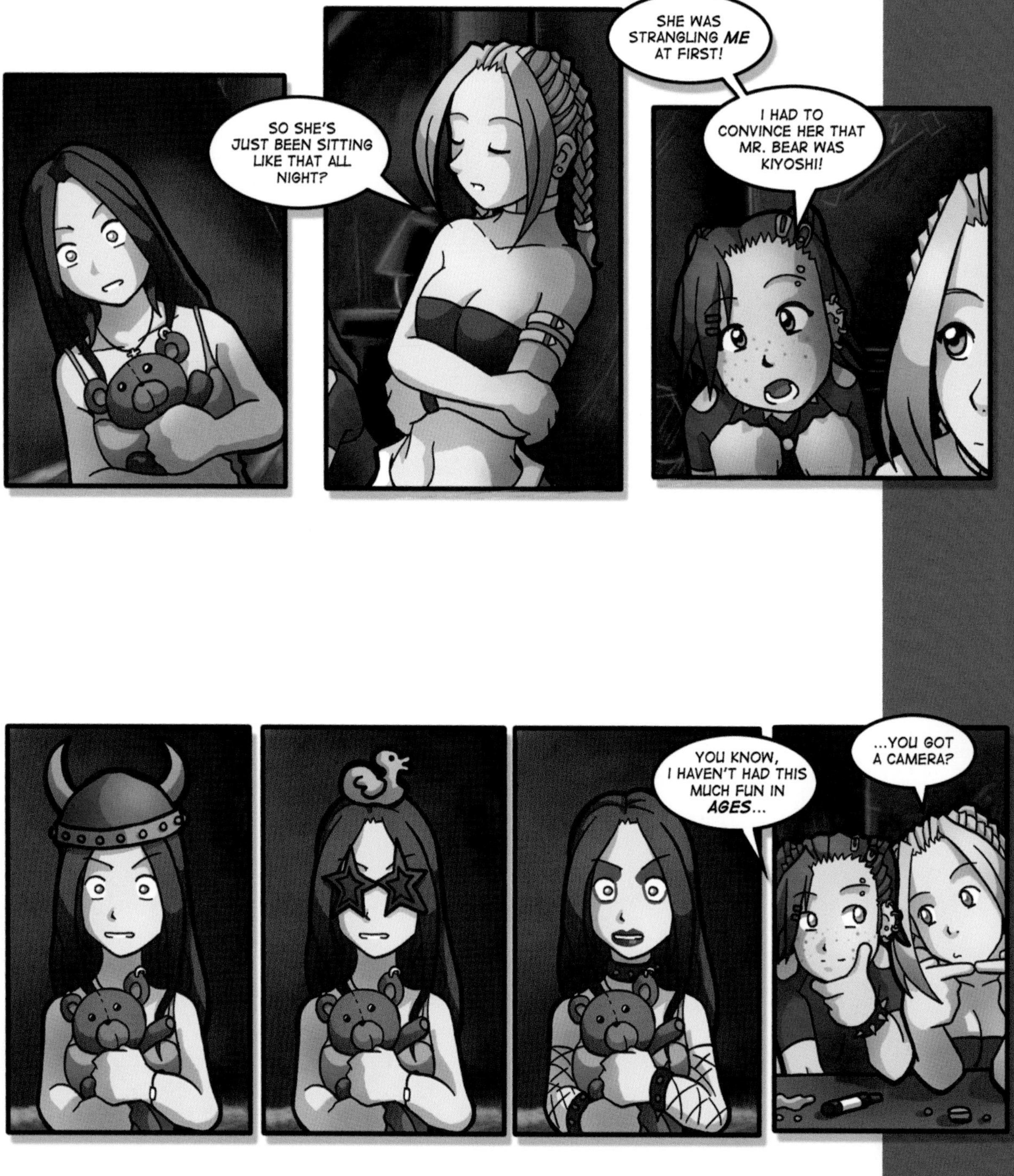
SO SHE'S JUST BEEN SITTING LIKE THAT ALL NIGHT?
SHE WAS STRANGLING *ME* AT FIRST!
I HAD TO CONVINCE HER THAT MR. BEAR WAS KIYOSHI!
YOU KNOW, I HAVEN'T HAD THIS MUCH FUN IN *AGES*...
...YOU GOT A CAMERA?

#38

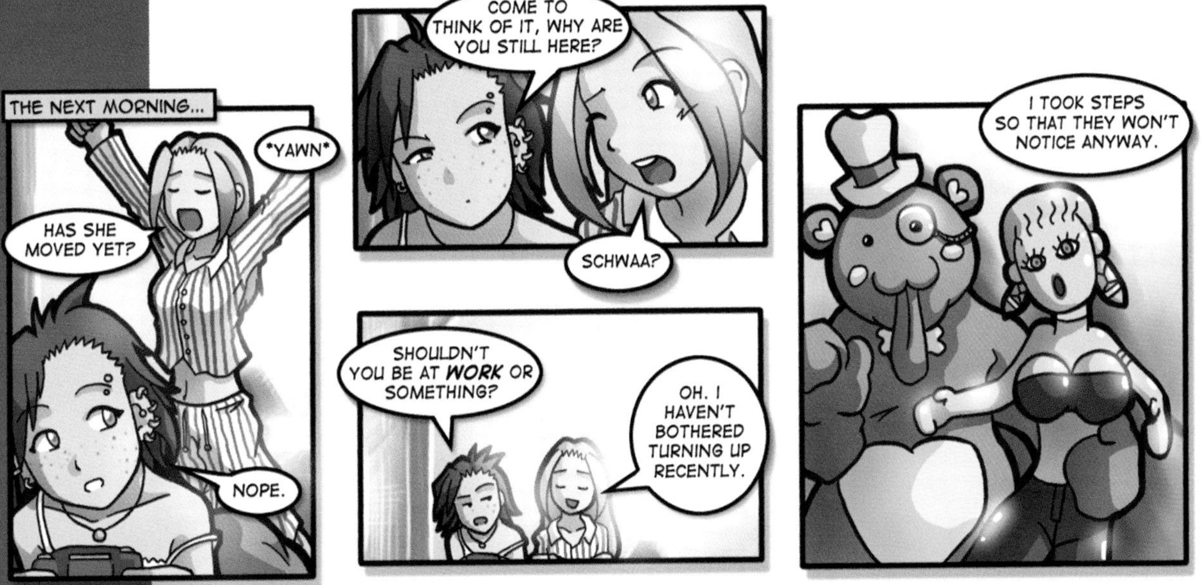
THE NEXT MORNING...
YAWN
HAS SHE MOVED YET?
NOPE.
COME TO THINK OF IT, WHY ARE YOU STILL HERE?
SCHWAA?
SHOULDN'T YOU BE AT WORK OR SOMETHING?
OH. I HAVEN'T BOTHERED TURNING UP RECENTLY.
I TOOK STEPS SO THAT THEY WON'T NOTICE ANYWAY.

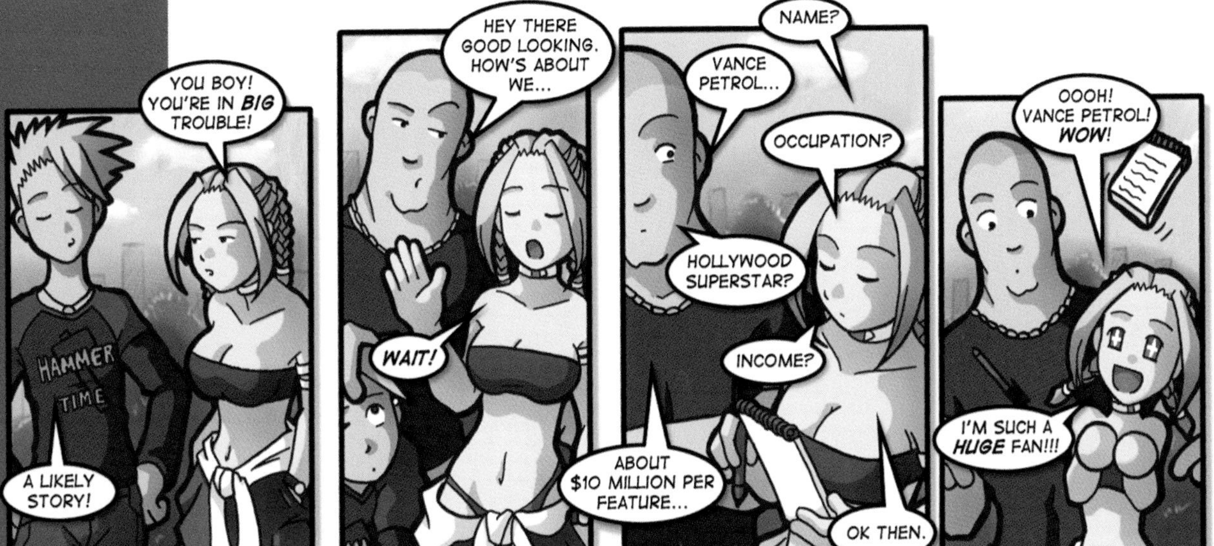
YOU BOY! YOU'RE IN BIG TROUBLE!
HAMMER TIME
A LIKELY STORY!
HEY THERE GOOD LOOKING. HOW'S ABOUT WE...
WAIT!
NAME?
VANCE PETROL...
OCCUPATION?
HOLLYWOOD SUPERSTAR?
INCOME?
ABOUT $10 MILLION PER FEATURE...
OK THEN.
OOOH! VANCE PETROL! WOW!
I'M SUCH A HUGE FAN!!!

#39

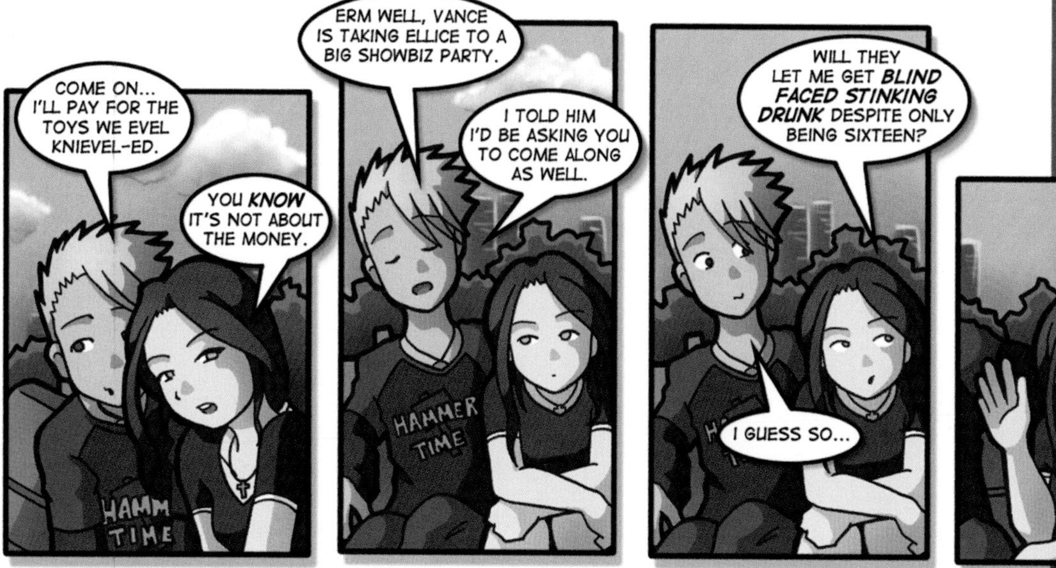
COME ON... I'LL PAY FOR THE TOYS WE EVEL KNIEVEL-ED.
YOU **KNOW** IT'S NOT ABOUT THE MONEY.
ERM WELL, VANCE IS TAKING ELLICE TO A BIG SHOWBIZ PARTY.
I TOLD HIM I'D BE ASKING YOU TO COME ALONG AS WELL.
HAMMER TIME
WILL THEY LET ME GET ***BLIND FACED STINKING DRUNK*** DESPITE ONLY BEING SIXTEEN?
I GUESS SO...
OKAY, I'M SOLD.

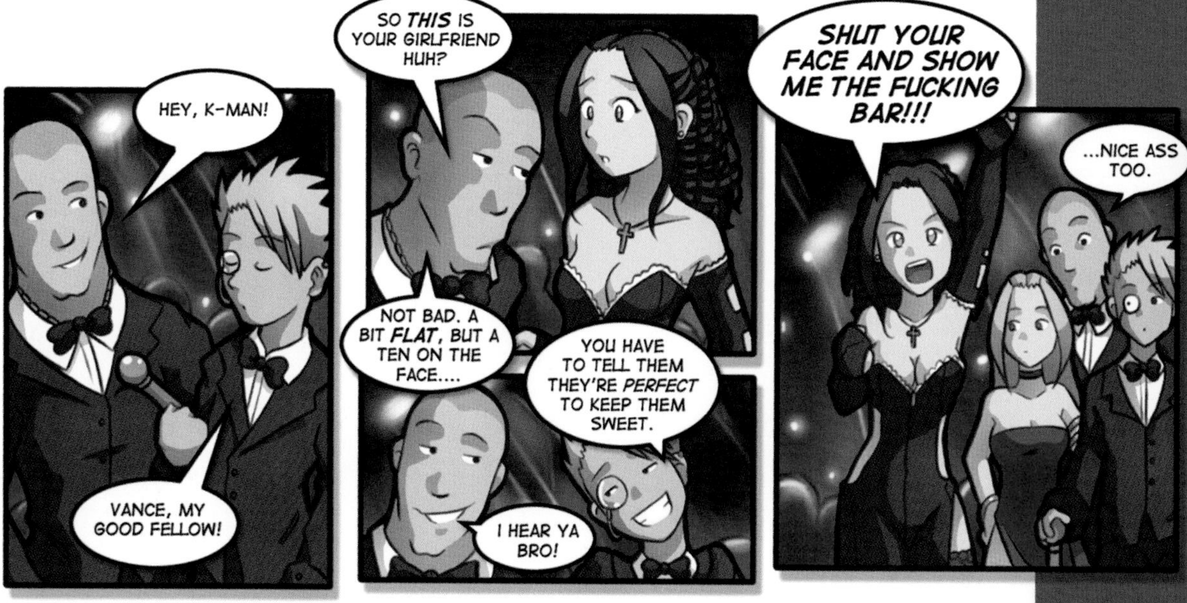
HEY, K-MAN!
VANCE, MY GOOD FELLOW!
SO ***THIS*** IS YOUR GIRLFRIEND HUH?
NOT BAD. A BIT ***FLAT***, BUT A TEN ON THE FACE....
YOU HAVE TO TELL THEM THEY'RE *PERFECT* TO KEEP THEM SWEET.
I HEAR YA BRO!
SHUT YOUR FACE AND SHOW ME THE FUCKING BAR!!!
...NICE ASS TOO.

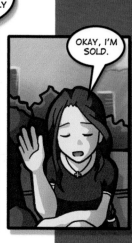

#40

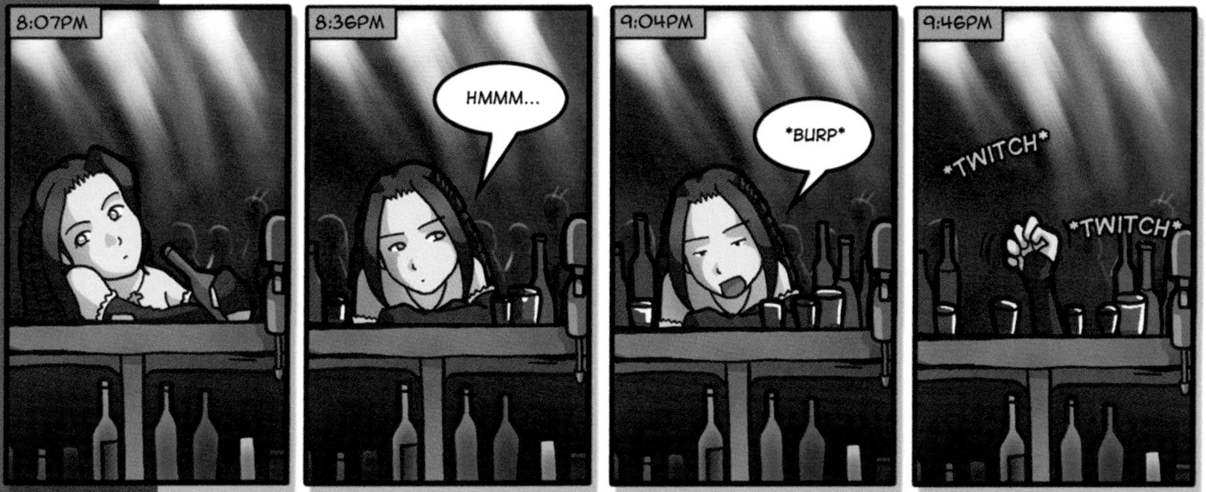
8:07PM
8:36PM
HMMM...
9:04PM
BURP
9:46PM
TWITCH
TWITCH

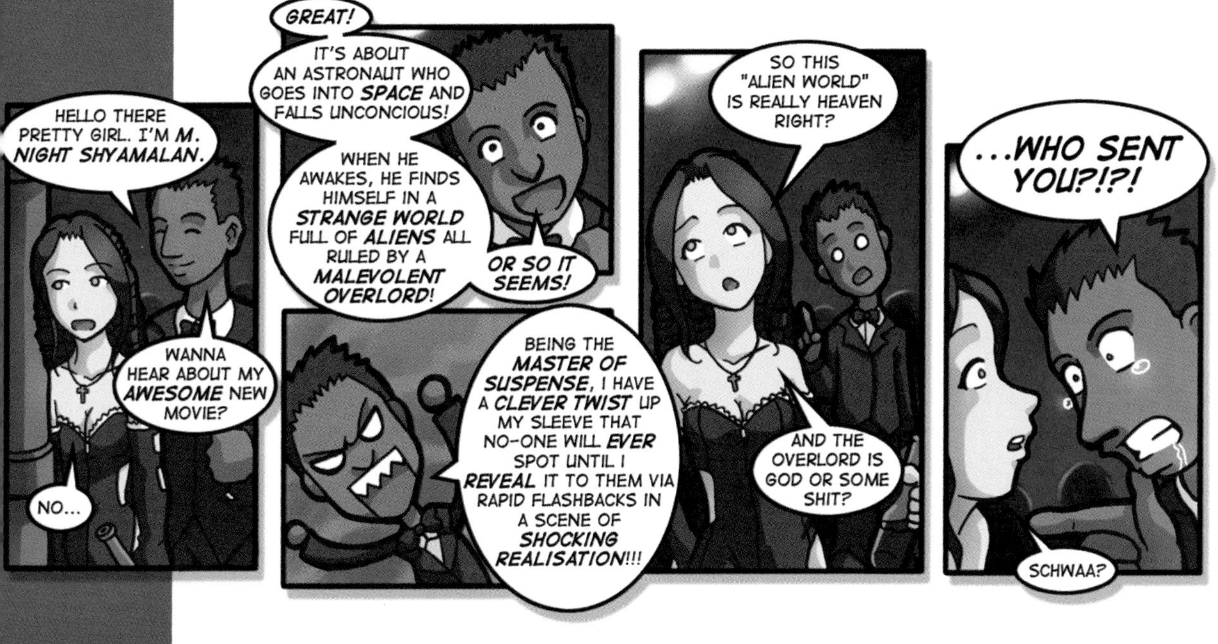
HELLO THERE PRETTY GIRL. I'M M. NIGHT SHYAMALAN.
WANNA HEAR ABOUT MY AWESOME NEW MOVIE?
NO...
GREAT!
IT'S ABOUT AN ASTRONAUT WHO GOES INTO SPACE AND FALLS UNCONCIOUS!
WHEN HE AWAKES, HE FINDS HIMSELF IN A STRANGE WORLD FULL OF ALIENS ALL RULED BY A MALEVOLENT OVERLORD!
OR SO IT SEEMS!
BEING THE MASTER OF SUSPENSE, I HAVE A CLEVER TWIST UP MY SLEEVE THAT NO-ONE WILL EVER SPOT UNTIL I REVEAL IT TO THEM VIA RAPID FLASHBACKS IN A SCENE OF SHOCKING REALISATION!!!
SO THIS "ALIEN WORLD" IS REALLY HEAVEN RIGHT?
AND THE OVERLORD IS GOD OR SOME SHIT?
...WHO SENT YOU?!?!
SCHWAA?

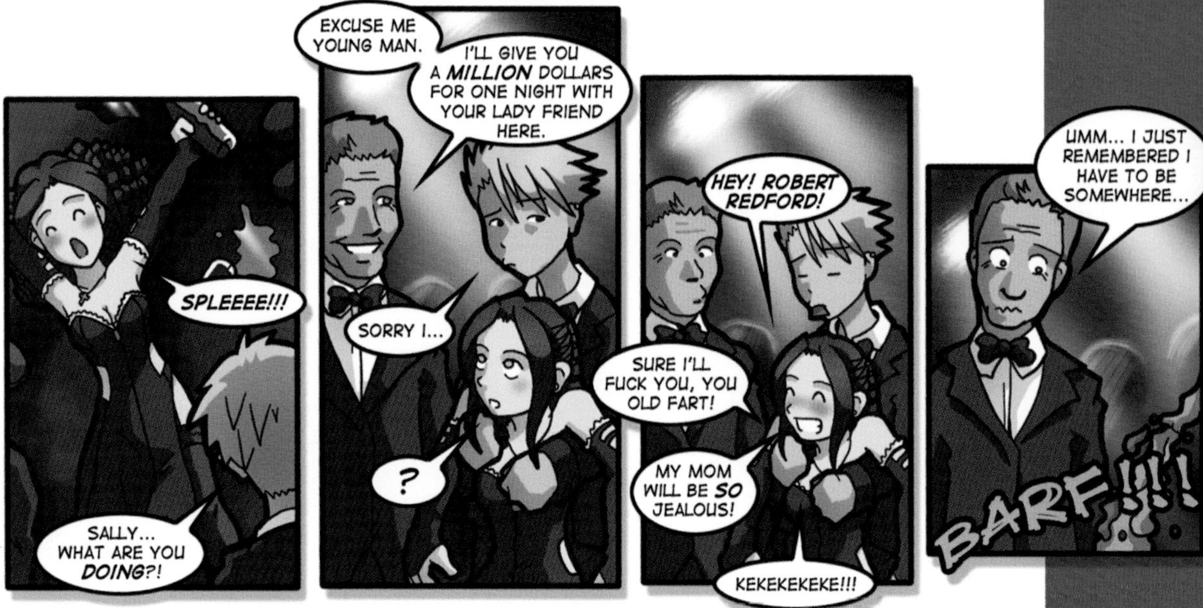
SPLEEEE!!!
SALLY... WHAT ARE YOU DOING?!
EXCUSE ME YOUNG MAN.
I'LL GIVE YOU A MILLION DOLLARS FOR ONE NIGHT WITH YOUR LADY FRIEND HERE.
SORRY I...
?
HEY! ROBERT REDFORD!
SURE I'LL FUCK YOU, YOU OLD FART!
MY MOM WILL BE SO JEALOUS!
KEKEKEKEKE!!!
UMM... I JUST REMEMBERED I HAVE TO BE SOMEWHERE...
BARF!!!!

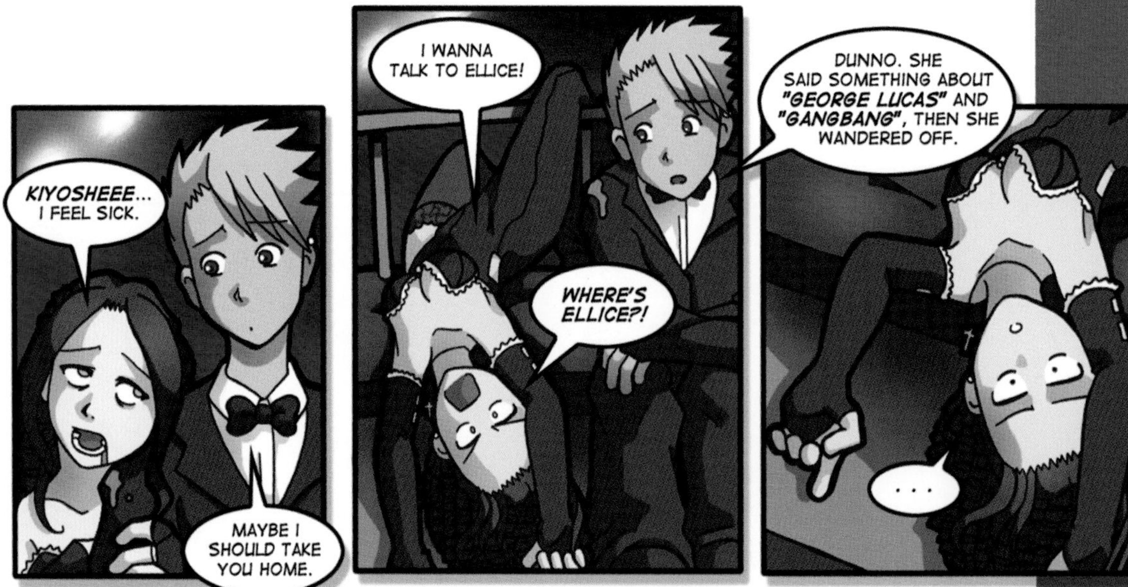
KIYOSHEEE... I FEEL SICK.
MAYBE I SHOULD TAKE YOU HOME.
I WANNA TALK TO ELLICE!
WHERE'S ELLICE?!
DUNNO. SHE SAID SOMETHING ABOUT "GEORGE LUCAS" AND "GANGBANG", THEN SHE WANDERED OFF.
. . .

#42

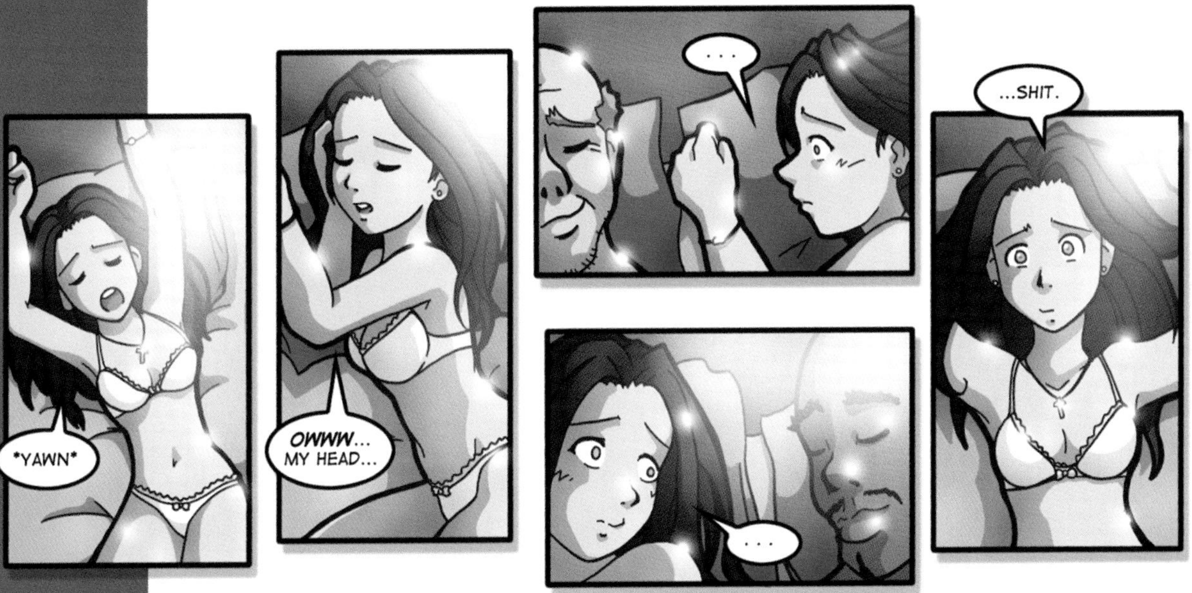
YAWN
OWWW... MY HEAD...
. . .
. . .
...SHIT.

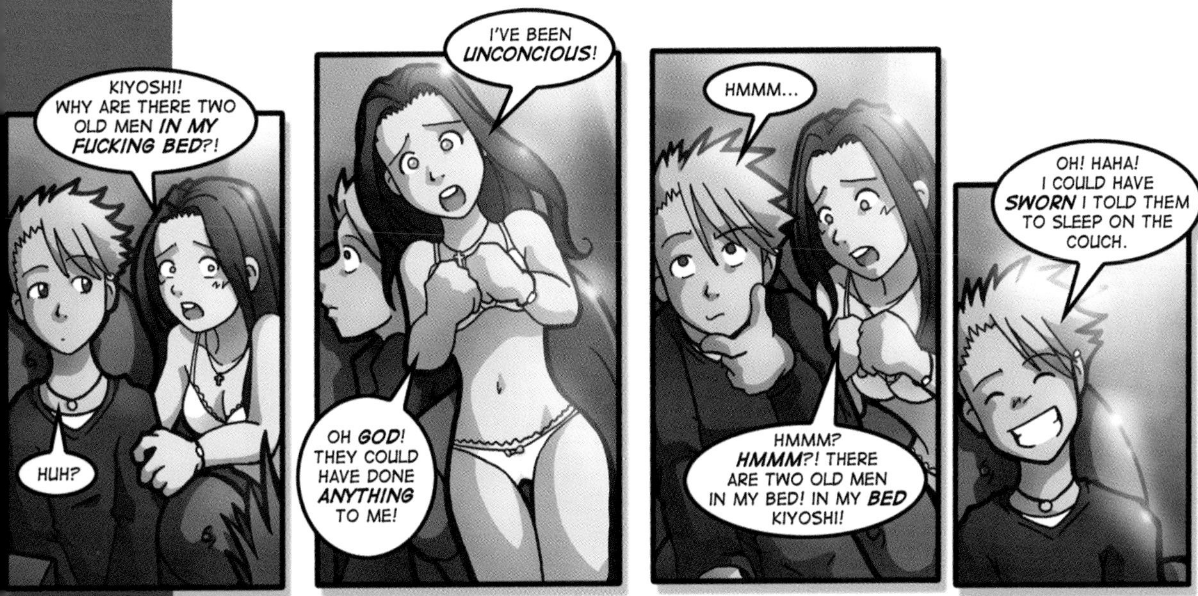
KIYOSHI! WHY ARE THERE TWO OLD MEN IN MY FUCKING BED?!
HUH?
I'VE BEEN UNCONCIOUS!
OH GOD! THEY COULD HAVE DONE ANYTHING TO ME!
HMMM...
HMMM? HMMM?! THERE ARE TWO OLD MEN IN MY BED! IN MY BED KIYOSHI!
OH! HAHA! I COULD HAVE SWORN I TOLD THEM TO SLEEP ON THE COUCH.

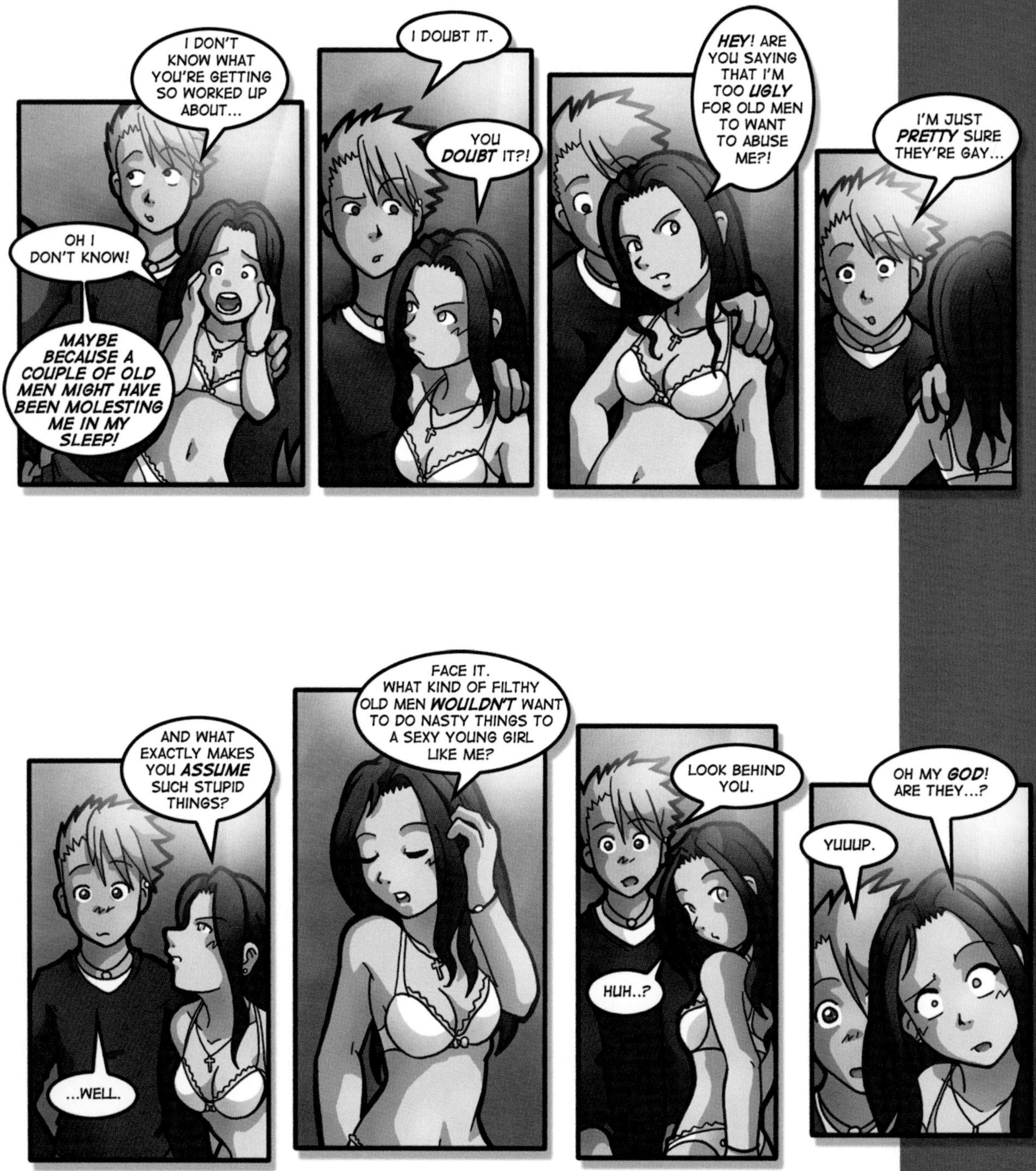
I DON'T KNOW WHAT YOU'RE GETTING SO WORKED UP ABOUT...
OH I DON'T KNOW!
MAYBE BECAUSE A COUPLE OF OLD MEN MIGHT HAVE BEEN MOLESTING ME IN MY SLEEP!
I DOUBT IT.
YOU DOUBT IT?!
HEY! ARE YOU SAYING THAT I'M TOO UGLY FOR OLD MEN TO WANT TO ABUSE ME?!
I'M JUST PRETTY SURE THEY'RE GAY...
AND WHAT EXACTLY MAKES YOU ASSUME SUCH STUPID THINGS?
...WELL.
FACE IT. WHAT KIND OF FILTHY OLD MEN WOULDN'T WANT TO DO NASTY THINGS TO A SEXY YOUNG GIRL LIKE ME?
LOOK BEHIND YOU.
HUH..?
OH MY GOD! ARE THEY...?
YUUUP.

#44

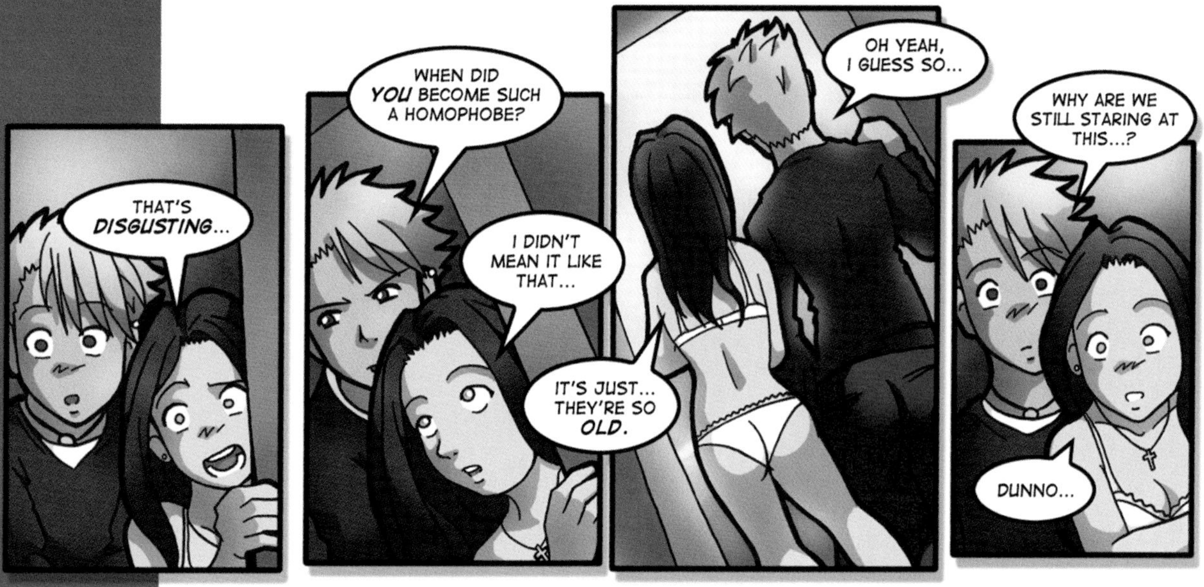
THAT'S *DISGUSTING*...
WHEN DID *YOU* BECOME SUCH A HOMOPHOBE?
I DIDN'T MEAN IT LIKE THAT...
IT'S JUST... THEY'RE SO *OLD*.
OH YEAH, I GUESS SO...
WHY ARE WE STILL STARING AT THIS...?
DUNNO...

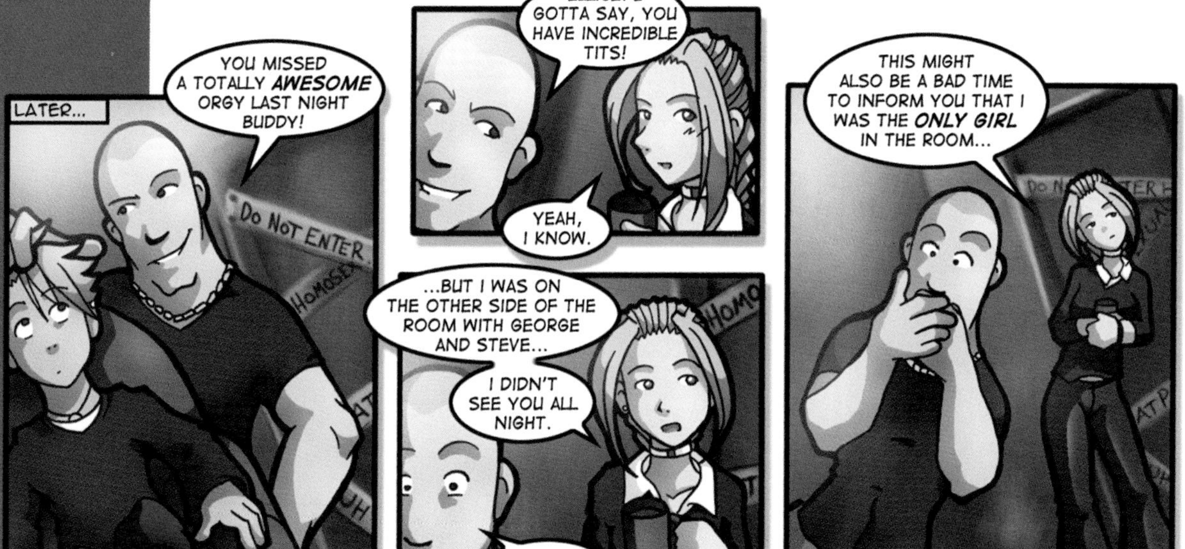
LATER...
YOU MISSED A TOTALLY *AWESOME* ORGY LAST NIGHT BUDDY!
DO NOT ENTER.
ELLICE. I GOTTA SAY, YOU HAVE INCREDIBLE TITS!
YEAH, I KNOW.
...BUT I WAS ON THE OTHER SIDE OF THE ROOM WITH GEORGE AND STEVE...
I DIDN'T SEE YOU ALL NIGHT.
...WHAT?
THIS MIGHT ALSO BE A BAD TIME TO INFORM YOU THAT I WAS THE *ONLY GIRL* IN THE ROOM...

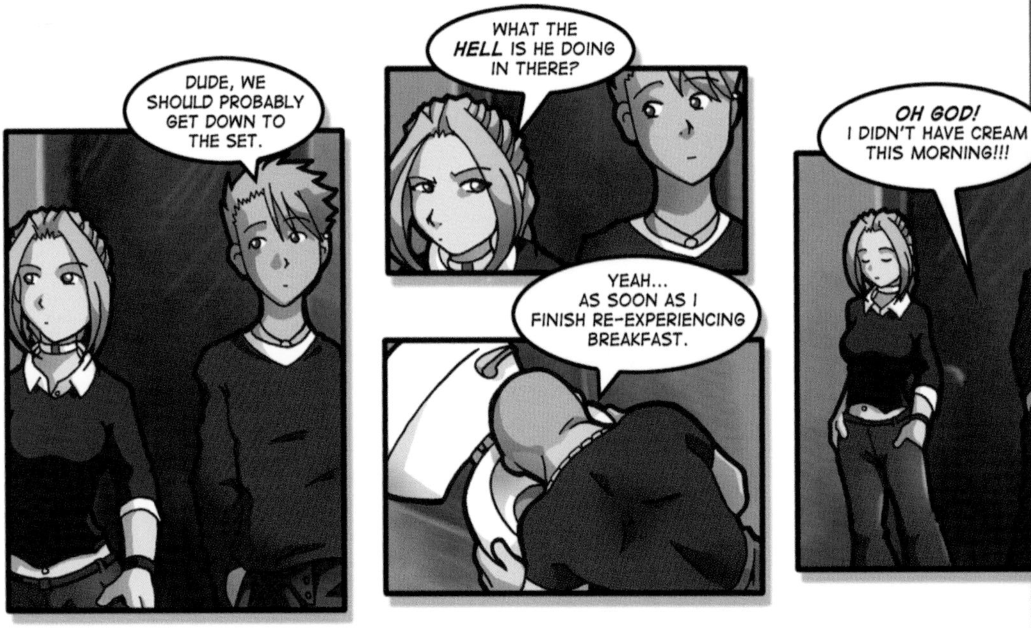
DUDE, WE SHOULD PROBABLY GET DOWN TO THE SET.
WHAT THE ***HELL*** IS HE DOING IN THERE?
YEAH... AS SOON AS I FINISH RE-EXPERIENCING BREAKFAST.
OH GOD! I DIDN'T HAVE CREAM THIS MORNING!!!

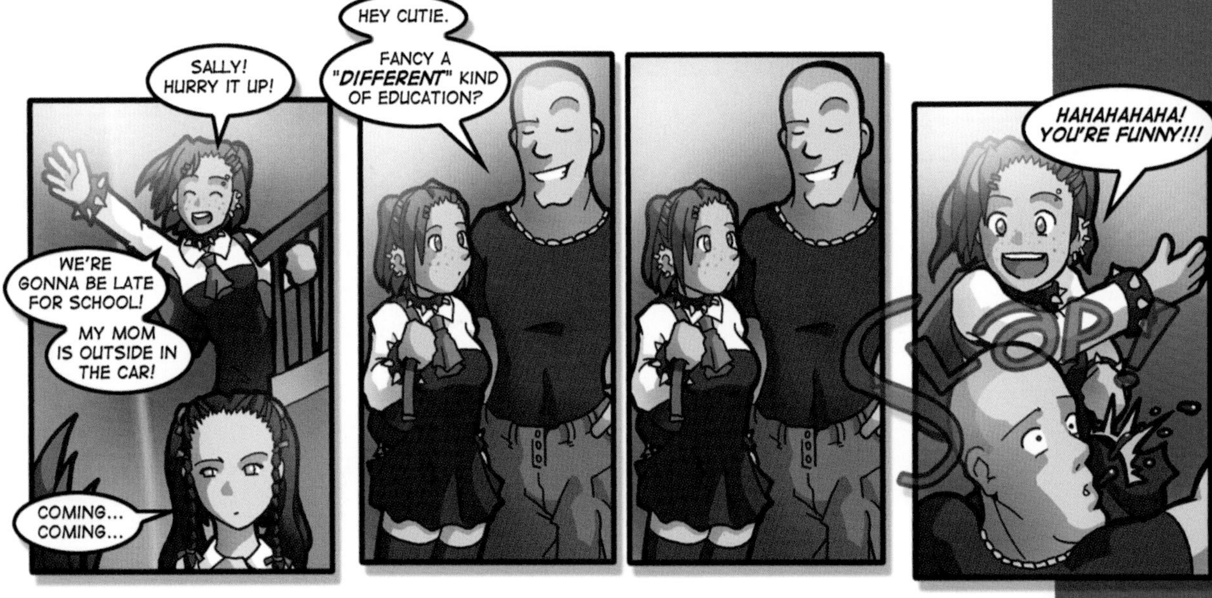
SALLY! HURRY IT UP!
WE'RE GONNA BE LATE FOR SCHOOL!
MY MOM IS OUTSIDE IN THE CAR!
COMING... COMING...
HEY CUTIE.
FANCY A "***DIFFERENT***" KIND OF EDUCATION?
HAHAHAHAHA! YOU'RE FUNNY!!!
SLOP!

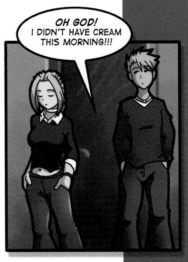

#46

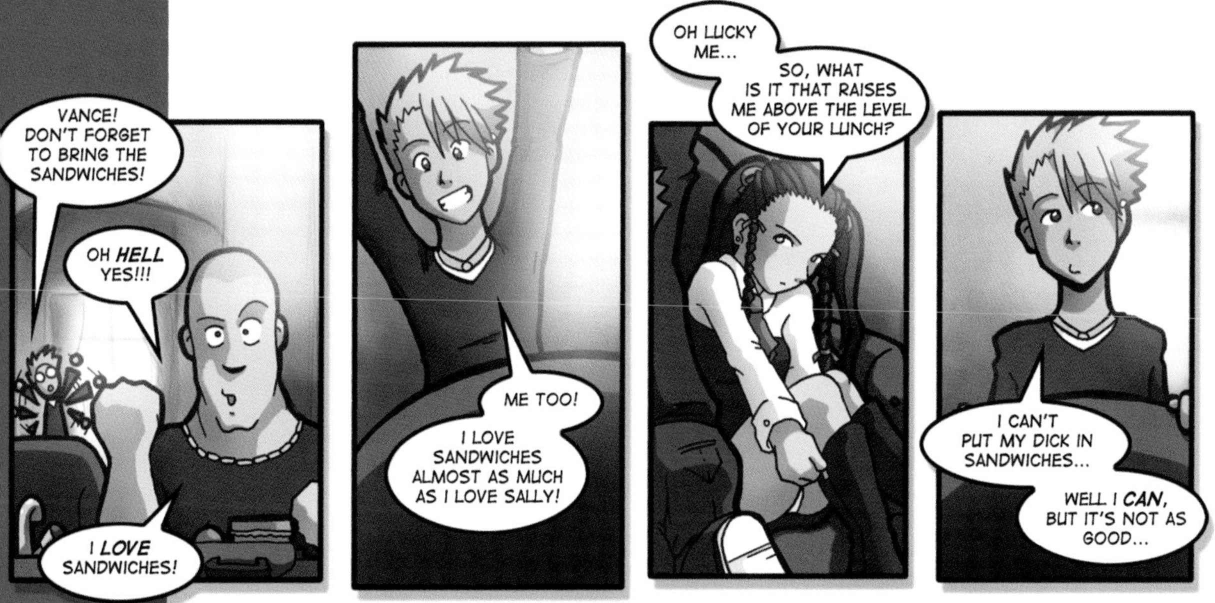
VANCE! DON'T FORGET TO BRING THE SANDWICHES!
OH *HELL* YES!!!
I *LOVE* SANDWICHES!
ME TOO!
I LOVE SANDWICHES ALMOST AS MUCH AS I LOVE SALLY!
OH LUCKY ME...
SO, WHAT IS IT THAT RAISES ME ABOVE THE LEVEL OF YOUR LUNCH?
I CAN'T PUT MY DICK IN SANDWICHES...
WELL I *CAN*, BUT IT'S NOT AS GOOD...

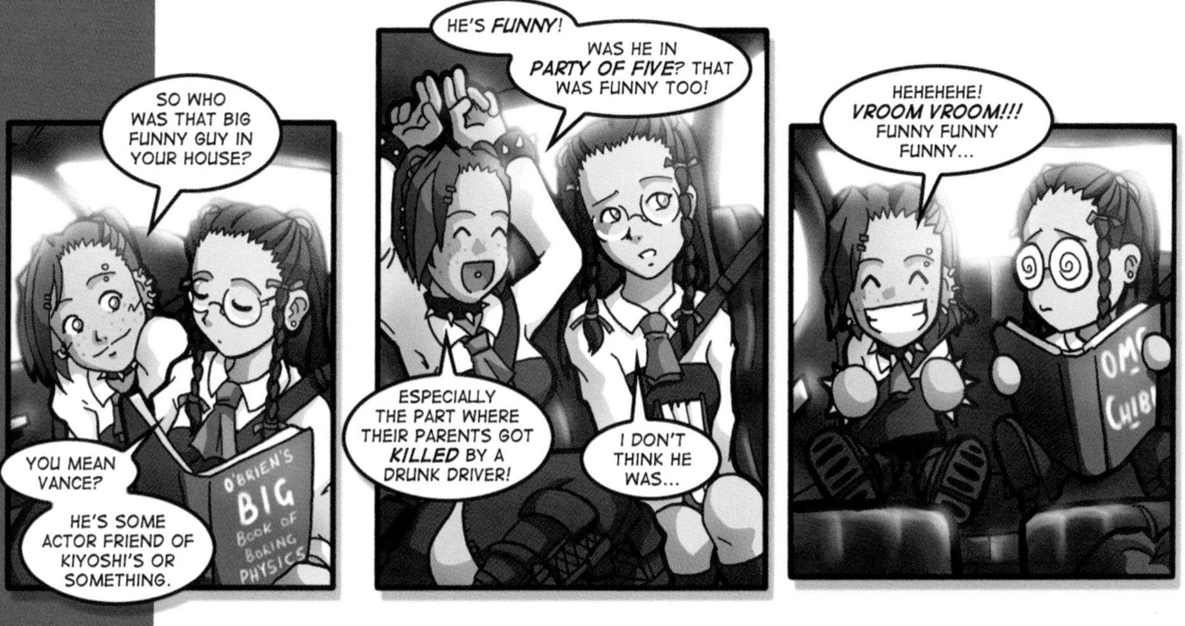
SO WHO WAS THAT BIG FUNNY GUY IN YOUR HOUSE?
YOU MEAN VANCE?
HE'S SOME ACTOR FRIEND OF KIYOSHI'S OR SOMETHING.
O'BRIEN'S BIG Book of Boring PHYSICS
HE'S *FUNNY*!
WAS HE IN *PARTY OF FIVE*? THAT WAS FUNNY TOO!
ESPECIALLY THE PART WHERE THEIR PARENTS GOT *KILLED* BY A DRUNK DRIVER!
I DON'T THINK HE WAS...
HEHEHEHE! *VROOM VROOM!!!* FUNNY FUNNY FUNNY...
OMG CHIBI

#47

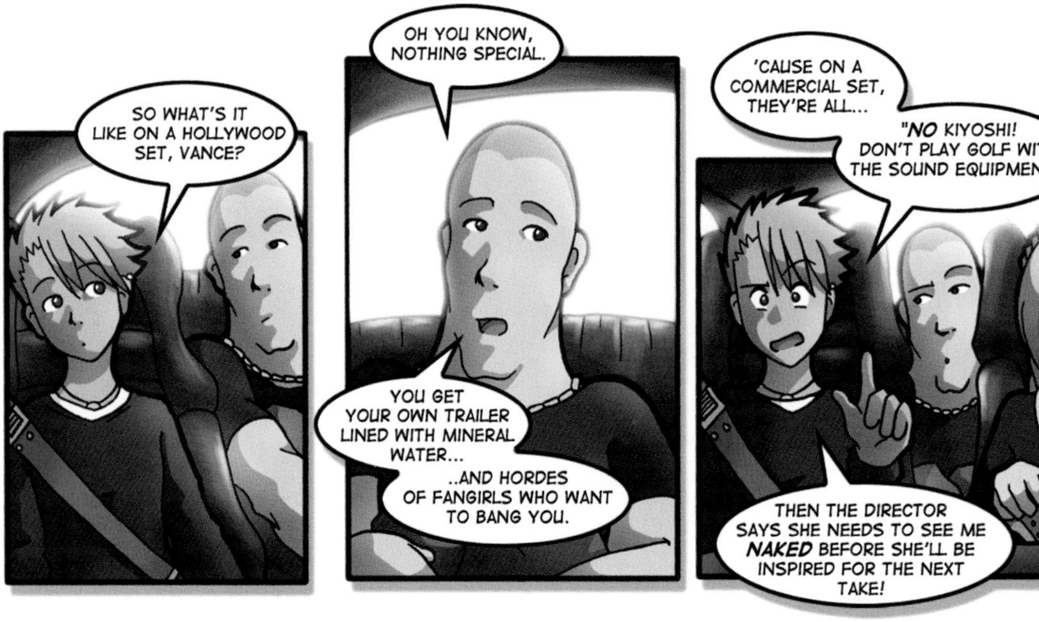
SO WHAT'S IT LIKE ON A HOLLYWOOD SET, VANCE?
OH YOU KNOW, NOTHING SPECIAL.
YOU GET YOUR OWN TRAILER LINED WITH MINERAL WATER...
..AND HORDES OF FANGIRLS WHO WANT TO BANG YOU.
'CAUSE ON A COMMERCIAL SET, THEY'RE ALL...
"*NO* KIYOSHI! DON'T PLAY GOLF WITH THE SOUND EQUIPMENT!"
THEN THE DIRECTOR SAYS SHE NEEDS TO SEE ME *NAKED* BEFORE SHE'LL BE INSPIRED FOR THE NEXT TAKE!

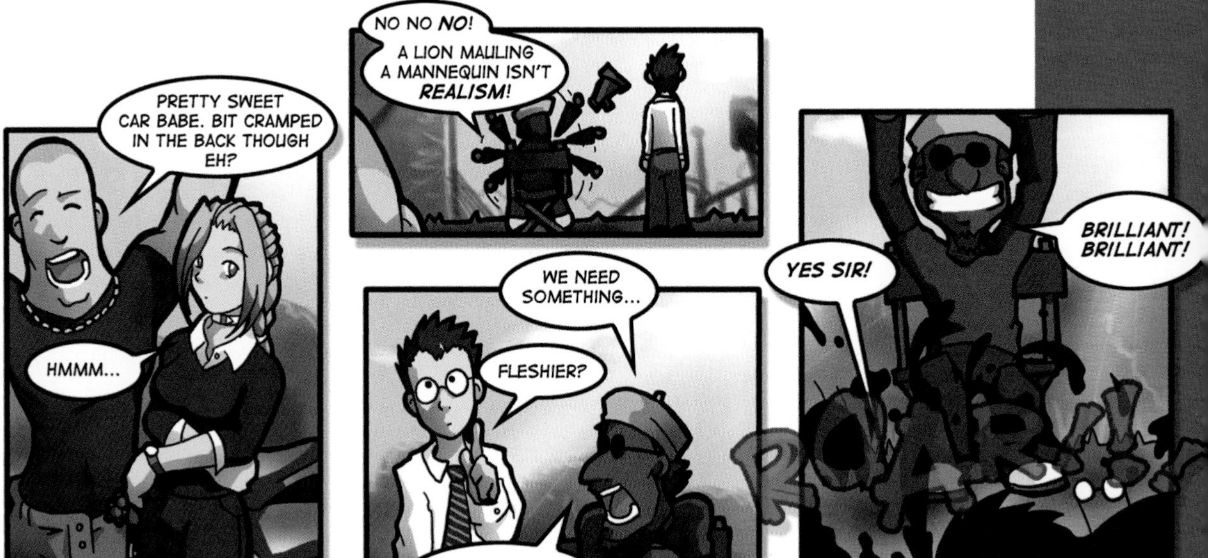
PRETTY SWEET CAR BABE. BIT CRAMPED IN THE BACK THOUGH EH?
HMMM...
NO NO *NO*! A LION MAULING A MANNEQUIN ISN'T *REALISM*!
WE NEED SOMETHING...
FLESHIER?
YES! *FLESHIER*! GET IN THERE!
YES SIR!
BRILLIANT! BRILLIANT!
ROAR

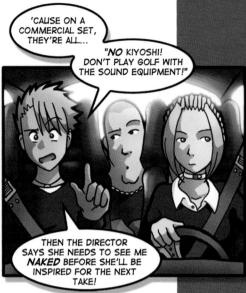

#48

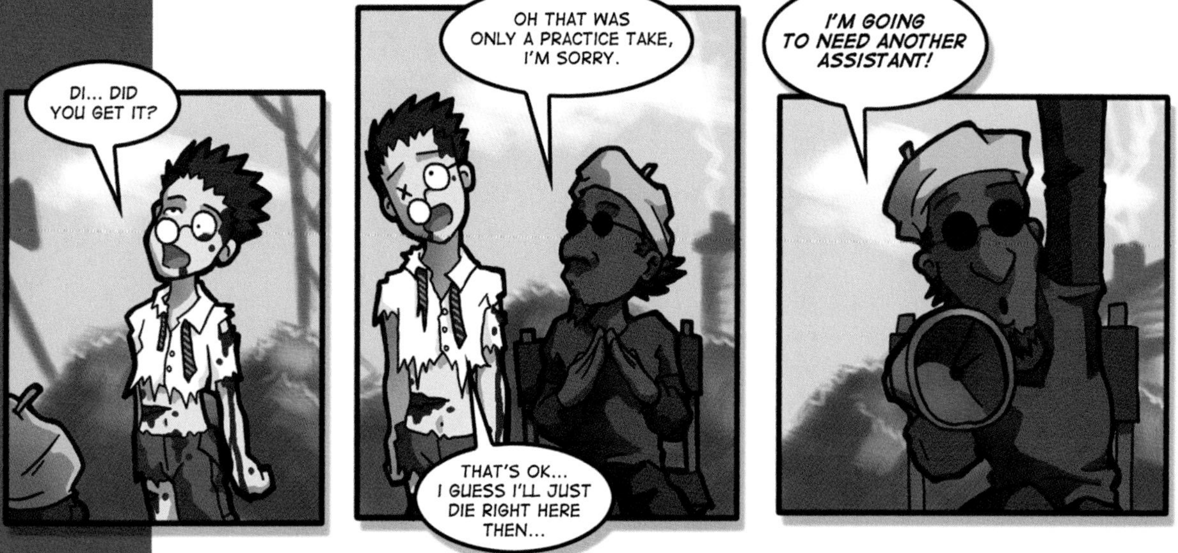
DI... DID YOU GET IT?
OH THAT WAS ONLY A PRACTICE TAKE, I'M SORRY.
THAT'S OK... I GUESS I'LL JUST DIE RIGHT HERE THEN...
I'M GOING TO NEED ANOTHER ASSISTANT!

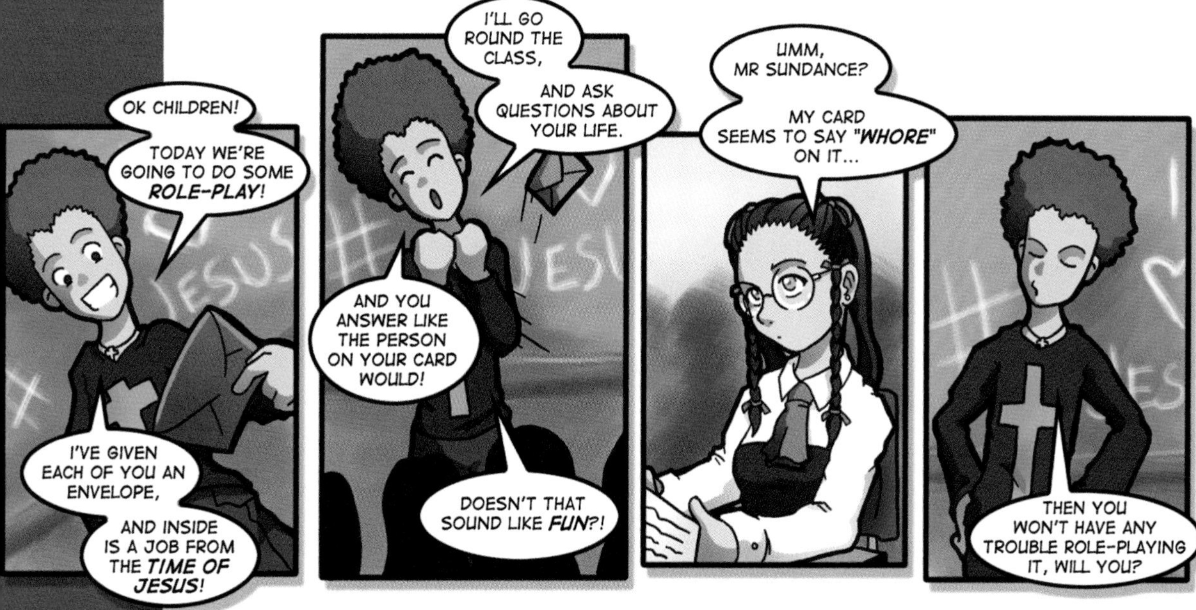
OK CHILDREN!
TODAY WE'RE GOING TO DO SOME *ROLE-PLAY*!
I'VE GIVEN EACH OF YOU AN ENVELOPE,
AND INSIDE IS A JOB FROM THE *TIME OF JESUS*!
I'LL GO ROUND THE CLASS,
AND ASK QUESTIONS ABOUT YOUR LIFE.
AND YOU ANSWER LIKE THE PERSON ON YOUR CARD WOULD!
DOESN'T THAT SOUND LIKE *FUN*?!
UMM, MR SUNDANCE?
MY CARD SEEMS TO SAY "*WHORE*" ON IT...
THEN YOU WON'T HAVE ANY TROUBLE ROLE-PLAYING IT, WILL YOU?

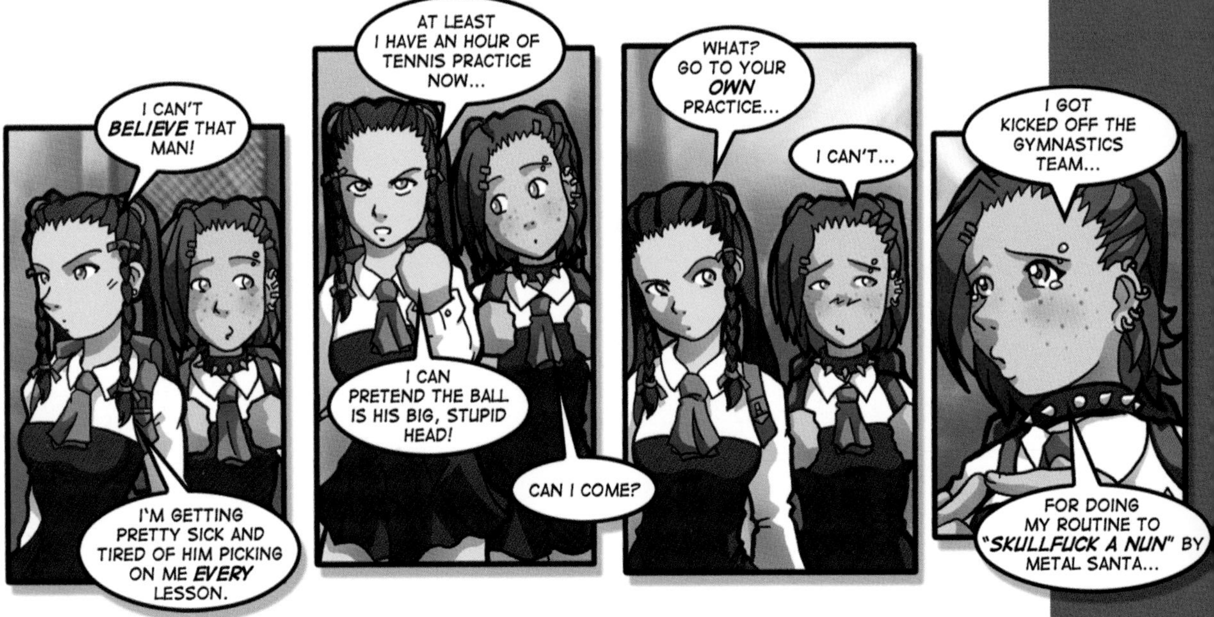
I CAN'T *BELIEVE* THAT MAN!
I'M GETTING PRETTY SICK AND TIRED OF HIM PICKING ON ME *EVERY* LESSON.
AT LEAST I HAVE AN HOUR OF TENNIS PRACTICE NOW...
I CAN PRETEND THE BALL IS HIS BIG, STUPID HEAD!
CAN I COME?
WHAT? GO TO YOUR *OWN* PRACTICE...
I CAN'T...
I GOT KICKED OFF THE GYMNASTICS TEAM...
FOR DOING MY ROUTINE TO "*SKULLFUCK A NUN*" BY METAL SANTA...

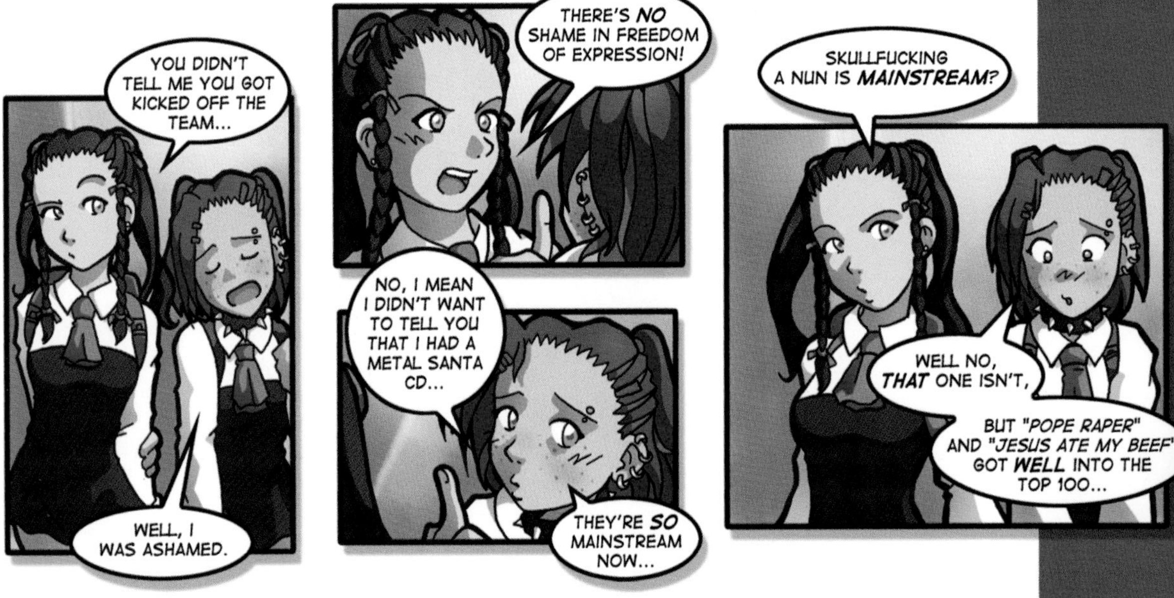
YOU DIDN'T TELL ME YOU GOT KICKED OFF THE TEAM...
WELL, I WAS ASHAMED.
THERE'S *NO* SHAME IN FREEDOM OF EXPRESSION!
NO, I MEAN I DIDN'T WANT TO TELL YOU THAT I HAD A METAL SANTA CD...
THEY'RE *SO* MAINSTREAM NOW...
SKULLFUCKING A NUN IS *MAINSTREAM*?
WELL NO, *THAT* ONE ISN'T,
BUT "*POPE RAPER*" AND "*JESUS ATE MY BEEF*" GOT *WELL* INTO THE TOP 100...

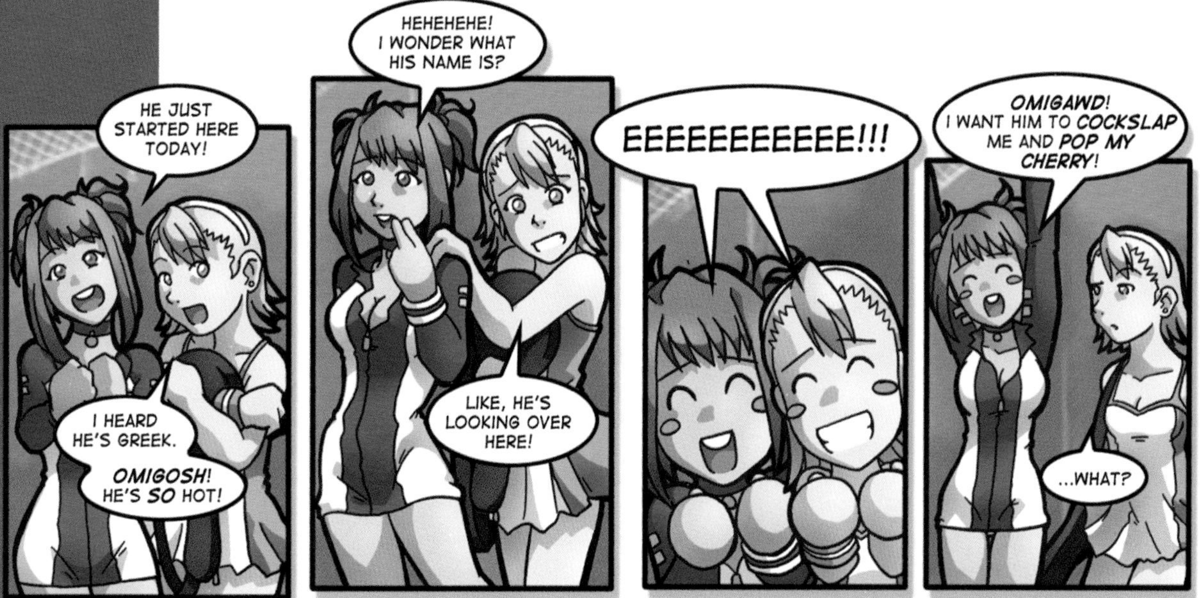
HE JUST STARTED HERE TODAY!
I HEARD HE'S GREEK.
OMIGOSH! HE'S SO HOT!
HEHEHEHE! I WONDER WHAT HIS NAME IS?
LIKE, HE'S LOOKING OVER HERE!
EEEEEEEEEEEE!!!
OMIGAWD! I WANT HIM TO COCKSLAP ME AND POP MY CHERRY!
...WHAT?

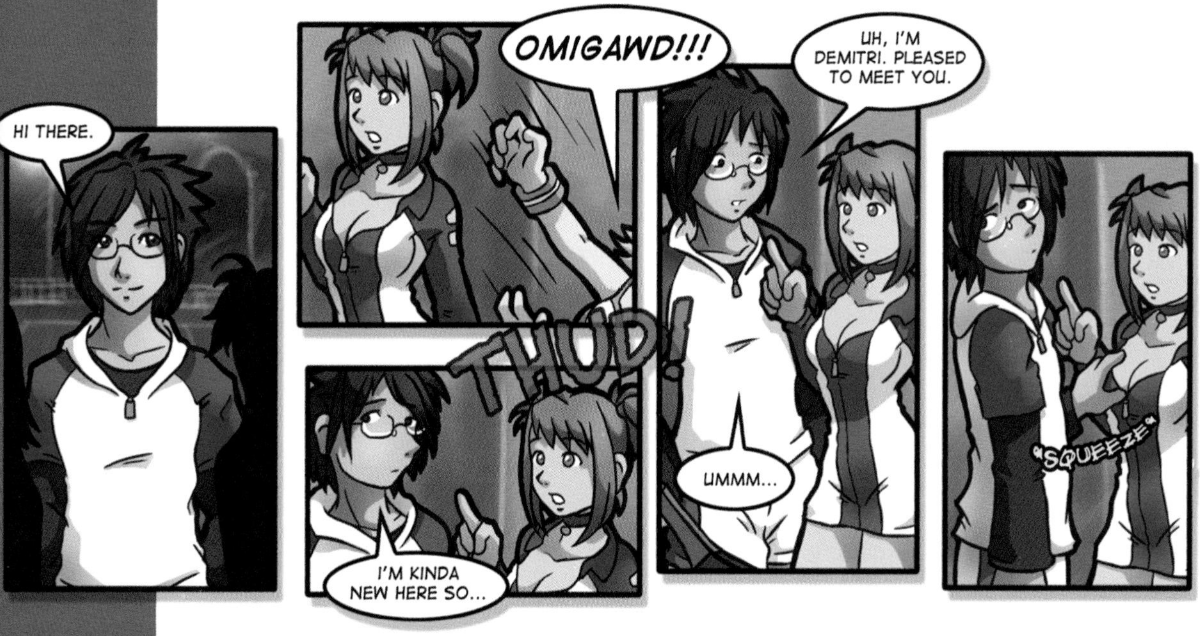
HI THERE.
OMIGAWD!!!
THUD!
I'M KINDA NEW HERE SO...
UH, I'M DEMITRI. PLEASED TO MEET YOU.
UMMM...
SQUEEZE

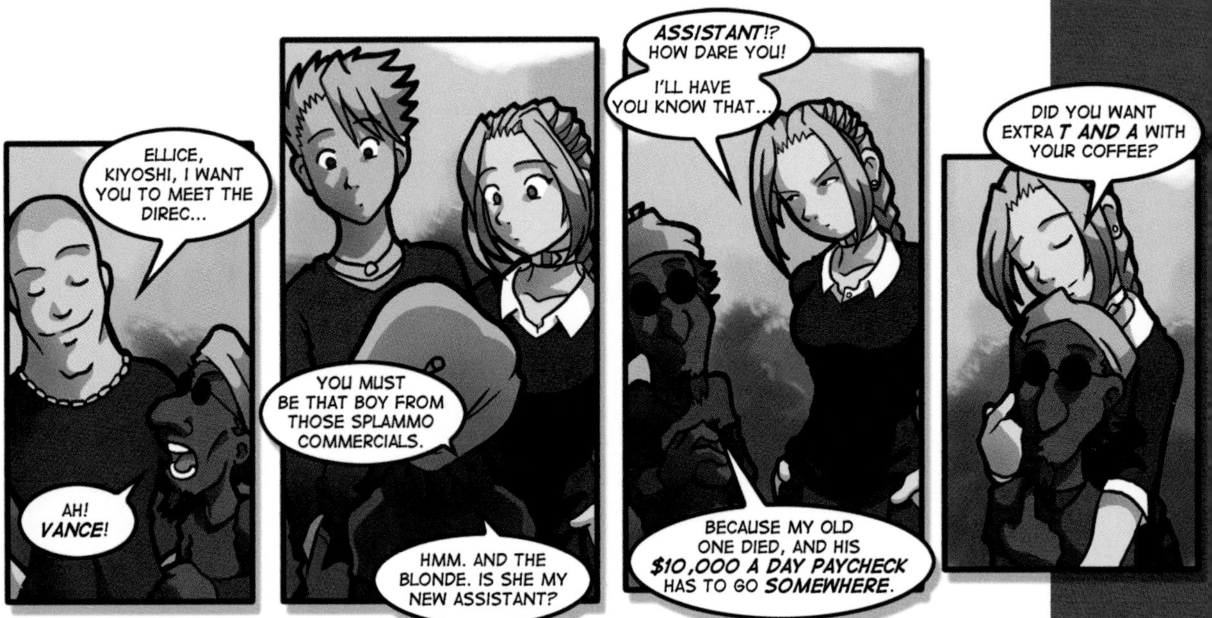
ELLICE, KIYOSHI, I WANT YOU TO MEET THE DIREC...
AH! **VANCE!**
YOU MUST BE THAT BOY FROM THOSE SPLAMMO COMMERCIALS.
HMM. AND THE BLONDE. IS SHE MY NEW ASSISTANT?
***ASSISTANT*!?** HOW DARE YOU!
I'LL HAVE YOU KNOW THAT...
BECAUSE MY OLD ONE DIED, AND HIS ***$10,000 A DAY PAYCHECK*** HAS TO GO ***SOMEWHERE***.
DID YOU WANT EXTRA ***T AND A*** WITH YOUR COFFEE?

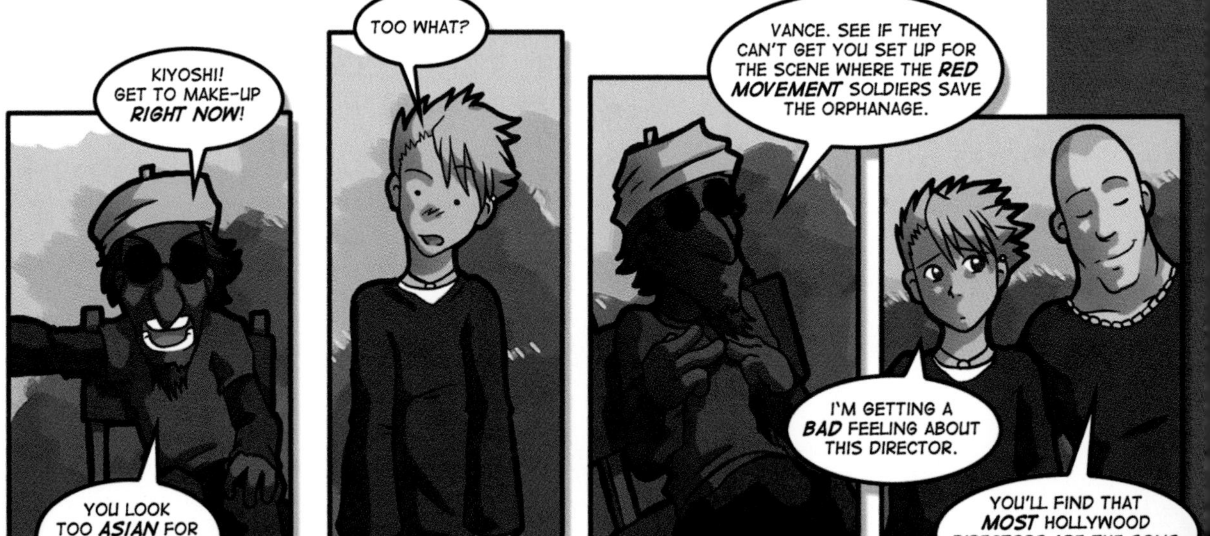
KIYOSHI! GET TO MAKE-UP ***RIGHT NOW***!
YOU LOOK TOO ***ASIAN*** FOR THE PART RIGHT NOW!
TOO WHAT?
VANCE. SEE IF THEY CAN'T GET YOU SET UP FOR THE SCENE WHERE THE ***RED MOVEMENT*** SOLDIERS SAVE THE ORPHANAGE.
I'M GETTING A ***BAD*** FEELING ABOUT THIS DIRECTOR.
YOU'LL FIND THAT ***MOST*** HOLLYWOOD DIRECTORS ARE THE SONS OF EVIL DICTATORS.

#52

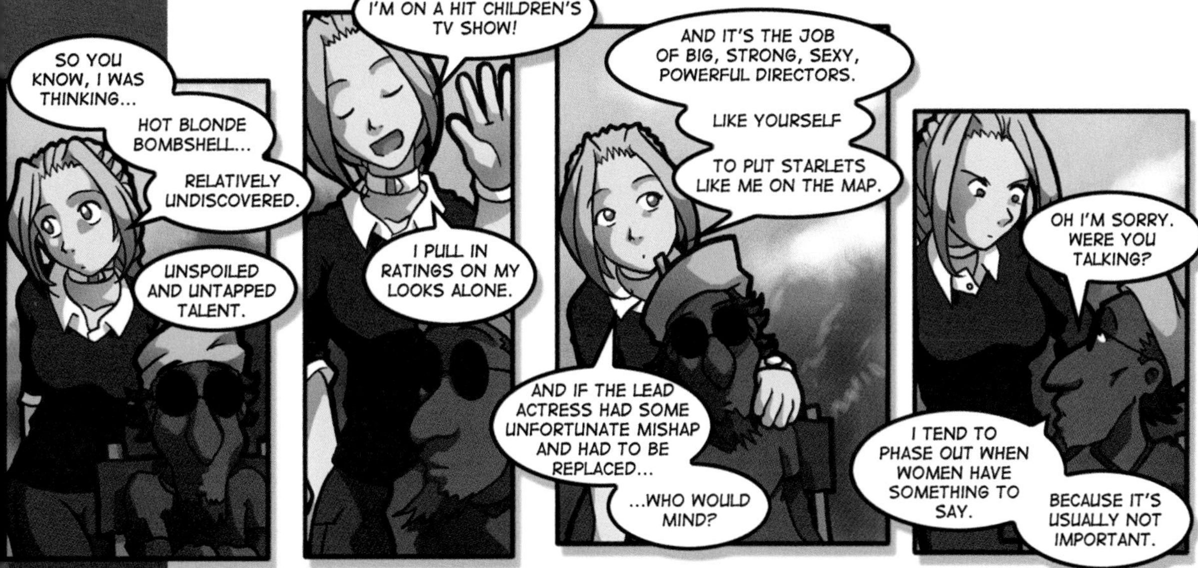
SO YOU KNOW, I WAS THINKING...
HOT BLONDE BOMBSHELL...
RELATIVELY UNDISCOVERED.
UNSPOILED AND UNTAPPED TALENT.
I MEAN, I'M ON A HIT CHILDREN'S TV SHOW!
I PULL IN RATINGS ON MY LOOKS ALONE.
AND IT'S THE JOB OF BIG, STRONG, SEXY, POWERFUL DIRECTORS.
LIKE YOURSELF
TO PUT STARLETS LIKE ME ON THE MAP.
AND IF THE LEAD ACTRESS HAD SOME UNFORTUNATE MISHAP AND HAD TO BE REPLACED...
...WHO WOULD MIND?
OH I'M SORRY. WERE YOU TALKING?
I TEND TO PHASE OUT WHEN WOMEN HAVE SOMETHING TO SAY.
BECAUSE IT'S USUALLY NOT IMPORTANT.

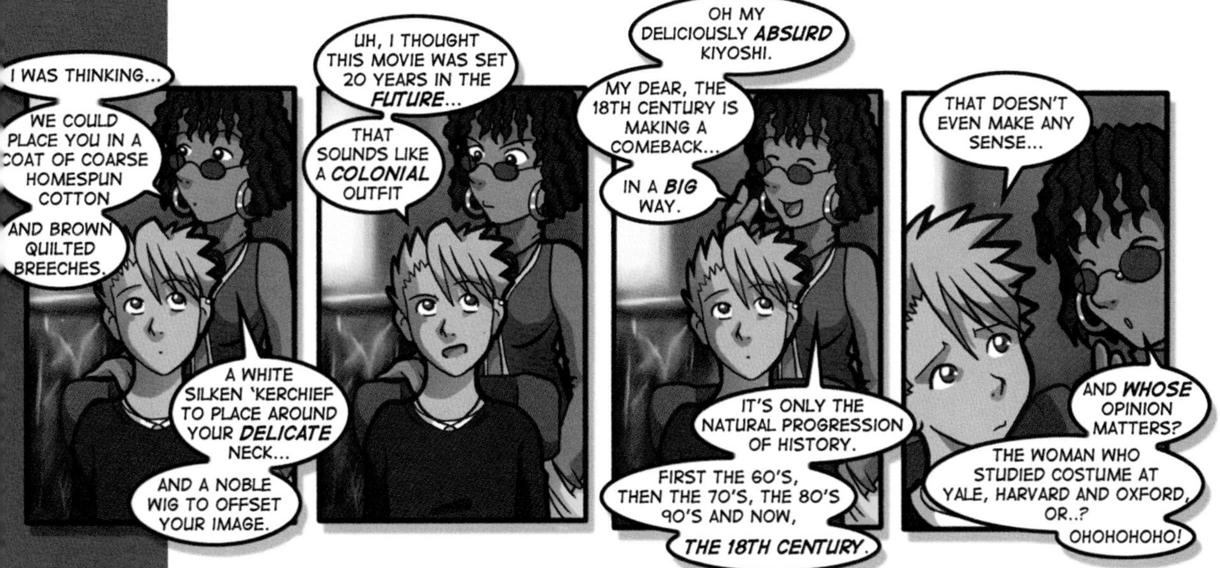
I WAS THINKING...
WE COULD PLACE YOU IN A COAT OF COARSE HOMESPUN COTTON
AND BROWN QUILTED BREECHES.
A WHITE SILKEN 'KERCHIEF TO PLACE AROUND YOUR DELICATE NECK...
AND A NOBLE WIG TO OFFSET YOUR IMAGE.
UH, I THOUGHT THIS MOVIE WAS SET 20 YEARS IN THE FUTURE...
THAT SOUNDS LIKE A COLONIAL OUTFIT
OH MY DELICIOUSLY ABSURD KIYOSHI.
MY DEAR, THE 18TH CENTURY IS MAKING A COMEBACK...
IN A BIG WAY.
IT'S ONLY THE NATURAL PROGRESSION OF HISTORY.
FIRST THE 60'S, THEN THE 70'S, THE 80'S 90'S AND NOW, THE 18TH CENTURY.
THAT DOESN'T EVEN MAKE ANY SENSE...
AND WHOSE OPINION MATTERS?
THE WOMAN WHO STUDIED COSTUME AT YALE, HARVARD AND OXFORD, OR..?
OHOHOHOHO!

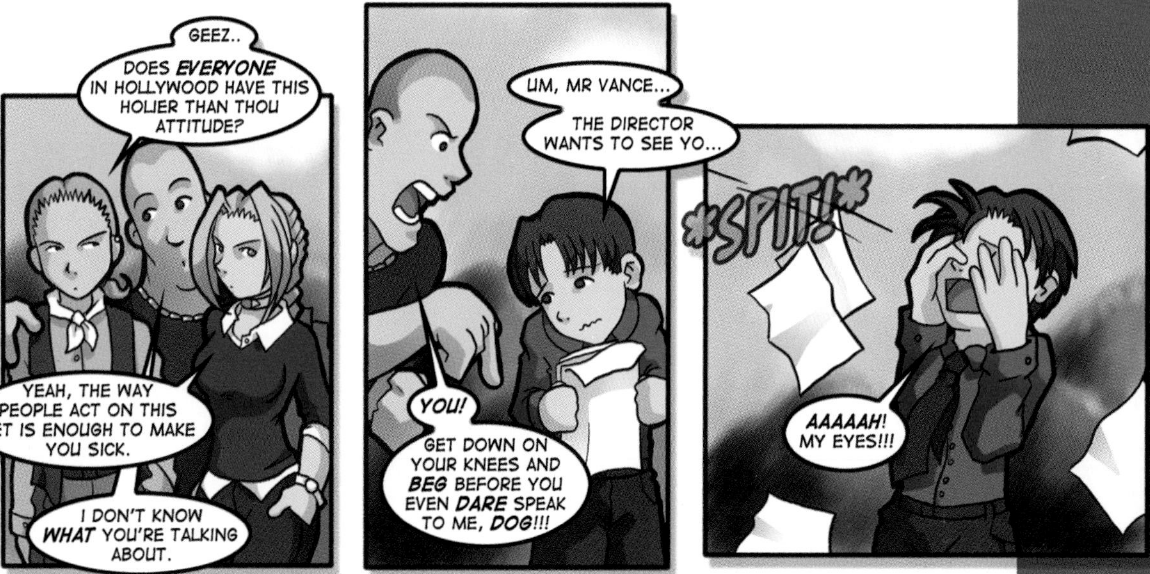
GEEZ..
DOES **EVERYONE** IN HOLLYWOOD HAVE THIS HOLIER THAN THOU ATTITUDE?
YEAH, THE WAY PEOPLE ACT ON THIS SET IS ENOUGH TO MAKE YOU SICK.
I DON'T KNOW **WHAT** YOU'RE TALKING ABOUT.
UM, MR VANCE...
THE DIRECTOR WANTS TO SEE YO...
YOU!
GET DOWN ON YOUR KNEES AND **BEG** BEFORE YOU EVEN **DARE** SPEAK TO ME, **DOG**!!!
SPIT!
AAAAAH! MY EYES!!!

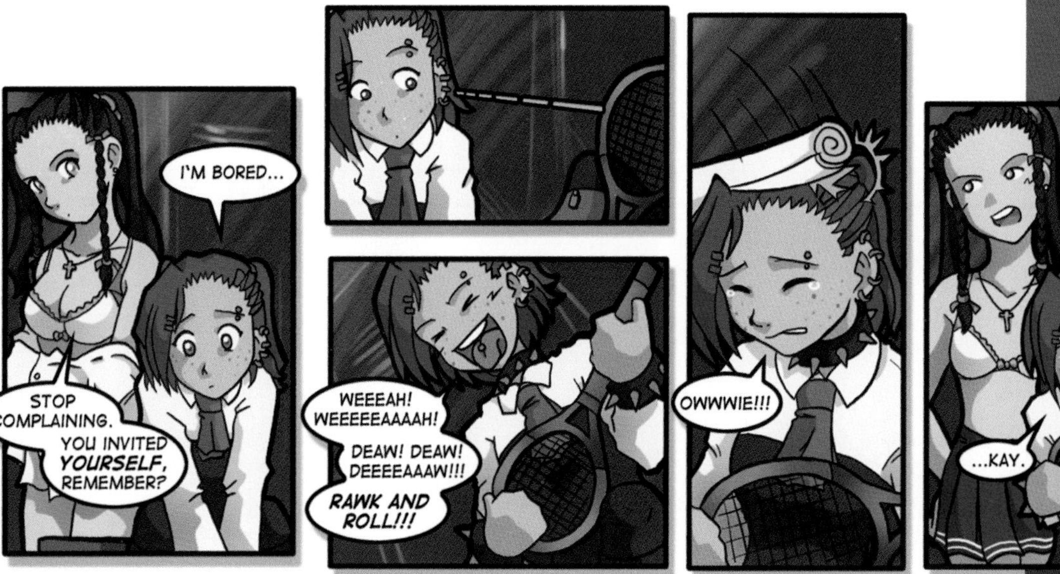
I'M BORED...
STOP COMPLAINING.
YOU INVITED **YOURSELF**, REMEMBER?
WEEEAH! WEEEEEEAAAAH!
DEAW! DEAW! DEEEEAAAW!!!
RAWK AND ROLL!!!
OWWWIE!!!
THE RACKET. **NOW**.
...KAY.

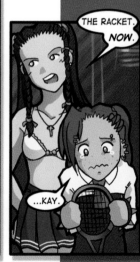

#54

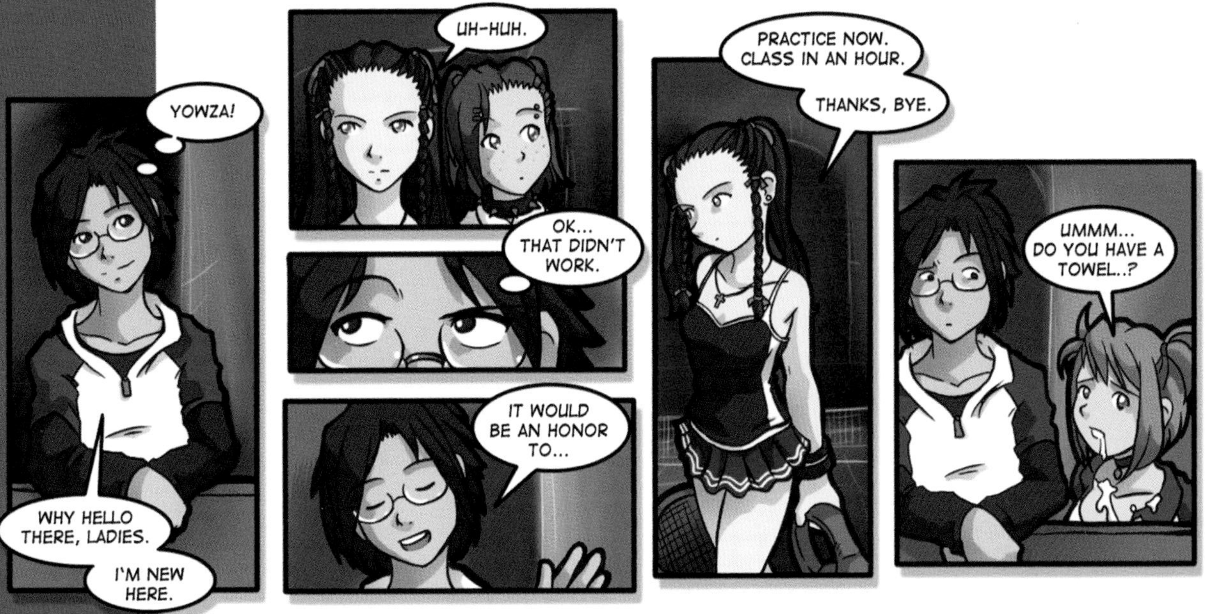
YOWZA!
WHY HELLO THERE, LADIES.
I'M NEW HERE.
UH-HUH.
OK... THAT DIDN'T WORK.
IT WOULD BE AN HONOR TO...
PRACTICE NOW. CLASS IN AN HOUR.
THANKS, BYE.
UMMM... DO YOU HAVE A TOWEL..?

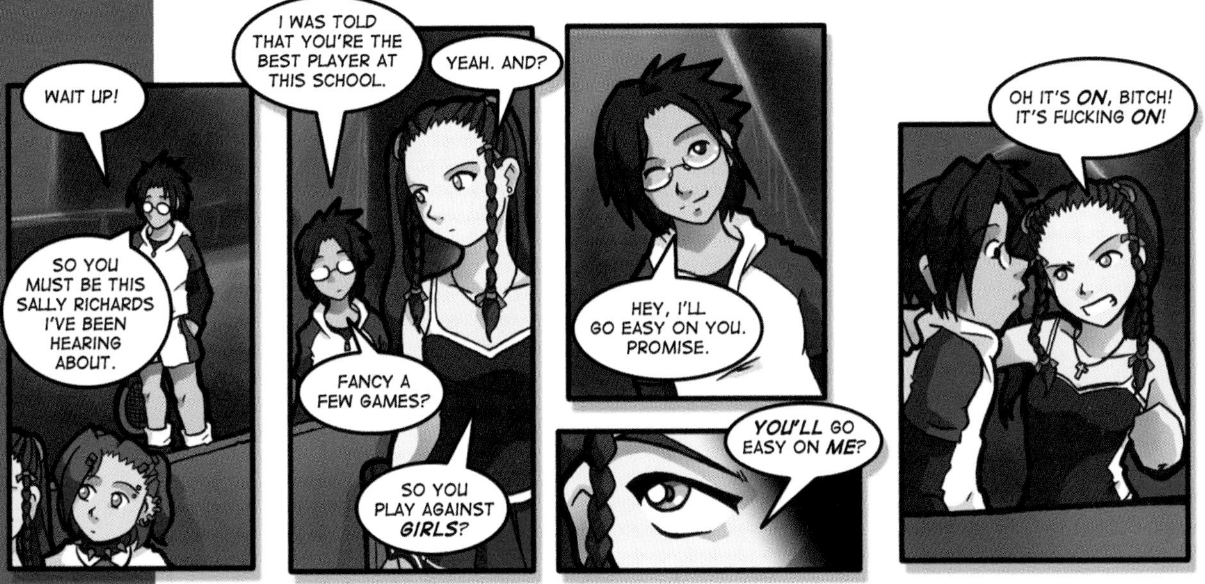
WAIT UP!
SO YOU MUST BE THIS SALLY RICHARDS I'VE BEEN HEARING ABOUT.
I WAS TOLD THAT YOU'RE THE BEST PLAYER AT THIS SCHOOL.
YEAH. AND?
FANCY A FEW GAMES?
SO YOU PLAY AGAINST *GIRLS*?
HEY, I'LL GO EASY ON YOU. PROMISE.
YOU'LL GO EASY ON *ME*?
OH IT'S *ON*, BITCH! IT'S FUCKING *ON*!

#55

GO SALLY! GO SALLY!
MEXICAN WAVE!
YAAAAY!!!
YOU KNOW, IT ISN'T ANY FUN IF ***YOU*** DON'T JOIN IN TOO...

ALRIGHT, I'LL ADMIT IT...
YOU'RE PRETTY GOOD.
ONLY *PRETTY GOOD?*
YEAH YEAH. YOU BEAT ME.
GET OVER IT.
I DIDN'T GET A CHANCE TO WARM UP ANYWAY.
DON'T LET IT GO TO YOUR HEAD.
SO NOW, YOU'RE LIKE SO IMPRESSED, YOU'VE FALLEN MADLY IN LOVE WITH ME...
RIGHT?
UH, NO.
DAMN.

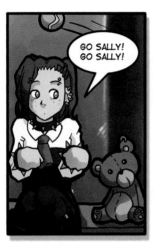

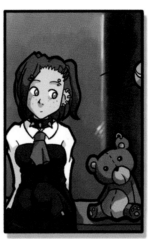

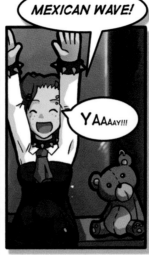

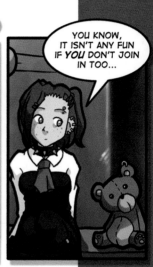

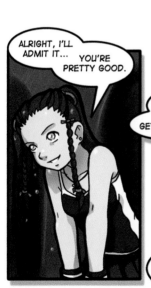

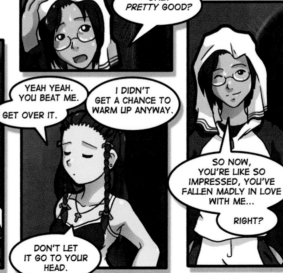

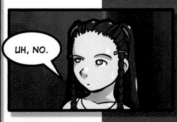

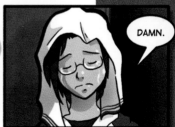

#56

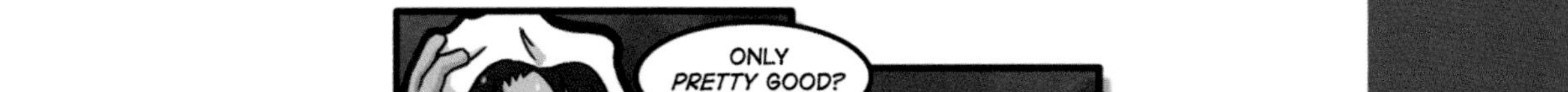

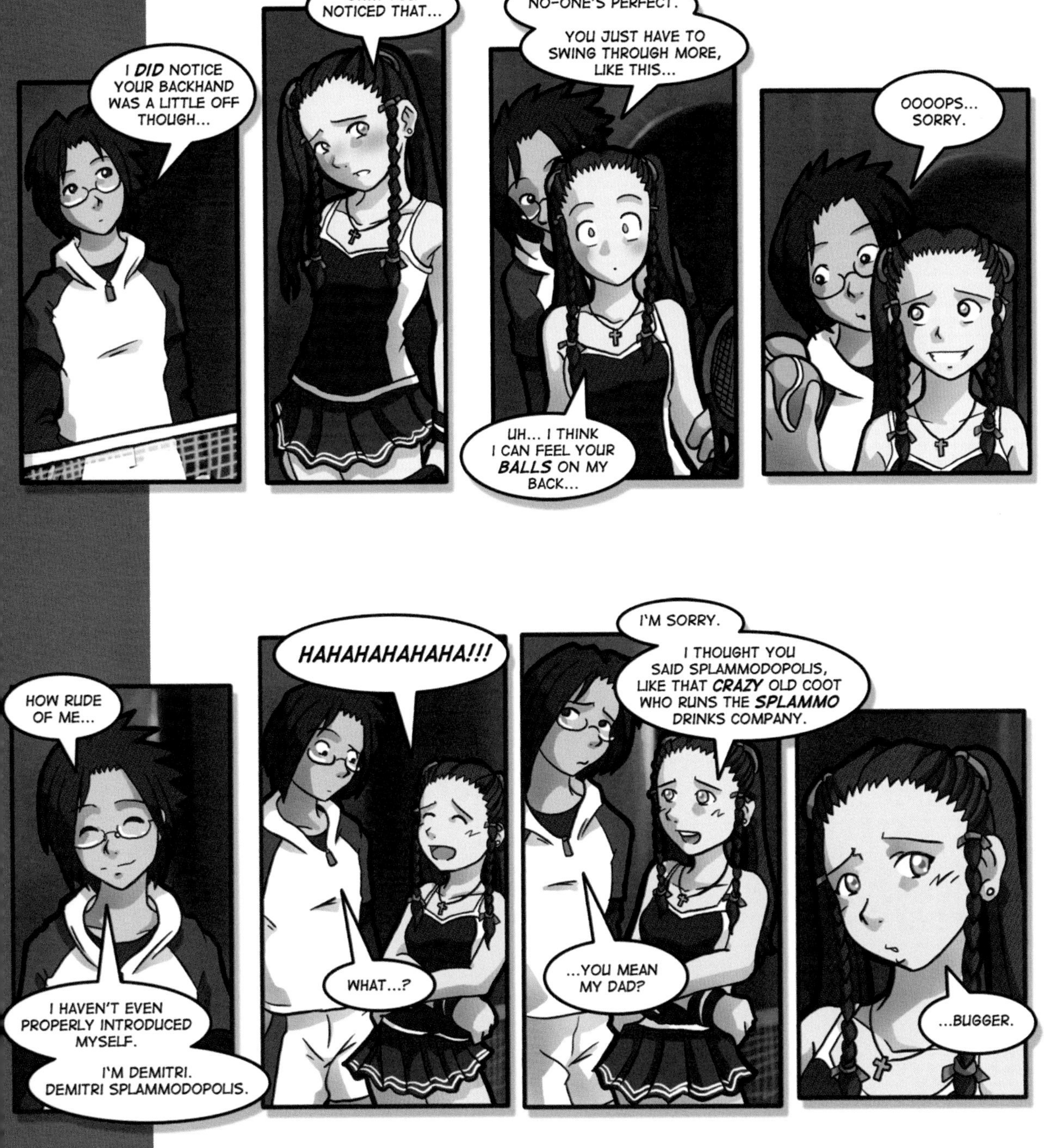
I DID NOTICE YOUR BACKHAND WAS A LITTLE OFF THOUGH...
OH... YOU NOTICED THAT...
NO-ONE'S PERFECT.
YOU JUST HAVE TO SWING THROUGH MORE, LIKE THIS...
UH... I THINK I CAN FEEL YOUR BALLS ON MY BACK...
OOOOPS... SORRY.
HOW RUDE OF ME...
I HAVEN'T EVEN PROPERLY INTRODUCED MYSELF.
I'M DEMITRI. DEMITRI SPLAMMODOPOLIS.
HAHAHAHAHAHA!!!
WHAT...?
I'M SORRY.
I THOUGHT YOU SAID SPLAMMODOPOLIS, LIKE THAT CRAZY OLD COOT WHO RUNS THE SPLAMMO DRINKS COMPANY.
...YOU MEAN MY DAD?
...BUGGER.

#57

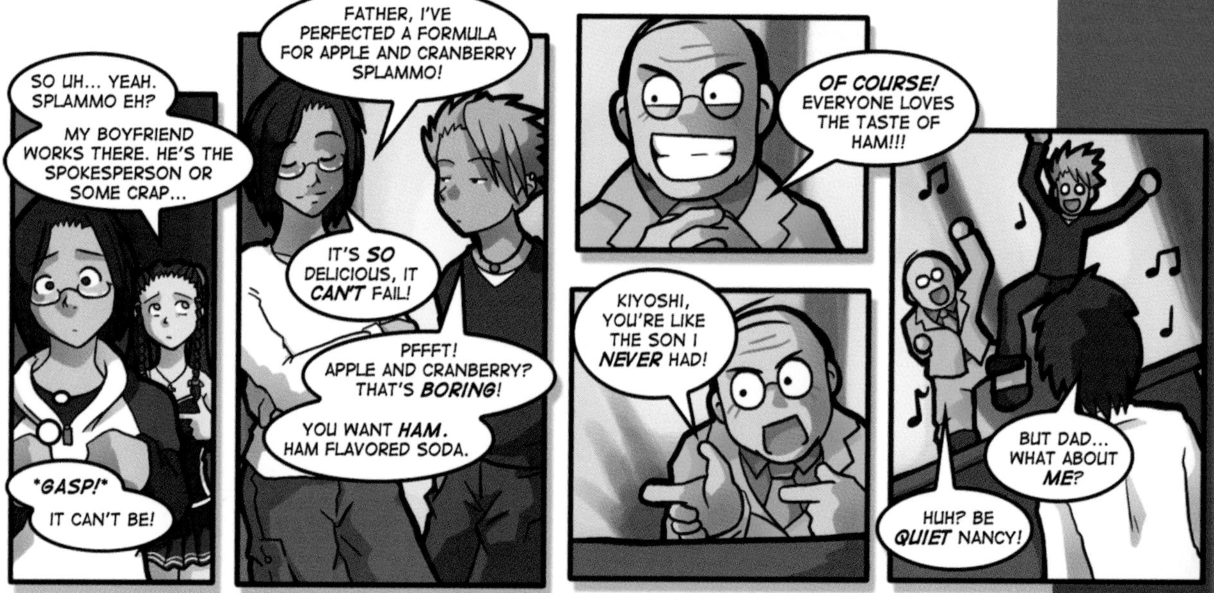
SO UH... YEAH. SPLAMMO EH?
MY BOYFRIEND WORKS THERE. HE'S THE SPOKESPERSON OR SOME CRAP...
GASP!
IT CAN'T BE!
FATHER, I'VE PERFECTED A FORMULA FOR APPLE AND CRANBERRY SPLAMMO!
IT'S SO DELICIOUS, IT CAN'T FAIL!
PFFFT! APPLE AND CRANBERRY? THAT'S BORING!
YOU WANT HAM. HAM FLAVORED SODA.
OF COURSE! EVERYONE LOVES THE TASTE OF HAM!!!
KIYOSHI, YOU'RE LIKE THE SON I NEVER HAD!
BUT DAD... WHAT ABOUT ME?
HUH? BE QUIET NANCY!

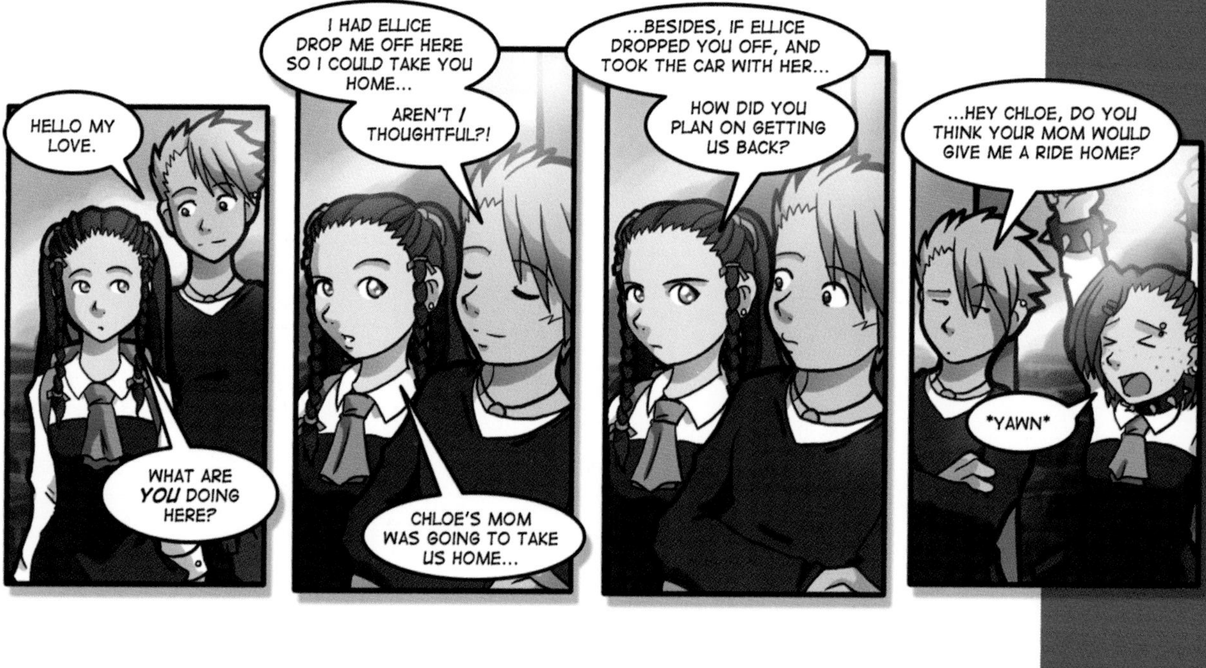
HELLO MY LOVE.
WHAT ARE YOU DOING HERE?
I HAD ELLICE DROP ME OFF HERE SO I COULD TAKE YOU HOME...
AREN'T I THOUGHTFUL?!
CHLOE'S MOM WAS GOING TO TAKE US HOME...
...BESIDES, IF ELLICE DROPPED YOU OFF, AND TOOK THE CAR WITH HER...
HOW DID YOU PLAN ON GETTING US BACK?
...HEY CHLOE, DO YOU THINK YOUR MOM WOULD GIVE ME A RIDE HOME?
YAWN

#58

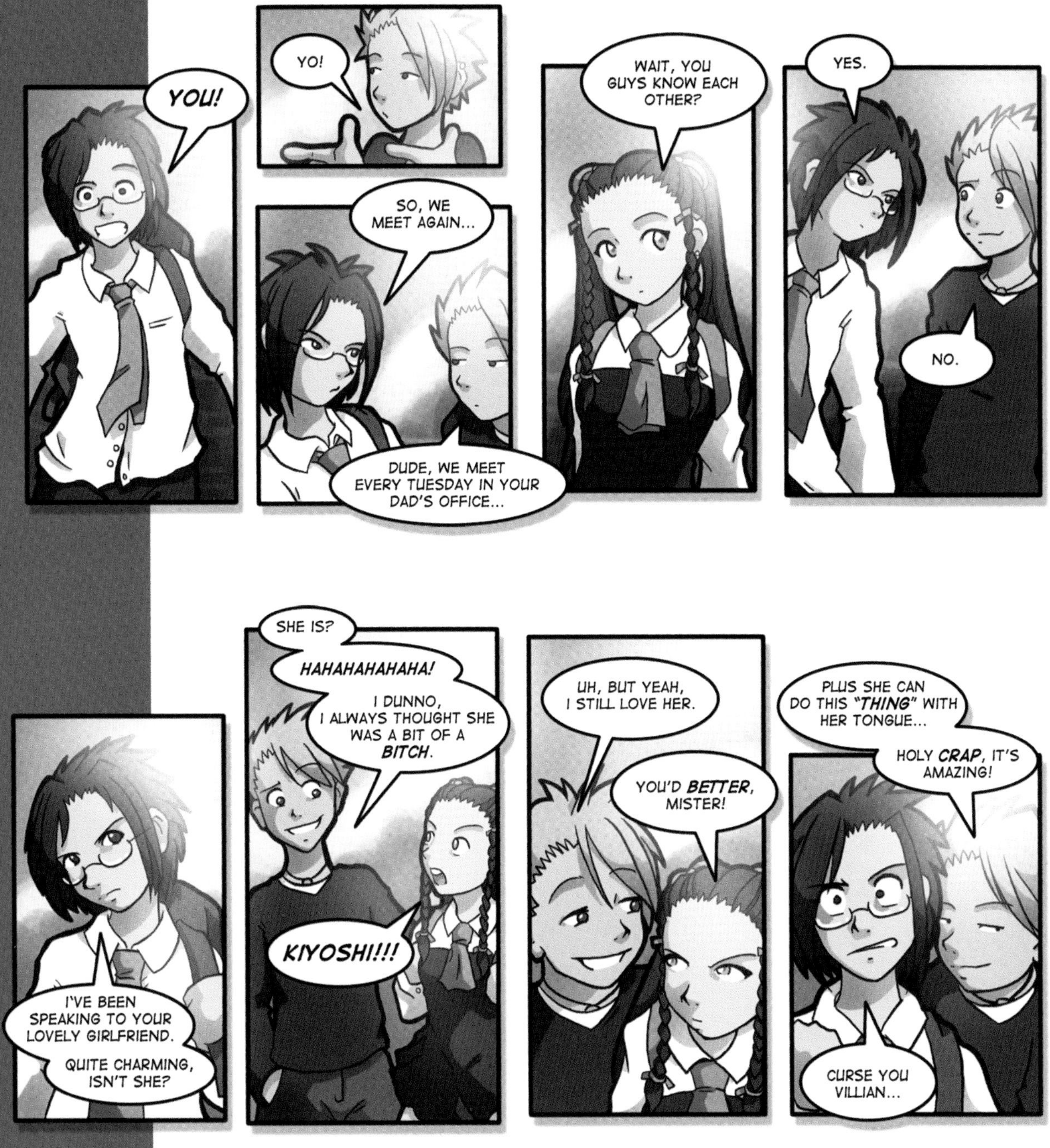
YOU!
YO!
SO, WE MEET AGAIN...
DUDE, WE MEET EVERY TUESDAY IN YOUR DAD'S OFFICE...
WAIT, YOU GUYS KNOW EACH OTHER?
YES.
NO.
I'VE BEEN SPEAKING TO YOUR LOVELY GIRLFRIEND.
QUITE CHARMING, ISN'T SHE?
SHE IS?
HAHAHAHAHAHA!
I DUNNO, I ALWAYS THOUGHT SHE WAS A BIT OF A BITCH.
KIYOSHI!!!
UH, BUT YEAH, I STILL LOVE HER.
YOU'D BETTER, MISTER!
PLUS SHE CAN DO THIS "THING" WITH HER TONGUE...
HOLY CRAP, IT'S AMAZING!
CURSE YOU VILLIAN...

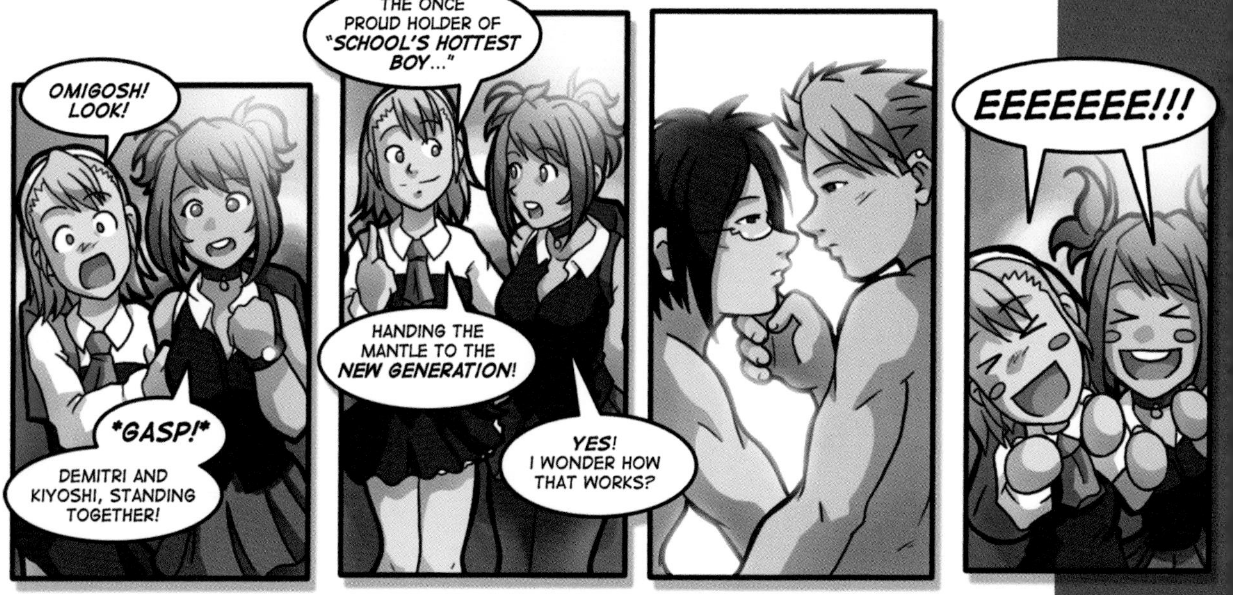
OMIGOSH! LOOK!
GASP!
DEMITRI AND KIYOSHI, STANDING TOGETHER!
THE ONCE PROUD HOLDER OF "SCHOOL'S HOTTEST BOY..."
HANDING THE MANTLE TO THE NEW GENERATION!
YES! I WONDER HOW THAT WORKS?
EEEEEEE!!!

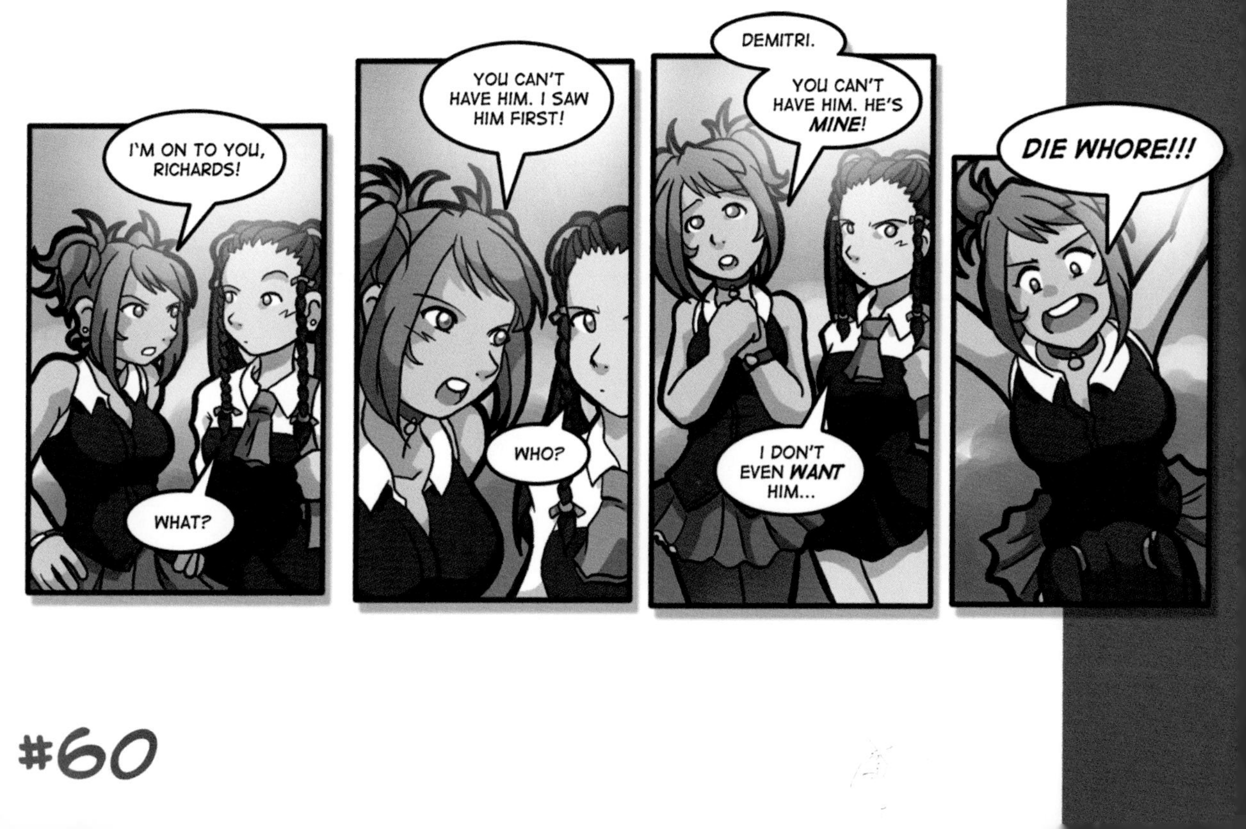
I'M ON TO YOU, RICHARDS!
WHAT?
YOU CAN'T HAVE HIM. I SAW HIM FIRST!
WHO?
DEMITRI.
YOU CAN'T HAVE HIM. HE'S MINE!
I DON'T EVEN WANT HIM...
DIE WHORE!!!

#60

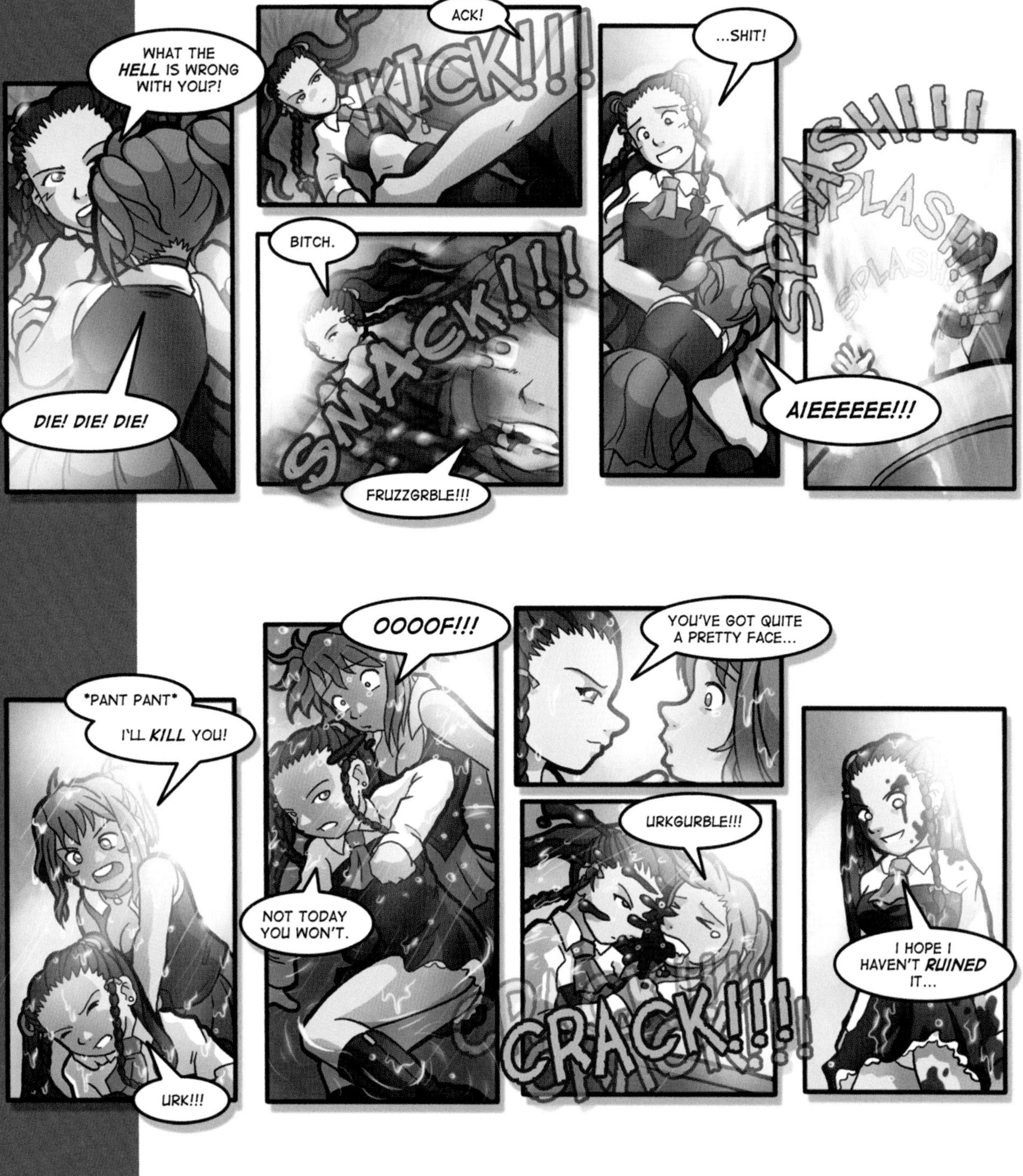
WHAT THE *HELL* IS WRONG WITH YOU?!
DIE! DIE! DIE!
ACK!
KICK!!!
BITCH.
SMACK!!!
FRUZZGRBLE!!!
...SHIT!
AIEEEEEE!!!
SPLASH!!!
SPLASH!!!
SPLASH!!!
PANT PANT
I'LL *KILL* YOU!
URK!!!
OOOOF!!!
NOT TODAY YOU WON'T.
YOU'VE GOT QUITE A PRETTY FACE...
URKGURBLE!!!
CRACK!!!
I HOPE I HAVEN'T *RUINED* IT...

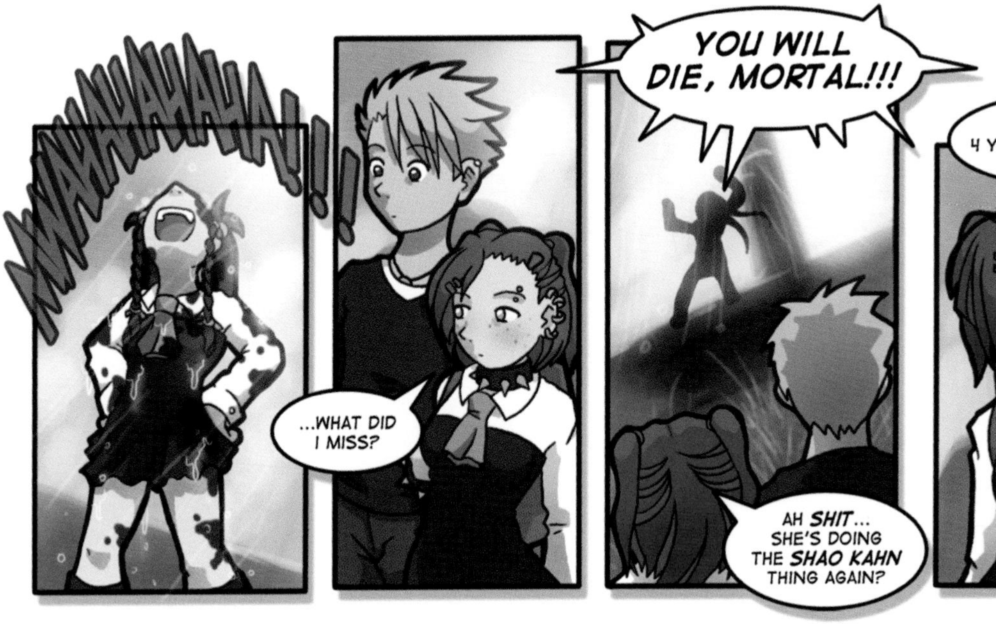
MWAHAHAHAHAHA!!!
...WHAT DID I MISS?
YOU WILL DIE, MORTAL!!!
AH *SHIT*... SHE'S DOING THE *SHAO KAHN* THING AGAIN?
THERE GOES 4 YEARS OF THERAPY...

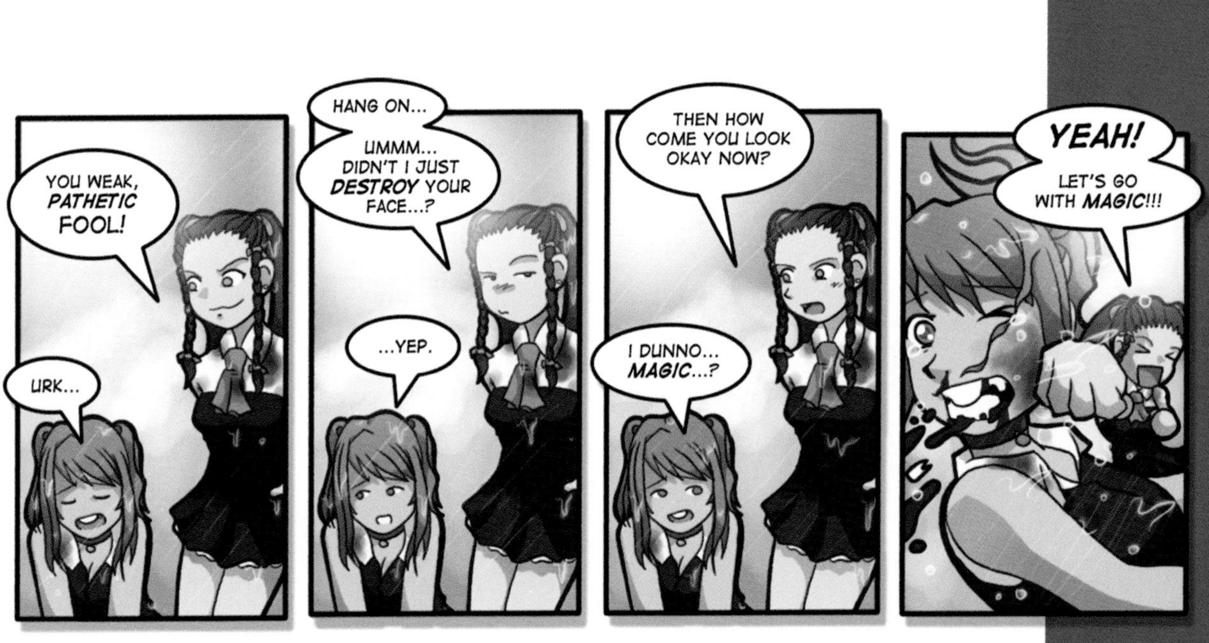
YOU WEAK, *PATHETIC* FOOL!
URK...
HANG ON...
UMMM... DIDN'T I JUST *DESTROY* YOUR FACE...?
...YEP.
THEN HOW COME YOU LOOK OKAY NOW?
I DUNNO... *MAGIC*...?
YEAH!
LET'S GO WITH *MAGIC*!!!

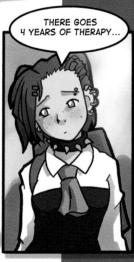

#62

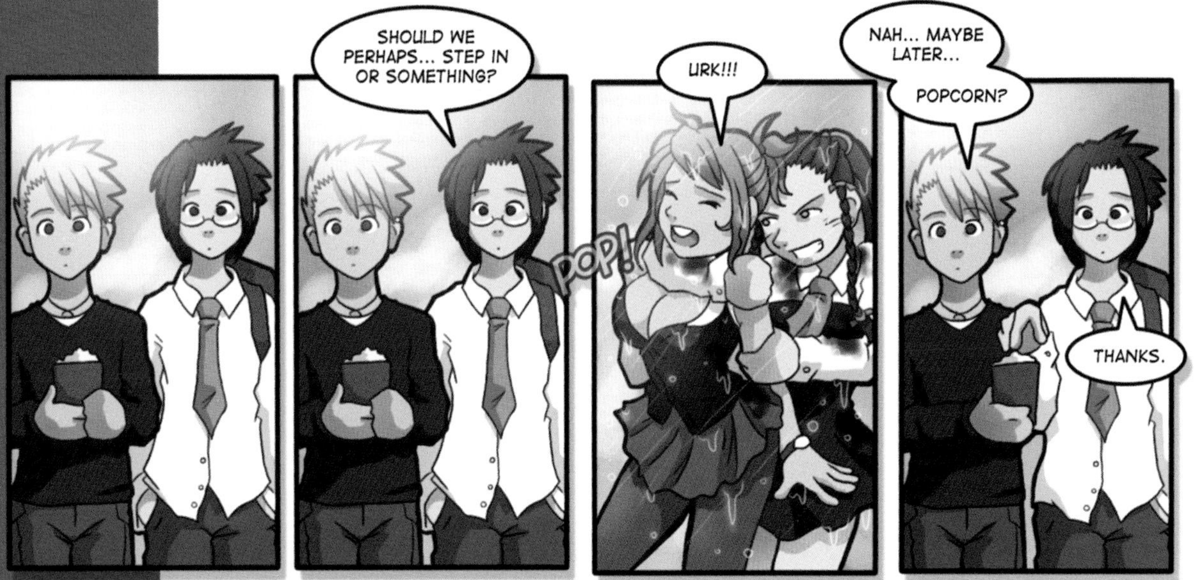
SHOULD WE PERHAPS... STEP IN OR SOMETHING?
URK!!!
POP!
NAH... MAYBE LATER...
POPCORN?
THANKS.

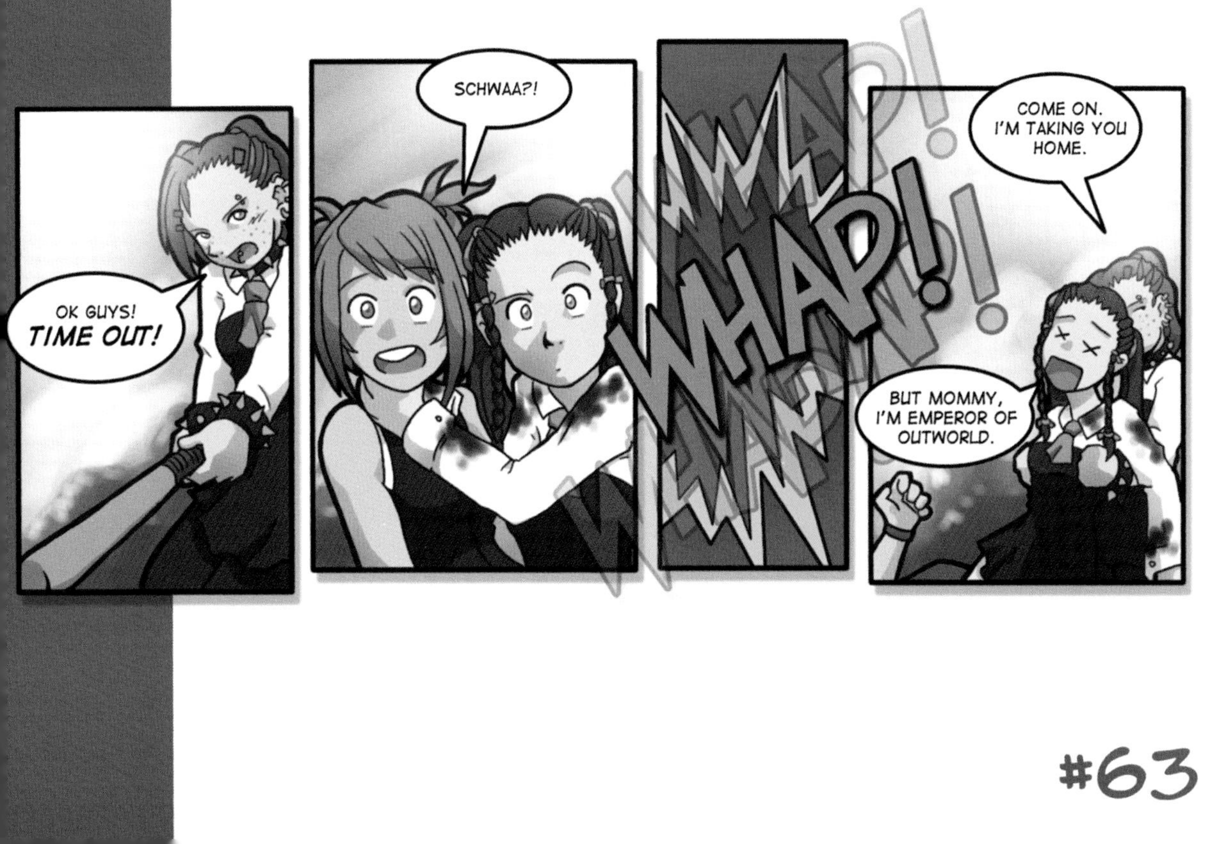
OK GUYS! ***TIME OUT!***
SCHWAA?!
WHAP!
COME ON. I'M TAKING YOU HOME.
BUT MOMMY, I'M EMPEROR OF OUTWORLD.

#63

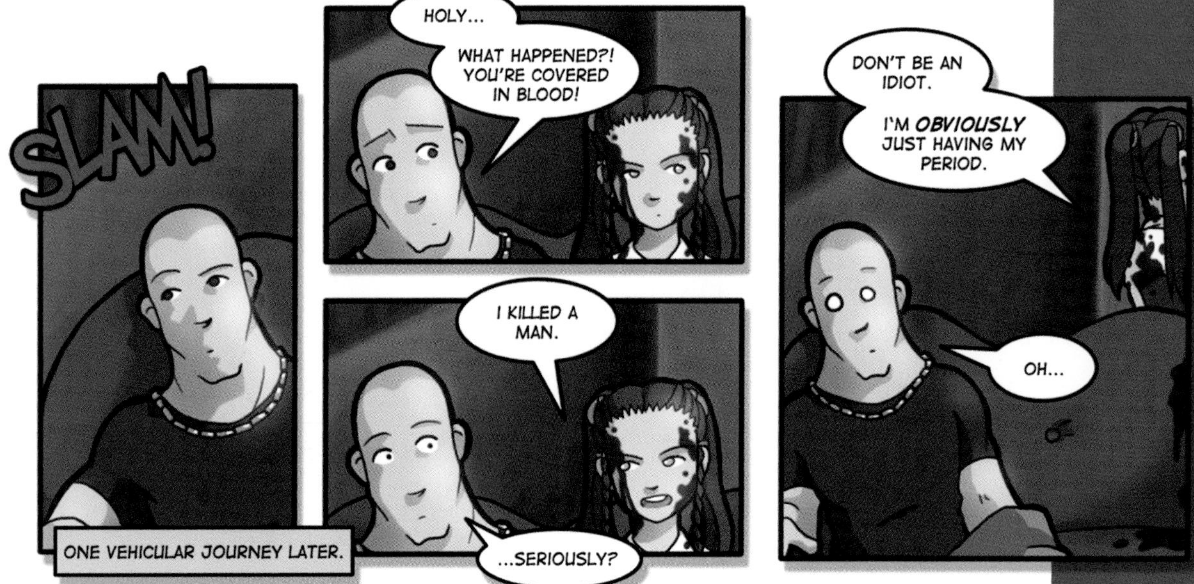
SLAM!
ONE VEHICULAR JOURNEY LATER.
HOLY...
WHAT HAPPENED?! YOU'RE COVERED IN BLOOD!
I KILLED A MAN.
...SERIOUSLY?
DON'T BE AN IDIOT.
I'M *OBVIOUSLY* JUST HAVING MY PERIOD.
OH...

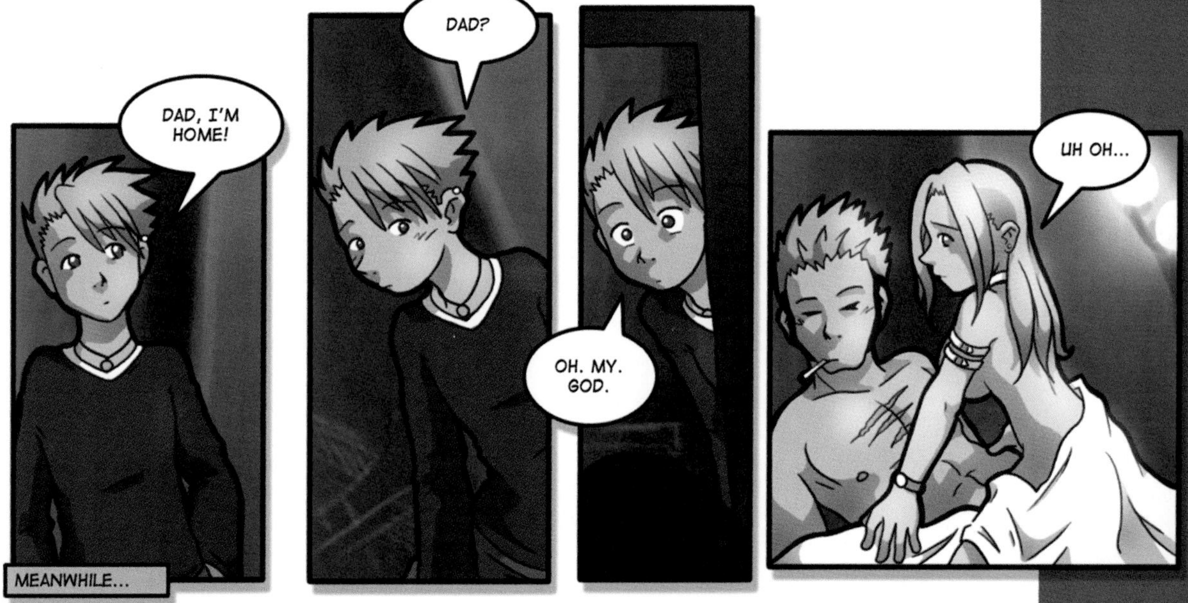
DAD, I'M HOME!
MEANWHILE...
DAD?
OH. MY. GOD.
UH OH...

#64

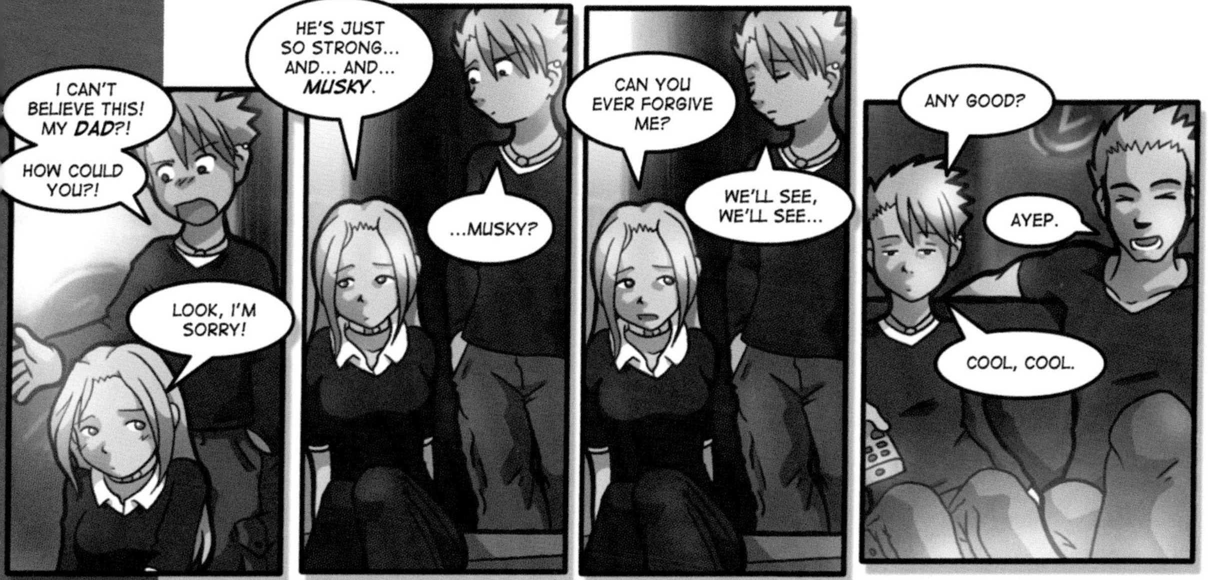
I CAN'T BELIEVE THIS! MY *DAD*?!
HOW COULD YOU?!
LOOK, I'M SORRY!
HE'S JUST SO STRONG... AND... AND... *MUSKY*.
...MUSKY?
CAN YOU EVER FORGIVE ME?
WE'LL SEE, WE'LL SEE...
ANY GOOD?
AYEP.
COOL, COOL.

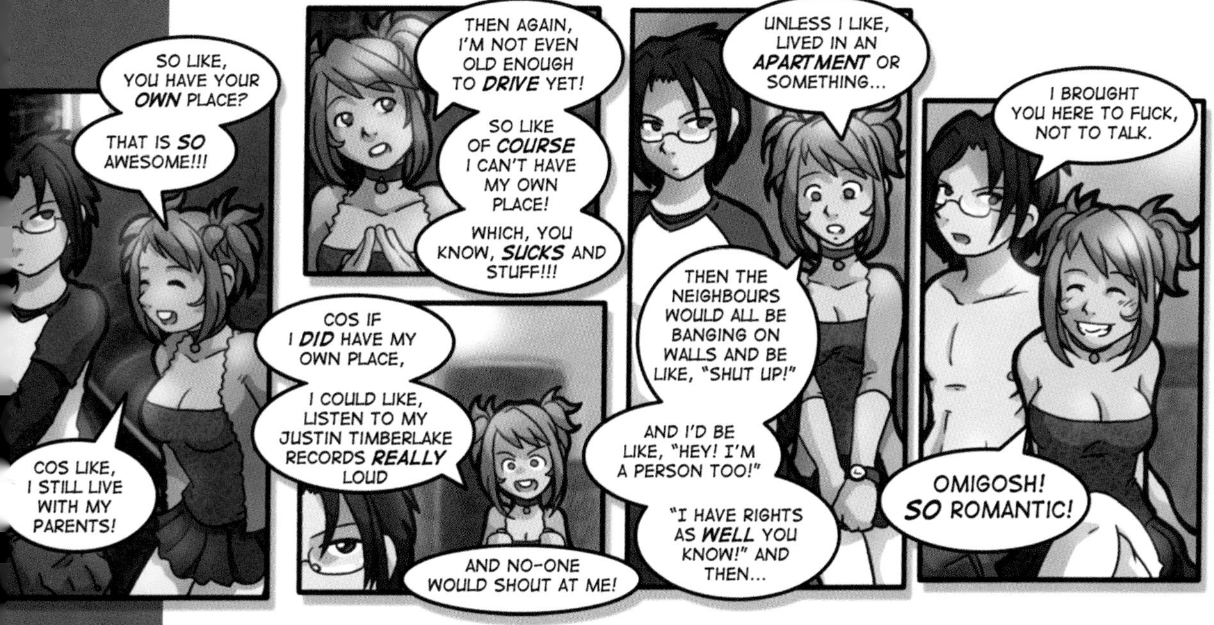
SO LIKE, YOU HAVE YOUR *OWN* PLACE?
THAT IS *SO* AWESOME!!!
COS LIKE, I STILL LIVE WITH MY PARENTS!
THEN AGAIN, I'M NOT EVEN OLD ENOUGH TO *DRIVE* YET!
SO LIKE OF *COURSE* I CAN'T HAVE MY OWN PLACE!
WHICH, YOU KNOW, *SUCKS* AND STUFF!!!
COS IF I *DID* HAVE MY OWN PLACE,
I COULD LIKE, LISTEN TO MY JUSTIN TIMBERLAKE RECORDS *REALLY* LOUD
AND NO-ONE WOULD SHOUT AT ME!
UNLESS I LIKE, LIVED IN AN *APARTMENT* OR SOMETHING...
THEN THE NEIGHBOURS WOULD ALL BE BANGING ON WALLS AND BE LIKE, "SHUT UP!"
AND I'D BE LIKE, "HEY! I'M A PERSON TOO!"
"I HAVE RIGHTS AS *WELL* YOU KNOW!" AND THEN...
I BROUGHT YOU HERE TO FUCK, NOT TO TALK.
OMIGOSH! *SO* ROMANTIC!

#65

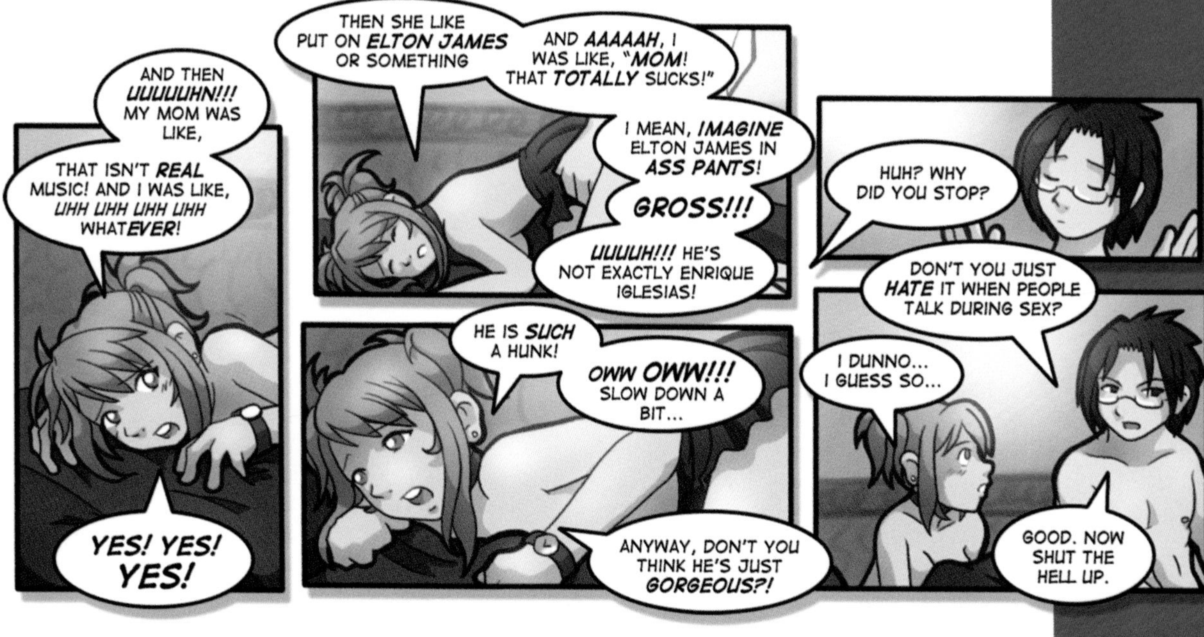
AND THEN UUUUUHN!!! MY MOM WAS LIKE,
THAT ISN'T REAL MUSIC! AND I WAS LIKE, UHH UHH UHH UHH WHATEVER!
YES! YES! YES!
THEN SHE LIKE PUT ON ELTON JAMES OR SOMETHING
AND AAAAAH, I WAS LIKE, "MOM! THAT TOTALLY SUCKS!"
I MEAN, IMAGINE ELTON JAMES IN ASS PANTS!
GROSS!!!
UUUUH!!! HE'S NOT EXACTLY ENRIQUE IGLESIAS!
HE IS SUCH A HUNK!
OWW OWW!!! SLOW DOWN A BIT...
ANYWAY, DON'T YOU THINK HE'S JUST GORGEOUS?!
HUH? WHY DID YOU STOP?
DON'T YOU JUST HATE IT WHEN PEOPLE TALK DURING SEX?
I DUNNO... I GUESS SO...
GOOD. NOW SHUT THE HELL UP.

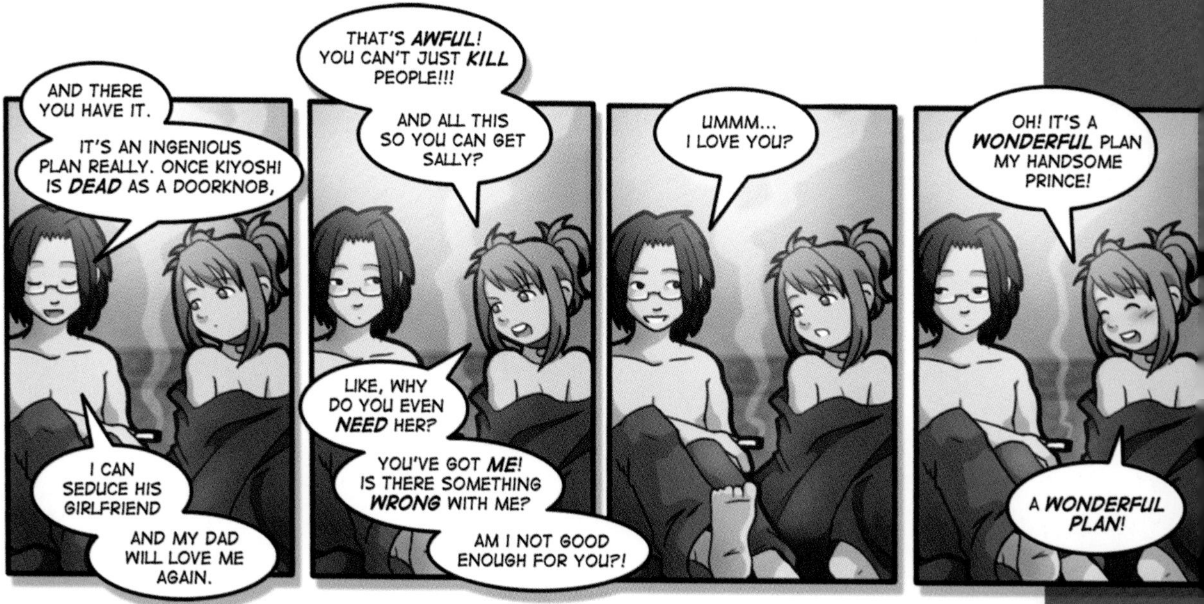
AND THERE YOU HAVE IT.
IT'S AN INGENIOUS PLAN REALLY. ONCE KIYOSHI IS DEAD AS A DOORKNOB,
I CAN SEDUCE HIS GIRLFRIEND
AND MY DAD WILL LOVE ME AGAIN.
THAT'S AWFUL! YOU CAN'T JUST KILL PEOPLE!!!
AND ALL THIS SO YOU CAN GET SALLY?
LIKE, WHY DO YOU EVEN NEED HER?
YOU'VE GOT ME! IS THERE SOMETHING WRONG WITH ME?
AM I NOT GOOD ENOUGH FOR YOU?!
UMMM... I LOVE YOU?
OH! IT'S A WONDERFUL PLAN MY HANDSOME PRINCE!
A WONDERFUL PLAN!

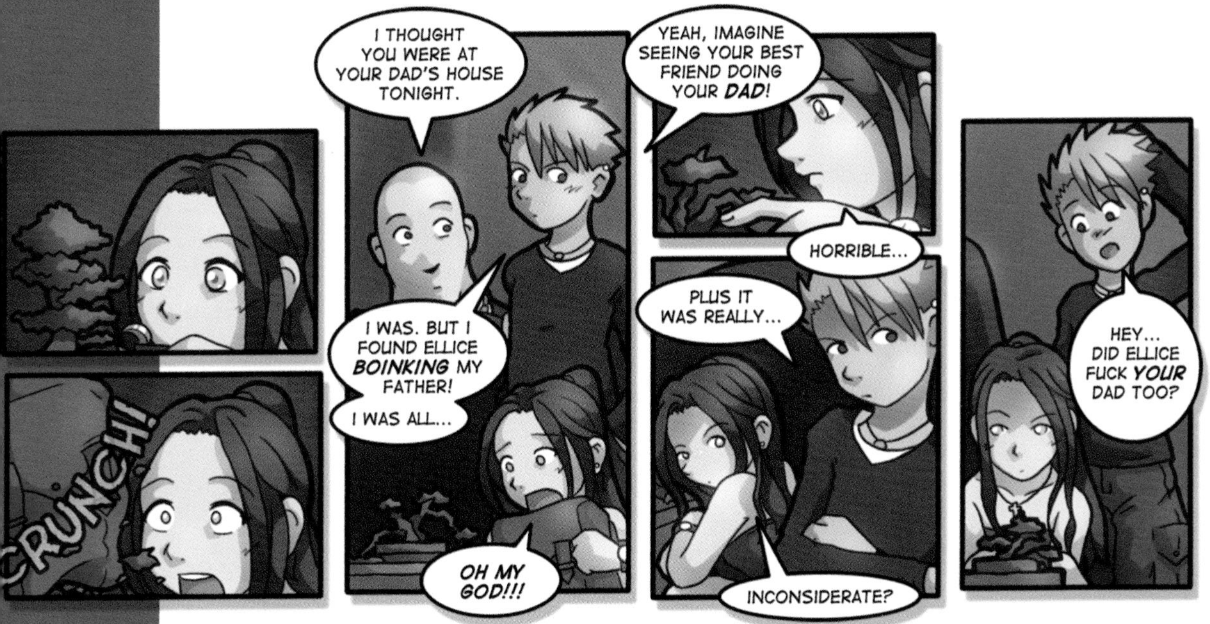
CRUNCH!
I THOUGHT YOU WERE AT YOUR DAD'S HOUSE TONIGHT.
I WAS. BUT I FOUND ELLICE **BOINKING** MY FATHER!
I WAS ALL...
OH MY GOD!!!
YEAH, IMAGINE SEEING YOUR BEST FRIEND DOING YOUR **DAD**!
HORRIBLE...
PLUS IT WAS REALLY...
INCONSIDERATE?
HEY... DID ELLICE FUCK **YOUR** DAD TOO?

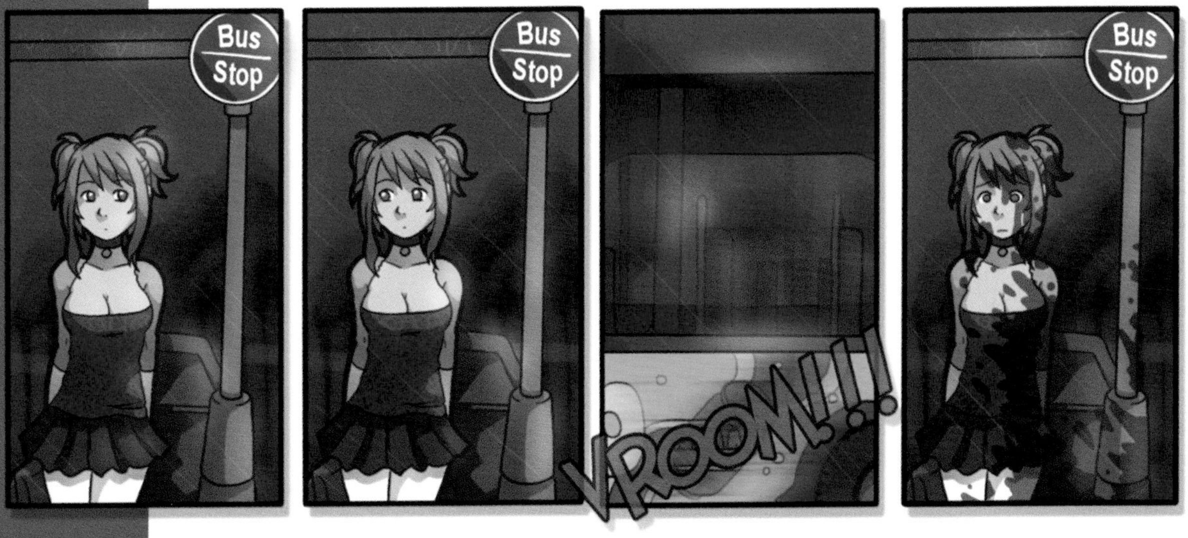
Bus Stop
Bus Stop
VROOM!!!!
Bus Stop

#67

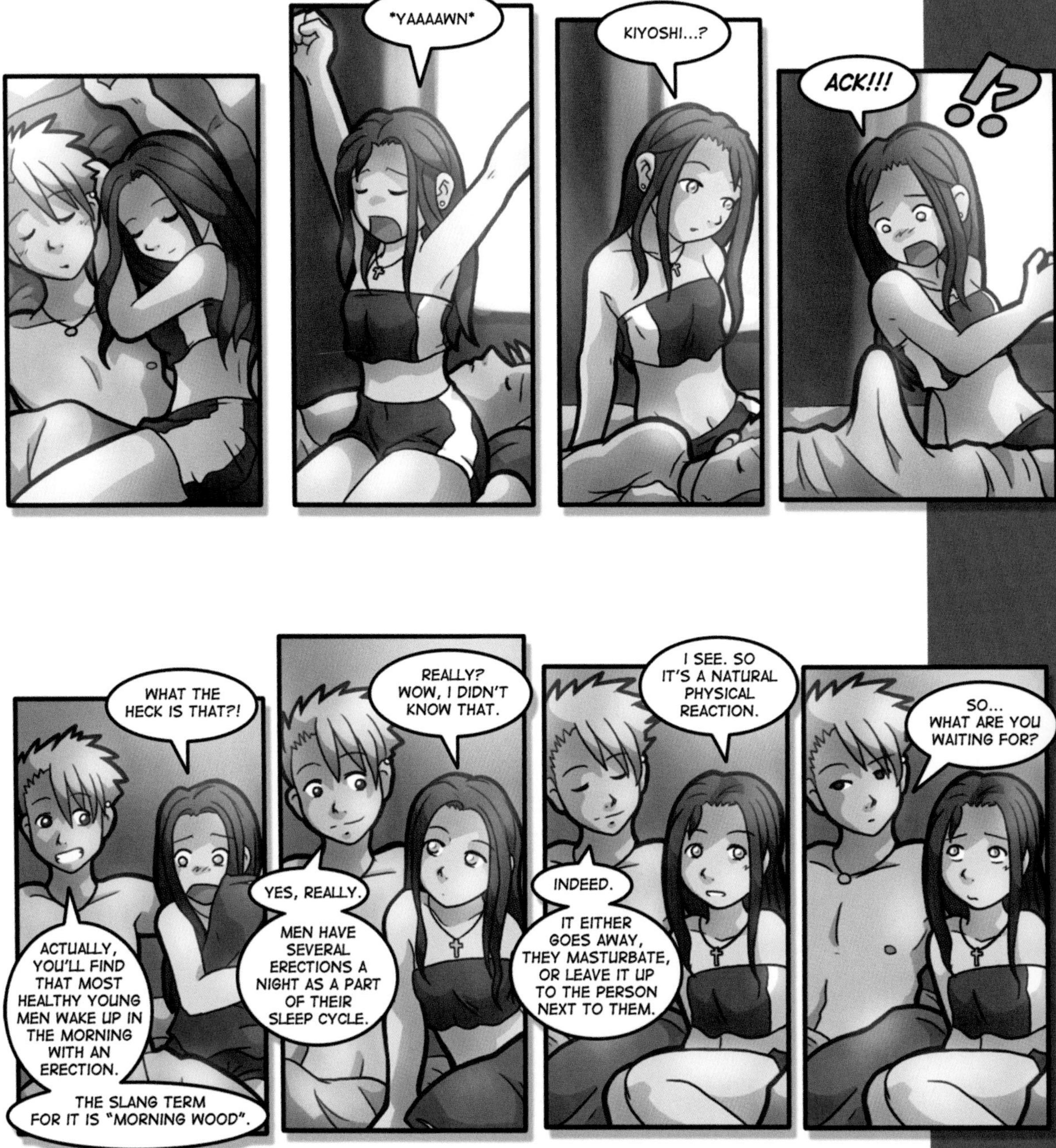
YAAAAWN
KIYOSHI...?
ACK!!!
!?
WHAT THE HECK IS THAT?!
ACTUALLY, YOU'LL FIND THAT MOST HEALTHY YOUNG MEN WAKE UP IN THE MORNING WITH AN ERECTION.
THE SLANG TERM FOR IT IS "MORNING WOOD".
REALLY? WOW, I DIDN'T KNOW THAT.
YES, REALLY.
MEN HAVE SEVERAL ERECTIONS A NIGHT AS A PART OF THEIR SLEEP CYCLE.
I SEE. SO IT'S A NATURAL PHYSICAL REACTION.
INDEED.
IT EITHER GOES AWAY, THEY MASTURBATE, OR LEAVE IT UP TO THE PERSON NEXT TO THEM.
SO... WHAT ARE YOU WAITING FOR?

#68

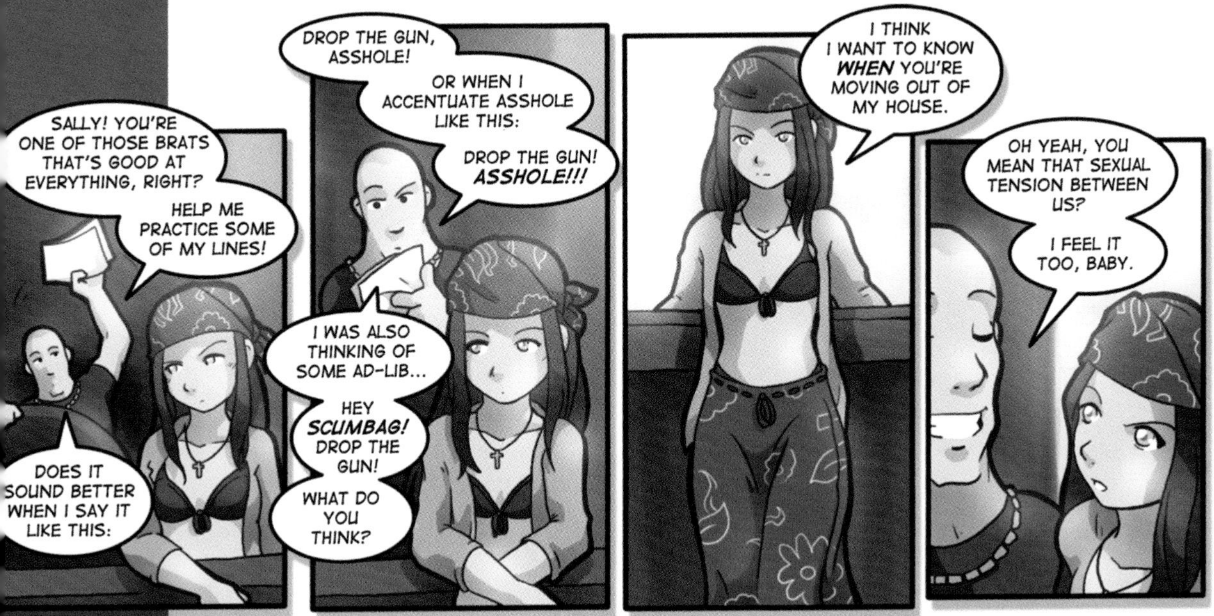
SALLY! YOU'RE ONE OF THOSE BRATS THAT'S GOOD AT EVERYTHING, RIGHT?
HELP ME PRACTICE SOME OF MY LINES!
DOES IT SOUND BETTER WHEN I SAY IT LIKE THIS:
DROP THE GUN, ASSHOLE!
OR WHEN I ACCENTUATE ASSHOLE LIKE THIS:
DROP THE GUN! **ASSHOLE!!!**
I WAS ALSO THINKING OF SOME AD-LIB...
HEY ***SCUMBAG!*** DROP THE GUN!
WHAT DO YOU THINK?
I THINK I WANT TO KNOW ***WHEN*** YOU'RE MOVING OUT OF MY HOUSE.
OH YEAH, YOU MEAN THAT SEXUAL TENSION BETWEEN US?
I FEEL IT TOO, BABY.

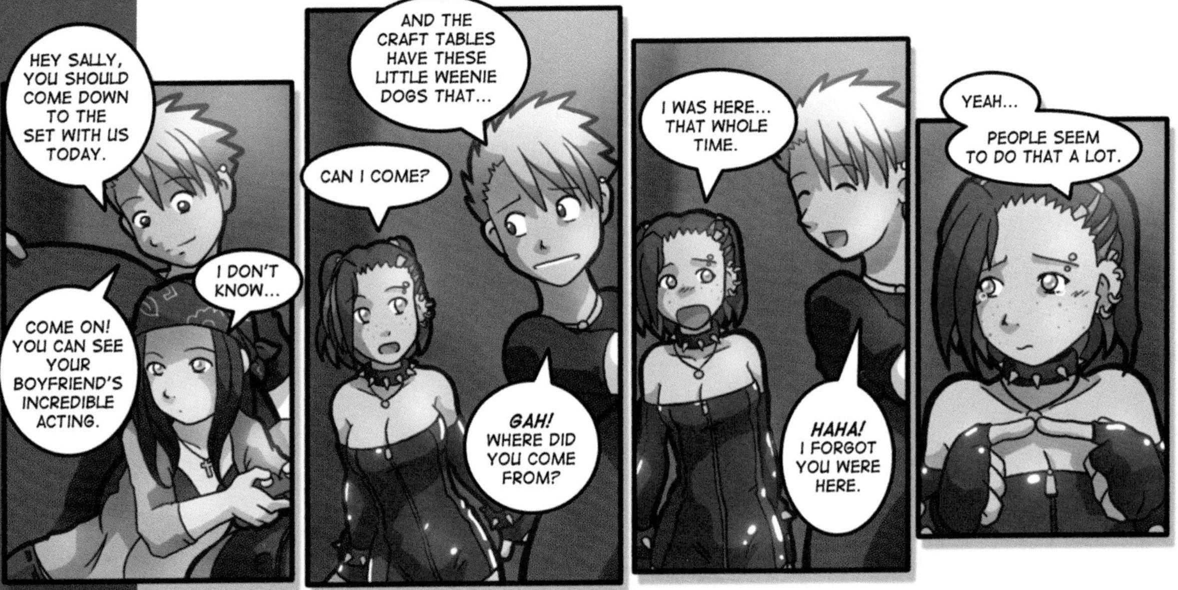
HEY SALLY, YOU SHOULD COME DOWN TO THE SET WITH US TODAY.
I DON'T KNOW...
COME ON! YOU CAN SEE YOUR BOYFRIEND'S INCREDIBLE ACTING.
AND THE CRAFT TABLES HAVE THESE LITTLE WEENIE DOGS THAT...
CAN I COME?
GAH! WHERE DID YOU COME FROM?
I WAS HERE... THAT WHOLE TIME.
HAHA! I FORGOT YOU WERE HERE.
YEAH...
PEOPLE SEEM TO DO THAT A LOT.

#69

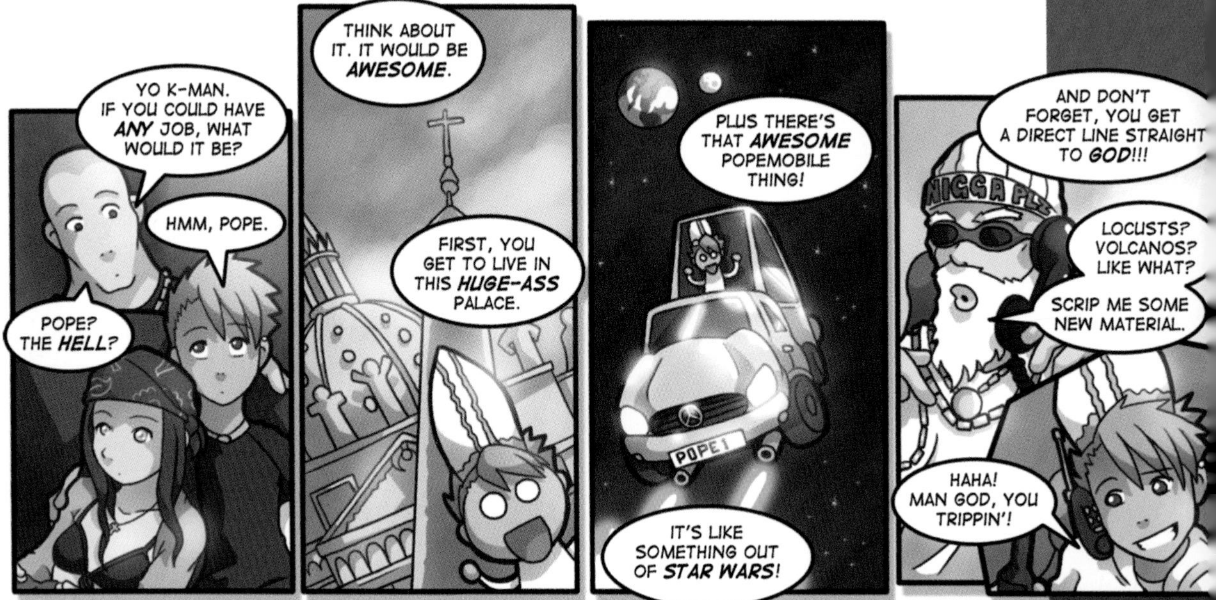
YO K-MAN. IF YOU COULD HAVE ANY JOB, WHAT WOULD IT BE?
HMM, POPE.
POPE? THE HELL?
THINK ABOUT IT. IT WOULD BE AWESOME.
FIRST, YOU GET TO LIVE IN THIS HUGE-ASS PALACE.
PLUS THERE'S THAT AWESOME POPEMOBILE THING!
POPE 1
IT'S LIKE SOMETHING OUT OF STAR WARS!
AND DON'T FORGET, YOU GET A DIRECT LINE STRAIGHT TO GOD!!!
LOCUSTS? VOLCANOS? LIKE WHAT?
SCRIP ME SOME NEW MATERIAL.
HAHA! MAN GOD, YOU TRIPPIN'!

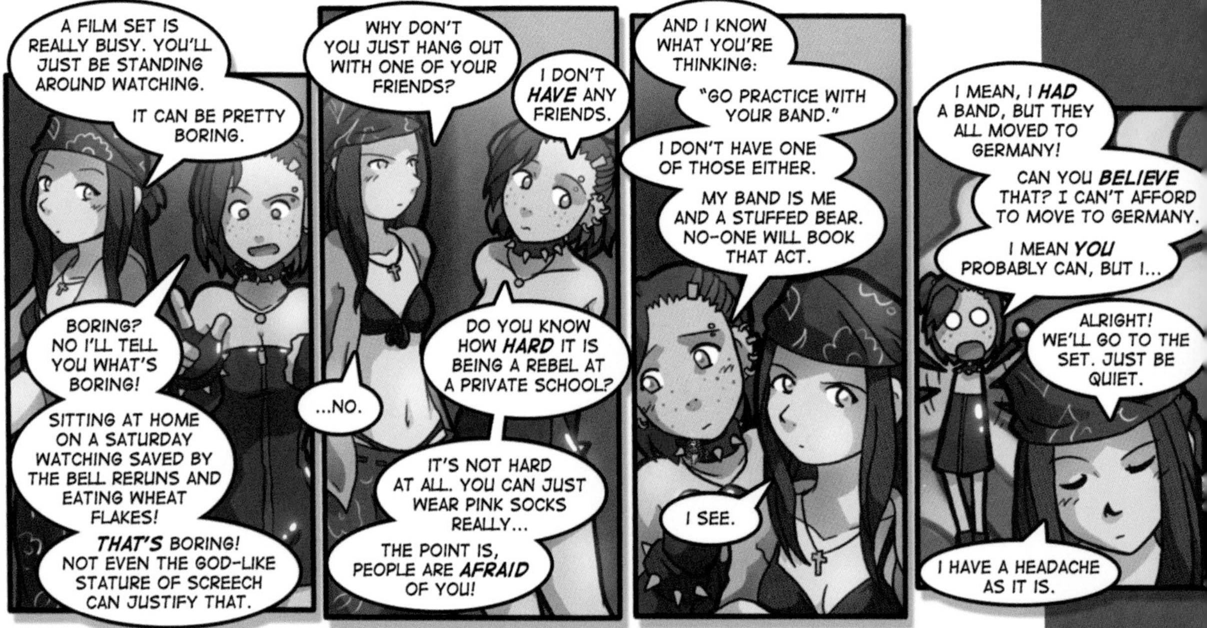
A FILM SET IS REALLY BUSY. YOU'LL JUST BE STANDING AROUND WATCHING.
IT CAN BE PRETTY BORING.
BORING? NO I'LL TELL YOU WHAT'S BORING!
SITTING AT HOME ON A SATURDAY WATCHING SAVED BY THE BELL RERUNS AND EATING WHEAT FLAKES!
THAT'S BORING! NOT EVEN THE GOD-LIKE STATURE OF SCREECH CAN JUSTIFY THAT.
WHY DON'T YOU JUST HANG OUT WITH ONE OF YOUR FRIENDS?
I DON'T HAVE ANY FRIENDS.
DO YOU KNOW HOW HARD IT IS BEING A REBEL AT A PRIVATE SCHOOL?
...NO.
IT'S NOT HARD AT ALL. YOU CAN JUST WEAR PINK SOCKS REALLY...
THE POINT IS, PEOPLE ARE AFRAID OF YOU!
AND I KNOW WHAT YOU'RE THINKING:
"GO PRACTICE WITH YOUR BAND."
I DON'T HAVE ONE OF THOSE EITHER.
MY BAND IS ME AND A STUFFED BEAR. NO-ONE WILL BOOK THAT ACT.
I SEE.
I MEAN, I HAD A BAND, BUT THEY ALL MOVED TO GERMANY!
CAN YOU BELIEVE THAT? I CAN'T AFFORD TO MOVE TO GERMANY.
I MEAN YOU PROBABLY CAN, BUT I...
ALRIGHT! WE'LL GO TO THE SET. JUST BE QUIET.
I HAVE A HEADACHE AS IT IS.

#70

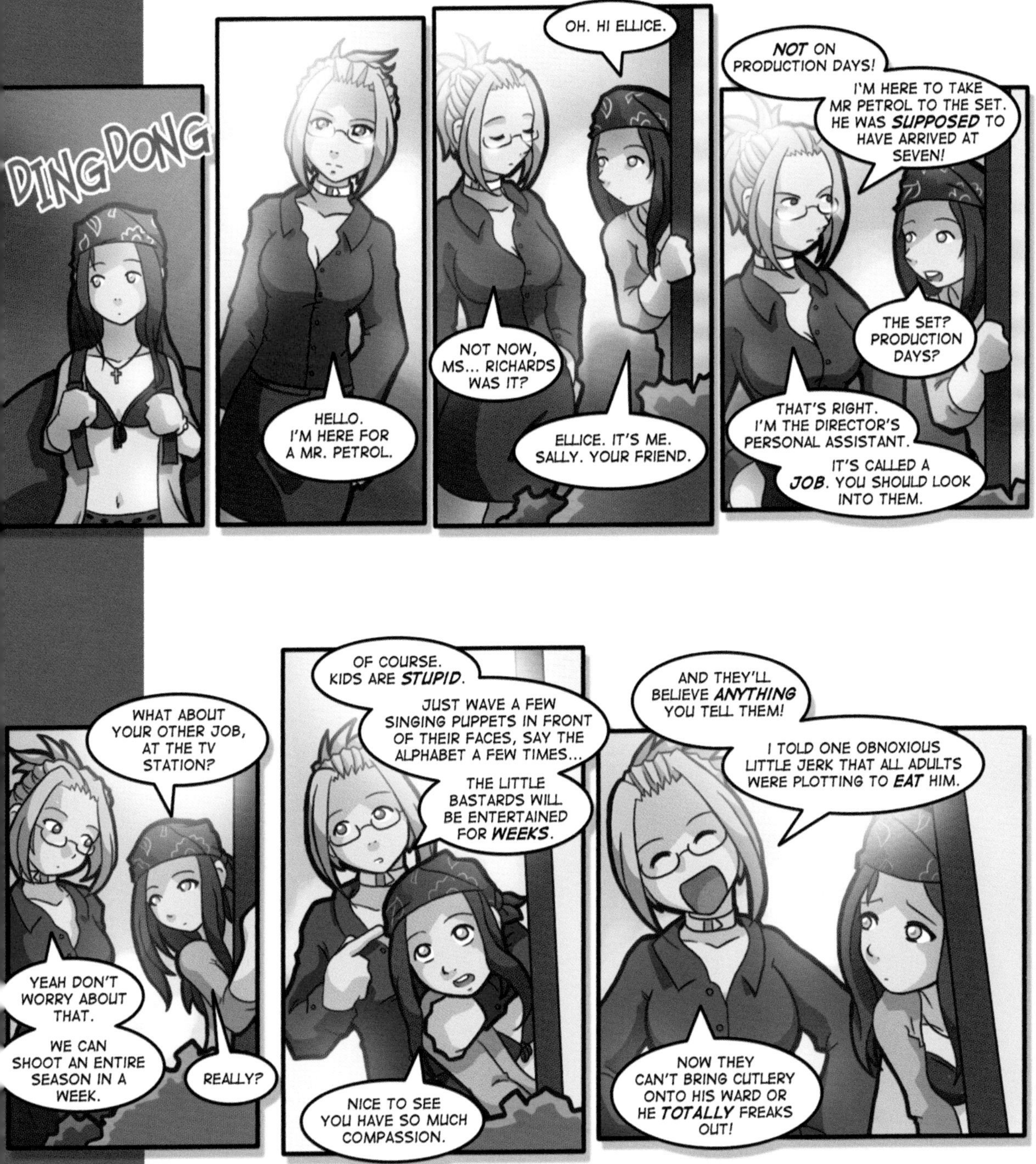
DING DONG
HELLO. I'M HERE FOR A MR. PETROL.
OH. HI ELLICE.
NOT NOW, MS... RICHARDS WAS IT?
ELLICE. IT'S ME. SALLY. YOUR FRIEND.
NOT ON PRODUCTION DAYS!
I'M HERE TO TAKE MR PETROL TO THE SET. HE WAS SUPPOSED TO HAVE ARRIVED AT SEVEN!
THE SET? PRODUCTION DAYS?
THAT'S RIGHT. I'M THE DIRECTOR'S PERSONAL ASSISTANT.
IT'S CALLED A JOB. YOU SHOULD LOOK INTO THEM.
WHAT ABOUT YOUR OTHER JOB, AT THE TV STATION?
YEAH DON'T WORRY ABOUT THAT.
WE CAN SHOOT AN ENTIRE SEASON IN A WEEK.
REALLY?
OF COURSE. KIDS ARE STUPID.
JUST WAVE A FEW SINGING PUPPETS IN FRONT OF THEIR FACES, SAY THE ALPHABET A FEW TIMES...
THE LITTLE BASTARDS WILL BE ENTERTAINED FOR WEEKS.
NICE TO SEE YOU HAVE SO MUCH COMPASSION.
AND THEY'LL BELIEVE ANYTHING YOU TELL THEM!
I TOLD ONE OBNOXIOUS LITTLE JERK THAT ALL ADULTS WERE PLOTTING TO EAT HIM.
NOW THEY CAN'T BRING CUTLERY ONTO HIS WARD OR HE TOTALLY FREAKS OUT!

#71

WHY ARE YOU WEARING GLASSES?
I DON'T BELIEVE I NEED TO JUSTIFY MYSELF TO YOU.
I'M BLIND! AAAAAAH!!! I'M BLIND, I'M BLIND!!!
WHY GOD, WHY?!
...
I SAID, I'M BLIND! THE HORROR! I CANNOT SEE A THING!
HOW CRUEL!
...
LOOK, JUST GIVE ME BACK THE GLASSES. OK?
SALLY, I CAME HERE TO BRING BACK YOUR...
OH... HI KIYOSHI...
UMM, HELLO.
ALRIGHT! AWKWARD TENSION!
YEAH! TENSION!
NOW THIS STUFF IS BETTER THAN THE MOVIES!
BETTER THAN THAT MOVIE!
WILL OLD FRIENDS RECONCILE? OR WILL THIS SPIRAL INTO A HEART WRENCHING FEUD?
RECONCILIATION IS THE MARK OF THE DEVIL!
ONLY PIRATE WENCHES TEAR APART OLD FRIENDS!
WHAT!?

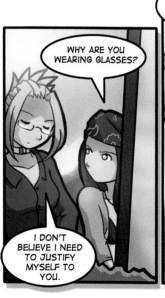

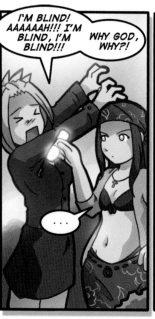

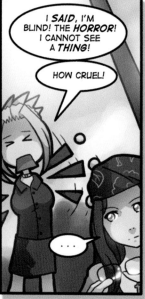

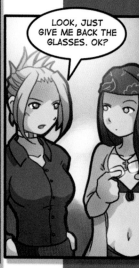

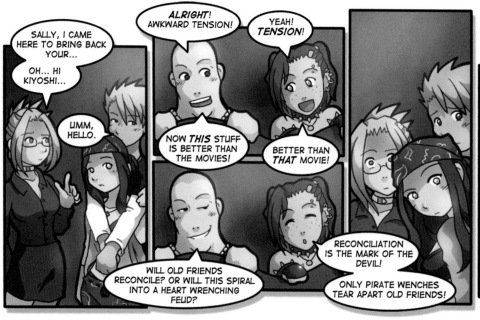

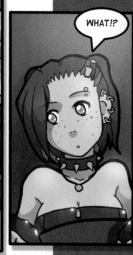

#72

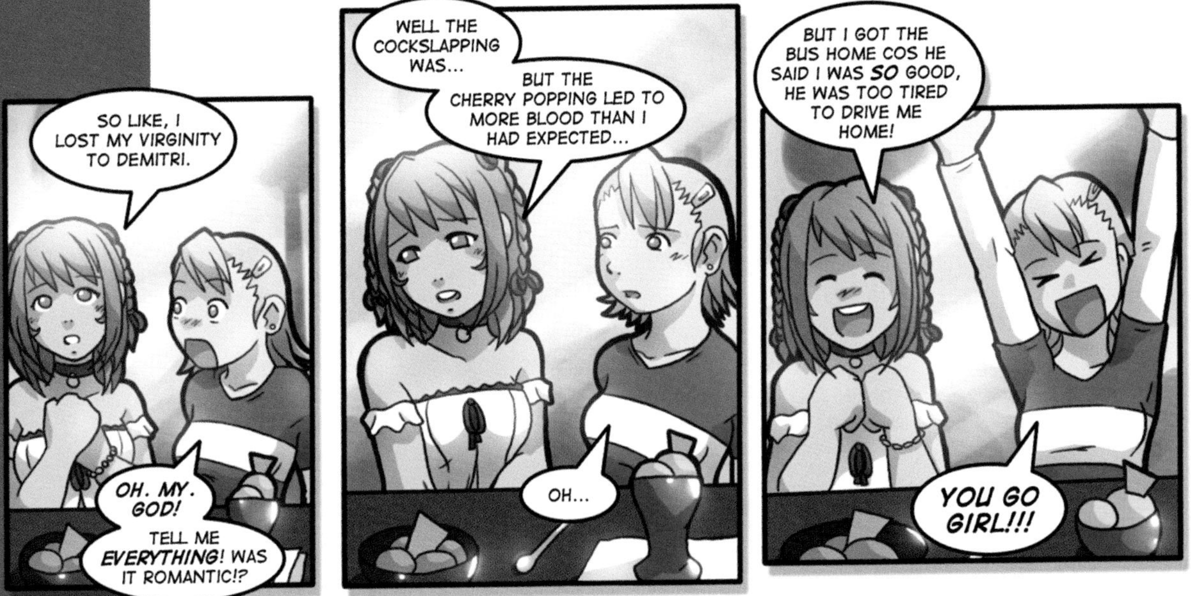
SO LIKE, I LOST MY VIRGINITY TO DEMITRI.
OH. MY. GOD!
TELL ME EVERYTHING! WAS IT ROMANTIC!?
WELL THE COCKSLAPPING WAS...
BUT THE CHERRY POPPING LED TO MORE BLOOD THAN I HAD EXPECTED...
OH...
BUT I GOT THE BUS HOME COS HE SAID I WAS SO GOOD, HE WAS TOO TIRED TO DRIVE ME HOME!
YOU GO GIRL!!!

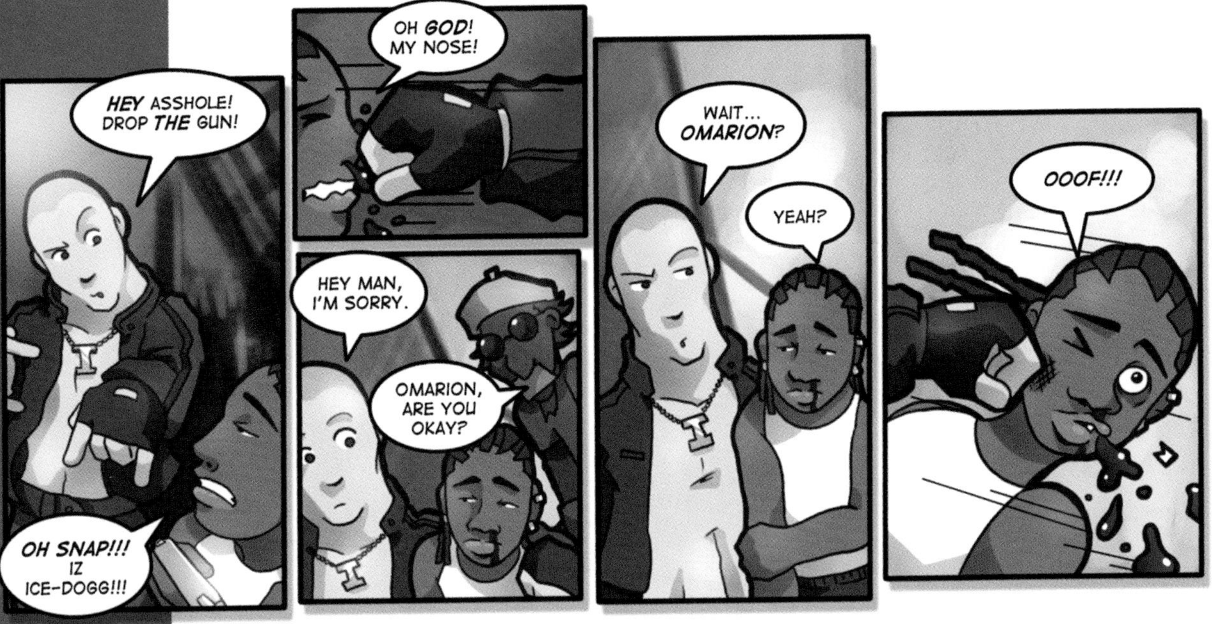
HEY ASSHOLE! DROP THE GUN!
OH SNAP!!! IZ ICE-DOGG!!!
OH GOD! MY NOSE!
HEY MAN, I'M SORRY.
OMARION, ARE YOU OKAY?
WAIT... OMARION?
YEAH?
OOOF!!!

MY *OTHER* JOB SET ME UP NICELY FOR THIS GIG.

THE STUDIO WANTED TO INVITE A BUNCH OF DYING KIDS TO MAKE US LOOK GOOD.

OBVIOUSLY *I* WAS THE PERFECT CHOICE TO HANDLE IT.

THE LITTLE BEGGARS *LOVE* ME.

I'M SO GREAT WITH KIDS.

EWWICE! EWWICE! I SAWED A *LION*!!!

THAT'S GREAT AMY, BUT ELLICE AND HER FRIEND ARE HAVING GROWN-UP TALK.

THAT ISN'T VERY NICE.

A *LION* HUH?! DID IT HAVE GREAT BIG SCARY TEETH?!

HEE HEE! *YUP!*

I WIKE YOU! IS EWWICE YOUR MOMMY?

NO. BUT SHE SURE LOOKS OLD ENOUGH TO BE, HUH?

YUP!

OH. THINK YOU'RE SMART EH?

WELL WATCH *THIS.*

AMY, YOU KNOW HOW YOU LOST YOUR ONLY GOOD KIDNEY LAST YEAR, AND NOW THE DOCTORS SAY YOU'RE GONNA DIE?

...YES.

WELL THAT'S COS SALLY HERE *STOLE* IT!

I DID NOT!

SNIFF

Y..YOU... YOU TOOK MY KIDNEY...?

WAA! WAA! GIVE IT BACK! GIVE IT BACK!

I... I...

I'LL LEAVE YOU TWO ALONE.

#74

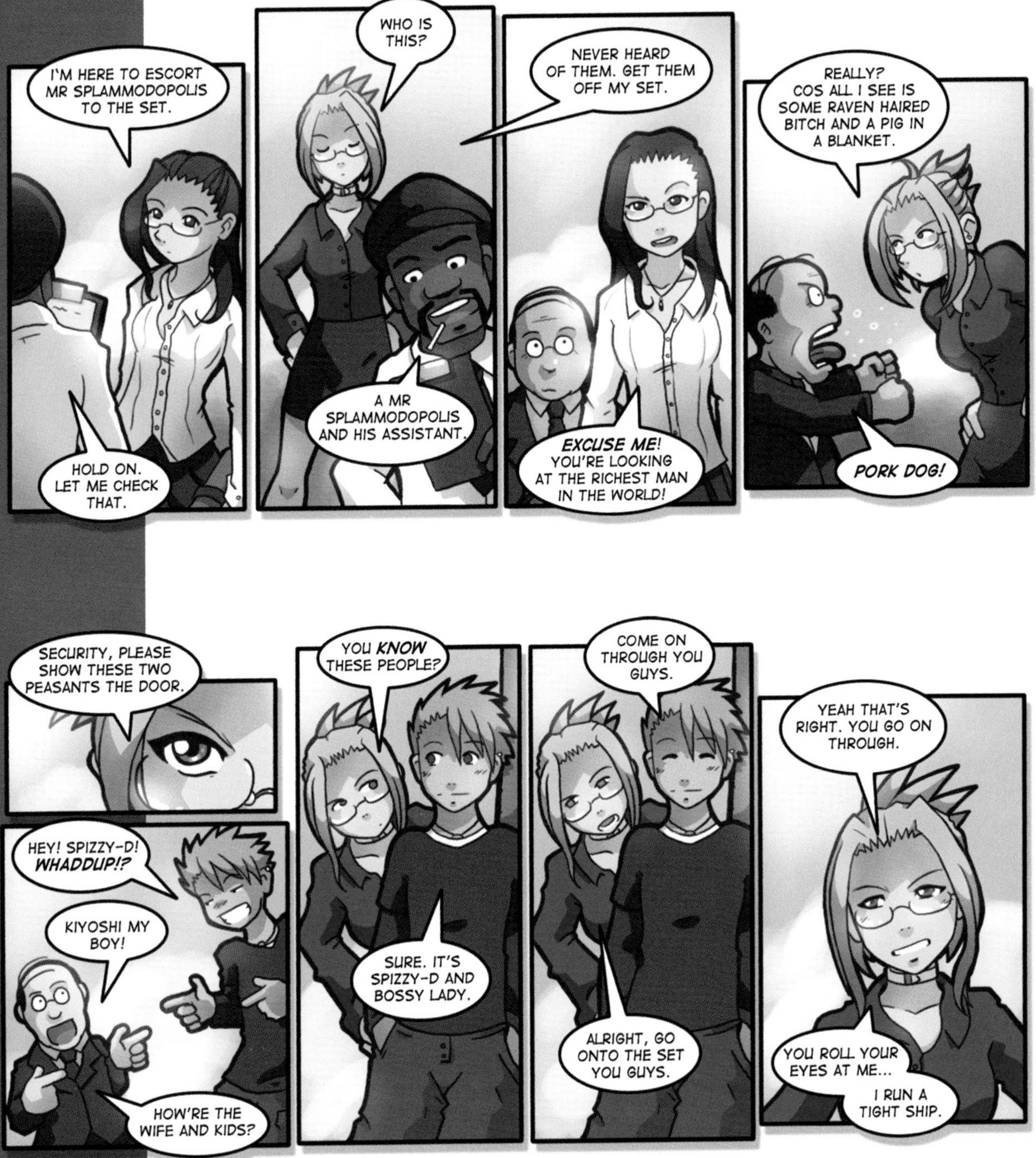
I'M HERE TO ESCORT MR SPLAMMODOPOLIS TO THE SET.
HOLD ON. LET ME CHECK THAT.
WHO IS THIS?
A MR SPLAMMODOPOLIS AND HIS ASSISTANT.
NEVER HEARD OF THEM. GET THEM OFF MY SET.
EXCUSE ME! YOU'RE LOOKING AT THE RICHEST MAN IN THE WORLD!
REALLY? COS ALL I SEE IS SOME RAVEN HAIRED BITCH AND A PIG IN A BLANKET.
PORK DOG!
SECURITY, PLEASE SHOW THESE TWO PEASANTS THE DOOR.
HEY! SPIZZY-D! *WHADDUP!?*
KIYOSHI MY BOY!
HOW'RE THE WIFE AND KIDS?
YOU *KNOW* THESE PEOPLE?
SURE. IT'S SPIZZY-D AND BOSSY LADY.
COME ON THROUGH YOU GUYS.
ALRIGHT, GO ONTO THE SET YOU GUYS.
YEAH THAT'S RIGHT. YOU GO ON THROUGH.
YOU ROLL YOUR EYES AT ME...
I RUN A TIGHT SHIP.

#75

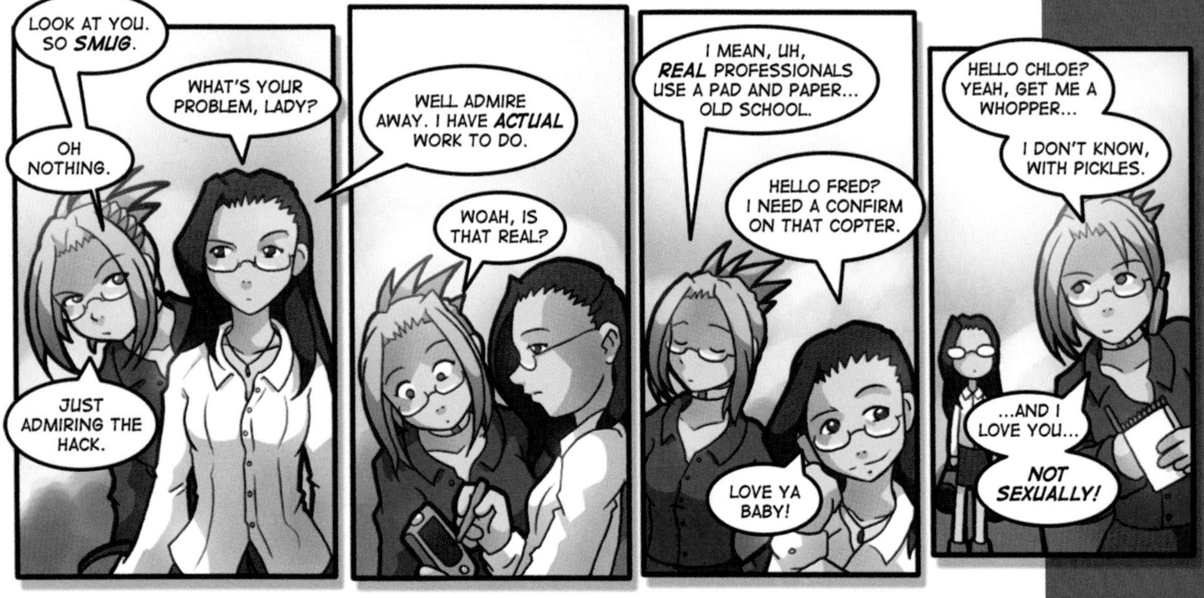
LOOK AT YOU. SO SMUG.
OH NOTHING.
JUST ADMIRING THE HACK.
WHAT'S YOUR PROBLEM, LADY?
WELL ADMIRE AWAY. I HAVE ACTUAL WORK TO DO.
WOAH, IS THAT REAL?
I MEAN, UH, REAL PROFESSIONALS USE A PAD AND PAPER... OLD SCHOOL.
HELLO FRED? I NEED A CONFIRM ON THAT COPTER.
LOVE YA BABY!
HELLO CHLOE? YEAH, GET ME A WHOPPER...
I DON'T KNOW, WITH PICKLES.
...AND I LOVE YOU...
NOT SEXUALLY!

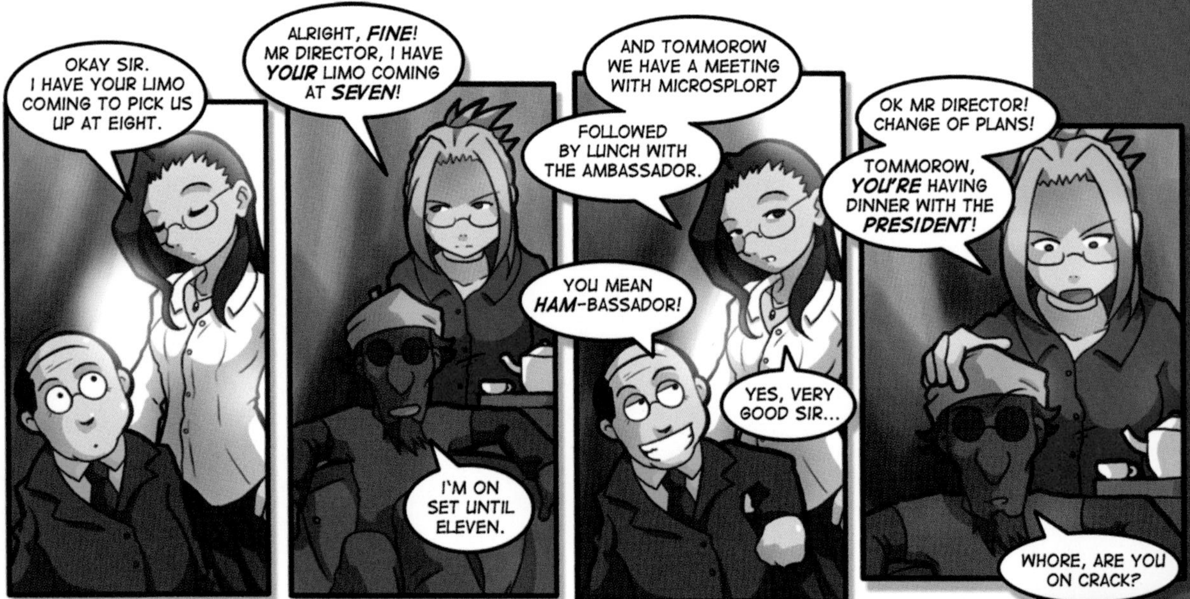
OKAY SIR. I HAVE YOUR LIMO COMING TO PICK US UP AT EIGHT.
ALRIGHT, FINE! MR DIRECTOR, I HAVE YOUR LIMO COMING AT SEVEN!
I'M ON SET UNTIL ELEVEN.
AND TOMMOROW WE HAVE A MEETING WITH MICROSPLORT
FOLLOWED BY LUNCH WITH THE AMBASSADOR.
YOU MEAN HAM-BASSADOR!
YES, VERY GOOD SIR...
OK MR DIRECTOR! CHANGE OF PLANS!
TOMMOROW, YOU'RE HAVING DINNER WITH THE PRESIDENT!
WHORE, ARE YOU ON CRACK?

#76

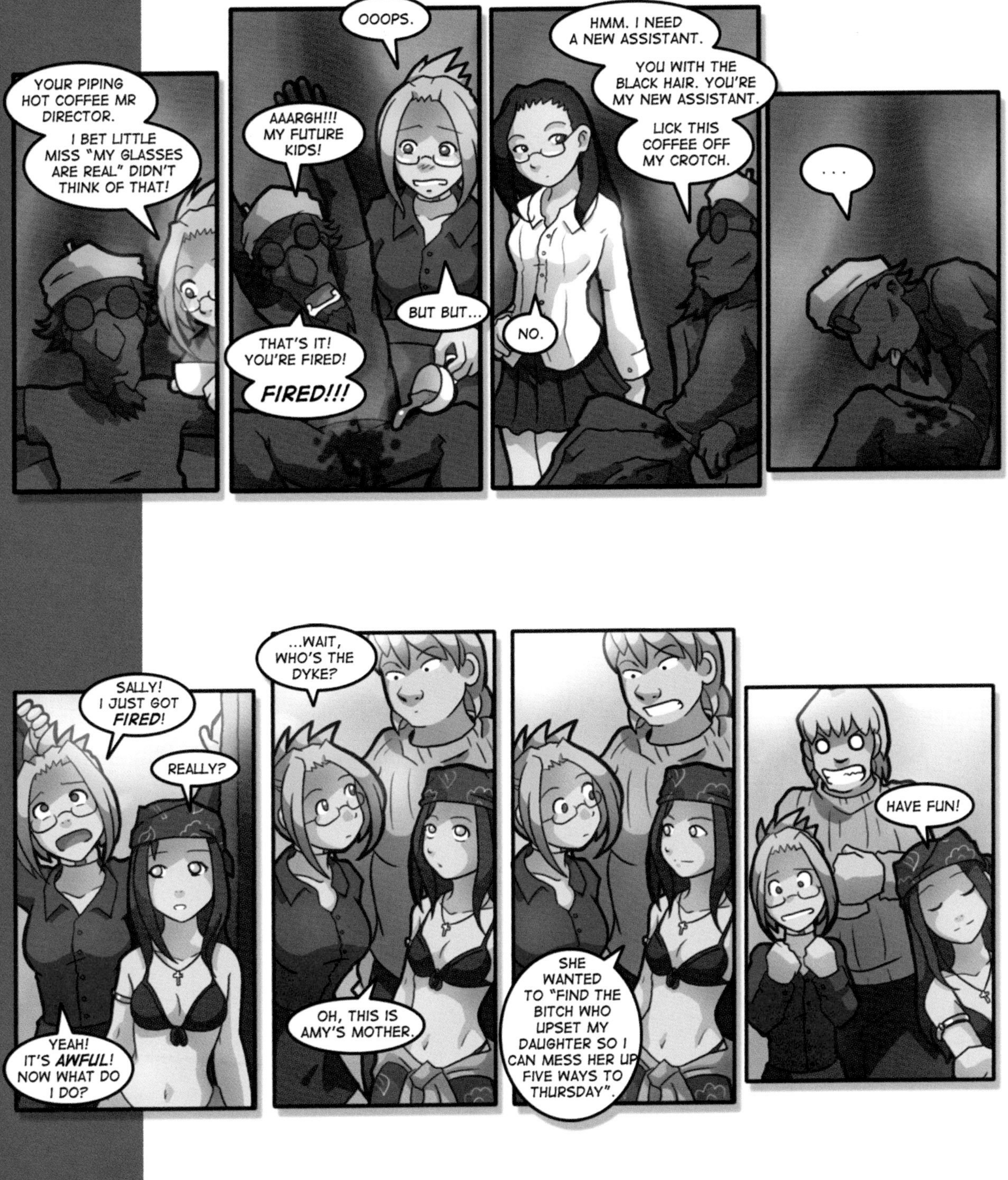
YOUR PIPING HOT COFFEE MR DIRECTOR.
I BET LITTLE MISS "MY GLASSES ARE REAL" DIDN'T THINK OF THAT!
OOOPS.
AAARGH!!! MY FUTURE KIDS!
THAT'S IT! YOU'RE FIRED!
FIRED!!!
BUT BUT...
HMM. I NEED A NEW ASSISTANT.
YOU WITH THE BLACK HAIR. YOU'RE MY NEW ASSISTANT.
LICK THIS COFFEE OFF MY CROTCH.
NO.
...
SALLY! I JUST GOT FIRED!
REALLY?
YEAH! IT'S AWFUL! NOW WHAT DO I DO?
...WAIT, WHO'S THE DYKE?
OH, THIS IS AMY'S MOTHER.
SHE WANTED TO "FIND THE BITCH WHO UPSET MY DAUGHTER SO I CAN MESS HER UP FIVE WAYS TO THURSDAY".
HAVE FUN!

#77

OMIGOD! ***HI***!!!
OH. IT'S YOU.
WHAT DO YOU WANT? I REALLY HAVE TO BE SOMEWHERE.
I WAS JUST SAYING HI!
OH RIGHT. I GUESS I CAN SPARE 30 MINUTES OR SO.
WE'LL HAVE TO DO IT IN THE BACK OF MY CAR THOUGH.
HUH? DO WHAT?
JUST SHUT UP AND FOLLOW ME. I PARKED CLOSE ROUND THE CORNER.
CAN I COME?
HUH? WHAT? COME WHERE?
?
I ***LIKE*** WHERE THIS IS GOING, LADIES.
THANKS FOR A DECIDEDLY MEDIOCRE TIME.
I HAVE TO GO AND DO SOMETHING NOW.
VROOOOOM!!!
UM... DOES THIS MAKE ME A SLUT?

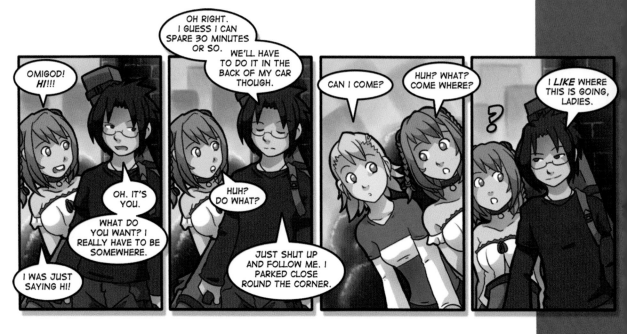

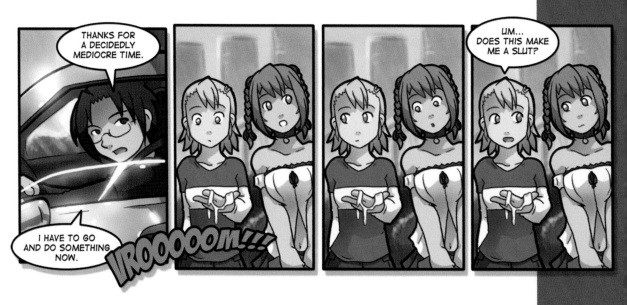

#78

OK... NOW WHAT?
WE COULD GO SEE A MOVIE.
SURE. WE CAN GO AND SEE SAW.
I ALREADY SAW SAW.
YOU SAW SAW?
YEAH, DID YOU NOT SEE SAW?
SEE SAW?
SAW SEE?

SEE SAW?
SAW SEE?
SAWED SEES?
SEE'D SAW SAWED SAWS SEE SO SAW SAID!
SPLORT!
NOT CANON!
SO DON'T BOTHER ASKING!

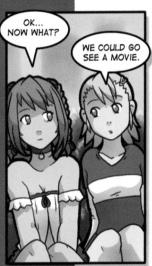

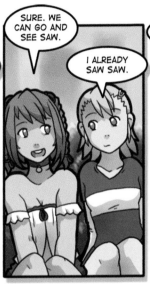

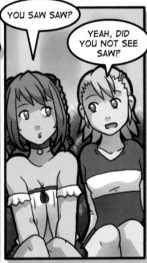

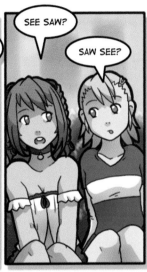

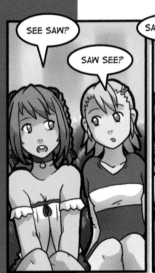

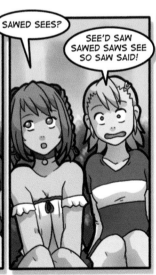

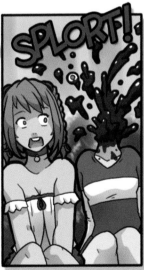

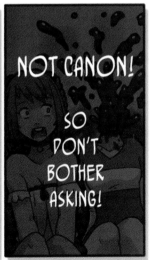

#79

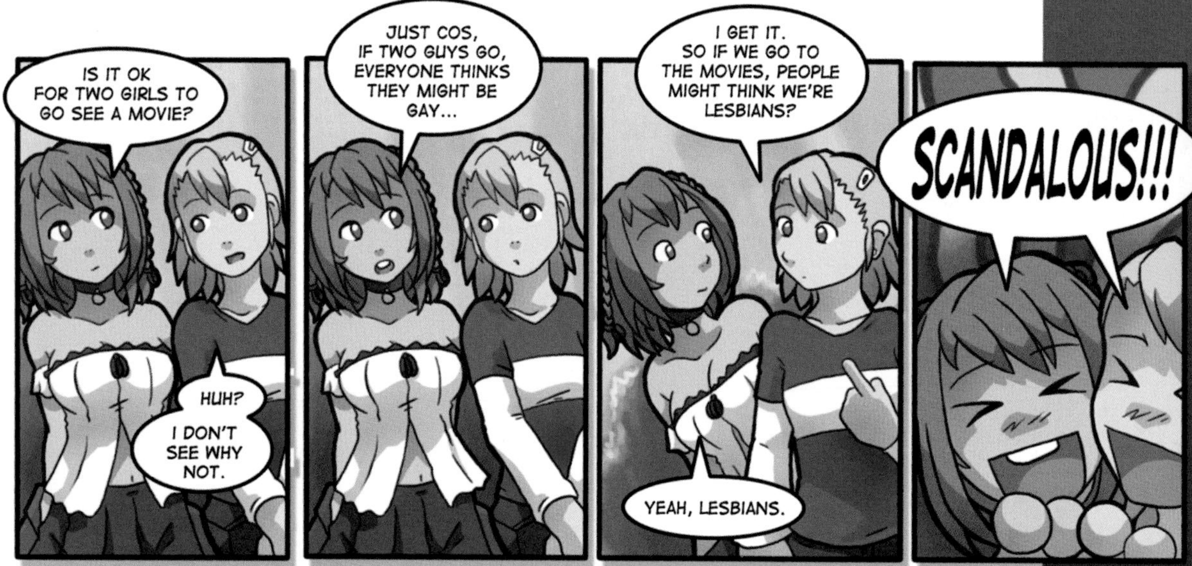
IS IT OK FOR TWO GIRLS TO GO SEE A MOVIE?
HUH?
I DON'T SEE WHY NOT.
JUST COS, IF TWO GUYS GO, EVERYONE THINKS THEY MIGHT BE GAY...
I GET IT. SO IF WE GO TO THE MOVIES, PEOPLE MIGHT THINK WE'RE LESBIANS?
YEAH, LESBIANS.
SCANDALOUS!!!

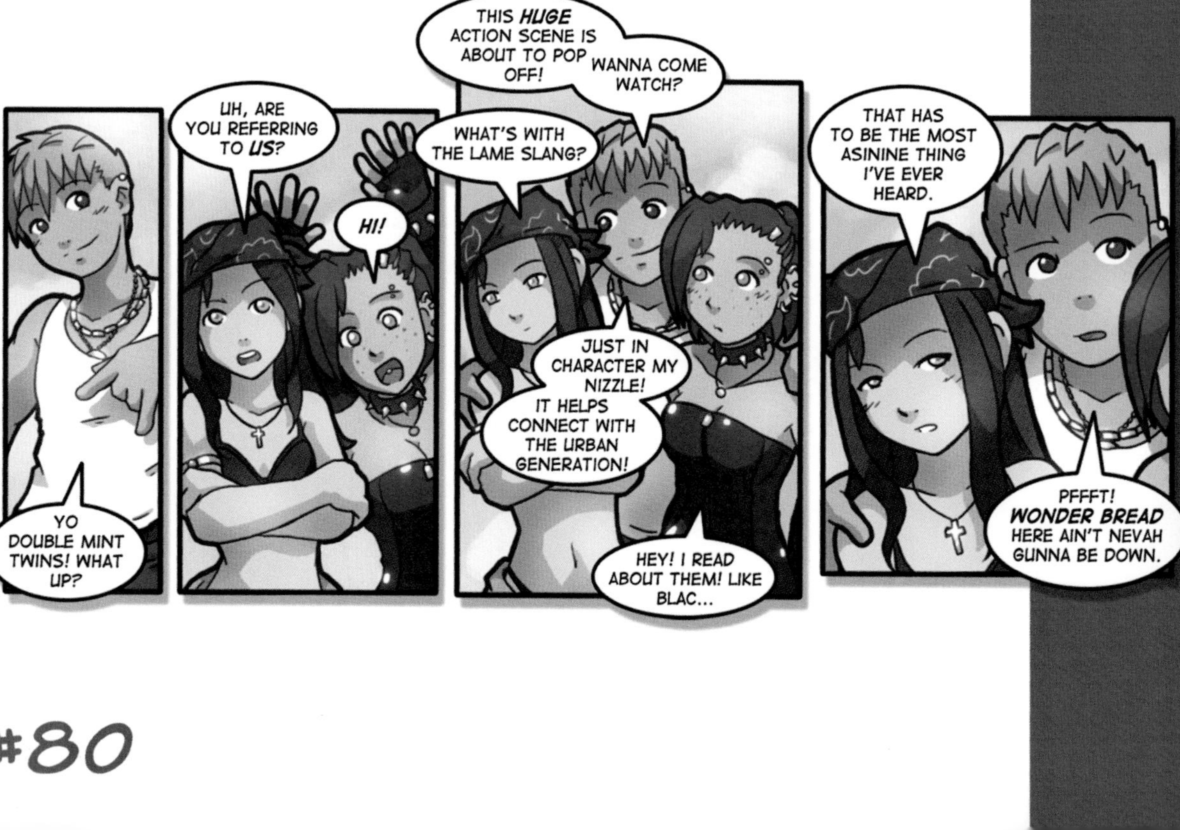
YO DOUBLE MINT TWINS! WHAT UP?
UH, ARE YOU REFERRING TO *US*?
HI!
THIS *HUGE* ACTION SCENE IS ABOUT TO POP OFF!
WANNA COME WATCH?
WHAT'S WITH THE LAME SLANG?
JUST IN CHARACTER MY NIZZLE!
IT HELPS CONNECT WITH THE URBAN GENERATION!
HEY! I READ ABOUT THEM! LIKE BLAC...
THAT HAS TO BE THE MOST ASININE THING I'VE EVER HEARD.
PFFFT! ***WONDER BREAD*** HERE AIN'T NEVAH GUNNA BE DOWN.

#80

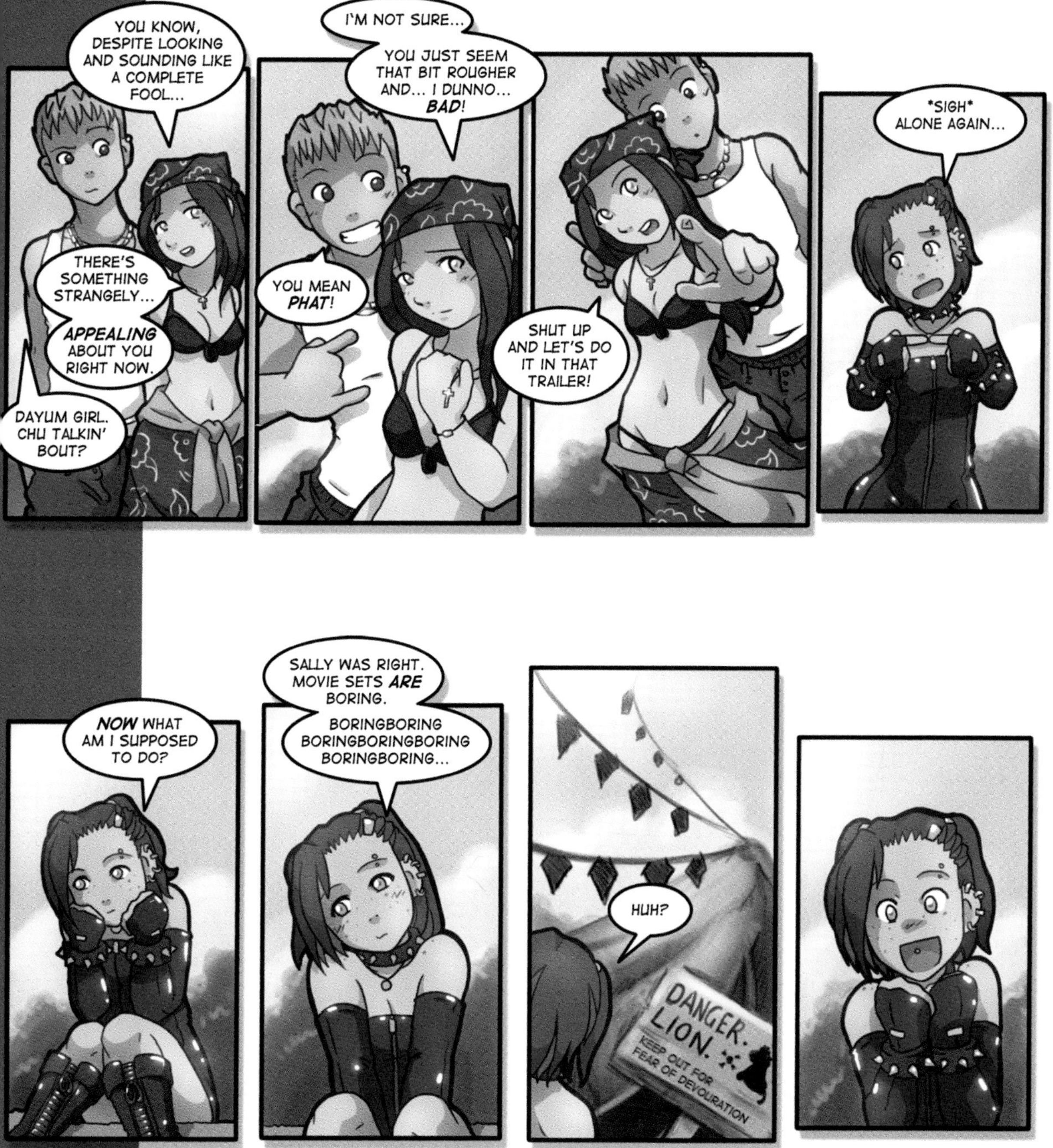
YOU KNOW, DESPITE LOOKING AND SOUNDING LIKE A COMPLETE FOOL...
THERE'S SOMETHING STRANGELY...
APPEALING ABOUT YOU RIGHT NOW.
DAYUM GIRL. CHU TALKIN' BOUT?
I'M NOT SURE...
YOU JUST SEEM THAT BIT ROUGHER AND... I DUNNO... BAD!
YOU MEAN PHAT!
SHUT UP AND LET'S DO IT IN THAT TRAILER!
SIGH ALONE AGAIN...
NOW WHAT AM I SUPPOSED TO DO?
SALLY WAS RIGHT. MOVIE SETS ARE BORING.
BORINGBORING BORINGBORINGBORING BORINGBORING...
HUH?
DANGER. LION.
KEEP OUT FOR FEAR OF DEVOURATION

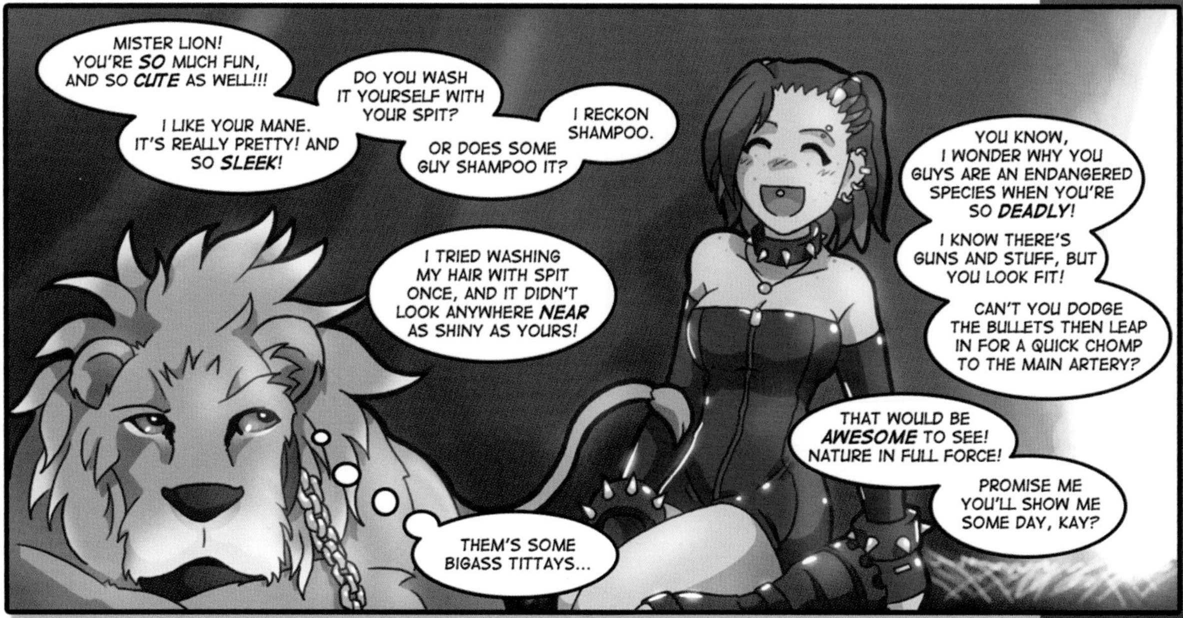
MISTER LION! YOU'RE SO MUCH FUN, AND SO CUTE AS WELL!!!
I LIKE YOUR MANE. IT'S REALLY PRETTY! AND SO SLEEK!
DO YOU WASH IT YOURSELF WITH YOUR SPIT?
OR DOES SOME GUY SHAMPOO IT?
I RECKON SHAMPOO.
I TRIED WASHING MY HAIR WITH SPIT ONCE, AND IT DIDN'T LOOK ANYWHERE NEAR AS SHINY AS YOURS!
YOU KNOW, I WONDER WHY YOU GUYS ARE AN ENDANGERED SPECIES WHEN YOU'RE SO DEADLY!
I KNOW THERE'S GUNS AND STUFF, BUT YOU LOOK FIT!
CAN'T YOU DODGE THE BULLETS THEN LEAP IN FOR A QUICK CHOMP TO THE MAIN ARTERY?
THAT WOULD BE AWESOME TO SEE! NATURE IN FULL FORCE!
PROMISE ME YOU'LL SHOW ME SOME DAY, KAY?
THEM'S SOME BIGASS TITTAYS...

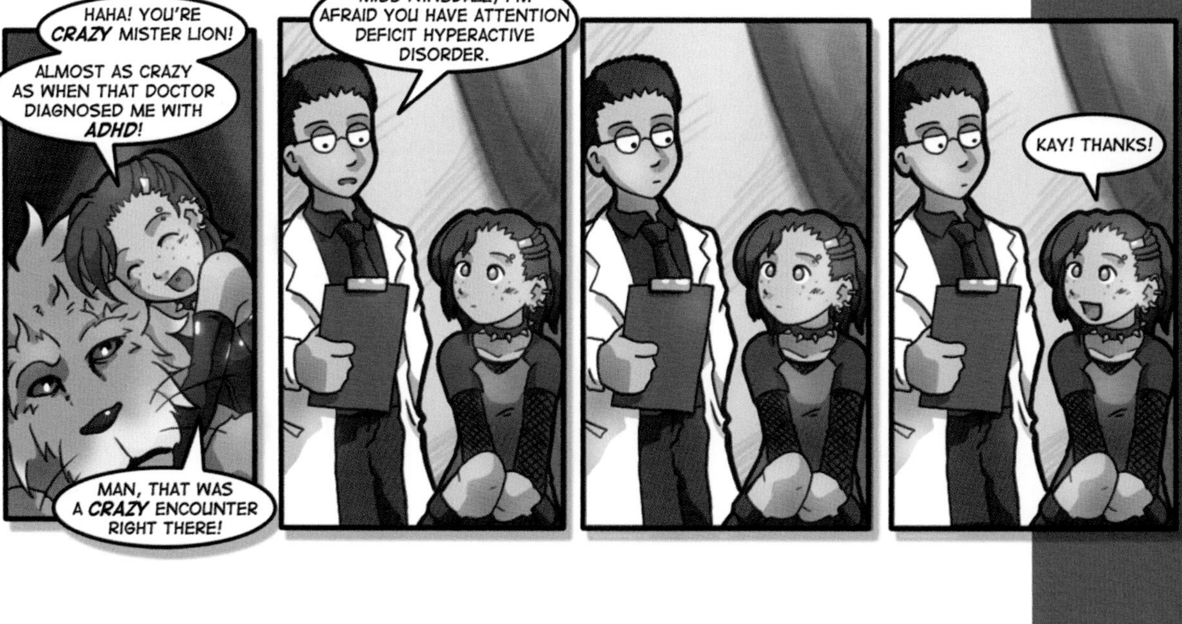
HAHA! YOU'RE CRAZY MISTER LION!
ALMOST AS CRAZY AS WHEN THAT DOCTOR DIAGNOSED ME WITH ADHD!
MAN, THAT WAS A CRAZY ENCOUNTER RIGHT THERE!
MISS WINSDALE, I'M AFRAID YOU HAVE ATTENTION DEFICIT HYPERACTIVE DISORDER.
KAY! THANKS!

#82

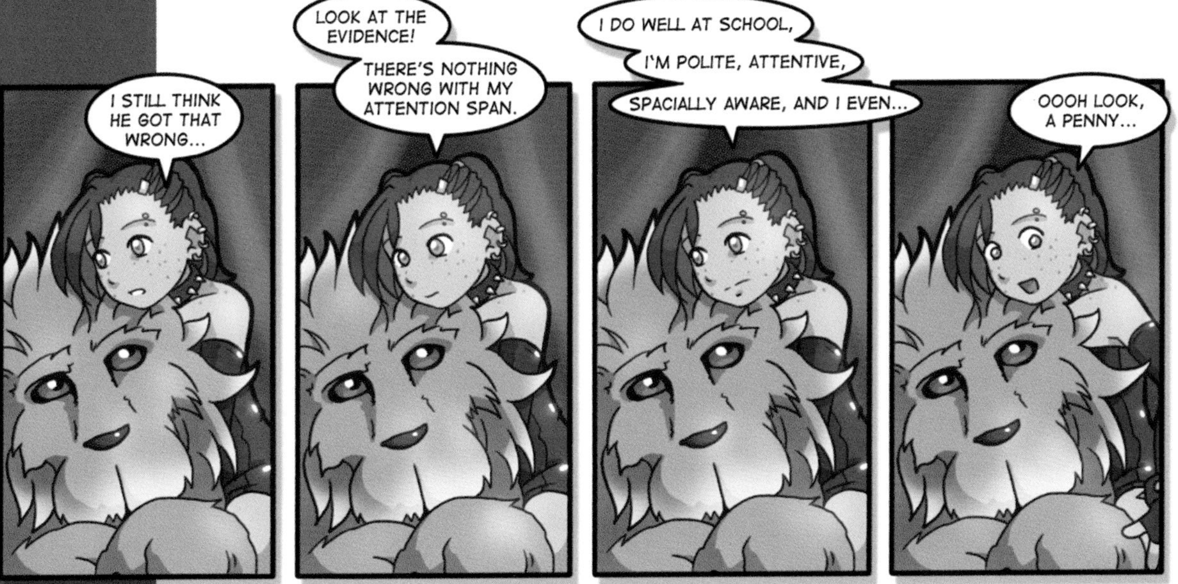
I STILL THINK HE GOT THAT WRONG...
LOOK AT THE EVIDENCE!
THERE'S NOTHING WRONG WITH MY ATTENTION SPAN.
I DO WELL AT SCHOOL,
I'M POLITE, ATTENTIVE,
SPACIALLY AWARE, AND I EVEN...
OOOH LOOK, A PENNY...

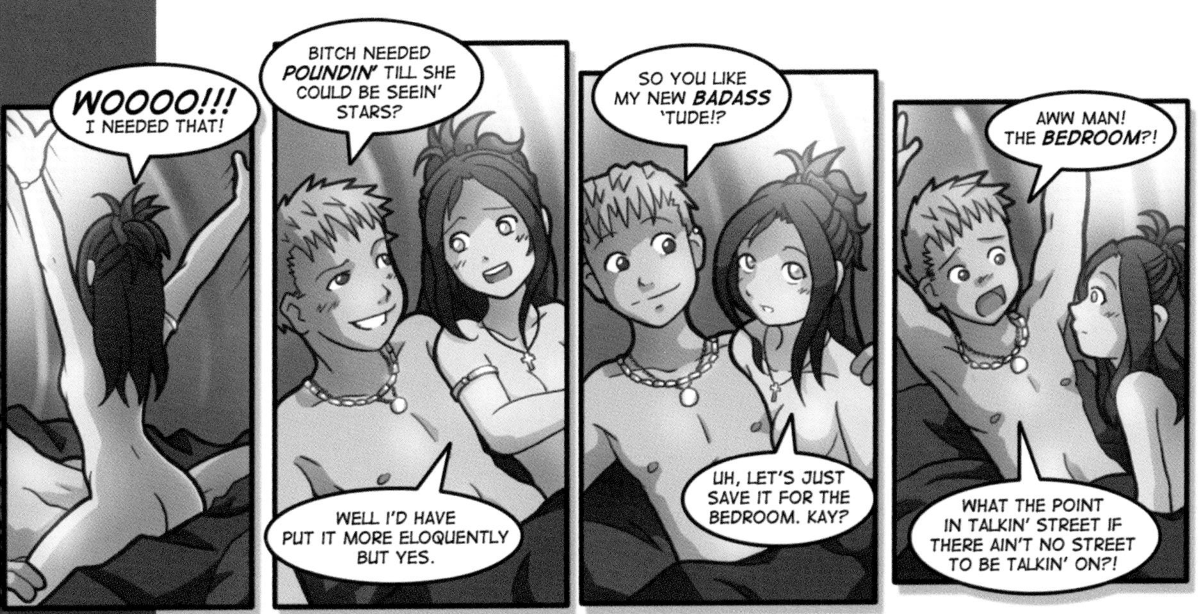
WOOOO!!! I NEEDED THAT!
BITCH NEEDED POUNDIN' TILL SHE COULD BE SEEIN' STARS?
WELL I'D HAVE PUT IT MORE ELOQUENTLY BUT YES.
SO YOU LIKE MY NEW BADASS 'TUDE!?
UH, LET'S JUST SAVE IT FOR THE BEDROOM. KAY?
AWW MAN! THE BEDROOM?!
WHAT THE POINT IN TALKIN' STREET IF THERE AIN'T NO STREET TO BE TALKIN' ON?!

#83

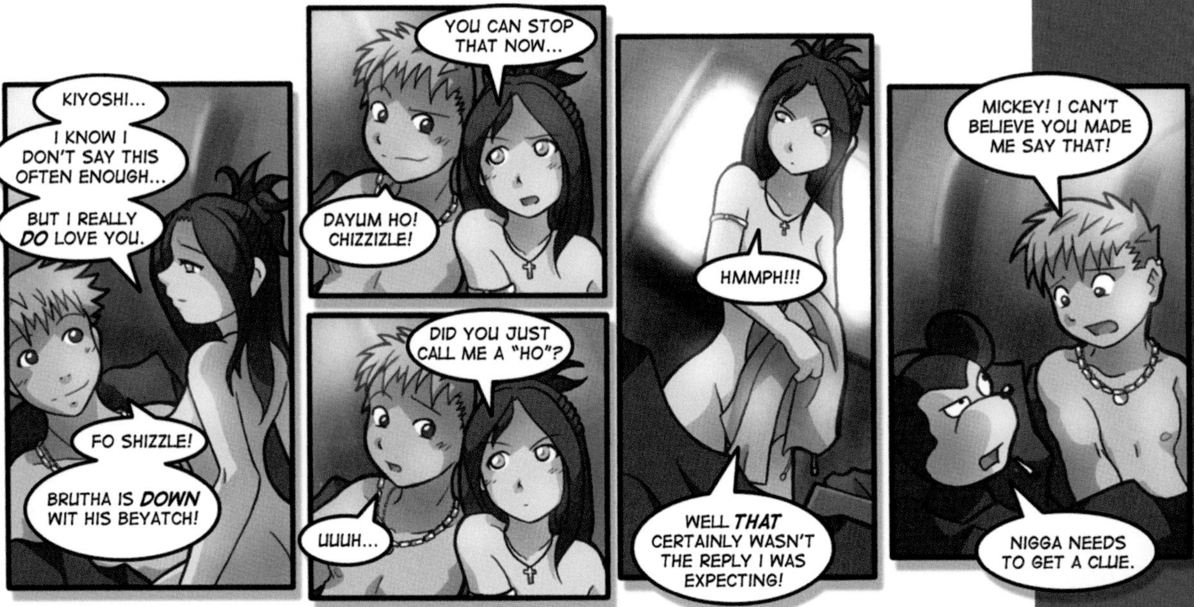
KIYOSHI...
I KNOW I DON'T SAY THIS OFTEN ENOUGH...
BUT I REALLY ***DO*** LOVE YOU.
FO SHIZZLE!
BRUTHA IS ***DOWN*** WIT HIS BEYATCH!
YOU CAN STOP THAT NOW...
DAYUM HO! CHIZZIZLE!
DID YOU JUST CALL ME A "HO"?
UUUH...
HMMPH!!!
WELL ***THAT*** CERTAINLY WASN'T THE REPLY I WAS EXPECTING!
MICKEY! I CAN'T BELIEVE YOU MADE ME SAY THAT!
NIGGA NEEDS TO GET A CLUE.

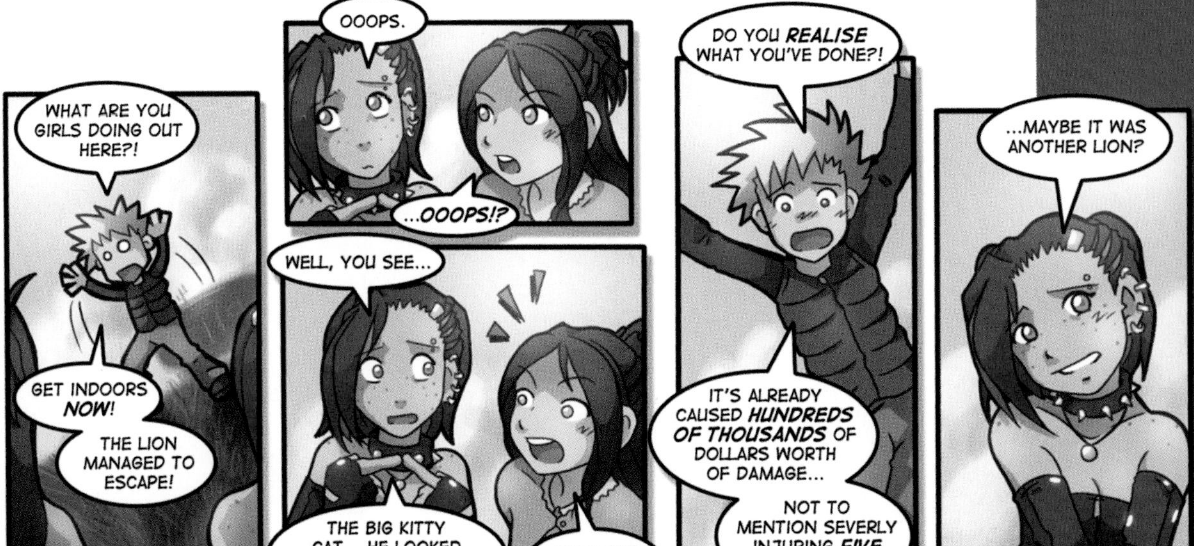
WHAT ARE YOU GIRLS DOING OUT HERE?!
GET INDOORS ***NOW!***
THE LION MANAGED TO ESCAPE!
OOOPS.
...***OOOPS!?***
WELL, YOU SEE...
THE BIG KITTY CAT... HE LOOKED SO SAD, SO I LET HIM OUT TO PLAY...
YOU DID WHAT?!
DO YOU ***REALISE*** WHAT YOU'VE DONE?!
IT'S ALREADY CAUSED ***HUNDREDS OF THOUSANDS*** OF DOLLARS WORTH OF DAMAGE...
NOT TO MENTION SEVERLY INJURING ***FIVE PEOPLE!***
...MAYBE IT WAS ANOTHER LION?

#84

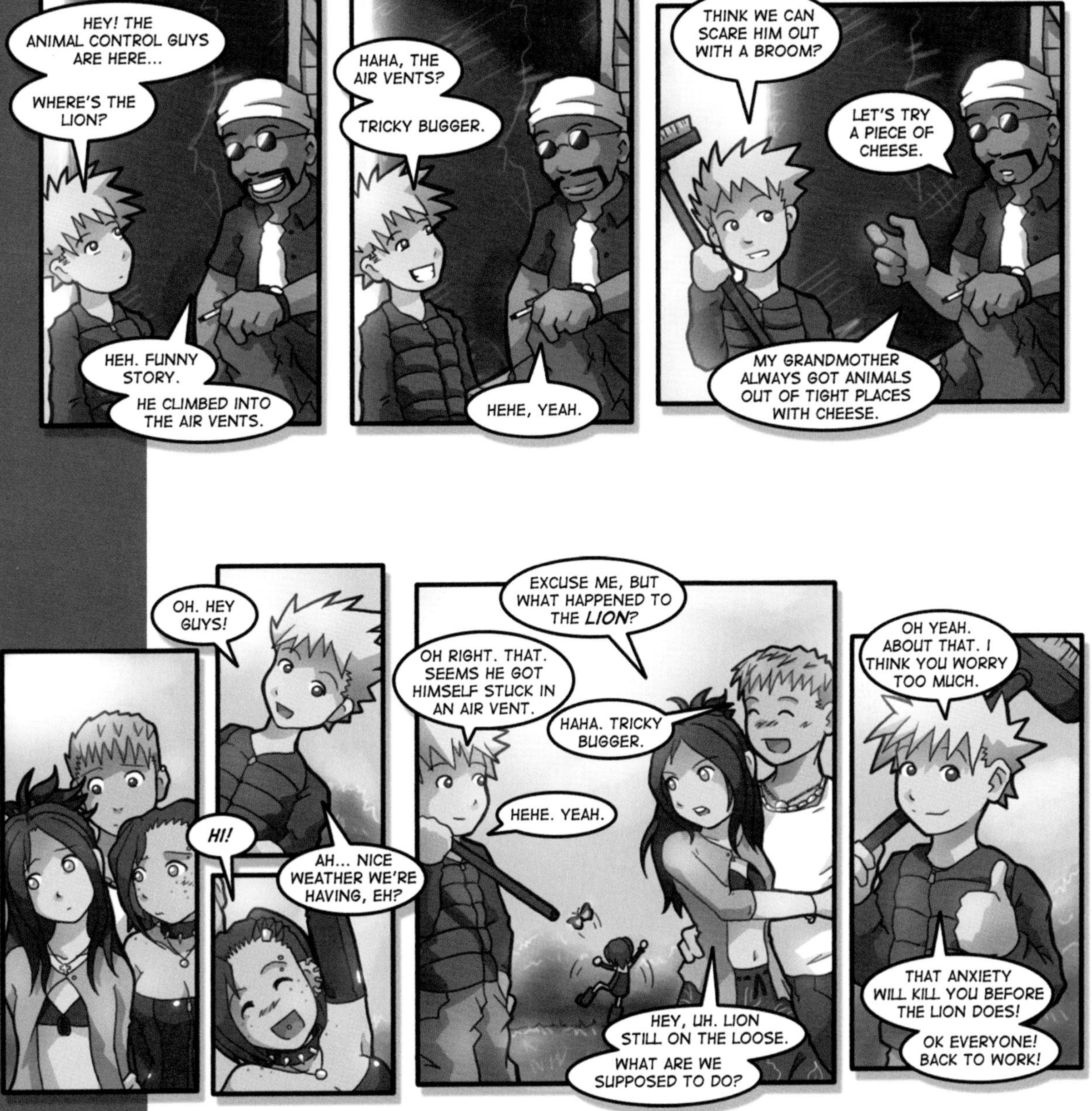
HEY! THE ANIMAL CONTROL GUYS ARE HERE...
WHERE'S THE LION?
HEH. FUNNY STORY.
HE CLIMBED INTO THE AIR VENTS.
HAHA, THE AIR VENTS?
TRICKY BUGGER.
HEHE, YEAH.
THINK WE CAN SCARE HIM OUT WITH A BROOM?
LET'S TRY A PIECE OF CHEESE.
MY GRANDMOTHER ALWAYS GOT ANIMALS OUT OF TIGHT PLACES WITH CHEESE.
OH. HEY GUYS!
HI!
AH... NICE WEATHER WE'RE HAVING, EH?
EXCUSE ME, BUT WHAT HAPPENED TO THE *LION*?
OH RIGHT. THAT. SEEMS HE GOT HIMSELF STUCK IN AN AIR VENT.
HAHA. TRICKY BUGGER.
HEHE. YEAH.
HEY, UH. LION STILL ON THE LOOSE.
WHAT ARE WE SUPPOSED TO DO?
OH YEAH. ABOUT THAT. I THINK YOU WORRY TOO MUCH.
THAT ANXIETY WILL KILL YOU BEFORE THE LION DOES!
OK EVERYONE! BACK TO WORK!

#85

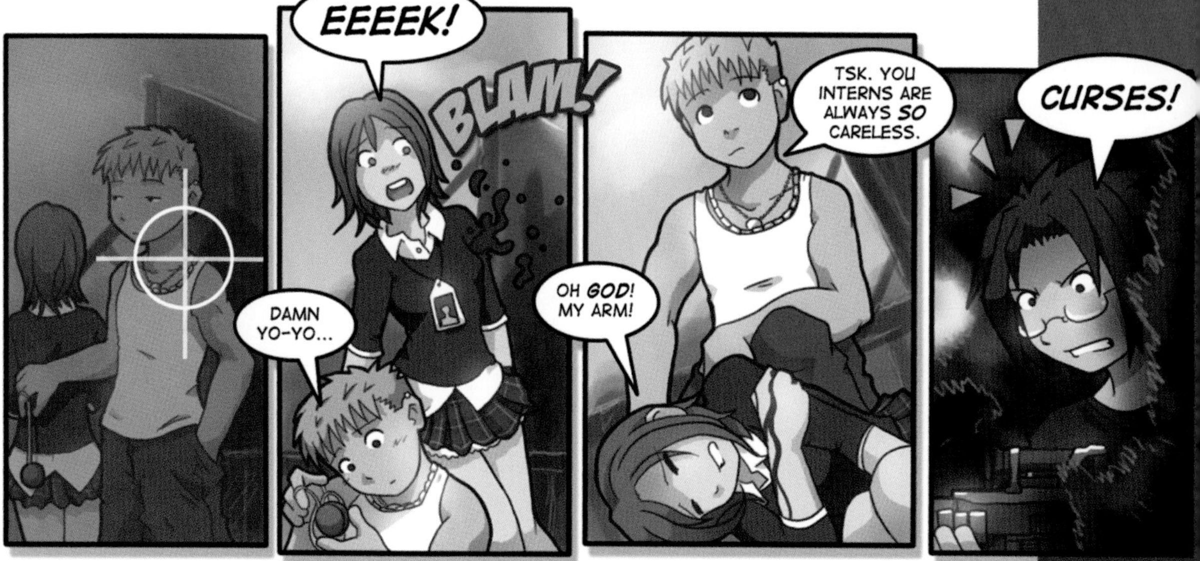
EEEEK!
BLAM!
DAMN YO-YO...
TSK. YOU INTERNS ARE ALWAYS *SO* CARELESS.
OH *GOD*! MY ARM!
CURSES!

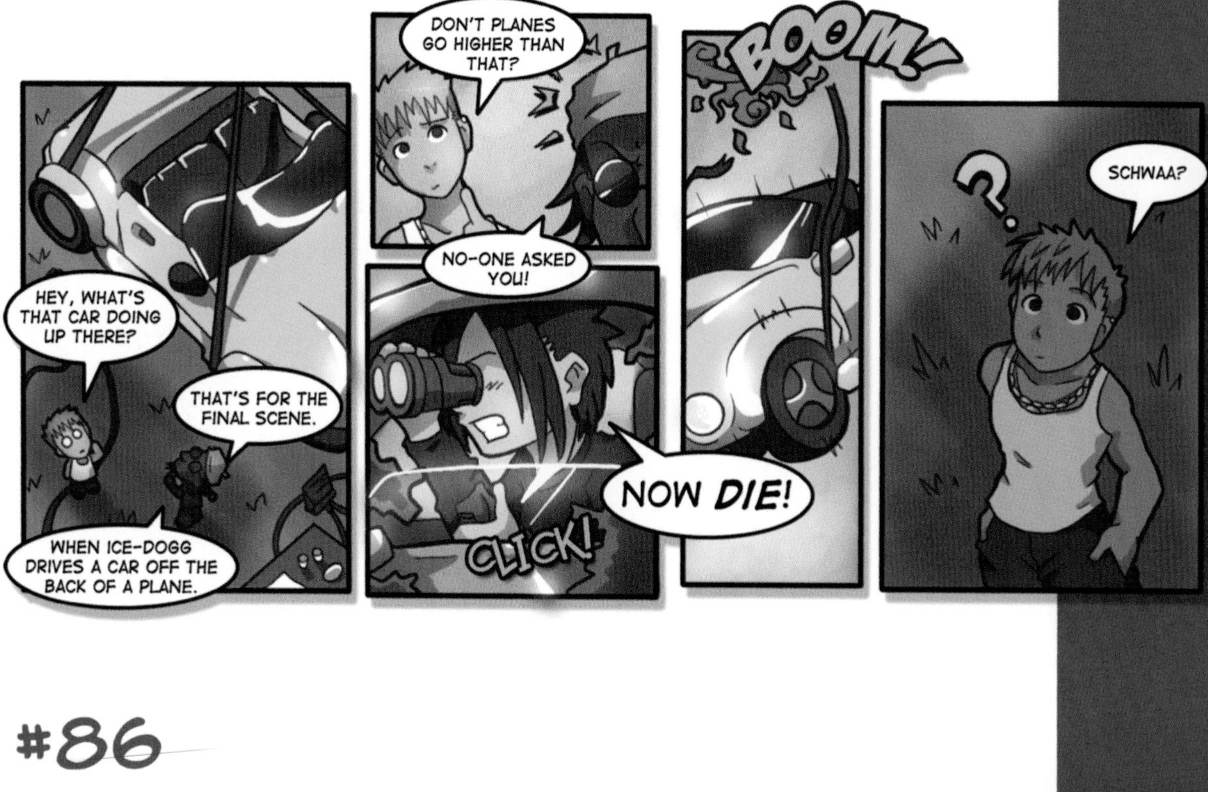
HEY, WHAT'S THAT CAR DOING UP THERE?
THAT'S FOR THE FINAL SCENE.
WHEN ICE-DOGG DRIVES A CAR OFF THE BACK OF A PLANE.
DON'T PLANES GO HIGHER THAN THAT?
NO-ONE ASKED YOU!
NOW *DIE*!
CLICK!
BOOM!
?
SCHWAA?

#86

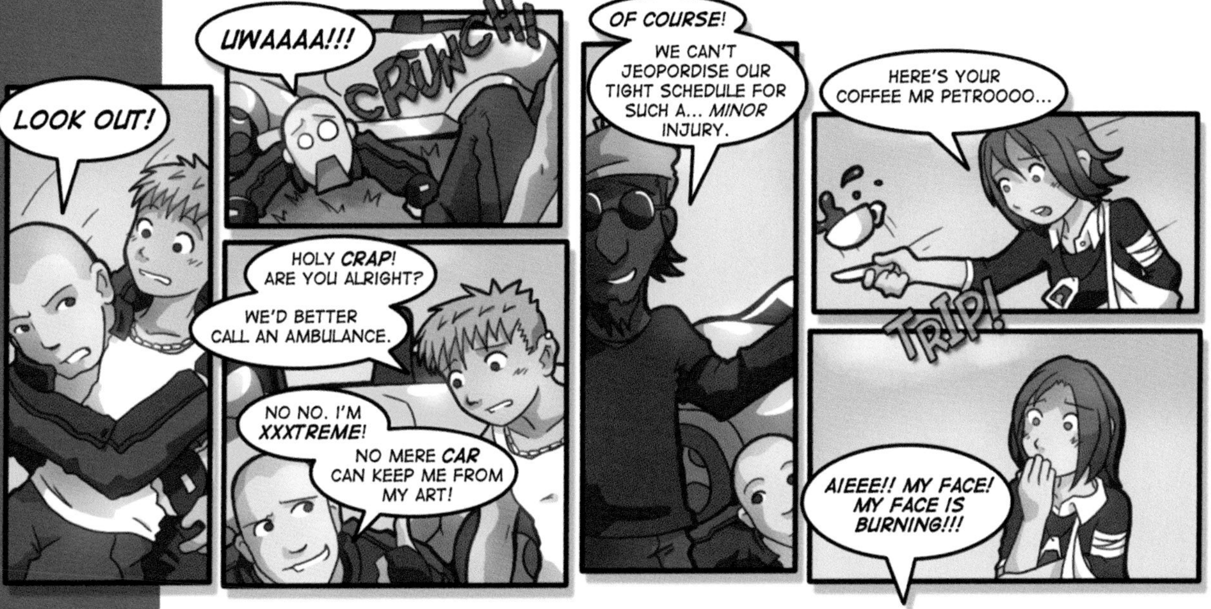

LOOK OUT!
UWAAAA!!!
CRUNCH!
HOLY CRAP! ARE YOU ALRIGHT?
WE'D BETTER CALL AN AMBULANCE.
NO NO. I'M XXXTREME!
NO MERE CAR CAN KEEP ME FROM MY ART!
OF COURSE!
WE CAN'T JEOPORDISE OUR TIGHT SCHEDULE FOR SUCH A... MINOR INJURY.
HERE'S YOUR COFFEE MR PETROOOO...
TRIP!
AIEEE!! MY FACE! MY FACE IS BURNING!!!

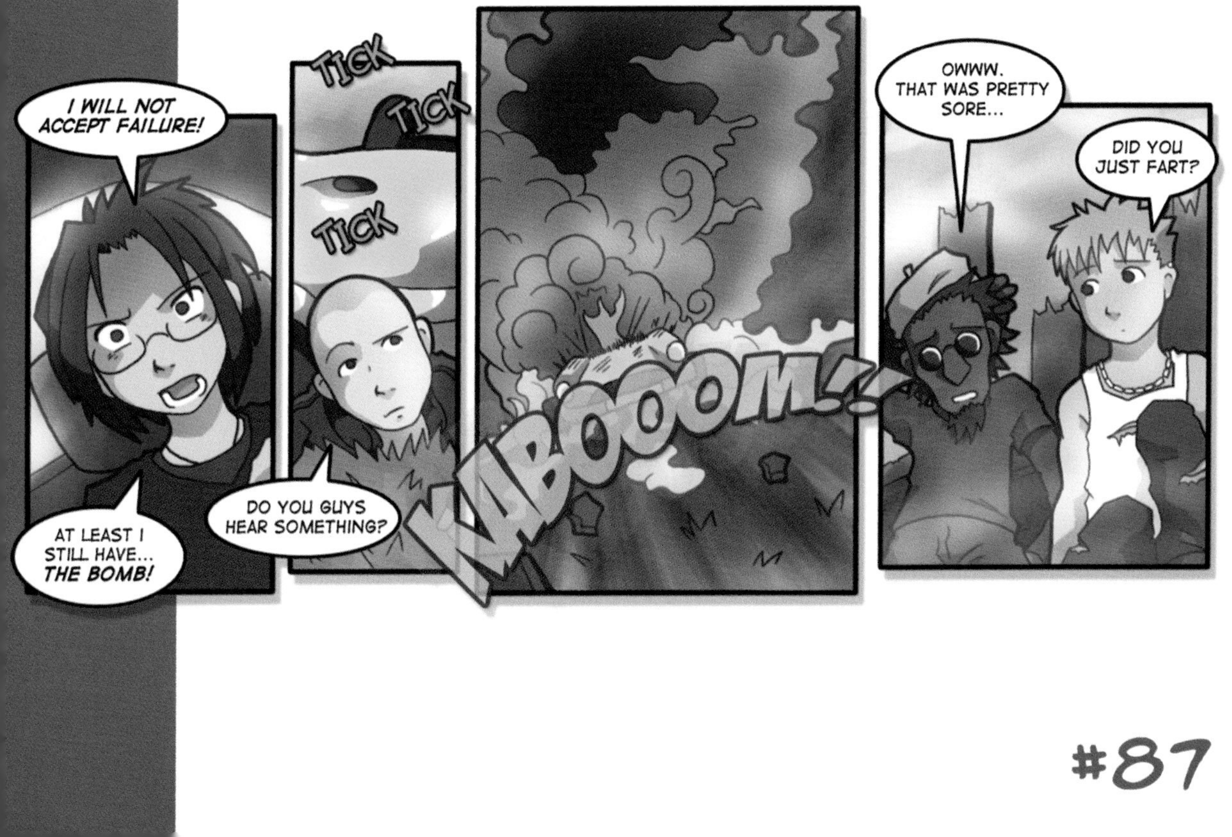

I WILL NOT ACCEPT FAILURE!
AT LEAST I STILL HAVE... THE BOMB!
TICK
TICK
TICK
DO YOU GUYS HEAR SOMETHING?
KABOOOM!!
OWWW. THAT WAS PRETTY SORE...
DID YOU JUST FART?

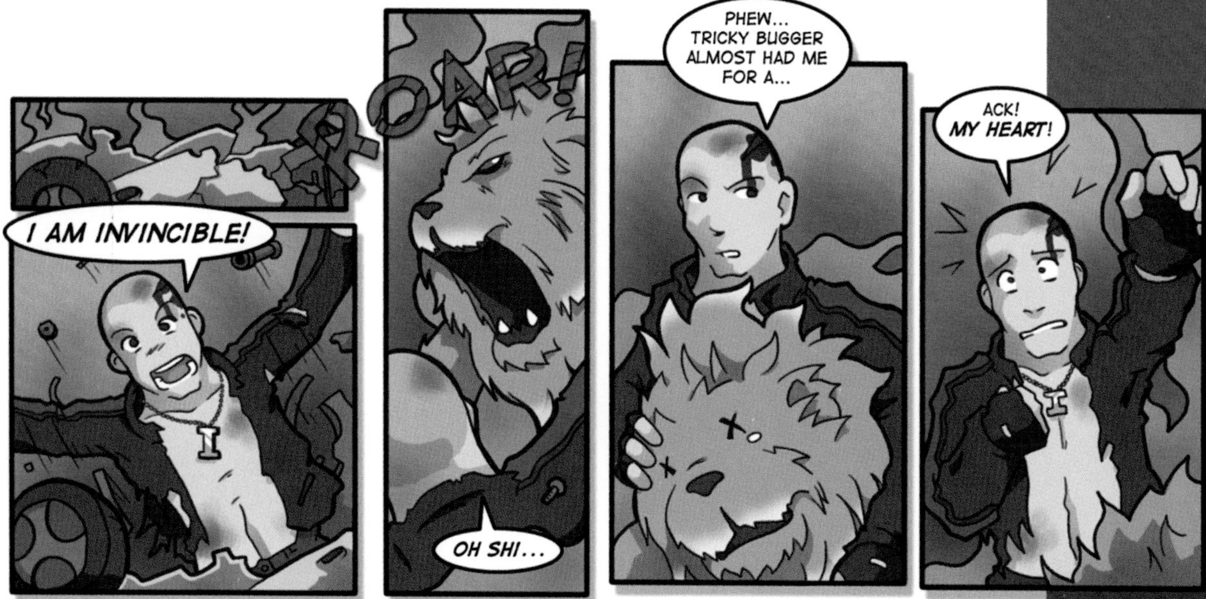
I AM INVINCIBLE!
ROAR!
OH SHI...
PHEW... TRICKY BUGGER ALMOST HAD ME FOR A...
ACK! MY HEART!

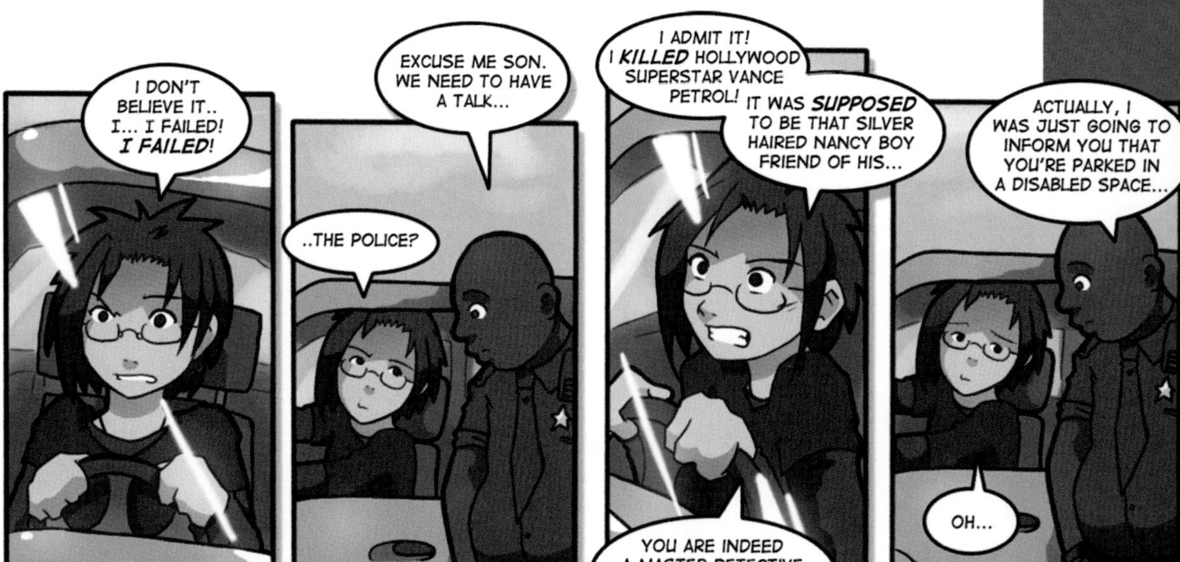
I DON'T BELIEVE IT.. I... I FAILED! I FAILED!
EXCUSE ME SON. WE NEED TO HAVE A TALK...
..THE POLICE?
I ADMIT IT! I KILLED HOLLYWOOD SUPERSTAR VANCE PETROL!
IT WAS SUPPOSED TO BE THAT SILVER HAIRED NANCY BOY FRIEND OF HIS...
YOU ARE INDEED A MASTER DETECTIVE TO HAVE FOUND ME OUT SO QUICKLY.
ACTUALLY, I WAS JUST GOING TO INFORM YOU THAT YOU'RE PARKED IN A DISABLED SPACE...
OH...

#88

FROM THE CONCRETE JUNGLE

TO THE JUNGLES OF SOUTH AMERICA.

A NEW TYPE OF SPECIAL AGENT IS KICKING ASS AND TAKING NAMES.

INTRODUCING TV'S KIYOSHI MASAMUNE!

OH SNIZZAP! THAT IS SOME *BULLSH...*

DROP *THE* GUNS BUTTHOLES!

HEY BUTTHOLES! THE GUN! DROP *IT!*

STARRING THE *DIGITALLY REMASTERED,* LATE VANCE PETROL!

USING THE OSCAR AWARD WINNER'S *OWN* ORIGINAL DIALOGUE!

THE SLOW AND THE MODERATELY ANGRY!

HEY BUTTHOLES!

SEE THIS MOVIE!

SOME TIME LATER

SO THERE I WAS, IN PRISON THANKS TO THAT INSUFFERABLE FOOL.

I WAS WASTING MY TIME IN THE YARD WHEN...

I HAPPENED TO SEE A YOUNG MAN SITTING ON A BENCH.

WOAH. HE LOOKS PRETTY FUCKING CREEPY...

JUST AS I WAS THINKING THAT,

THE MAN SUDDENLY STARTED UNZIPPING HIS OVERALLS...

RIGHT THERE IN FRONT OF MY EYES!

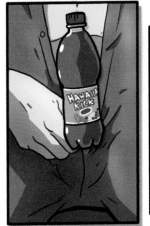

HAWAII KICK

SHALL WE DO IT?

#89

Dragon Rod Riders.

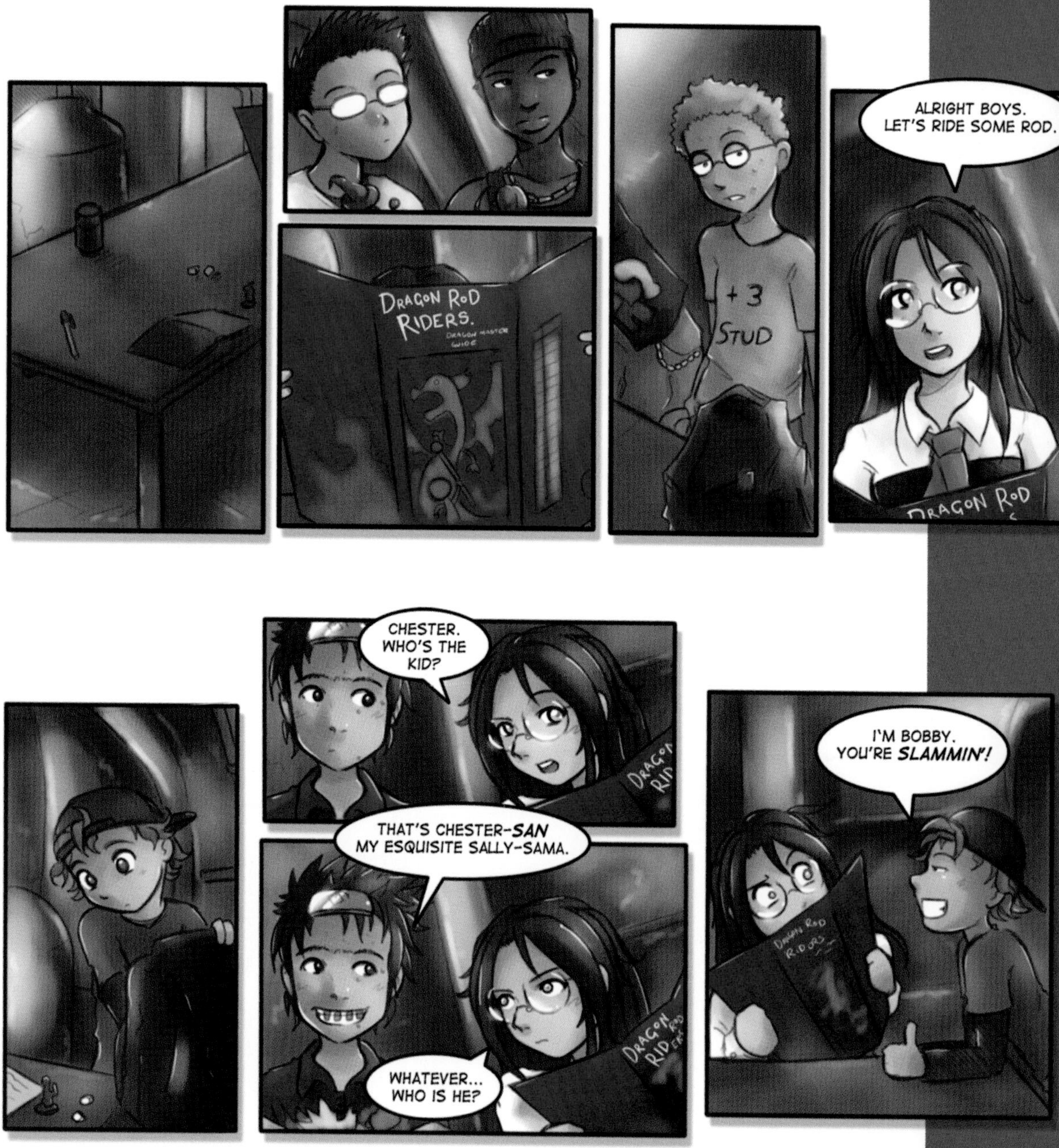
DRAGON ROD RIDERS.
DRAGON MASTER GUIDE
+3 STUD
ALRIGHT BOYS. LET'S RIDE SOME ROD.
DRAGON ROD
CHESTER. WHO'S THE KID?
THAT'S CHESTER-*SAN* MY ESQUISITE SALLY-SAMA.
DRAGON ROD RIDERS
WHATEVER... WHO IS HE?
DRAGON ROD RIDERS
I'M BOBBY. YOU'RE ***SLAMMIN'!***

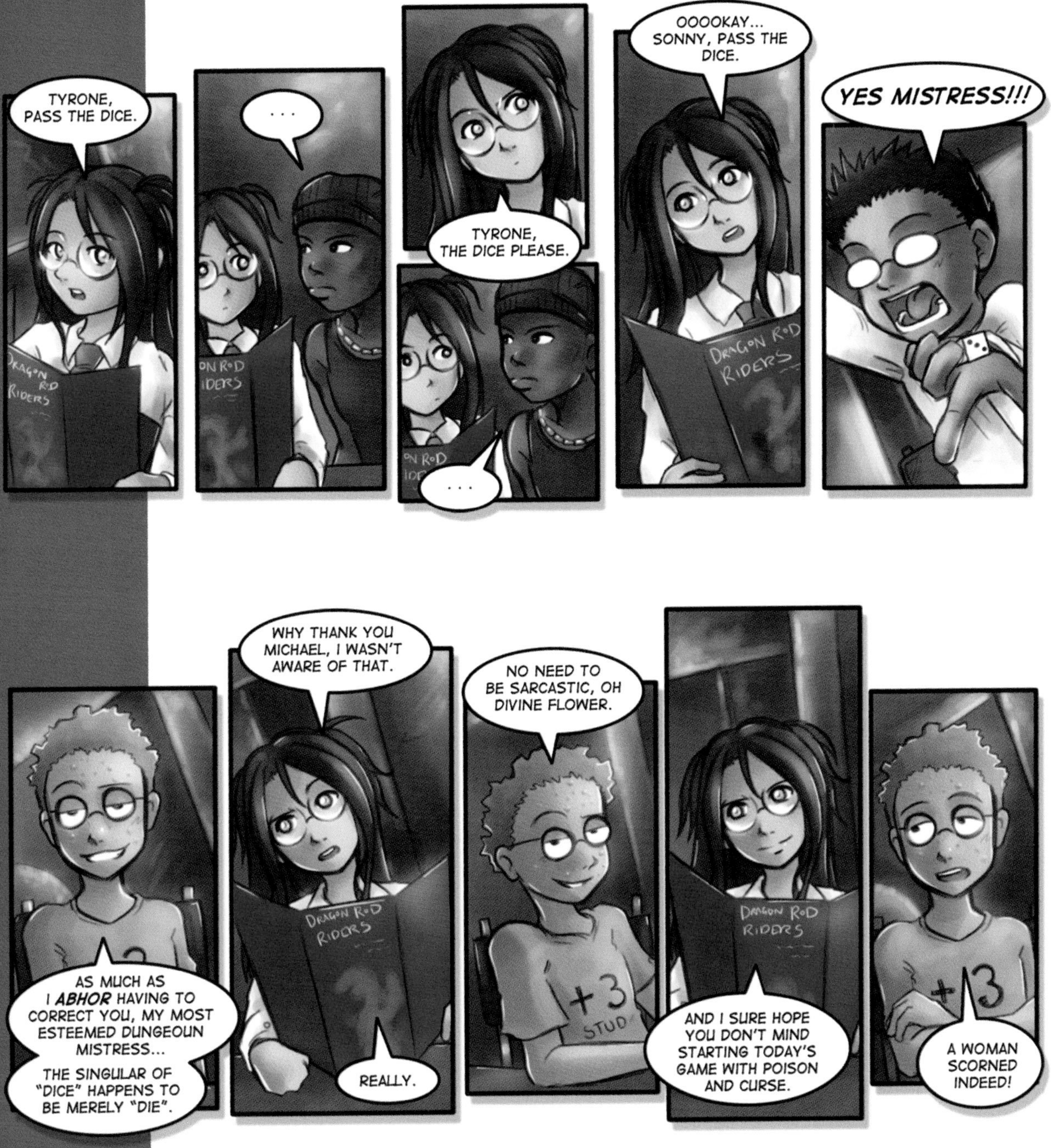

TYRONE, PASS THE DICE.
. . .
TYRONE, THE DICE PLEASE.
. . .
OOOOKAY... SONNY, PASS THE DICE.
YES MISTRESS!!!
AS MUCH AS I **ABHOR** HAVING TO CORRECT YOU, MY MOST ESTEEMED DUNGEOUN MISTRESS...
THE SINGULAR OF "DICE" HAPPENS TO BE MERELY "DIE".
WHY THANK YOU MICHAEL, I WASN'T AWARE OF THAT.
REALLY.
NO NEED TO BE SARCASTIC, OH DIVINE FLOWER.
AND I SURE HOPE YOU DON'T MIND STARTING TODAY'S GAME WITH POISON AND CURSE.
A WOMAN SCORNED INDEED!

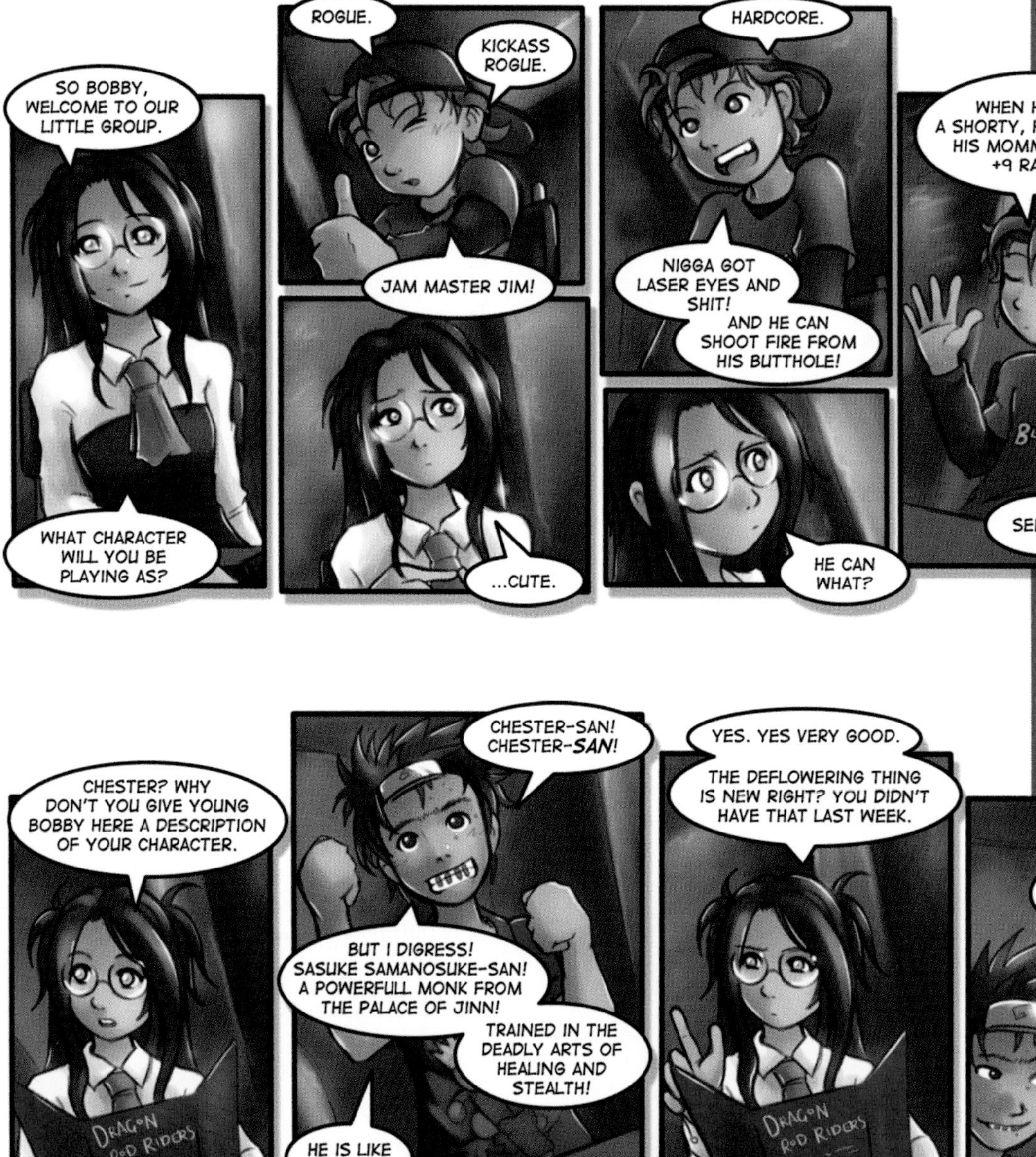
SO BOBBY, WELCOME TO OUR LITTLE GROUP.
WHAT CHARACTER WILL YOU BE PLAYING AS?
ROGUE.
KICKASS ROGUE.
JAM MASTER JIM!
...CUTE.
HARDCORE.
NIGGA GOT LASER EYES AND SHIT!
AND HE CAN SHOOT FIRE FROM HIS BUTTHOLE!
HE CAN WHAT?
WHEN HE WAS A SHORTY, HE STABBED HIS MOMMA WITH A +9 RAZOR.
BLING
SERIOUS.
CHESTER? WHY DON'T YOU GIVE YOUNG BOBBY HERE A DESCRIPTION OF YOUR CHARACTER.
DRAGON ROD RIDERS
MIGHT FUEL HIS IMAGINATION SOMEWHAT.
CHESTER-SAN! CHESTER-**SAN**!
BUT I DIGRESS! SASUKE SAMANOSUKE-SAN! A POWERFULL MONK FROM THE PALACE OF JINN!
TRAINED IN THE DEADLY ARTS OF HEALING AND STEALTH!
HE IS LIKE THE WIND!
ONLY WHISPERS REMAIN ON THE LIPS OF THE MANY FINE SHRINE MAIDENS HE HAS **DEFLOWERED**!
YES. YES VERY GOOD.
THE DEFLOWERING THING IS NEW RIGHT? YOU DIDN'T HAVE THAT LAST WEEK.
DRAGON ROD RIDERS
OR **DID** I!?

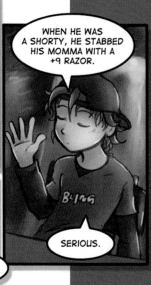

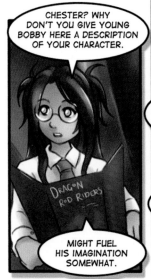

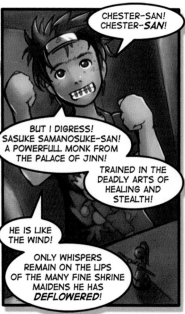

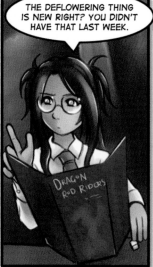

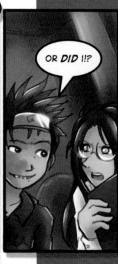

#92

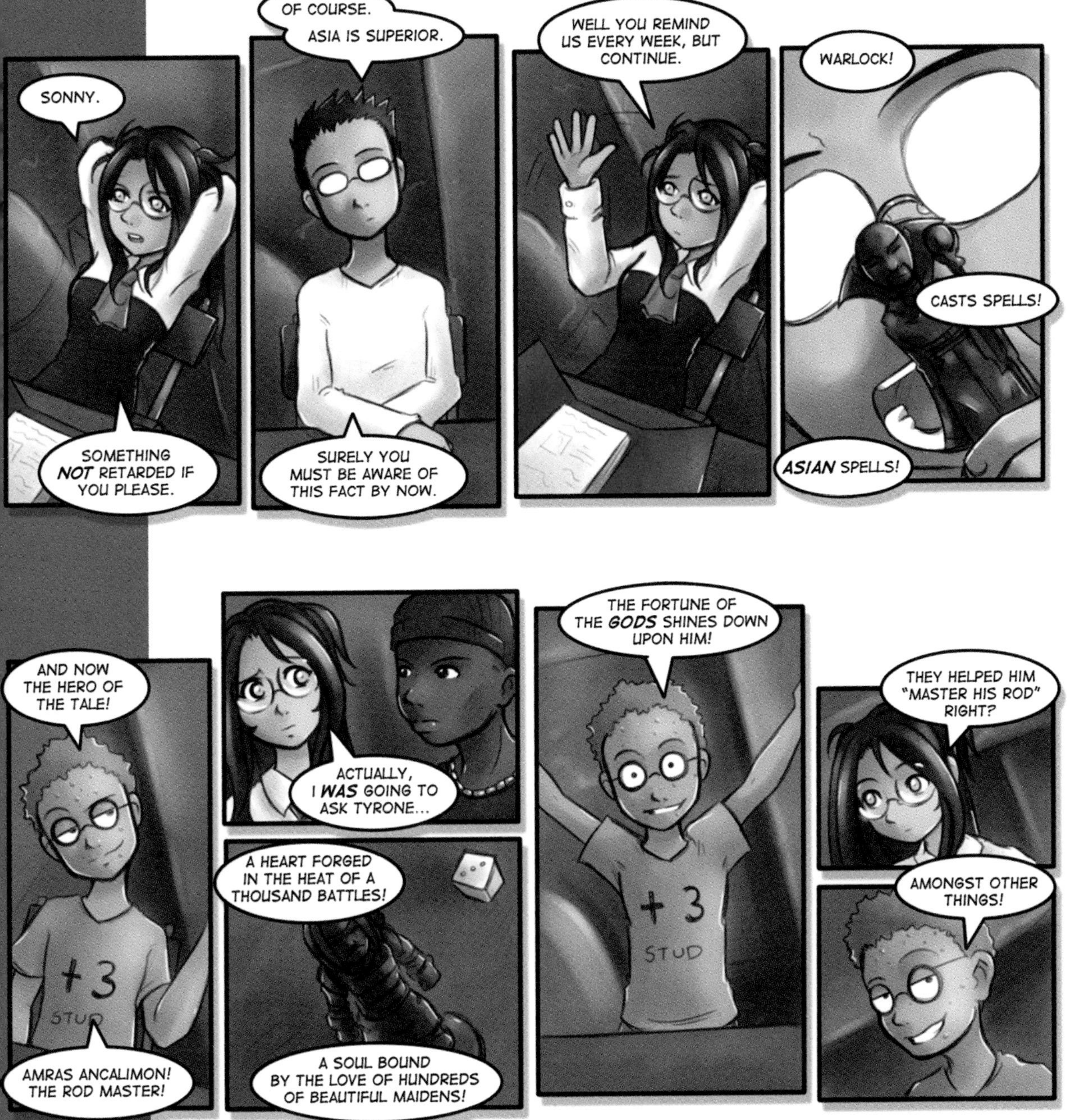

SONNY.
SOMETHING NOT RETARDED IF YOU PLEASE.
OF COURSE.
ASIA IS SUPERIOR.
SURELY YOU MUST BE AWARE OF THIS FACT BY NOW.
WELL YOU REMIND US EVERY WEEK, BUT CONTINUE.
WARLOCK!
CASTS SPELLS!
ASIAN SPELLS!
AND NOW THE HERO OF THE TALE!
+3
STUD
AMRAS ANCALIMON! THE ROD MASTER!
ACTUALLY, I WAS GOING TO ASK TYRONE...
A HEART FORGED IN THE HEAT OF A THOUSAND BATTLES!
A SOUL BOUND BY THE LOVE OF HUNDREDS OF BEAUTIFUL MAIDENS!
THE FORTUNE OF THE GODS SHINES DOWN UPON HIM!
+3
STUD
THEY HELPED HIM "MASTER HIS ROD" RIGHT?
AMONGST OTHER THINGS!

#93

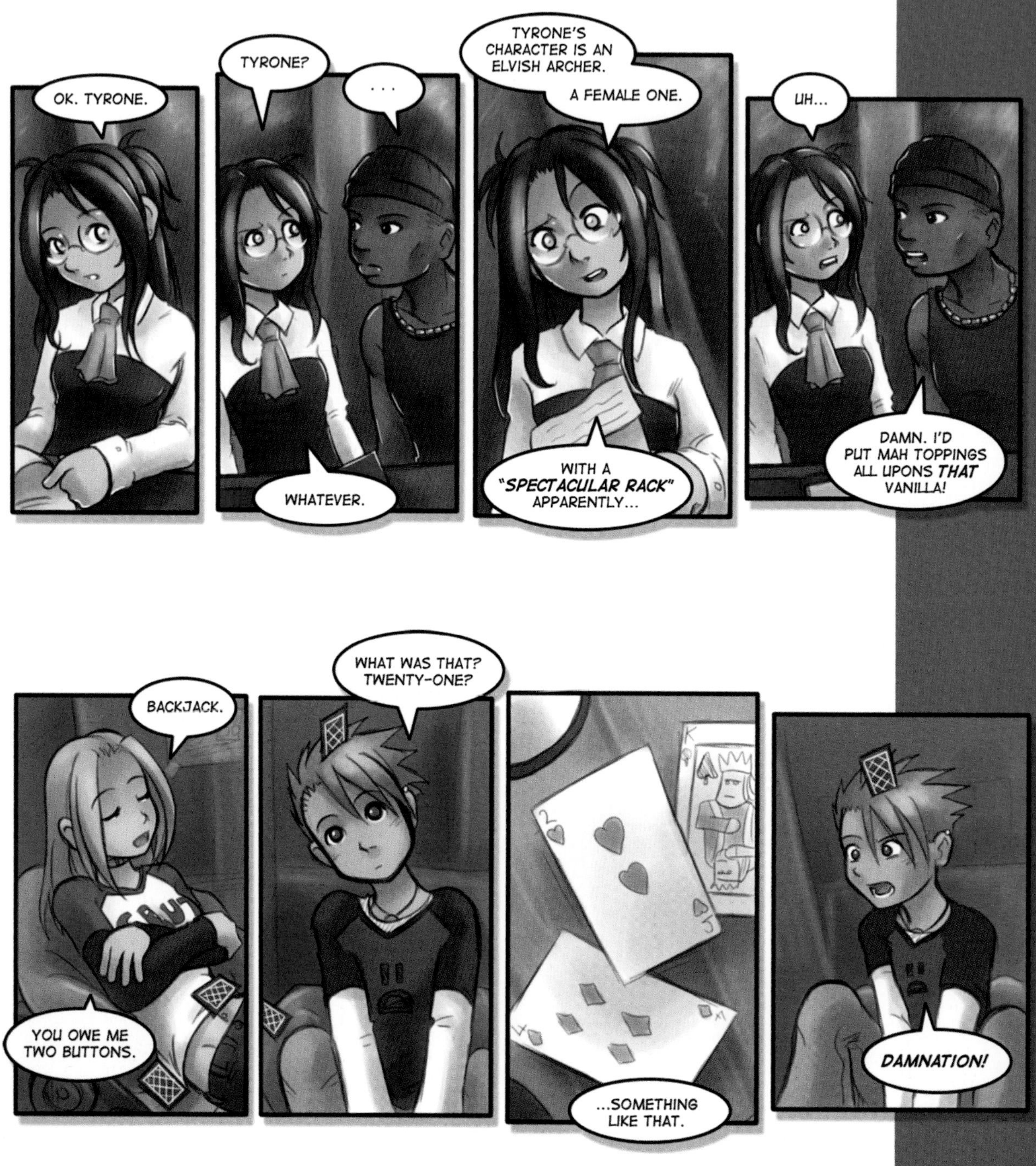
OK. TYRONE.
TYRONE?
. . .
WHATEVER.
TYRONE'S CHARACTER IS AN ELVISH ARCHER.
A FEMALE ONE.
WITH A "SPECTACULAR RACK" APPARENTLY...
UH...
DAMN. I'D PUT MAH TOPPINGS ALL UPONS THAT VANILLA!
BACKJACK.
YOU OWE ME TWO BUTTONS.
WHAT WAS THAT? TWENTY-ONE?
...SOMETHING LIKE THAT.
DAMNATION!

#94

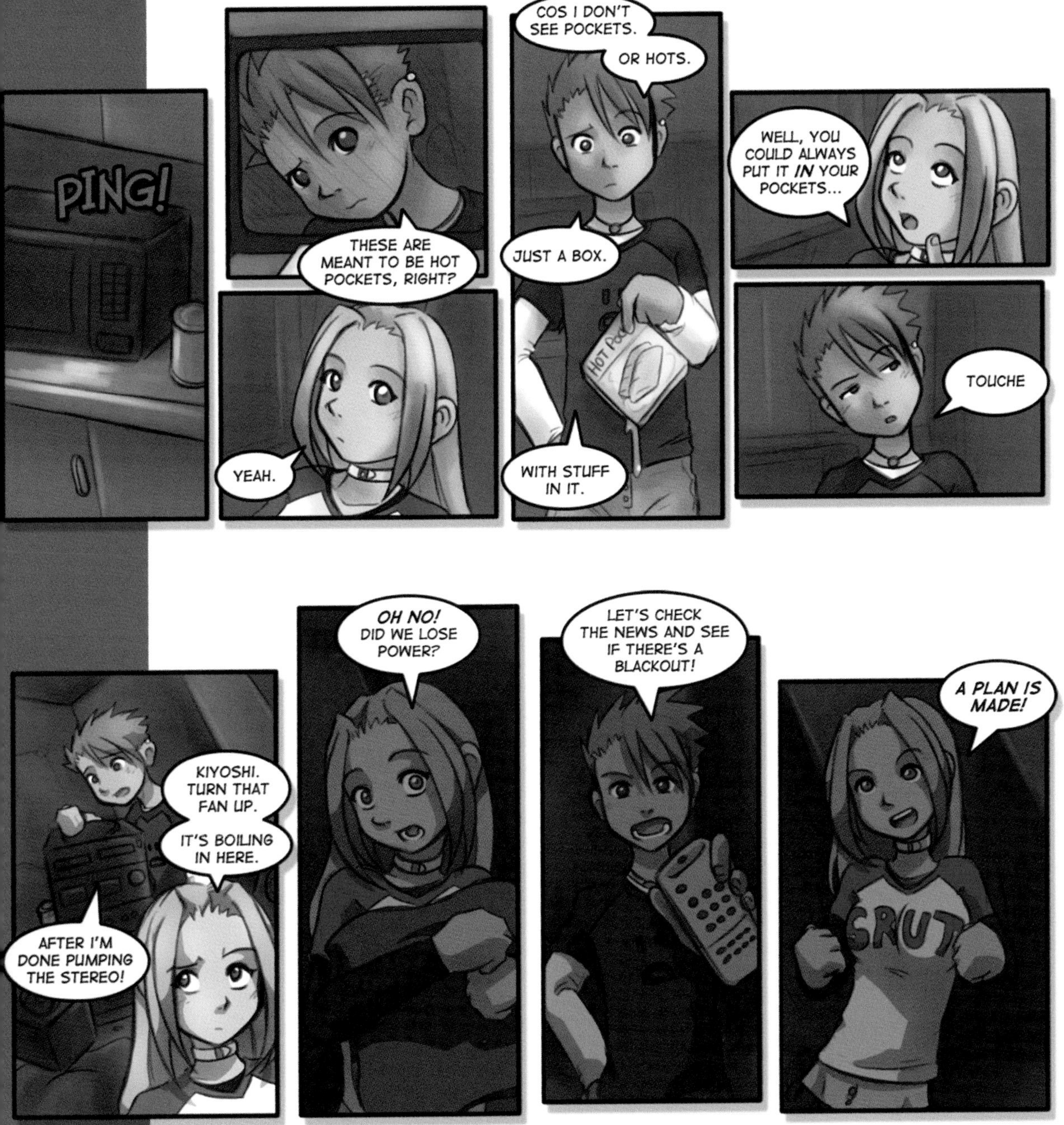
PING!
THESE ARE MEANT TO BE HOT POCKETS, RIGHT?
YEAH.
COS I DON'T SEE POCKETS.
OR HOTS.
JUST A BOX.
WITH STUFF IN IT.
WELL, YOU COULD ALWAYS PUT IT *IN* YOUR POCKETS...
TOUCHE
KIYOSHI. TURN THAT FAN UP.
IT'S BOILING IN HERE.
AFTER I'M DONE PUMPING THE STEREO!
OH NO! DID WE LOSE POWER?
LET'S CHECK THE NEWS AND SEE IF THERE'S A BLACKOUT!
A PLAN IS MADE!

#95

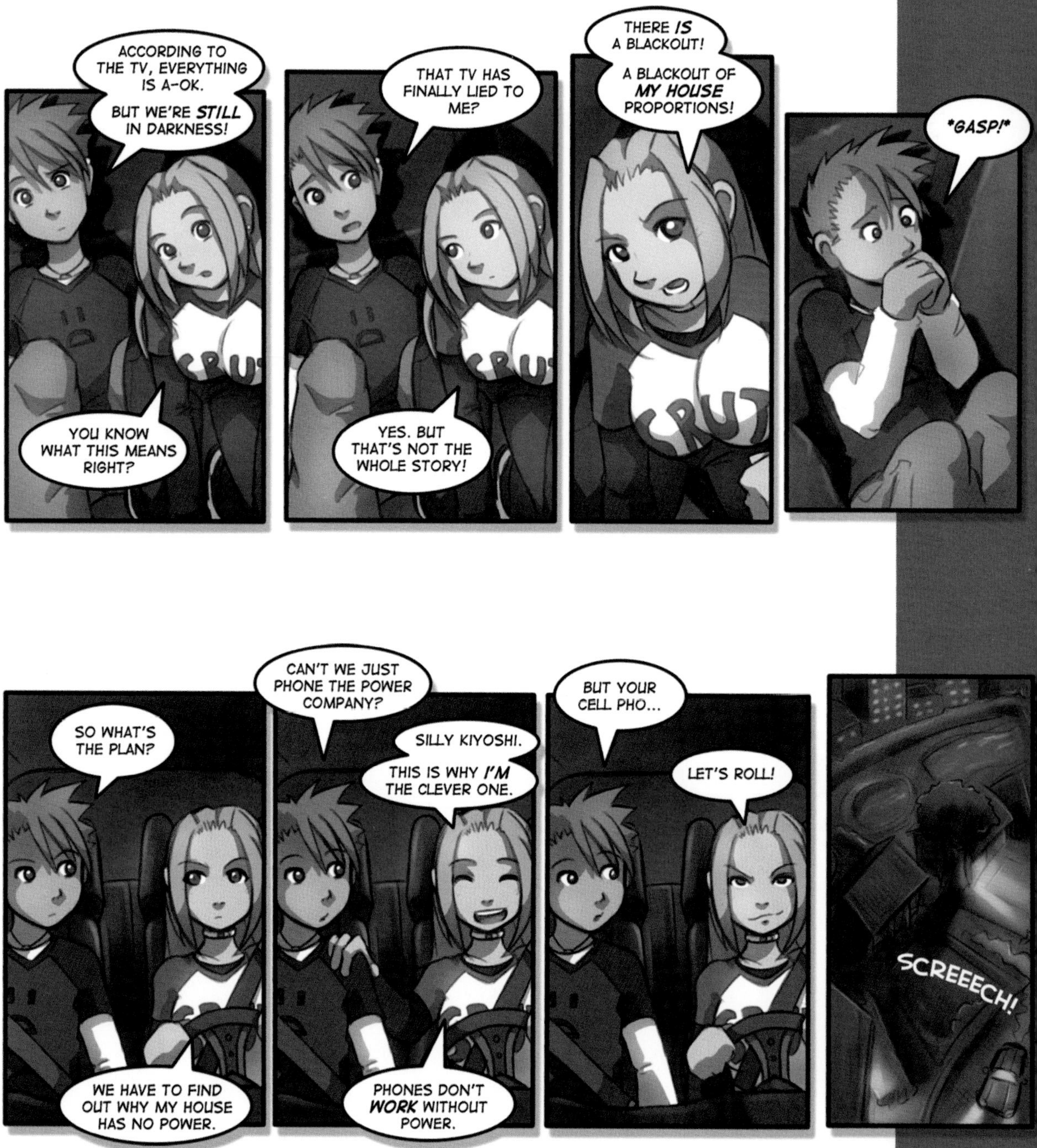
ACCORDING TO THE TV, EVERYTHING IS A-OK.
BUT WE'RE *STILL* IN DARKNESS!
YOU KNOW WHAT THIS MEANS RIGHT?
THAT TV HAS FINALLY LIED TO ME?
YES. BUT THAT'S NOT THE WHOLE STORY!
THERE *IS* A BLACKOUT!
A BLACKOUT OF ***MY HOUSE*** PROPORTIONS!
GASP!
SO WHAT'S THE PLAN?
WE HAVE TO FIND OUT WHY MY HOUSE HAS NO POWER.
CAN'T WE JUST PHONE THE POWER COMPANY?
SILLY KIYOSHI.
THIS IS WHY *I'M* THE CLEVER ONE.
PHONES DON'T ***WORK*** WITHOUT POWER.
BUT YOUR CELL PHO...
LET'S ROLL!
SCREEECH!

#96

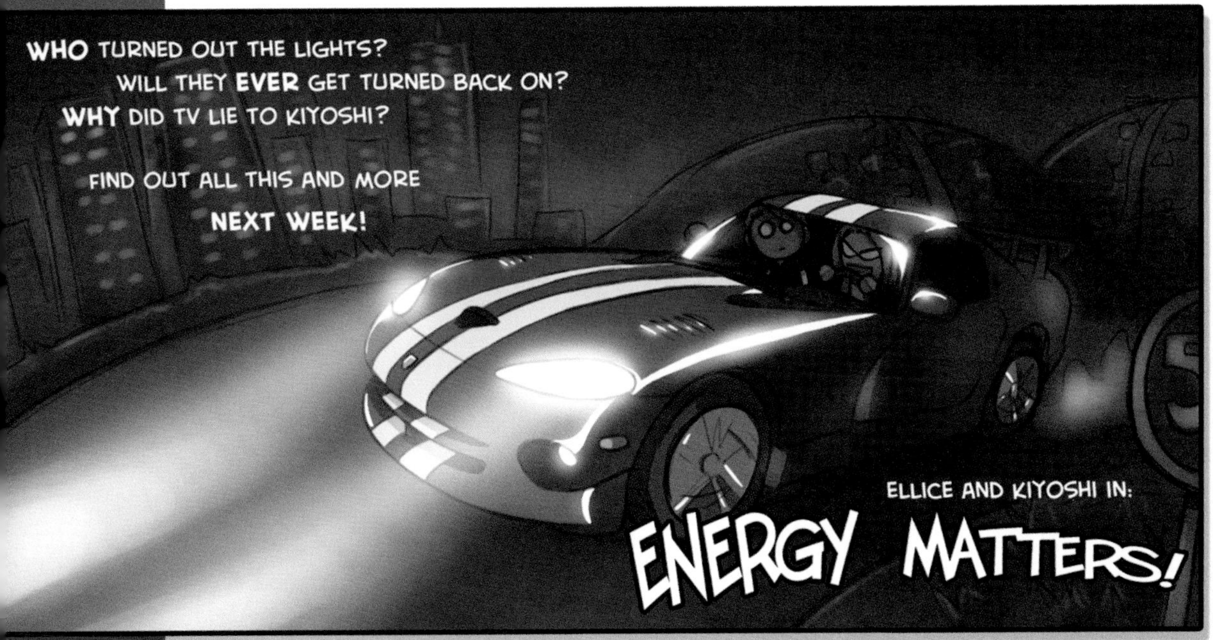
WHO TURNED OUT THE LIGHTS?
WILL THEY EVER GET TURNED BACK ON?
WHY DID TV LIE TO KIYOSHI?
FIND OUT ALL THIS AND MORE
NEXT WEEK!
ELLICE AND KIYOSHI IN:
ENERGY MATTERS!

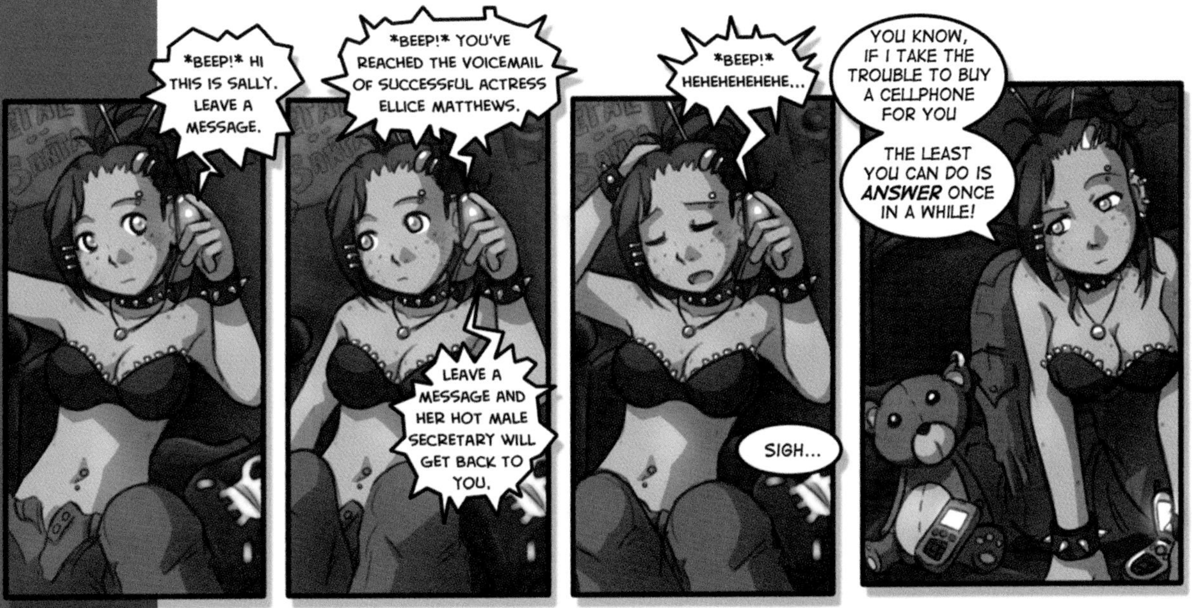
BEEP! HI THIS IS SALLY. LEAVE A MESSAGE.
BEEP! YOU'VE REACHED THE VOICEMAIL OF SUCCESSFUL ACTRESS ELLICE MATTHEWS.
LEAVE A MESSAGE AND HER HOT MALE SECRETARY WILL GET BACK TO YOU.
BEEP! HEHEHEHEHEHE...
SIGH...
YOU KNOW, IF I TAKE THE TROUBLE TO BUY A CELLPHONE FOR YOU
THE LEAST YOU CAN DO IS ANSWER ONCE IN A WHILE!

#97

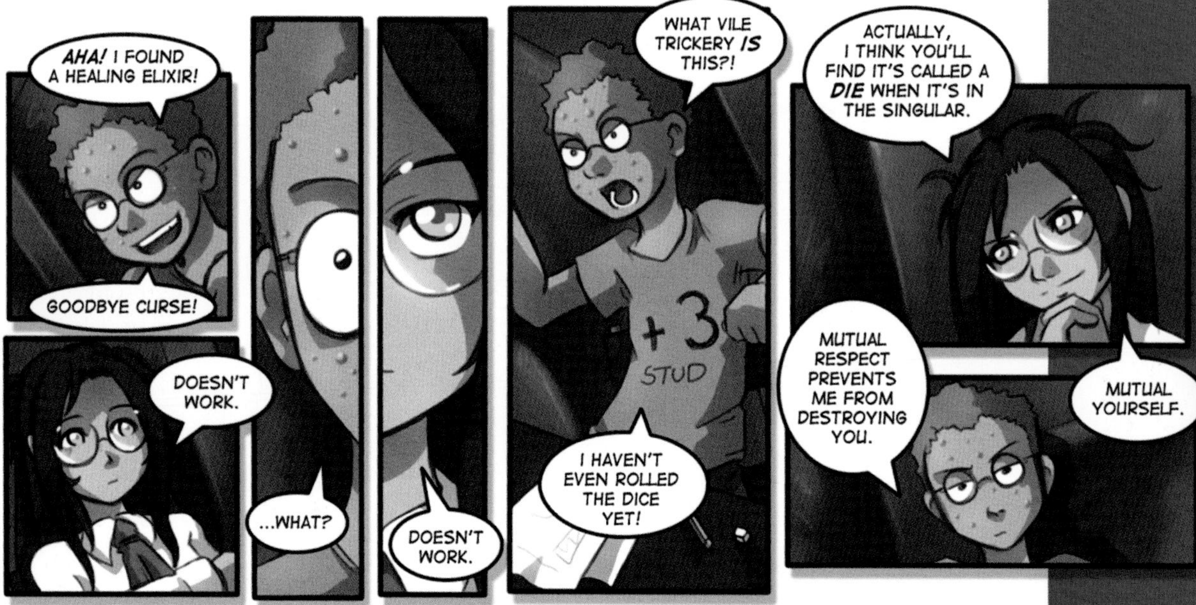
AHA! I FOUND A HEALING ELIXIR!
GOODBYE CURSE!
DOESN'T WORK.
...WHAT?
DOESN'T WORK.
WHAT VILE TRICKERY IS THIS?!
+3 STUD
I HAVEN'T EVEN ROLLED THE DICE YET!
ACTUALLY, I THINK YOU'LL FIND IT'S CALLED A DIE WHEN IT'S IN THE SINGULAR.
MUTUAL RESPECT PREVENTS ME FROM DESTROYING YOU.
MUTUAL YOURSELF.

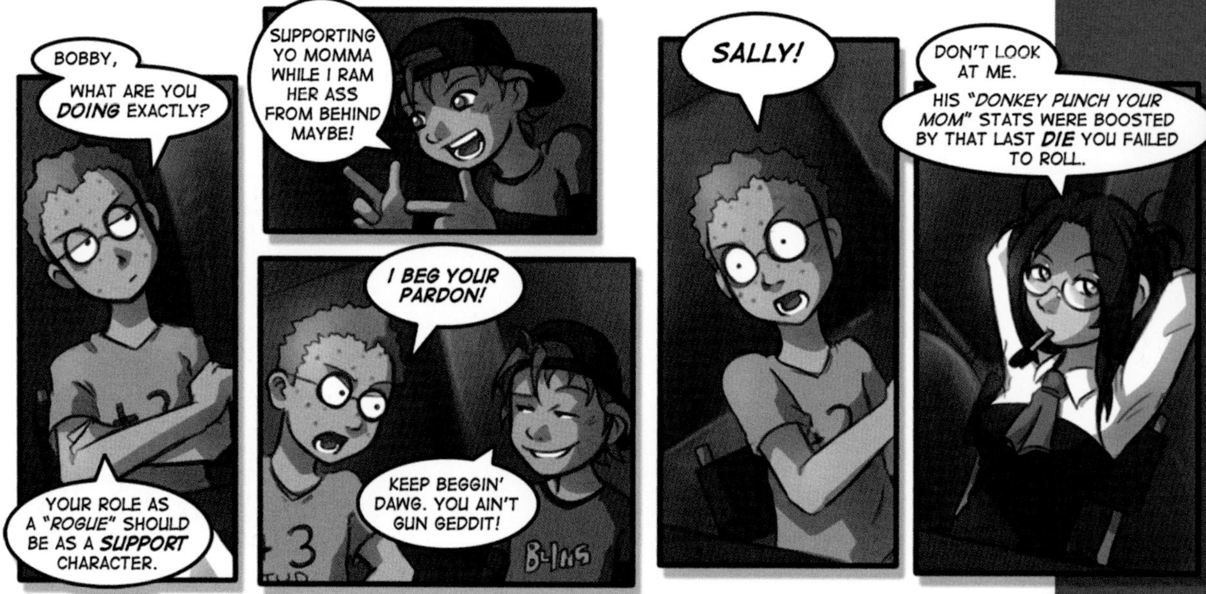
BOBBY,
WHAT ARE YOU DOING EXACTLY?
YOUR ROLE AS A "ROGUE" SHOULD BE AS A SUPPORT CHARACTER.
SUPPORTING YO MOMMA WHILE I RAM HER ASS FROM BEHIND MAYBE!
I BEG YOUR PARDON!
KEEP BEGGIN' DAWG. YOU AIN'T GUN GEDDIT!
SALLY!
DON'T LOOK AT ME.
HIS "DONKEY PUNCH YOUR MOM" STATS WERE BOOSTED BY THAT LAST DIE YOU FAILED TO ROLL.

#98

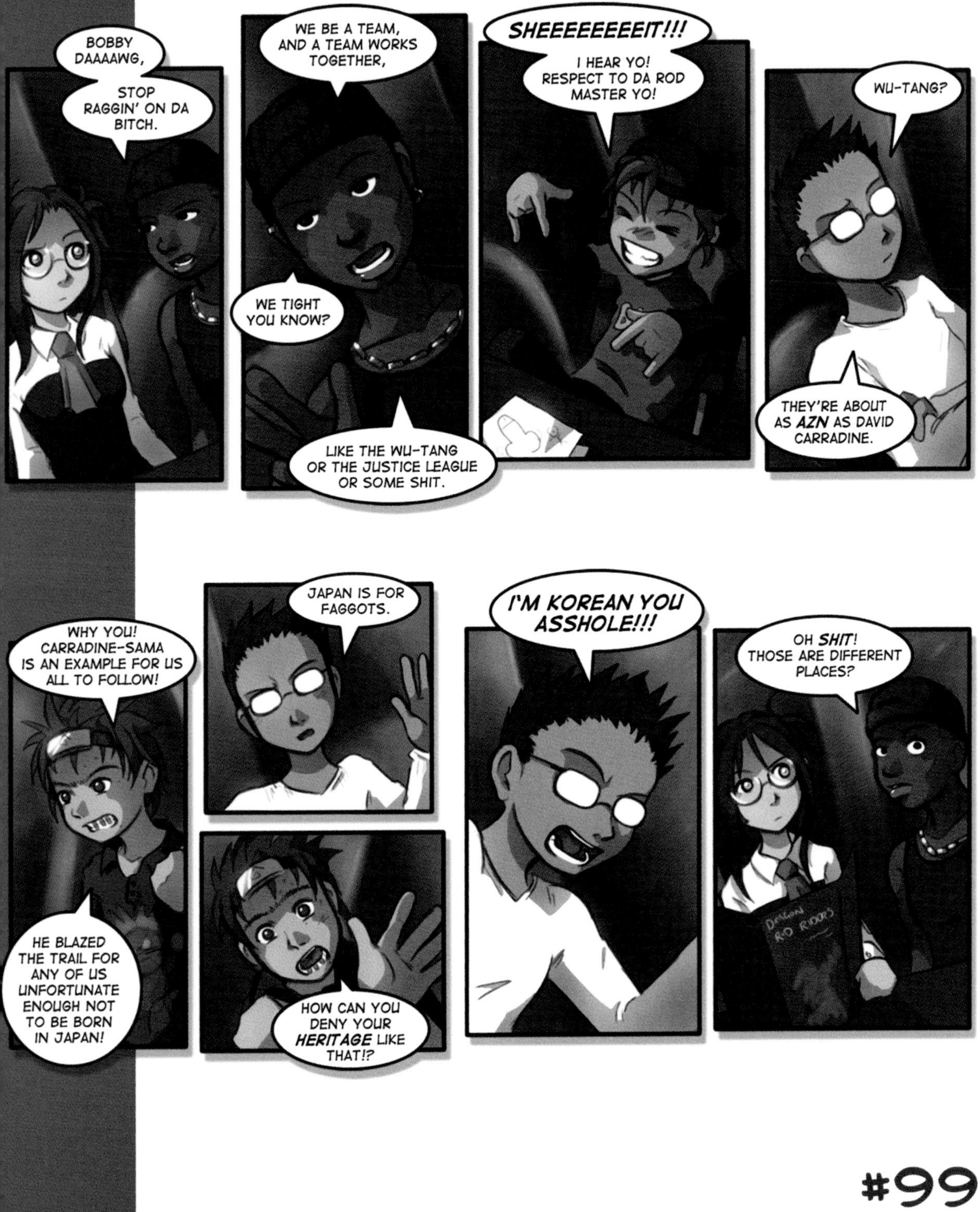
BOBBY DAAAAWG,
STOP RAGGIN' ON DA BITCH.
WE BE A TEAM, AND A TEAM WORKS TOGETHER,
WE TIGHT YOU KNOW?
LIKE THE WU-TANG OR THE JUSTICE LEAGUE OR SOME SHIT.
SHEEEEEEEEIT!!!
I HEAR YO! RESPECT TO DA ROD MASTER YO!
WU-TANG?
THEY'RE ABOUT AS AZN AS DAVID CARRADINE.
WHY YOU! CARRADINE-SAMA IS AN EXAMPLE FOR US ALL TO FOLLOW!
HE BLAZED THE TRAIL FOR ANY OF US UNFORTUNATE ENOUGH NOT TO BE BORN IN JAPAN!
JAPAN IS FOR FAGGOTS.
HOW CAN YOU DENY YOUR HERITAGE LIKE THAT!?
I'M KOREAN YOU ASSHOLE!!!
OH SHIT! THOSE ARE DIFFERENT PLACES?

#99

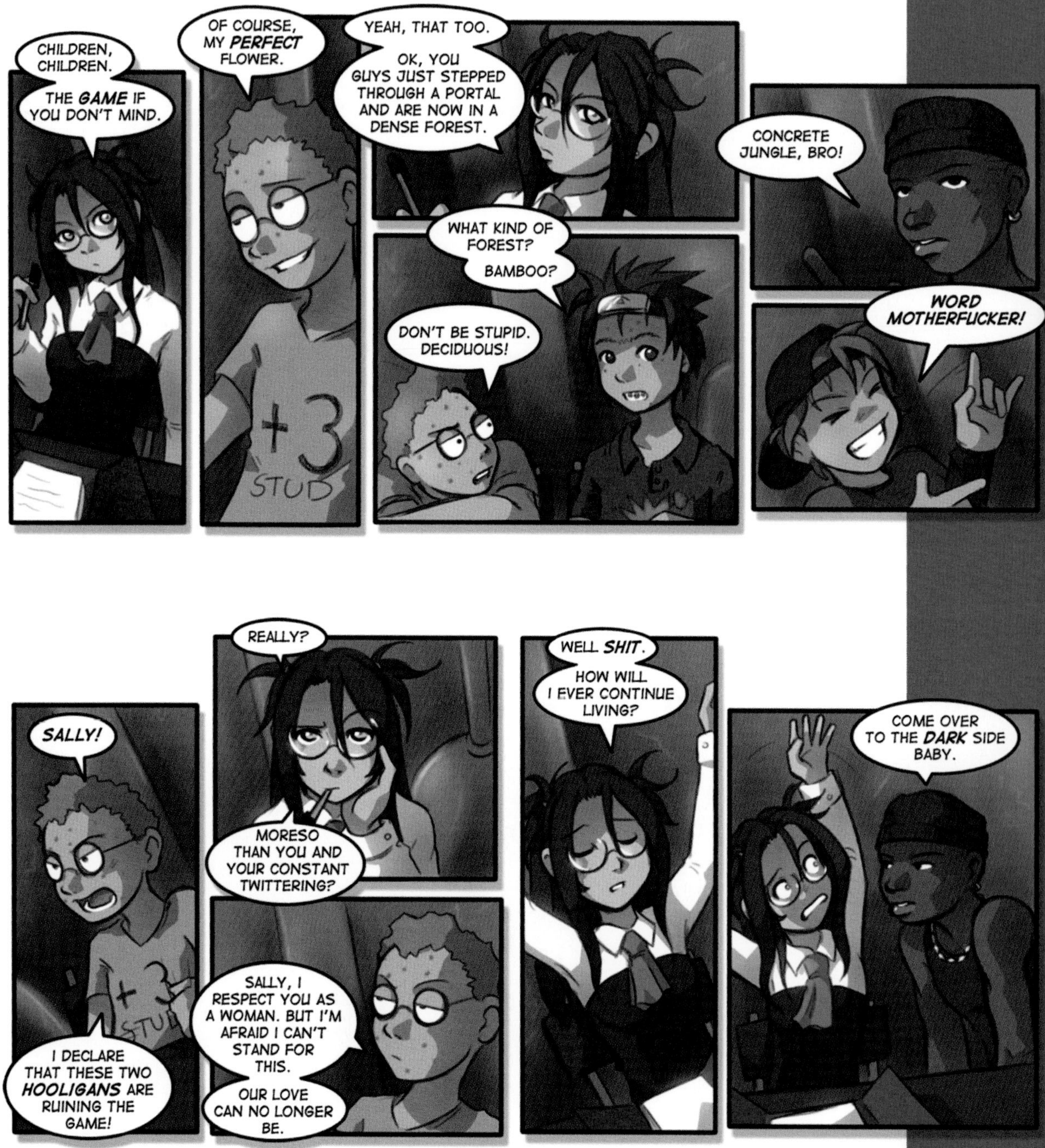
CHILDREN, CHILDREN.
THE GAME IF YOU DON'T MIND.
OF COURSE, MY PERFECT FLOWER.
+3 STUD
YEAH, THAT TOO.
OK, YOU GUYS JUST STEPPED THROUGH A PORTAL AND ARE NOW IN A DENSE FOREST.
WHAT KIND OF FOREST?
BAMBOO?
DON'T BE STUPID. DECIDUOUS!
CONCRETE JUNGLE, BRO!
WORD MOTHERFUCKER!
SALLY!
I DECLARE THAT THESE TWO HOOLIGANS ARE RUINING THE GAME!
REALLY?
MORESO THAN YOU AND YOUR CONSTANT TWITTERING?
SALLY, I RESPECT YOU AS A WOMAN. BUT I'M AFRAID I CAN'T STAND FOR THIS.
OUR LOVE CAN NO LONGER BE.
WELL SHIT.
HOW WILL I EVER CONTINUE LIVING?
COME OVER TO THE DARK SIDE BABY.

#100

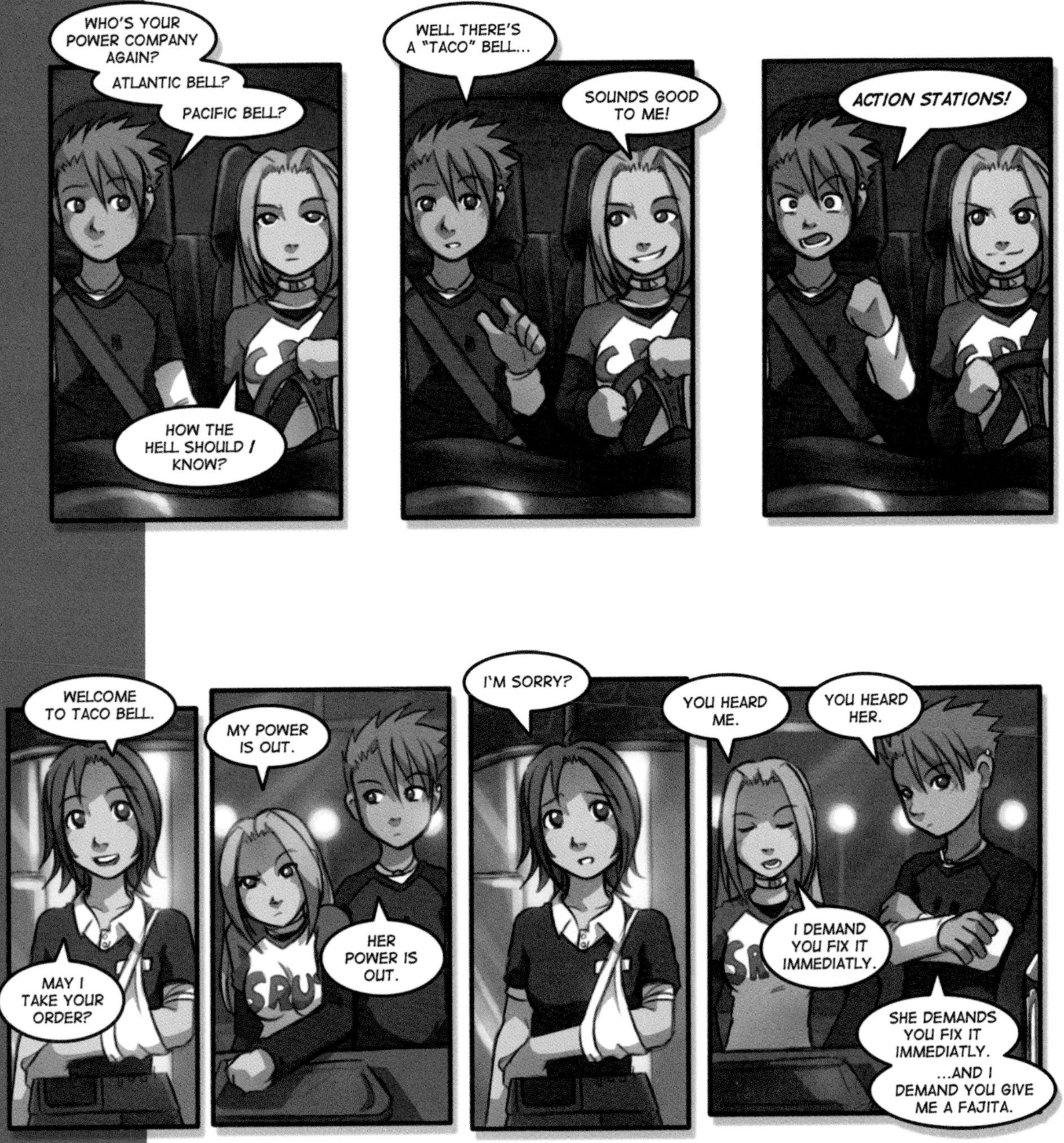
WHO'S YOUR POWER COMPANY AGAIN?
ATLANTIC BELL?
PACIFIC BELL?
HOW THE HELL SHOULD I KNOW?
WELL THERE'S A "TACO" BELL...
SOUNDS GOOD TO ME!
ACTION STATIONS!
WELCOME TO TACO BELL.
MAY I TAKE YOUR ORDER?
MY POWER IS OUT.
HER POWER IS OUT.
I'M SORRY?
YOU HEARD ME.
YOU HEARD HER.
I DEMAND YOU FIX IT IMMEDIATLY.
SHE DEMANDS YOU FIX IT IMMEDIATLY.
...AND I DEMAND YOU GIVE ME A FAJITA.

#101

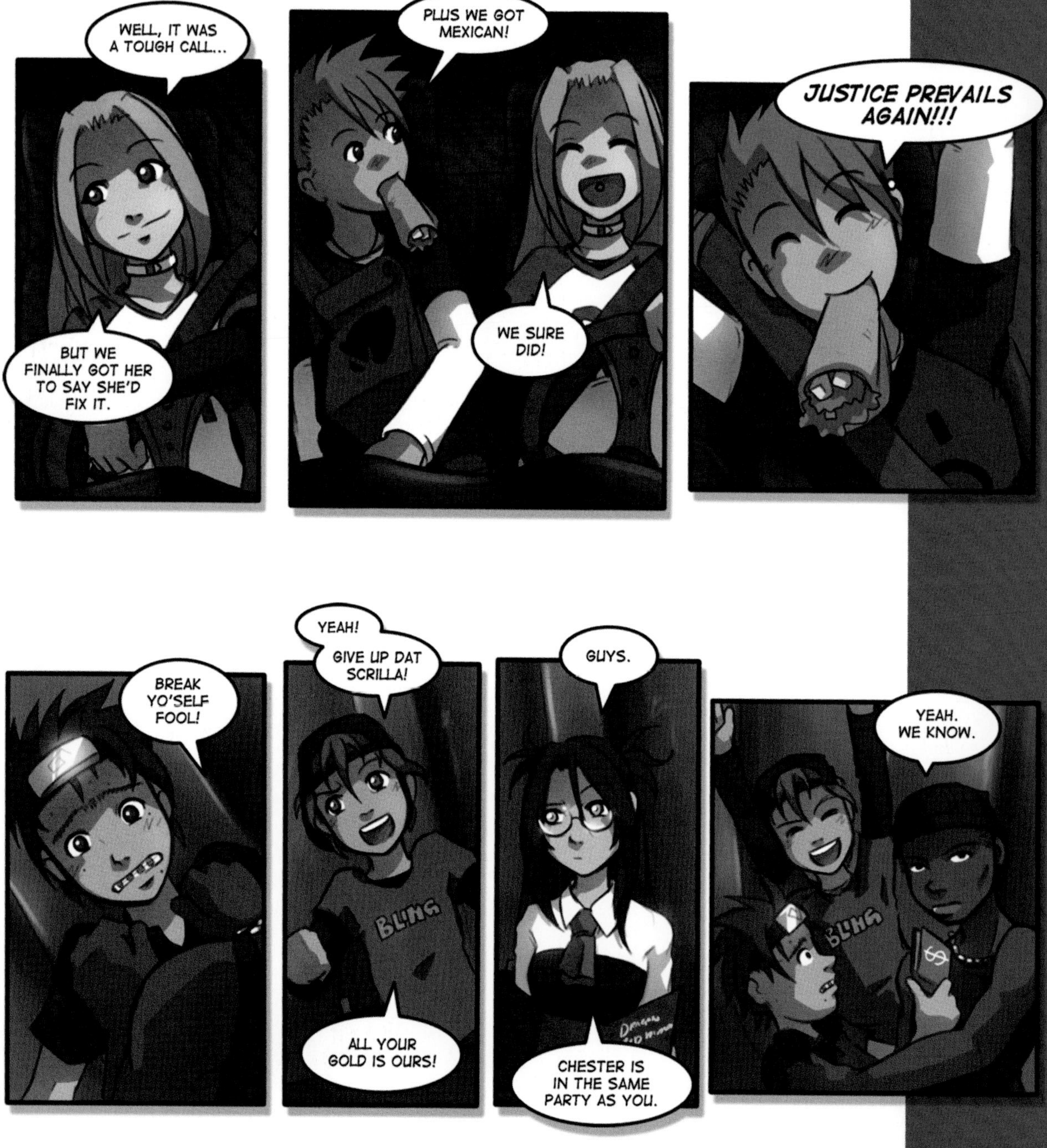
WELL, IT WAS A TOUGH CALL...
BUT WE FINALLY GOT HER TO SAY SHE'D FIX IT.
PLUS WE GOT MEXICAN!
WE SURE DID!
JUSTICE PREVAILS AGAIN!!!
BREAK YO'SELF FOOL!
YEAH!
GIVE UP DAT SCRILLA!
BLING
ALL YOUR GOLD IS OURS!
GUYS.
CHESTER IS IN THE SAME PARTY AS YOU.
YEAH. WE KNOW.
BLING

#102

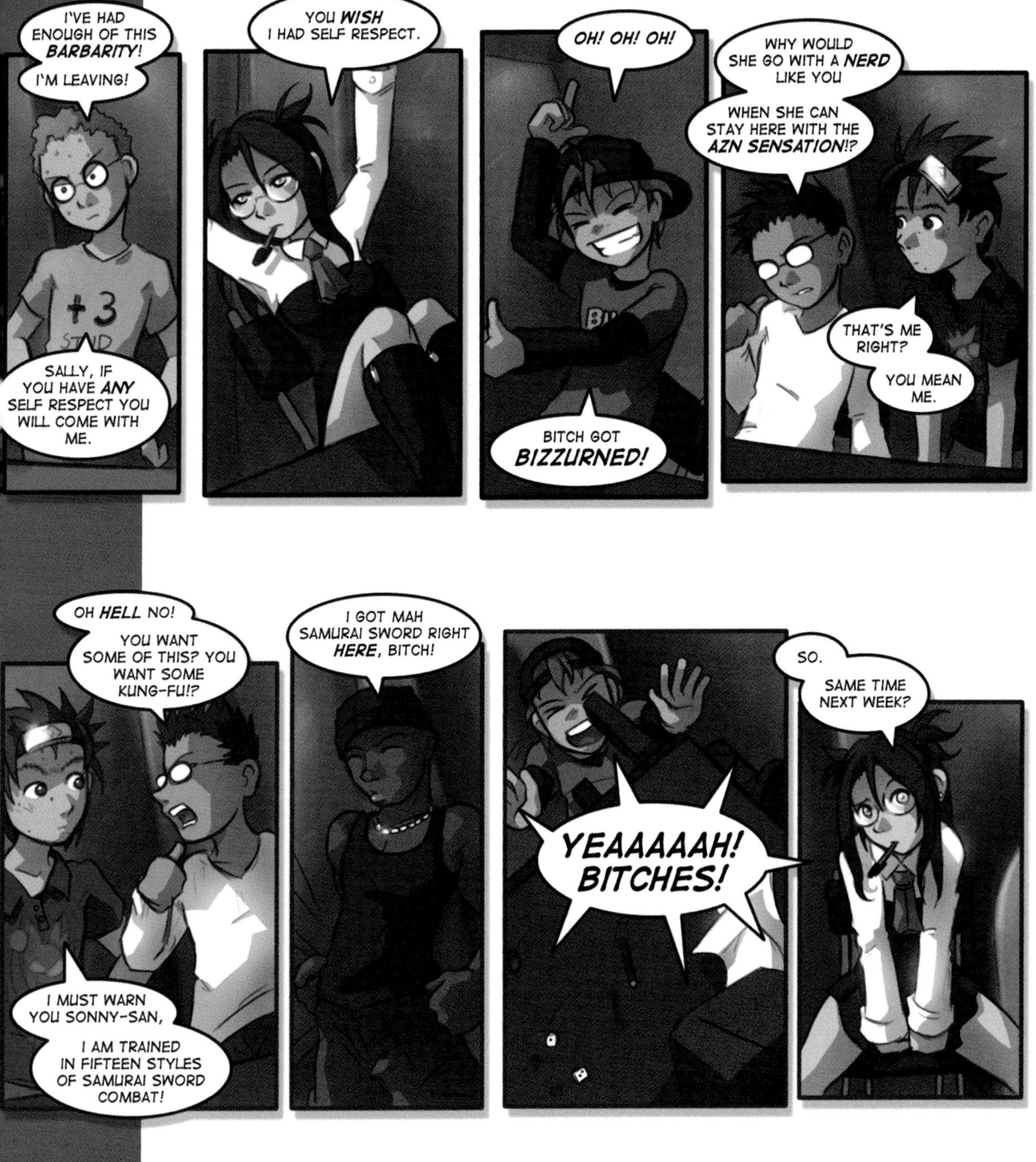
I'VE HAD ENOUGH OF THIS BARBARITY!
I'M LEAVING!
SALLY, IF YOU HAVE ANY SELF RESPECT YOU WILL COME WITH ME.
YOU WISH I HAD SELF RESPECT.
OH! OH! OH!
BITCH GOT BIZZURNED!
WHY WOULD SHE GO WITH A NERD LIKE YOU
WHEN SHE CAN STAY HERE WITH THE AZN SENSATION!?
THAT'S ME RIGHT?
YOU MEAN ME.
OH HELL NO!
YOU WANT SOME OF THIS? YOU WANT SOME KUNG-FU!?
I MUST WARN YOU SONNY-SAN,
I AM TRAINED IN FIFTEEN STYLES OF SAMURAI SWORD COMBAT!
I GOT MAH SAMURAI SWORD RIGHT HERE, BITCH!
YEAAAAAH! BITCHES!
SO.
SAME TIME NEXT WEEK?

#103

Random, Unrelated Strips.

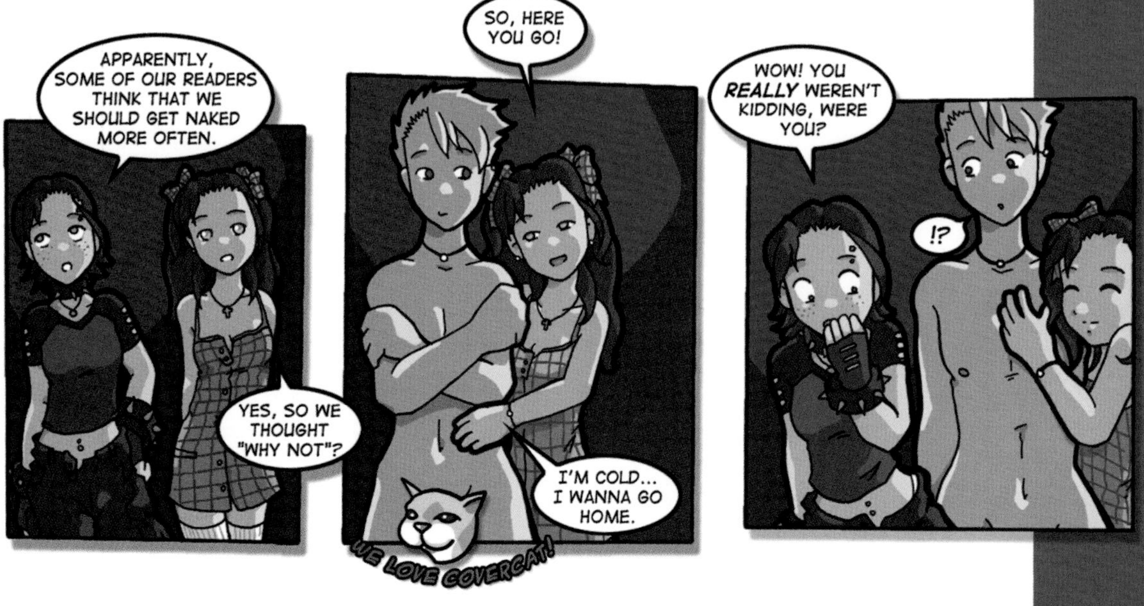
APPARENTLY, SOME OF OUR READERS THINK THAT WE SHOULD GET NAKED MORE OFTEN.
YES, SO WE THOUGHT "WHY NOT"?
SO, HERE YOU GO!
I'M COLD... I WANNA GO HOME.
WE LOVE COVERCAT!
WOW! YOU REALLY WEREN'T KIDDING, WERE YOU?
!?

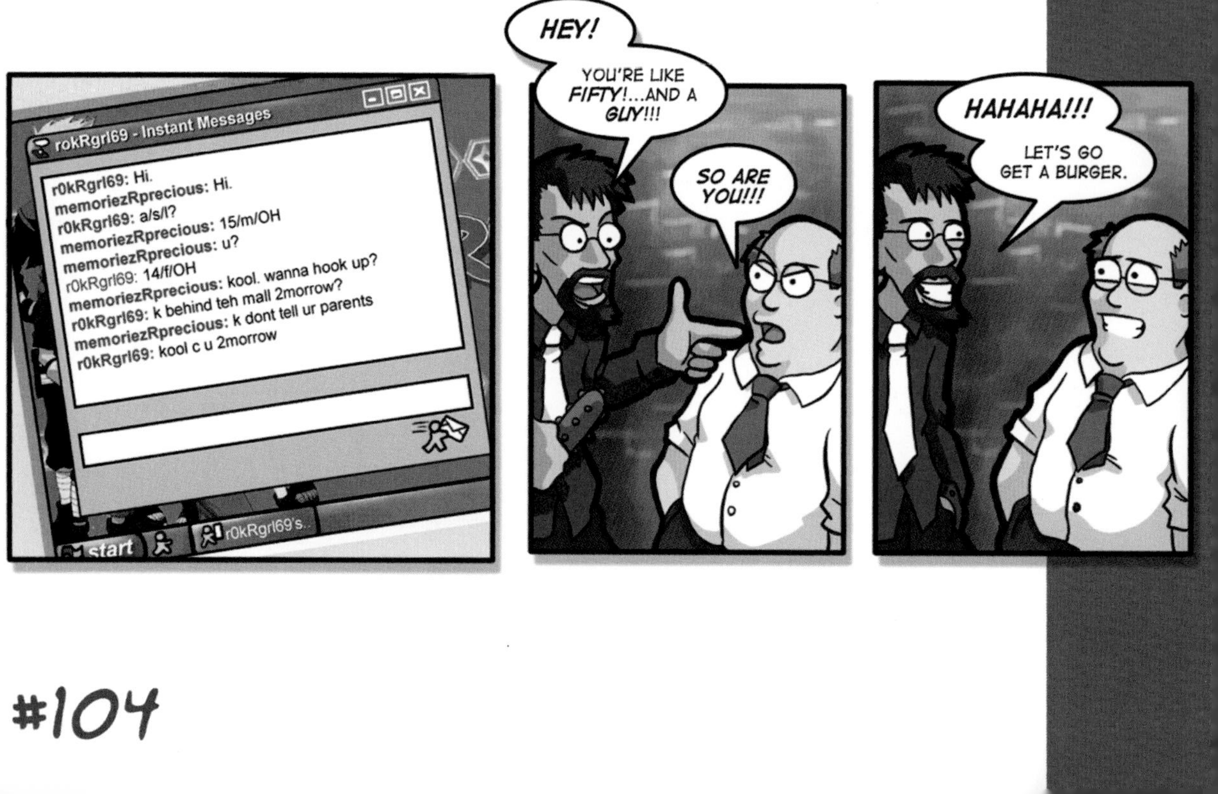
rokRgrl69 - Instant Messages
r0kRgrl69: Hi.
memoriezRprecious: Hi.
r0kRgrl69: a/s/l?
memoriezRprecious: 15/m/OH
memoriezRprecious: u?
r0kRgrl69: 14/f/OH
memoriezRprecious: kool. wanna hook up?
r0kRgrl69: k behind teh mall 2morrow?
memoriezRprecious: k dont tell ur parents
r0kRgrl69: kool c u 2morrow
start
r0kRgrl69's..
HEY!
YOU'RE LIKE FIFTY!...AND A GUY!!!
SO ARE YOU!!!
HAHAHA!!!
LET'S GO GET A BURGER.

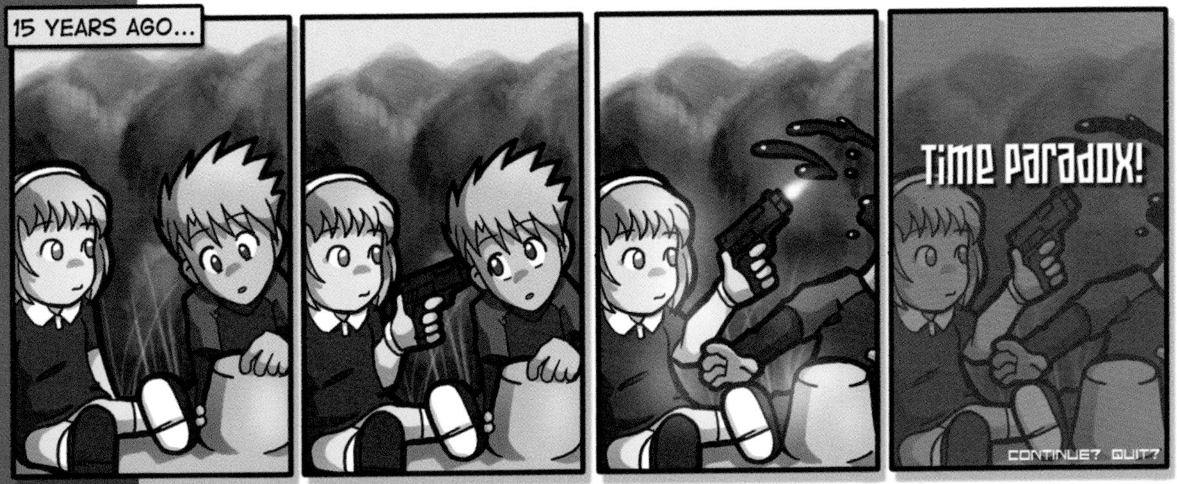
15 YEARS AGO...
TIME PARADOX!
CONTINUE? QUIT?

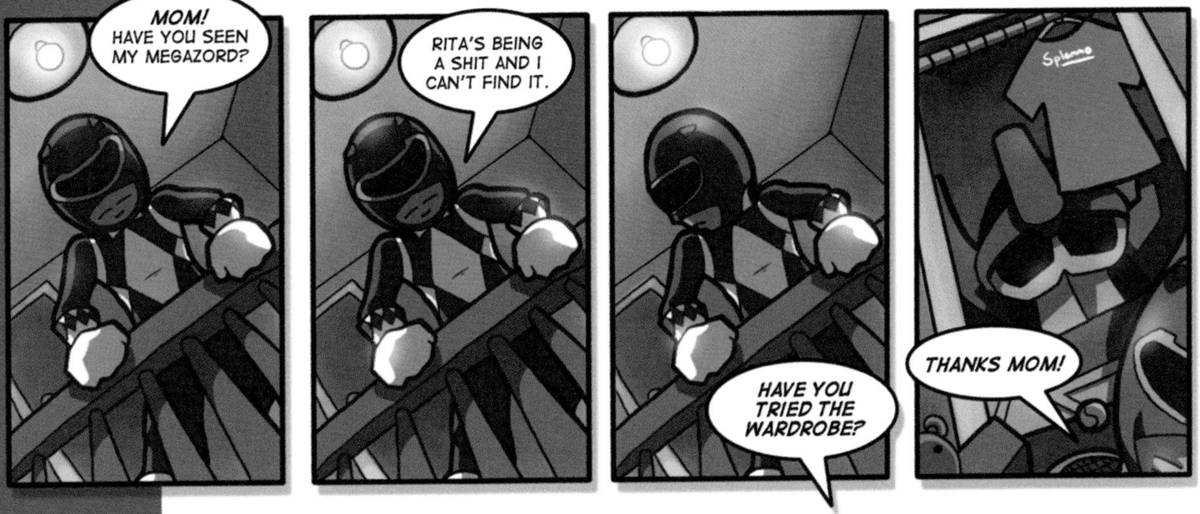
MOM! HAVE YOU SEEN MY MEGAZORD?
RITA'S BEING A SHIT AND I CAN'T FIND IT.
HAVE YOU TRIED THE WARDROBE?
THANKS MOM!

#105

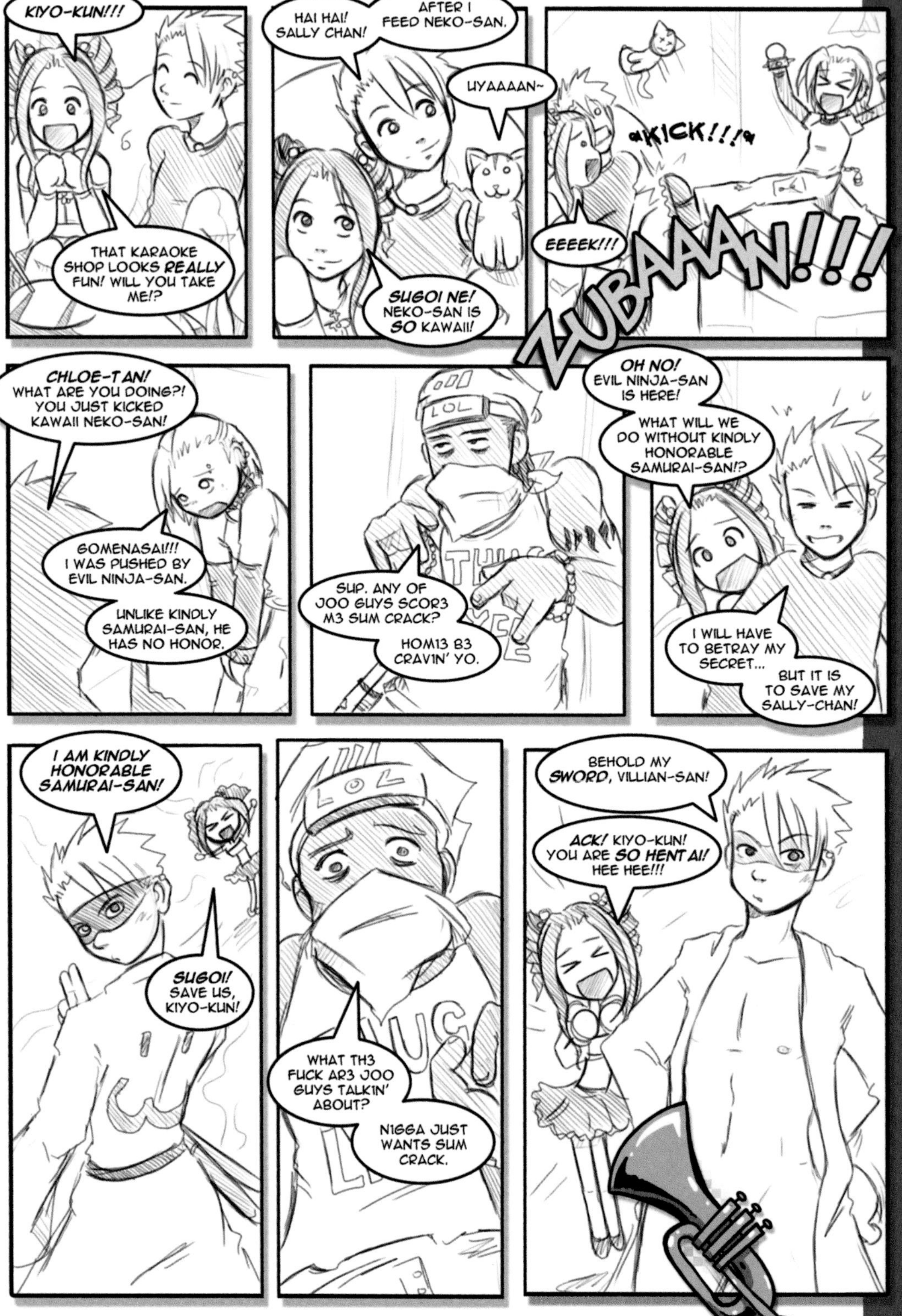
KIYO-KUN!!!
THAT KARAOKE SHOP LOOKS REALLY FUN! WILL YOU TAKE ME!?
HAI HAI! SALLY CHAN!
AFTER I FEED NEKO-SAN.
UYAAAAN~
SUGOI NE! NEKO-SAN IS SO KAWAII!
KICK!!!
EEEEK!!!
ZUBAAAN!!!!
CHLOE-TAN! WHAT ARE YOU DOING?! YOU JUST KICKED KAWAII NEKO-SAN!
GOMENASAI!!! I WAS PUSHED BY EVIL NINJA-SAN.
UNLIKE KINDLY SAMURAI-SAN, HE HAS NO HONOR.
SUP. ANY OF JOO GUYS SCOR3 M3 SUM CRACK?
HOM13 B3 CRAV1N' YO.
OH NO! EVIL NINJA-SAN IS HERE!
WHAT WILL WE DO WITHOUT KINDLY HONORABLE SAMURAI-SAN!?
I WILL HAVE TO BETRAY MY SECRET...
BUT IT IS TO SAVE MY SALLY-CHAN!
I AM KINDLY HONORABLE SAMURAI-SAN!
SUGOI! SAVE US, KIYO-KUN!
WHAT TH3 FUCK AR3 JOO GUYS TALKIN' ABOUT?
N1GGA JUST WANTS SUM CRACK.
BEHOLD MY SWORD, VILLIAN-SAN!
ACK! KIYO-KUN! YOU ARE SO HENTAI! HEE HEE!!!

#106

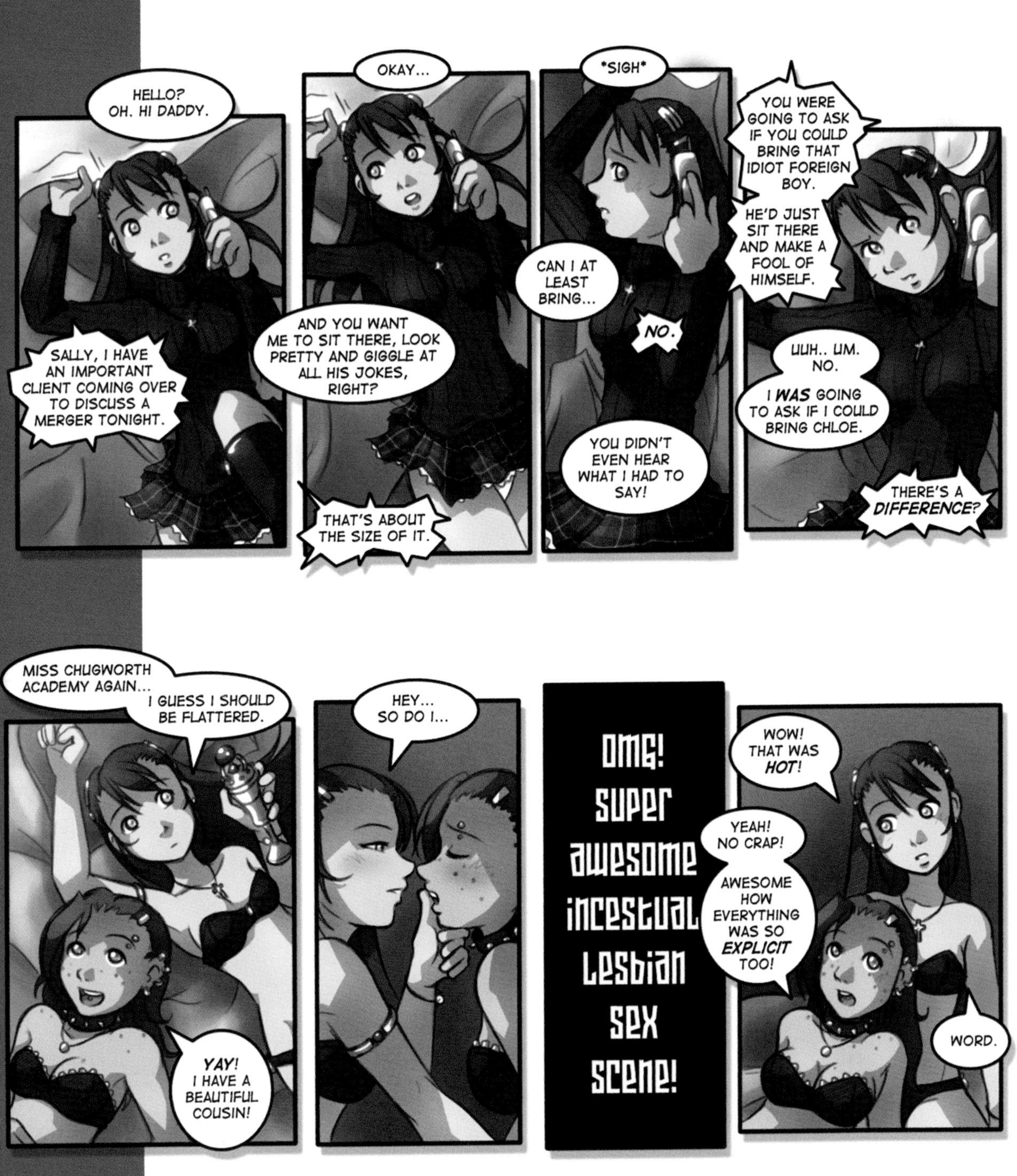
HELLO? OH. HI DADDY.
SALLY, I HAVE AN IMPORTANT CLIENT COMING OVER TO DISCUSS A MERGER TONIGHT.
OKAY...
AND YOU WANT ME TO SIT THERE, LOOK PRETTY AND GIGGLE AT ALL HIS JOKES, RIGHT?
THAT'S ABOUT THE SIZE OF IT.
SIGH
CAN I AT LEAST BRING...
NO.
YOU DIDN'T EVEN HEAR WHAT I HAD TO SAY!
YOU WERE GOING TO ASK IF YOU COULD BRING THAT IDIOT FOREIGN BOY.
HE'D JUST SIT THERE AND MAKE A FOOL OF HIMSELF.
UUH.. UM. NO.
I **WAS** GOING TO ASK IF I COULD BRING CHLOE.
THERE'S A ***DIFFERENCE***?
MISS CHUGWORTH ACADEMY AGAIN...
I GUESS I SHOULD BE FLATTERED.
YAY! I HAVE A BEAUTIFUL COUSIN!
HEY... SO DO I...
OMG! SUPER AWESOME INCESTUAL LESBIAN SEX SCENE!
WOW! THAT WAS *HOT*!
YEAH! NO CRAP!
AWESOME HOW EVERYTHING WAS SO ***EXPLICIT*** TOO!
WORD.

#107

The Beginning of the End.

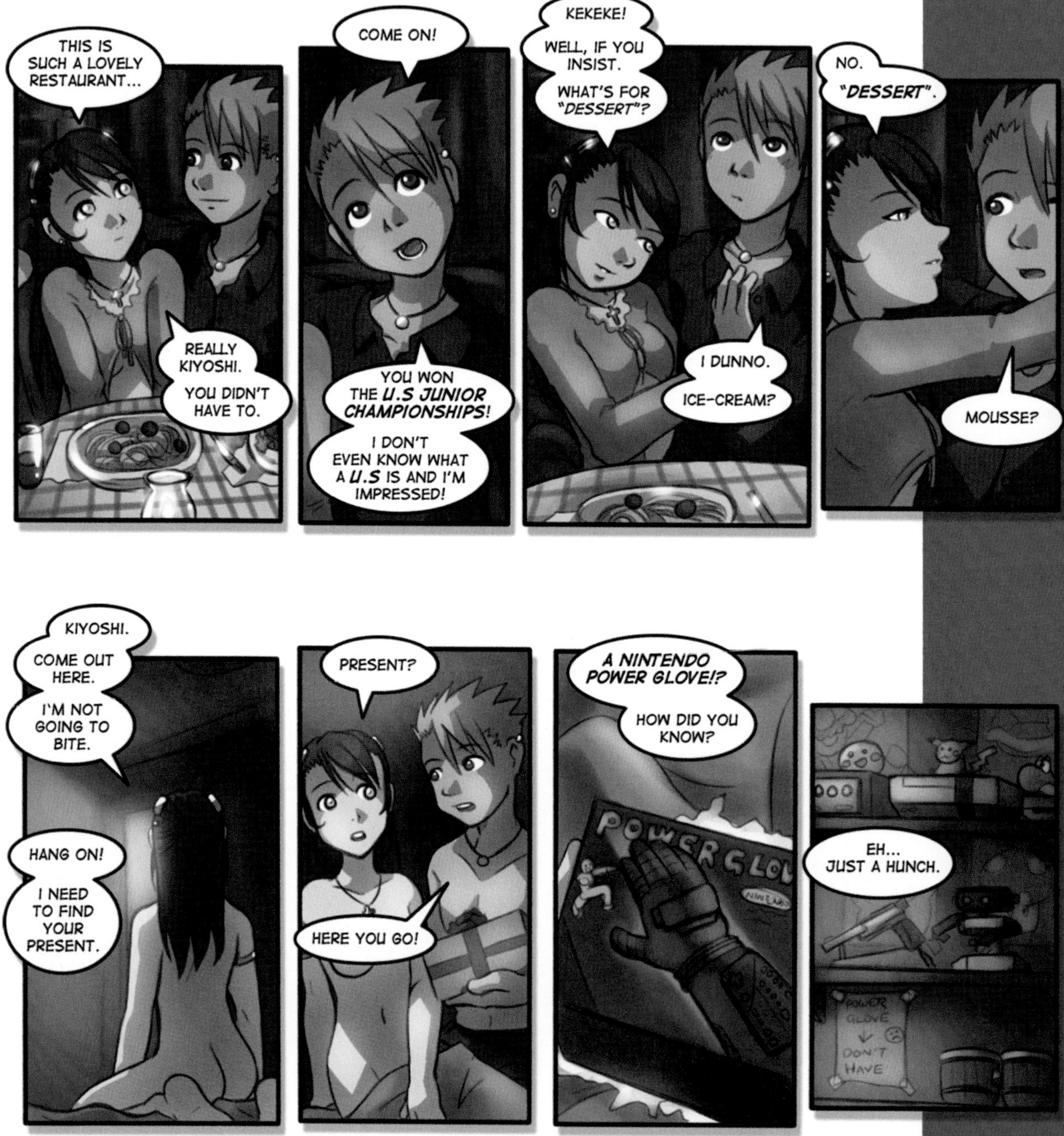
THIS IS SUCH A LOVELY RESTAURANT...
REALLY KIYOSHI.
YOU DIDN'T HAVE TO.
COME ON!
YOU WON THE U.S JUNIOR CHAMPIONSHIPS!
I DON'T EVEN KNOW WHAT A U.S IS AND I'M IMPRESSED!
KEKEKE!
WELL, IF YOU INSIST.
WHAT'S FOR "DESSERT"?
I DUNNO.
ICE-CREAM?
NO.
"DESSERT".
MOUSSE?
KIYOSHI.
COME OUT HERE.
I'M NOT GOING TO BITE.
HANG ON!
I NEED TO FIND YOUR PRESENT.
PRESENT?
HERE YOU GO!
A NINTENDO POWER GLOVE!?
HOW DID YOU KNOW?
EH... JUST A HUNCH.
POWER GLOVE
DON'T HAVE

#108

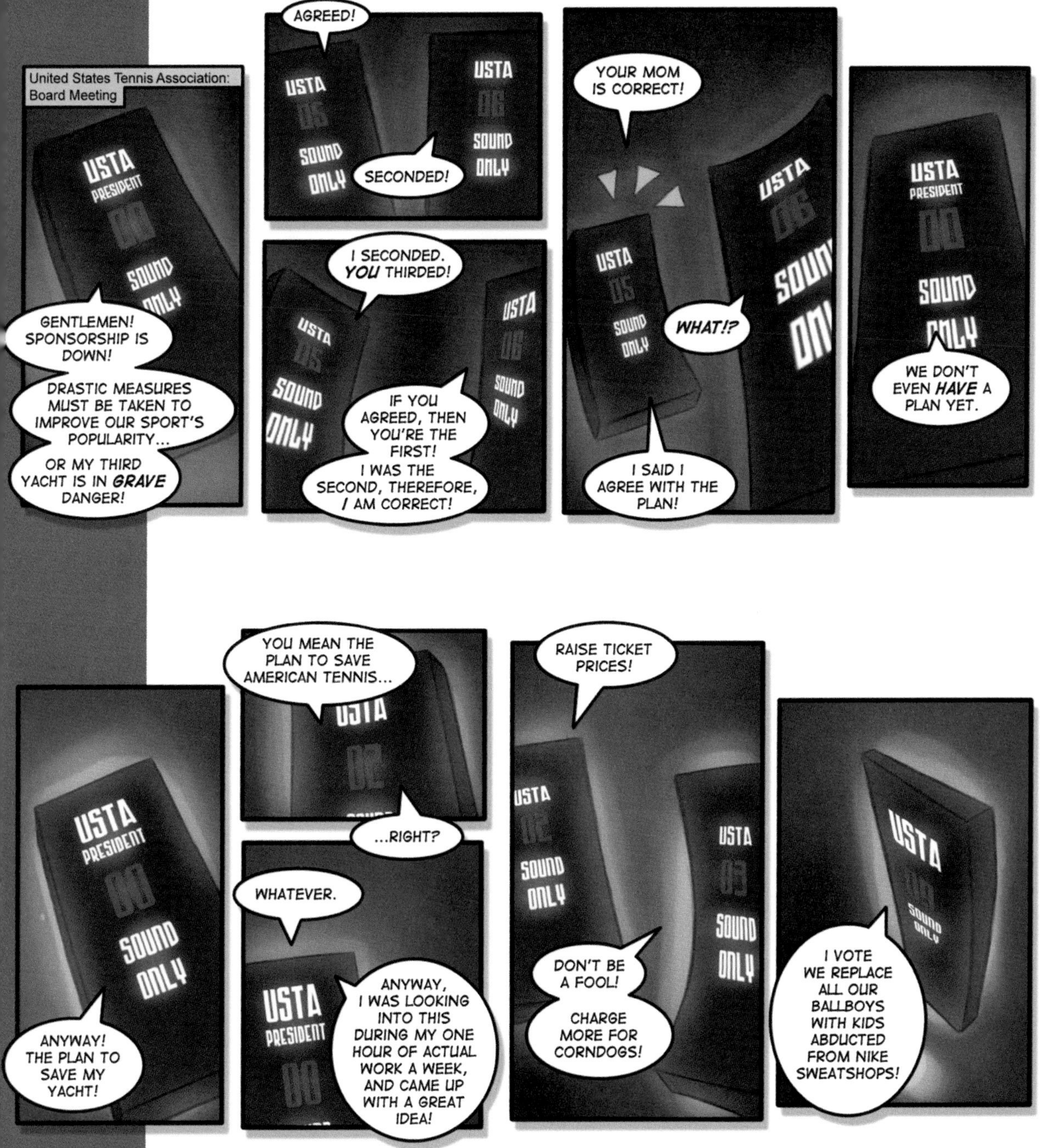
United States Tennis Association: Board Meeting
GENTLEMEN! SPONSORSHIP IS DOWN!
DRASTIC MEASURES MUST BE TAKEN TO IMPROVE OUR SPORT'S POPULARITY...
OR MY THIRD YACHT IS IN GRAVE DANGER!
AGREED!
SECONDED!
I SECONDED. YOU THIRDED!
IF YOU AGREED, THEN YOU'RE THE FIRST!
I WAS THE SECOND, THEREFORE, I AM CORRECT!
YOUR MOM IS CORRECT!
WHAT!?
I SAID I AGREE WITH THE PLAN!
WE DON'T EVEN HAVE A PLAN YET.
ANYWAY! THE PLAN TO SAVE MY YACHT!
YOU MEAN THE PLAN TO SAVE AMERICAN TENNIS...
...RIGHT?
WHATEVER.
ANYWAY, I WAS LOOKING INTO THIS DURING MY ONE HOUR OF ACTUAL WORK A WEEK, AND CAME UP WITH A GREAT IDEA!
RAISE TICKET PRICES!
DON'T BE A FOOL!
CHARGE MORE FOR CORNDOGS!
I VOTE WE REPLACE ALL OUR BALLBOYS WITH KIDS ABDUCTED FROM NIKE SWEATSHOPS!

#109

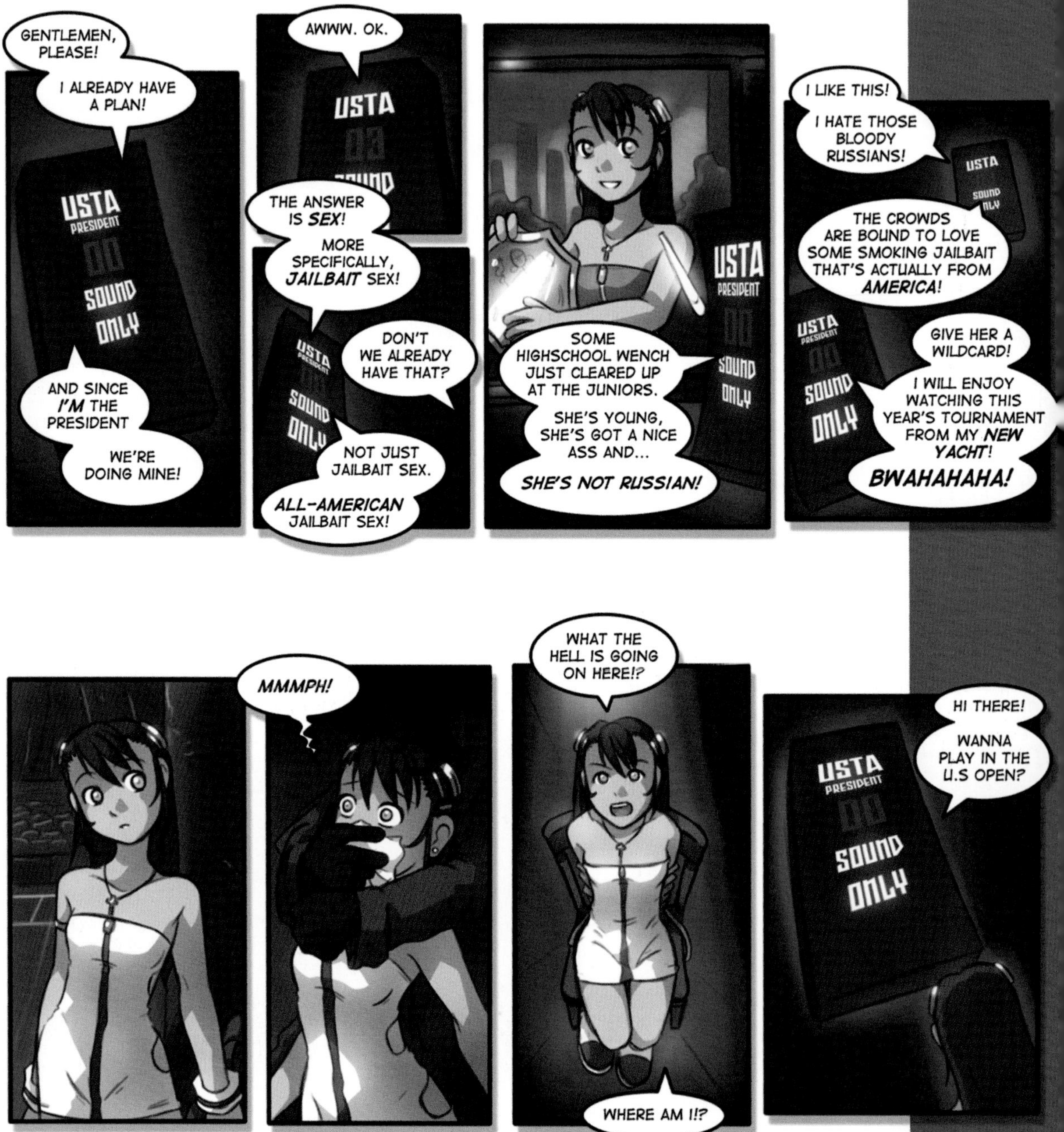
GENTLEMEN, PLEASE!
I ALREADY HAVE A PLAN!
USTA PRESIDENT 00 SOUND ONLY
AND SINCE *I'M* THE PRESIDENT
WE'RE DOING MINE!
AWWW. OK.
USTA 03
THE ANSWER IS ***SEX***!
MORE SPECIFICALLY, ***JAILBAIT*** SEX!
USTA PRESIDENT SOUND ONLY
DON'T WE ALREADY HAVE THAT?
NOT JUST JAILBAIT SEX.
ALL-AMERICAN JAILBAIT SEX!
USTA PRESIDENT 00 SOUND ONLY
SOME HIGHSCHOOL WENCH JUST CLEARED UP AT THE JUNIORS.
SHE'S YOUNG, SHE'S GOT A NICE ASS AND...
SHE'S NOT RUSSIAN!
I LIKE THIS!
I HATE THOSE BLOODY RUSSIANS!
USTA SOUND ONLY
THE CROWDS ARE BOUND TO LOVE SOME SMOKING JAILBAIT THAT'S ACTUALLY FROM ***AMERICA***!
USTA PRESIDENT 00 SOUND ONLY
GIVE HER A WILDCARD!
I WILL ENJOY WATCHING THIS YEAR'S TOURNAMENT FROM MY ***NEW YACHT***!
BWAHAHAHA!
MMMPH!
WHAT THE HELL IS GOING ON HERE!?
WHERE AM I!?
HI THERE!
WANNA PLAY IN THE U.S OPEN?
USTA PRESIDENT 00 SOUND ONLY

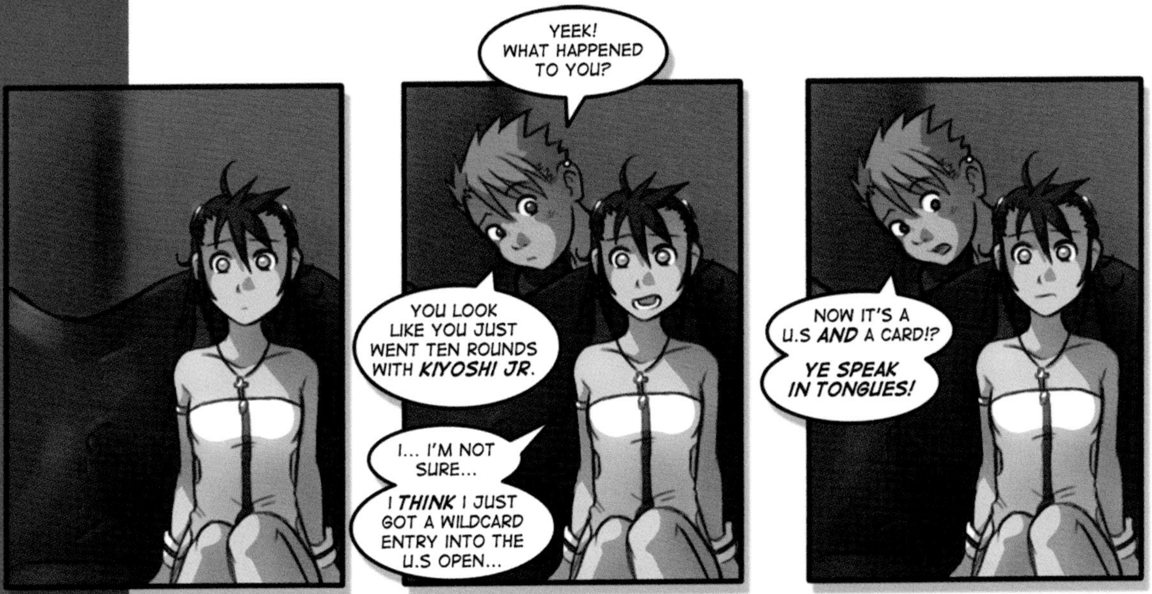
YEEK! WHAT HAPPENED TO YOU?
YOU LOOK LIKE YOU JUST WENT TEN ROUNDS WITH *KIYOSHI JR*.
I... I'M NOT SURE...
I *THINK* I JUST GOT A WILDCARD ENTRY INTO THE U.S OPEN...
NOW IT'S A U.S *AND* A CARD!?
YE SPEAK IN TONGUES!

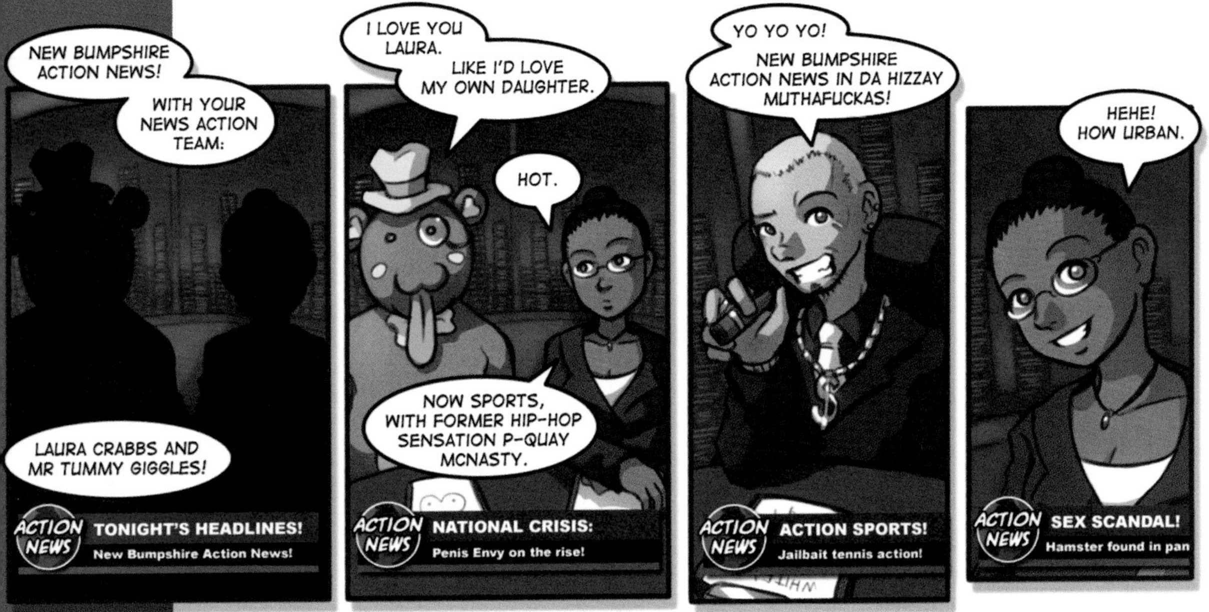
NEW BUMPSHIRE ACTION NEWS!
WITH YOUR NEWS ACTION TEAM:
LAURA CRABBS AND MR TUMMY GIGGLES!
ACTION NEWS
TONIGHT'S HEADLINES!
New Bumpshire Action News!
I LOVE YOU LAURA.
LIKE I'D LOVE MY OWN DAUGHTER.
HOT.
NOW SPORTS, WITH FORMER HIP-HOP SENSATION P-QUAY MCNASTY.
ACTION NEWS
NATIONAL CRISIS:
Penis Envy on the rise!
YO YO YO!
NEW BUMPSHIRE ACTION NEWS IN DA HIZZAY MUTHAFUCKAS!
ACTION NEWS
ACTION SPORTS!
Jailbait tennis action!
HEHE! HOW URBAN.
ACTION NEWS
SEX SCANDAL!
Hamster found in pan

#111

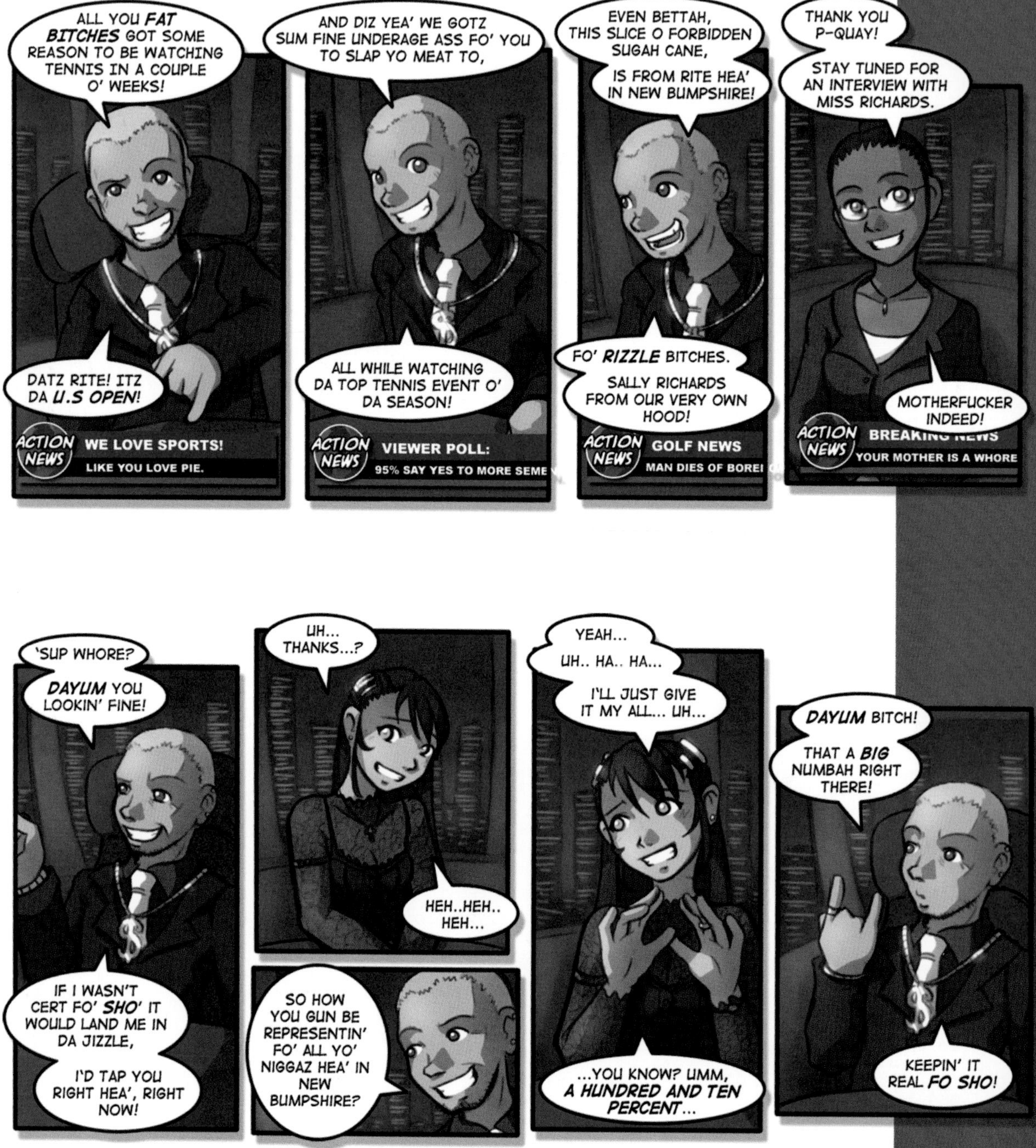
ALL YOU FAT BITCHES GOT SOME REASON TO BE WATCHING TENNIS IN A COUPLE O' WEEKS!
DATZ RITE! ITZ DA U.S OPEN!
ACTION NEWS
WE LOVE SPORTS!
LIKE YOU LOVE PIE.
AND DIZ YEA' WE GOTZ SUM FINE UNDERAGE ASS FO' YOU TO SLAP YO MEAT TO,
ALL WHILE WATCHING DA TOP TENNIS EVENT O' DA SEASON!
ACTION NEWS
VIEWER POLL:
95% SAY YES TO MORE SEME
EVEN BETTAH, THIS SLICE O FORBIDDEN SUGAH CANE,
IS FROM RITE HEA' IN NEW BUMPSHIRE!
FO' RIZZLE BITCHES.
SALLY RICHARDS FROM OUR VERY OWN HOOD!
ACTION NEWS
GOLF NEWS
MAN DIES OF BORE
THANK YOU P-QUAY!
STAY TUNED FOR AN INTERVIEW WITH MISS RICHARDS.
MOTHERFUCKER INDEED!
ACTION NEWS
BREAKING NEWS
YOUR MOTHER IS A WHORE
'SUP WHORE?
DAYUM YOU LOOKIN' FINE!
IF I WASN'T CERT FO' SHO' IT WOULD LAND ME IN DA JIZZLE,
I'D TAP YOU RIGHT HEA', RIGHT NOW!
UH... THANKS...?
HEH..HEH.. HEH...
SO HOW YOU GUN BE REPRESENTIN' FO' ALL YO' NIGGAZ HEA' IN NEW BUMPSHIRE?
YEAH...
UH.. HA.. HA...
I'LL JUST GIVE IT MY ALL... UH...
...YOU KNOW? UMM, A HUNDRED AND TEN PERCENT...
DAYUM BITCH!
THAT A BIG NUMBAH RIGHT THERE!
KEEPIN' IT REAL FO SHO!

#112

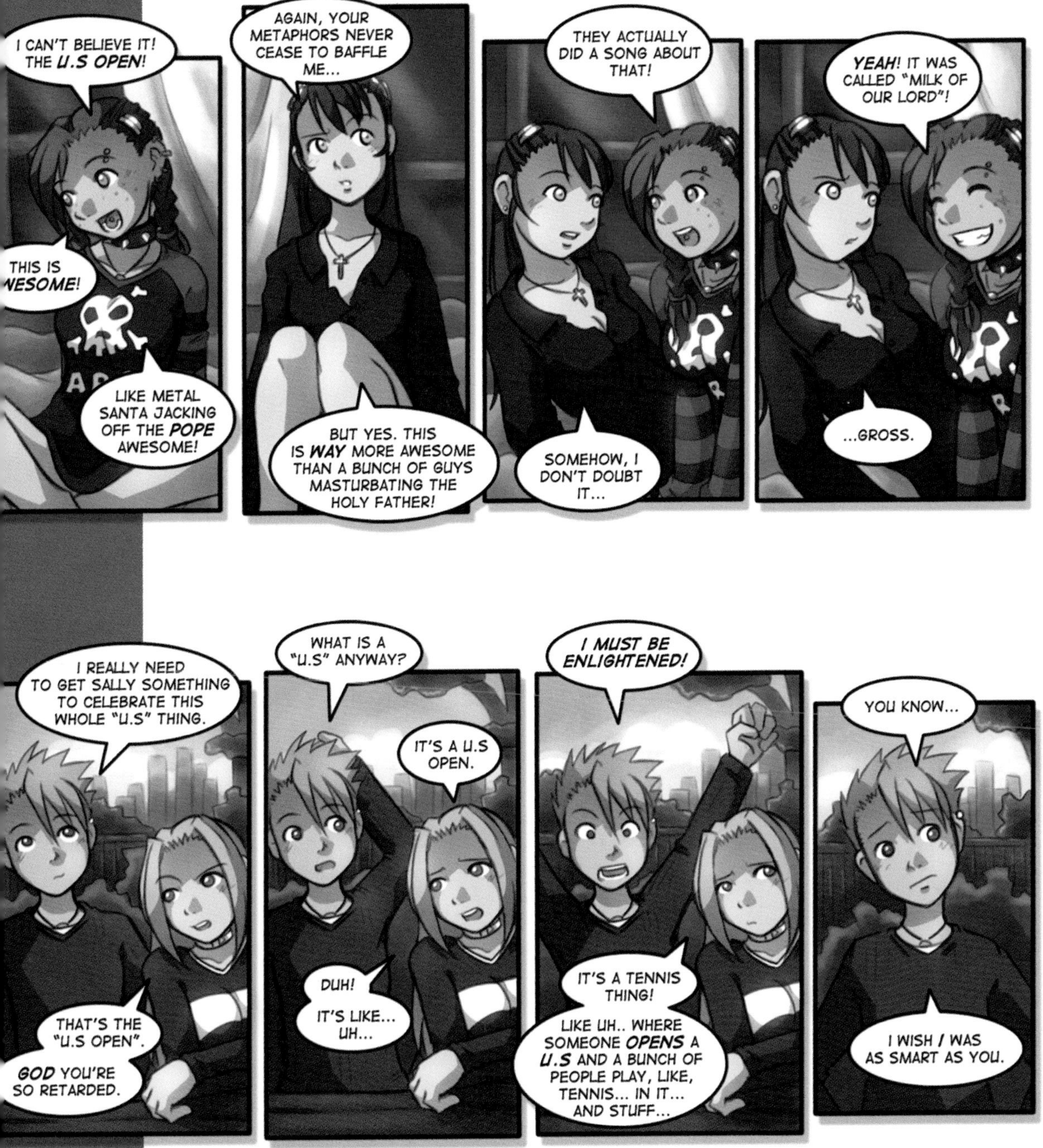
I CAN'T BELIEVE IT! THE U.S OPEN!
THIS IS ...WESOME!
LIKE METAL SANTA JACKING OFF THE POPE AWESOME!
AGAIN, YOUR METAPHORS NEVER CEASE TO BAFFLE ME...
BUT YES. THIS IS WAY MORE AWESOME THAN A BUNCH OF GUYS MASTURBATING THE HOLY FATHER!
THEY ACTUALLY DID A SONG ABOUT THAT!
SOMEHOW, I DON'T DOUBT IT...
YEAH! IT WAS CALLED "MILK OF OUR LORD"!
...GROSS.
I REALLY NEED TO GET SALLY SOMETHING TO CELEBRATE THIS WHOLE "U.S" THING.
THAT'S THE "U.S OPEN".
GOD YOU'RE SO RETARDED.
WHAT IS A "U.S" ANYWAY?
IT'S A U.S OPEN.
DUH!
IT'S LIKE... UH...
I MUST BE ENLIGHTENED!
IT'S A TENNIS THING!
LIKE UH.. WHERE SOMEONE OPENS A U.S AND A BUNCH OF PEOPLE PLAY, LIKE, TENNIS... IN IT... AND STUFF...
YOU KNOW...
I WISH I WAS AS SMART AS YOU.

#113

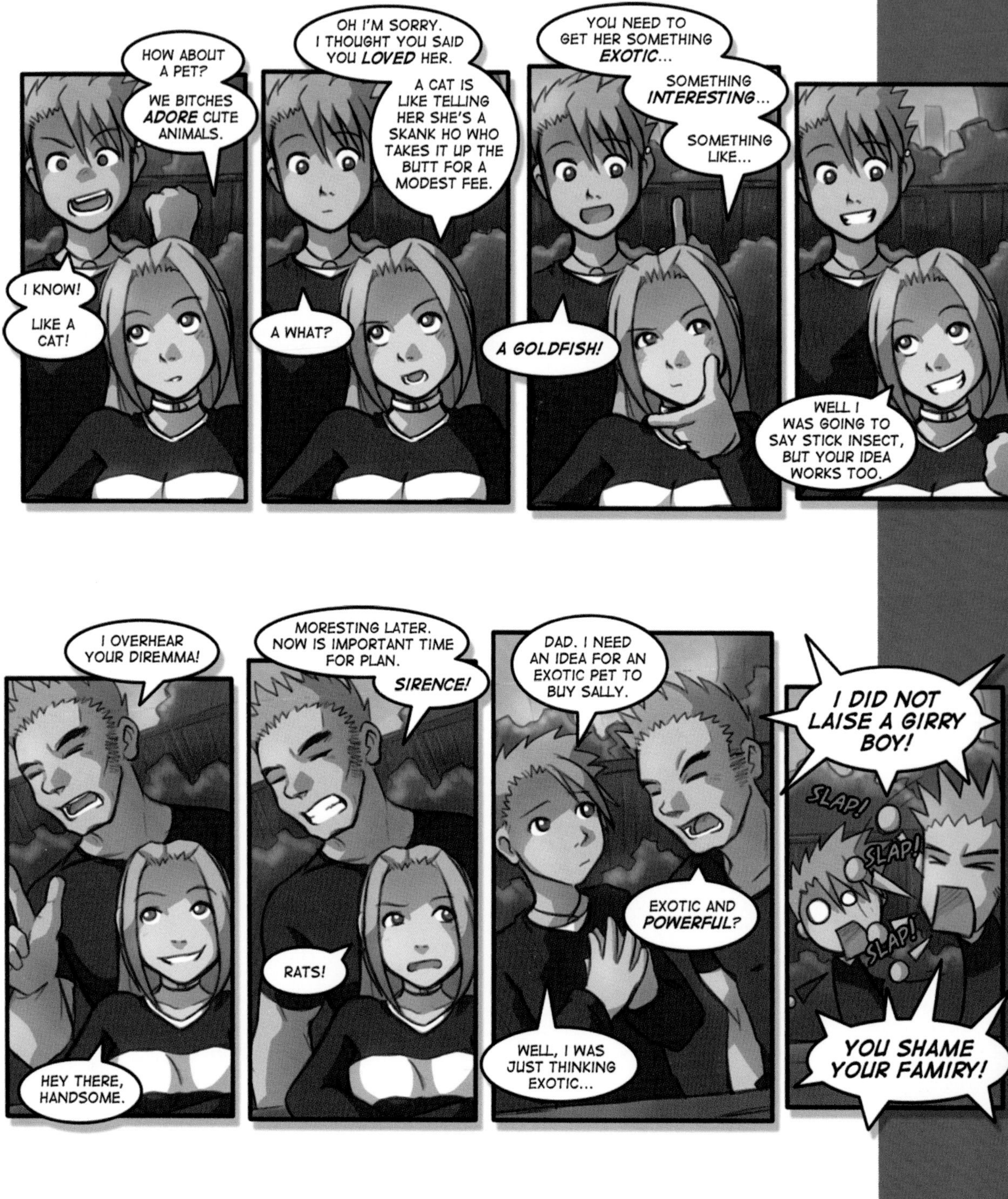
HOW ABOUT A PET?
WE BITCHES ADORE CUTE ANIMALS.
I KNOW!
LIKE A CAT!
OH I'M SORRY. I THOUGHT YOU SAID YOU LOVED HER.
A CAT IS LIKE TELLING HER SHE'S A SKANK HO WHO TAKES IT UP THE BUTT FOR A MODEST FEE.
A WHAT?
YOU NEED TO GET HER SOMETHING EXOTIC...
SOMETHING INTERESTING...
SOMETHING LIKE...
A GOLDFISH!
WELL I WAS GOING TO SAY STICK INSECT, BUT YOUR IDEA WORKS TOO.
I OVERHEAR YOUR DIREMMA!
HEY THERE, HANDSOME.
MORESTING LATER. NOW IS IMPORTANT TIME FOR PLAN.
SIRENCE!
RATS!
DAD. I NEED AN IDEA FOR AN EXOTIC PET TO BUY SALLY.
EXOTIC AND POWERFUL?
WELL, I WAS JUST THINKING EXOTIC...
I DID NOT LAISE A GIRRY BOY!
SLAP!
SLAP!
SLAP!
YOU SHAME YOUR FAMIRY!

#114

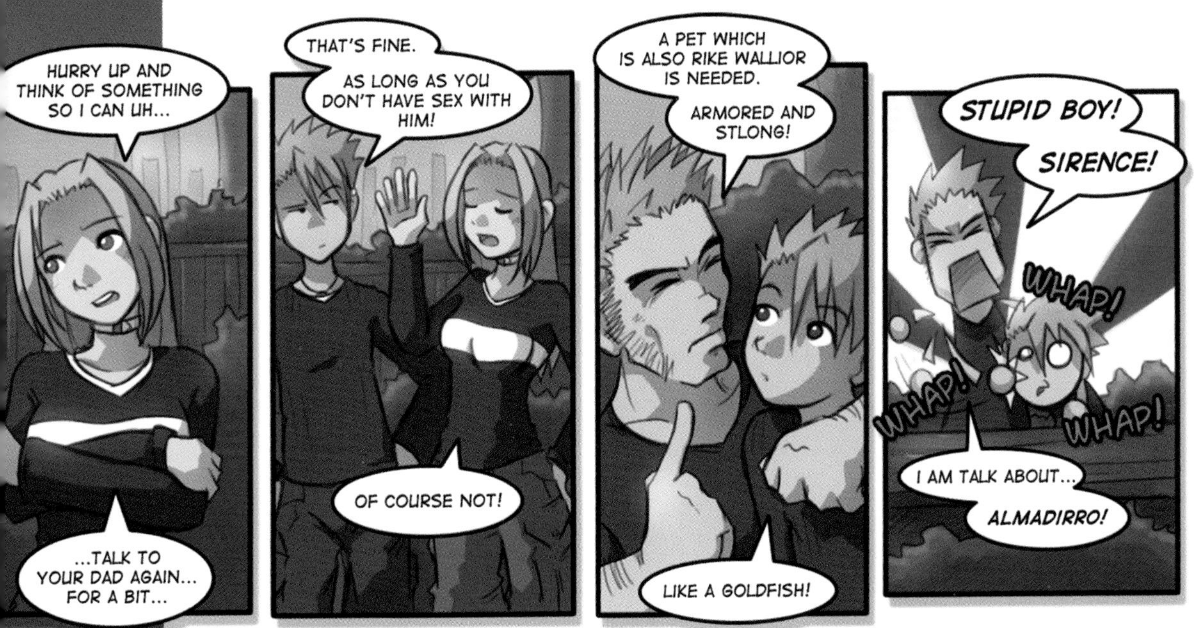
HURRY UP AND THINK OF SOMETHING SO I CAN UH...
...TALK TO YOUR DAD AGAIN... FOR A BIT...
THAT'S FINE.
AS LONG AS YOU DON'T HAVE SEX WITH HIM!
OF COURSE NOT!
A PET WHICH IS ALSO RIKE WALLIOR IS NEEDED.
ARMORED AND STLONG!
LIKE A GOLDFISH!
STUPID BOY!
SIRENCE!
WHAP!
WHAP!
WHAP!
I AM TALK ABOUT...
ALMADIRRO!

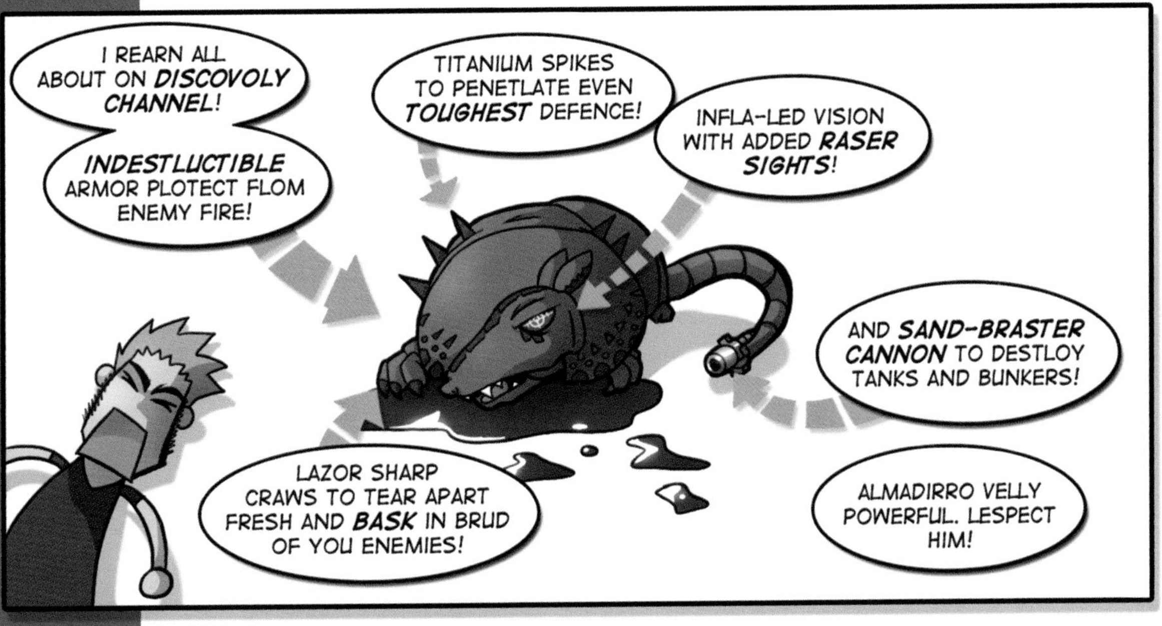
I REARN ALL ABOUT ON DISCOVOLY CHANNEL!
INDESTLUCTIBLE ARMOR PLOTECT FLOM ENEMY FIRE!
TITANIUM SPIKES TO PENETLATE EVEN TOUGHEST DEFENCE!
INFLA-LED VISION WITH ADDED RASER SIGHTS!
AND SAND-BRASTER CANNON TO DESTLOY TANKS AND BUNKERS!
LAZOR SHARP CRAWS TO TEAR APART FRESH AND BASK IN BRUD OF YOU ENEMIES!
ALMADIRRO VELLY POWERFUL. LESPECT HIM!

#115

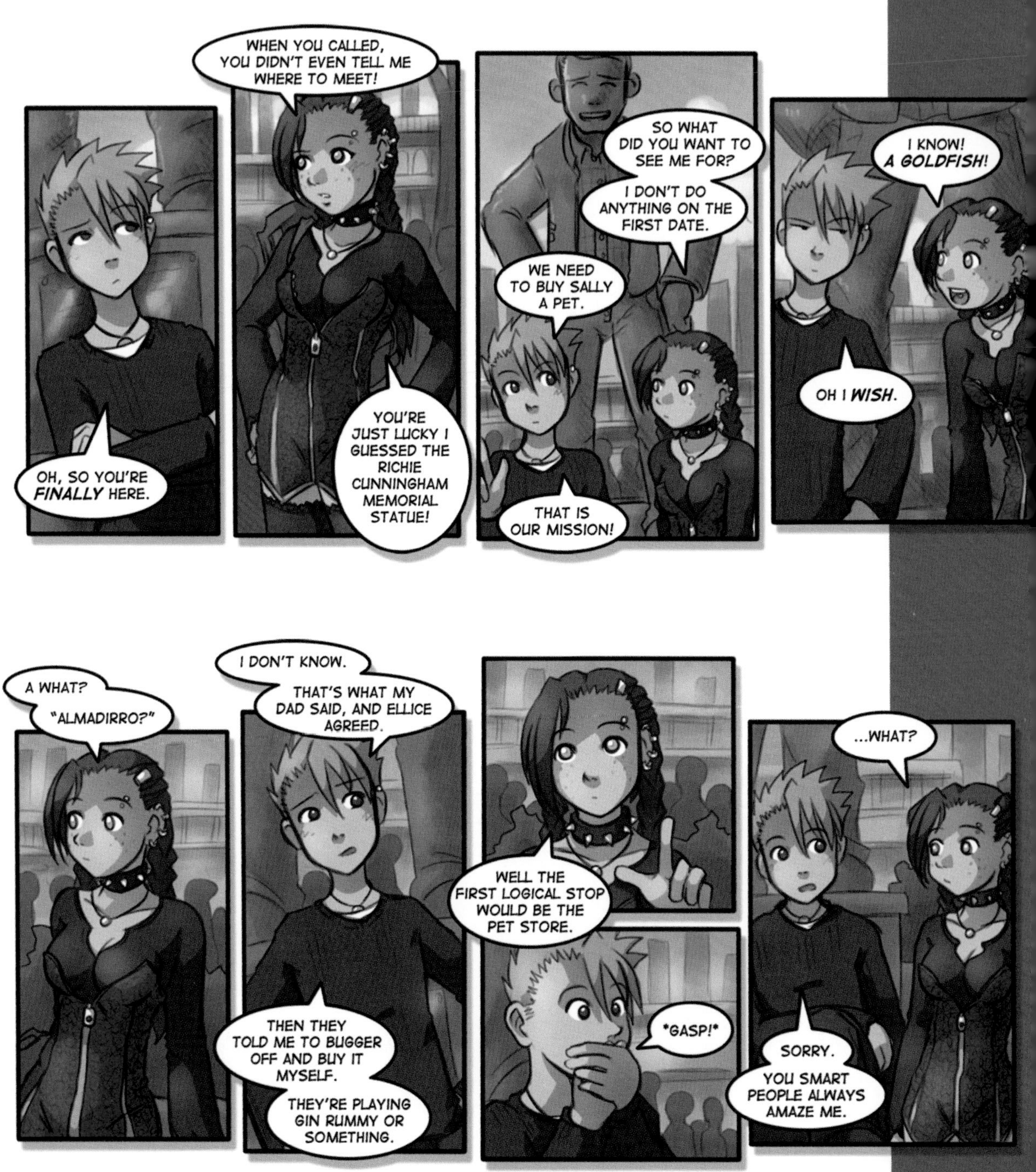
OH, SO YOU'RE *FINALLY* HERE.
WHEN YOU CALLED, YOU DIDN'T EVEN TELL ME WHERE TO MEET!
YOU'RE JUST LUCKY I GUESSED THE RICHIE CUNNINGHAM MEMORIAL STATUE!
SO WHAT DID YOU WANT TO SEE ME FOR?
I DON'T DO ANYTHING ON THE FIRST DATE.
WE NEED TO BUY SALLY A PET.
THAT IS OUR MISSION!
I KNOW! *A GOLDFISH*!
OH I *WISH*.
A WHAT?
"ALMADIRRO?"
I DON'T KNOW.
THAT'S WHAT MY DAD SAID, AND ELLICE AGREED.
THEN THEY TOLD ME TO BUGGER OFF AND BUY IT MYSELF.
THEY'RE PLAYING GIN RUMMY OR SOMETHING.
WELL THE FIRST LOGICAL STOP WOULD BE THE PET STORE.
GASP!
...WHAT?
SORRY.
YOU SMART PEOPLE ALWAYS AMAZE ME.

#116

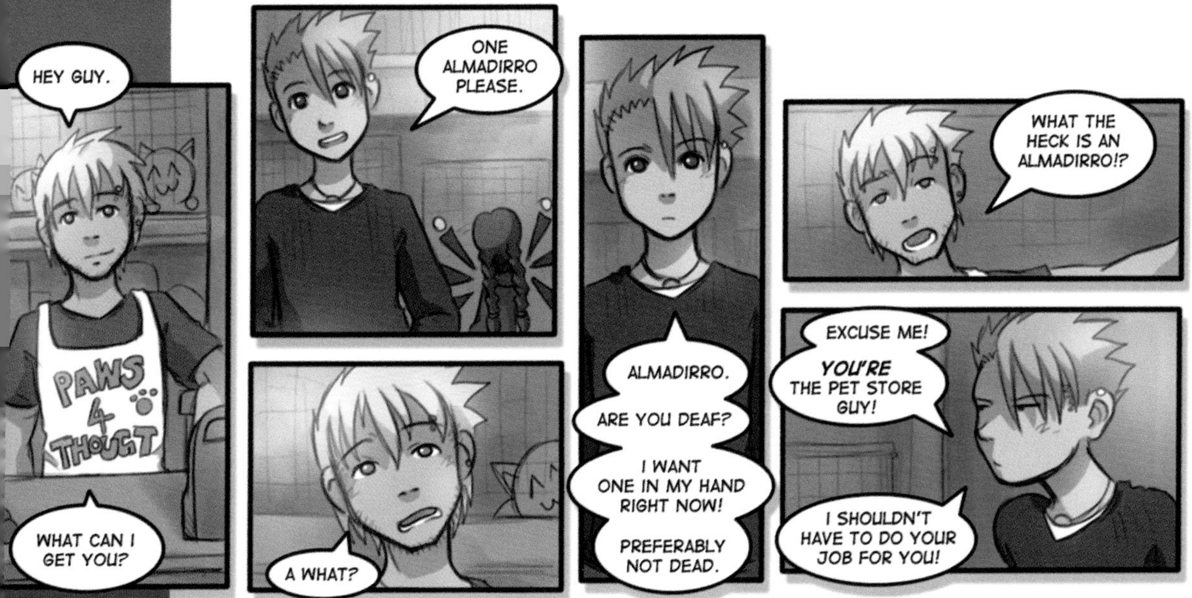
HEY GUY.
WHAT CAN I GET YOU?
ONE ALMADIRRO PLEASE.
A WHAT?
ALMADIRRO.
ARE YOU DEAF?
I WANT ONE IN MY HAND RIGHT NOW!
PREFERABLY NOT DEAD.
WHAT THE HECK IS AN ALMADIRRO!?
EXCUSE ME!
YOU'RE THE PET STORE GUY!
I SHOULDN'T HAVE TO DO YOUR JOB FOR YOU!

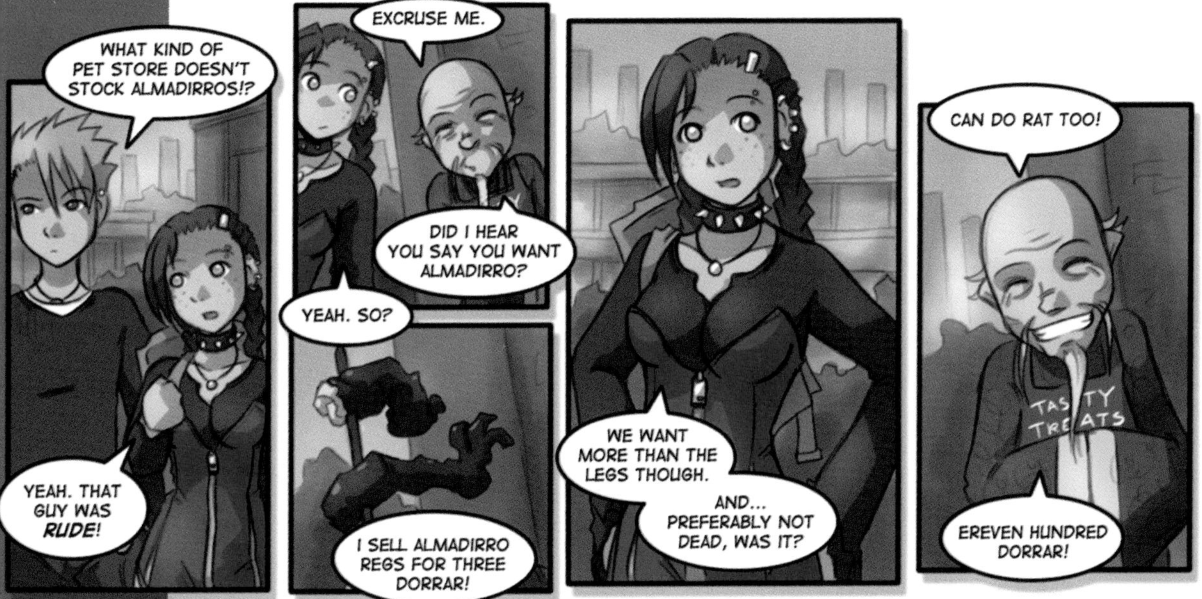
WHAT KIND OF PET STORE DOESN'T STOCK ALMADIRROS!?
YEAH. THAT GUY WAS ***RUDE***!
EXCRUSE ME.
DID I HEAR YOU SAY YOU WANT ALMADIRRO?
YEAH. SO?
I SELL ALMADIRRO REGS FOR THREE DORRAR!
WE WANT MORE THAN THE LEGS THOUGH.
AND... PREFERABLY NOT DEAD, WAS IT?
CAN DO RAT TOO!
EREVEN HUNDRED DORRAR!

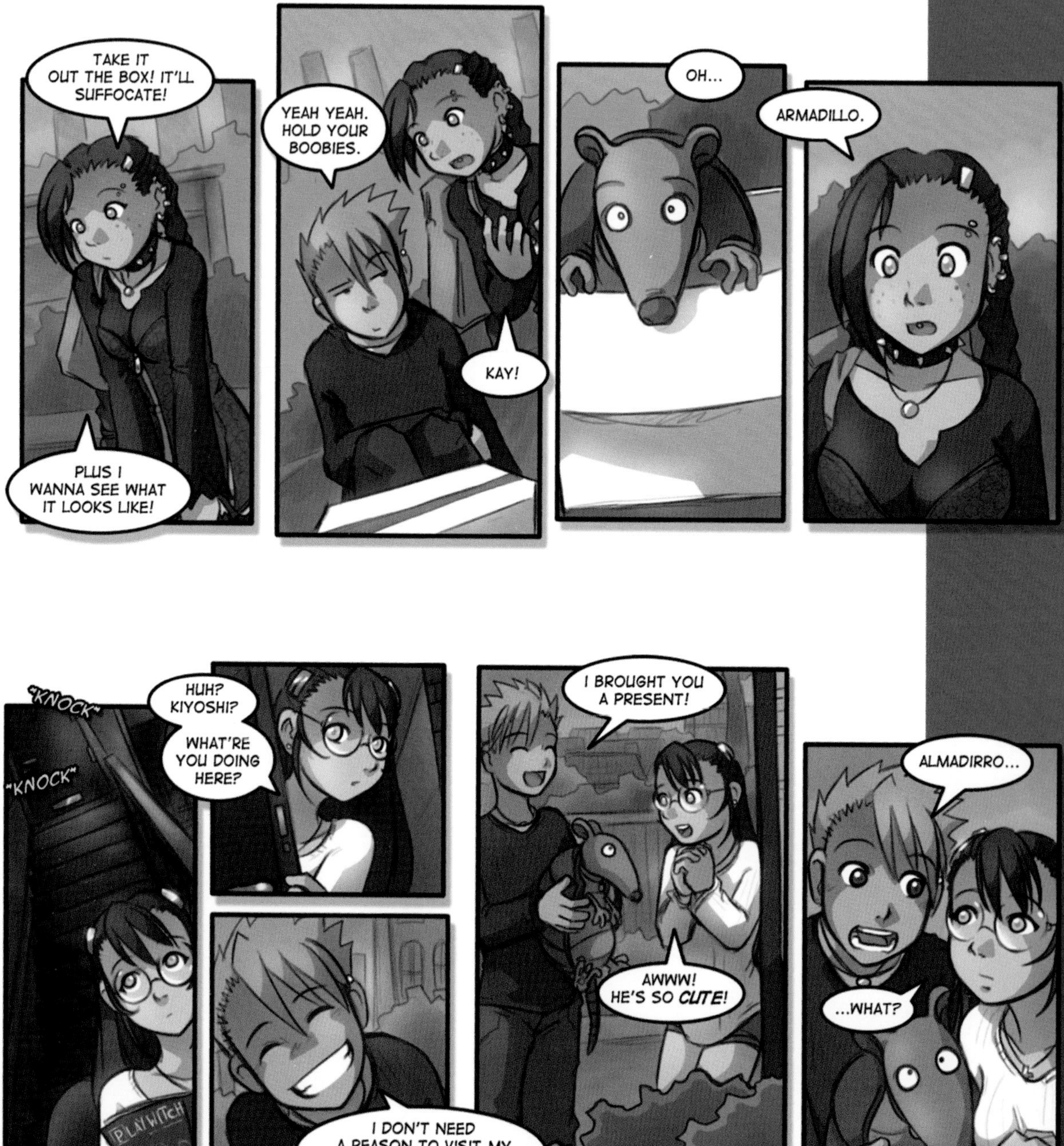
TAKE IT OUT THE BOX! IT'LL SUFFOCATE!
PLUS I WANNA SEE WHAT IT LOOKS LIKE!
YEAH YEAH. HOLD YOUR BOOBIES.
KAY!
OH...
ARMADILLO.
"KNOCK"
"KNOCK"
PLAYWITCH
HUH? KIYOSHI?
WHAT'RE YOU DOING HERE?
I DON'T NEED A REASON TO VISIT MY SWEET LITTLE SNUCKYPOOS DO I?
I BROUGHT YOU A PRESENT!
AWWW! HE'S SO *CUTE*!
ALMADIRRO...
...WHAT?

#118

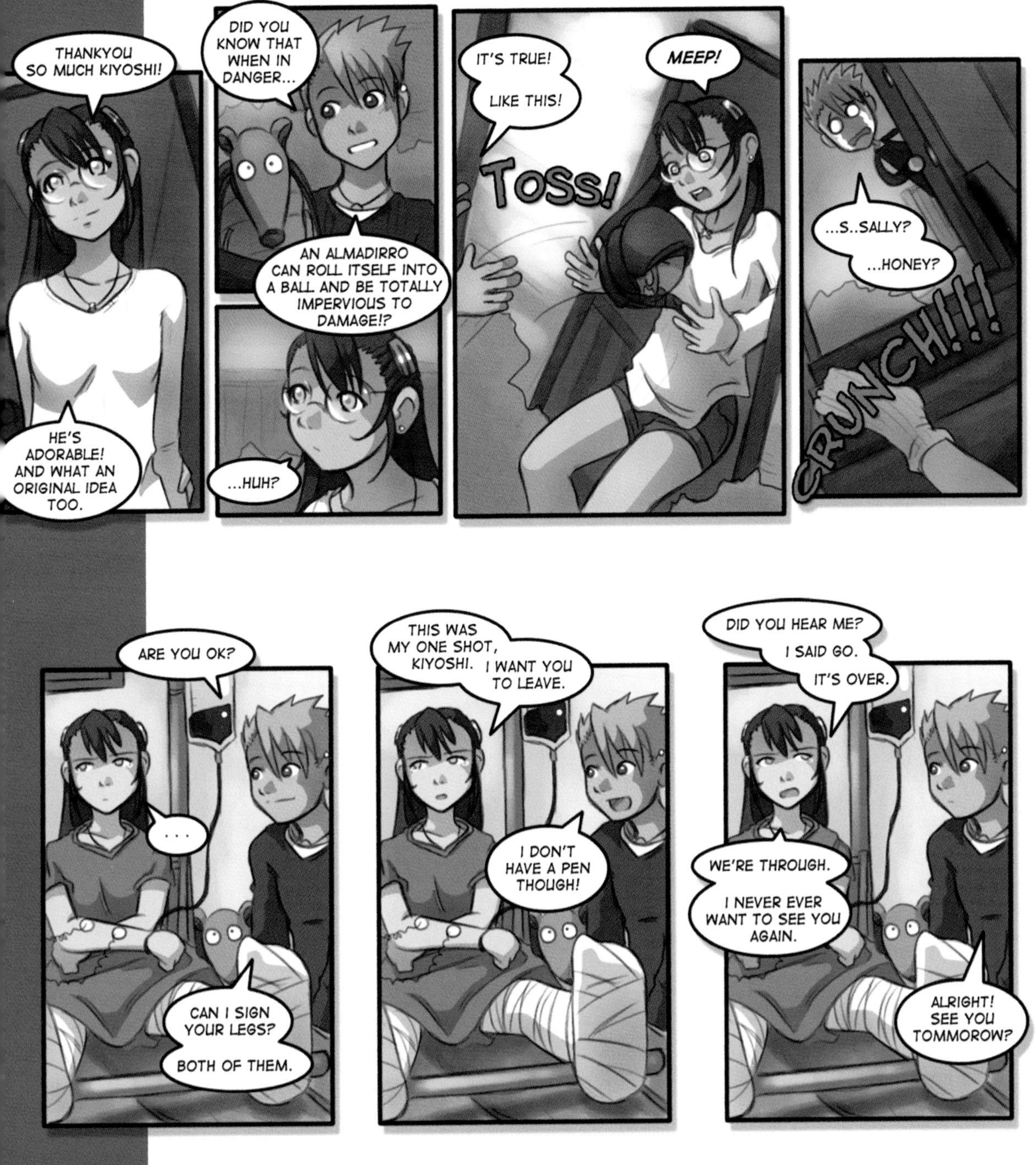
THANKYOU SO MUCH KIYOSHI!
HE'S ADORABLE! AND WHAT AN ORIGINAL IDEA TOO.
DID YOU KNOW THAT WHEN IN DANGER...
AN ALMADIRRO CAN ROLL ITSELF INTO A BALL AND BE TOTALLY IMPERVIOUS TO DAMAGE!?
...HUH?
IT'S TRUE!
LIKE THIS!
MEEP!
TOSS!
...S..SALLY?
...HONEY?
CRUNCH!!!!
ARE YOU OK?
. . .
CAN I SIGN YOUR LEGS?
BOTH OF THEM.
THIS WAS MY ONE SHOT, KIYOSHI.
I WANT YOU TO LEAVE.
I DON'T HAVE A PEN THOUGH!
DID YOU HEAR ME?
I SAID GO.
IT'S OVER.
WE'RE THROUGH.
I NEVER EVER WANT TO SEE YOU AGAIN.
ALRIGHT! SEE YOU TOMMOROW?

Pancake Motherfuckers.

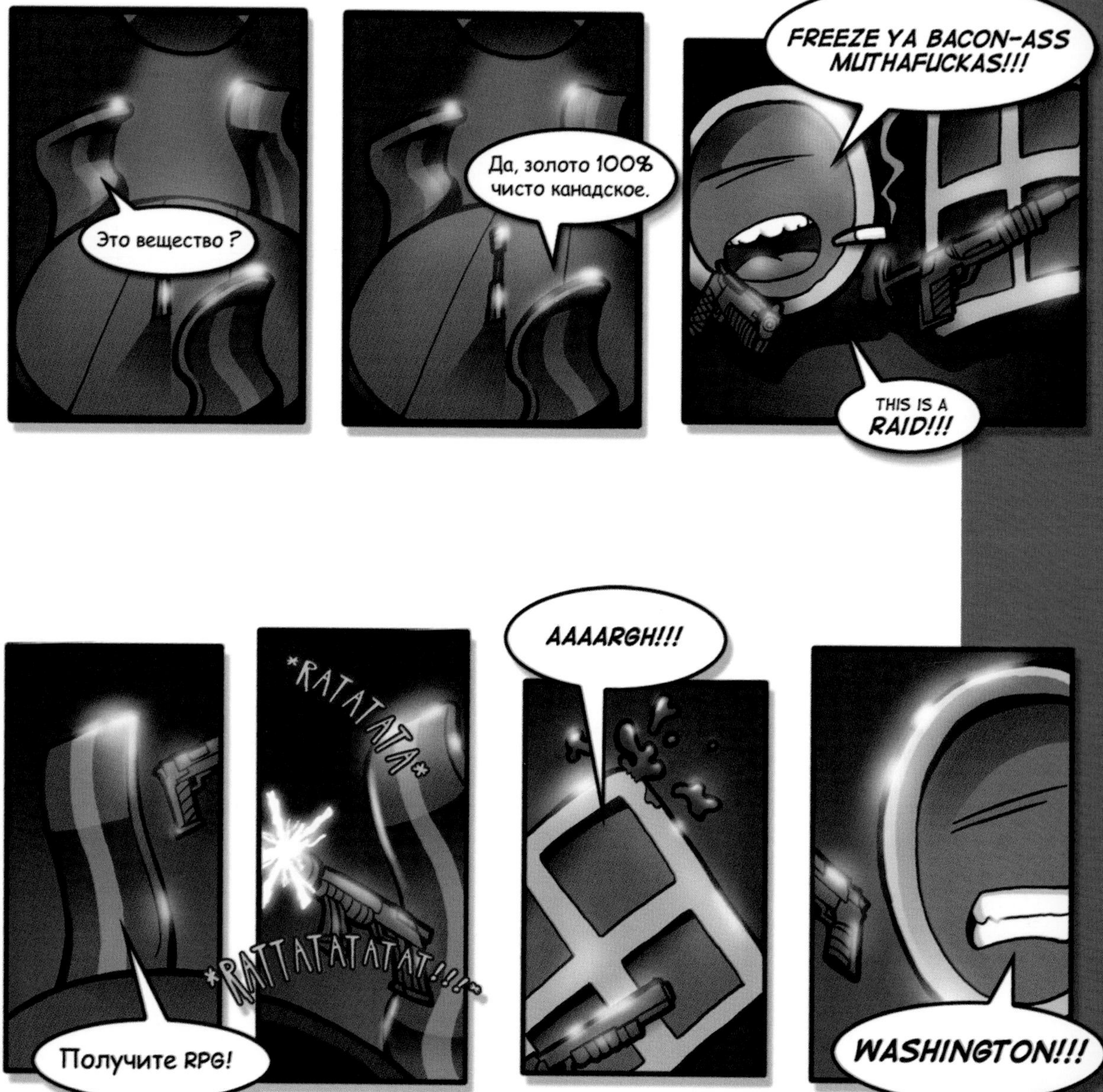

Это вещество ?
Да, золото 100% чисто канадское.
FREEZE YA BACON-ASS MUTHAFUCKAS!!!
THIS IS A RAID!!!
Получите RPG!
RATATATA
RATTATATATATAT!!!
AAAARGH!!!
WASHINGTON!!!

#120

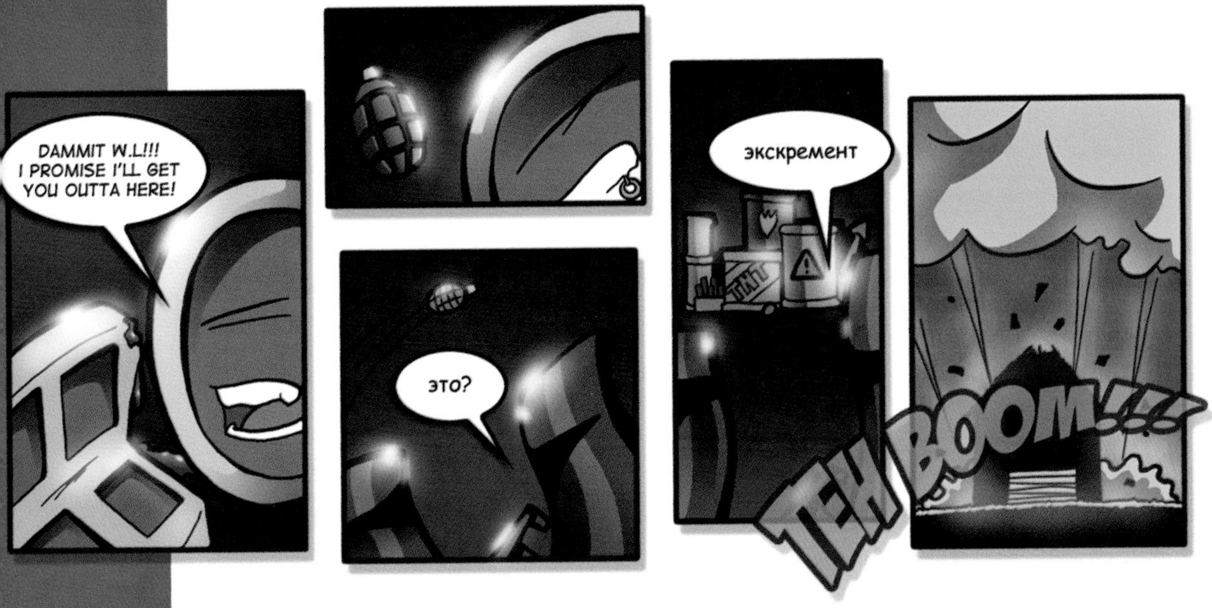
DAMMIT W.L!!! I PROMISE I'LL GET YOU OUTTA HERE!
это?
экскремент
TEH BOOM!!!

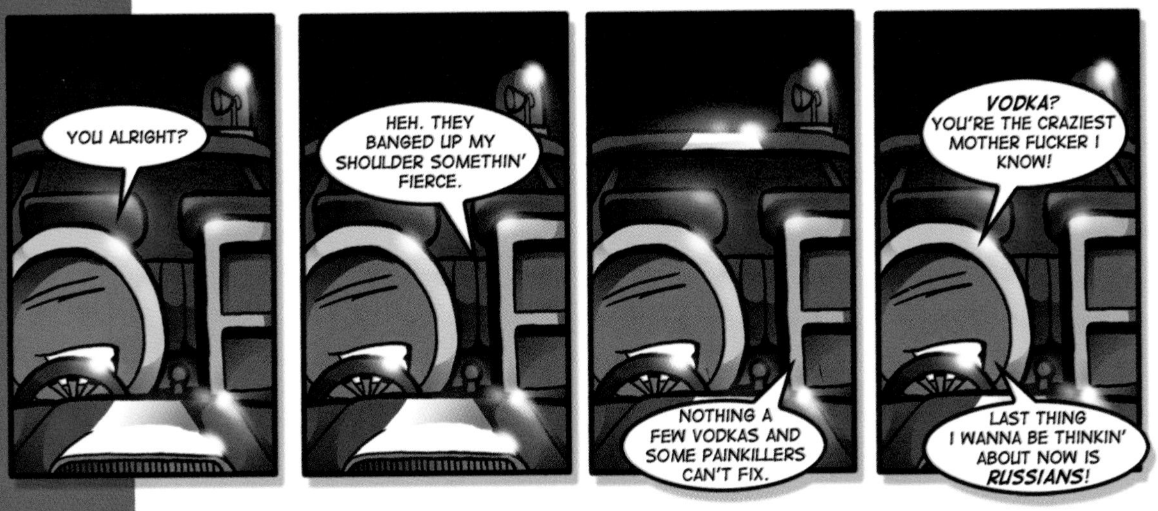
YOU ALRIGHT?
HEH. THEY BANGED UP MY SHOULDER SOMETHIN' FIERCE.
NOTHING A FEW VODKAS AND SOME PAINKILLERS CAN'T FIX.
VODKA? YOU'RE THE CRAZIEST MOTHER FUCKER I KNOW!
LAST THING I WANNA BE THINKIN' ABOUT NOW IS RUSSIANS!

#121

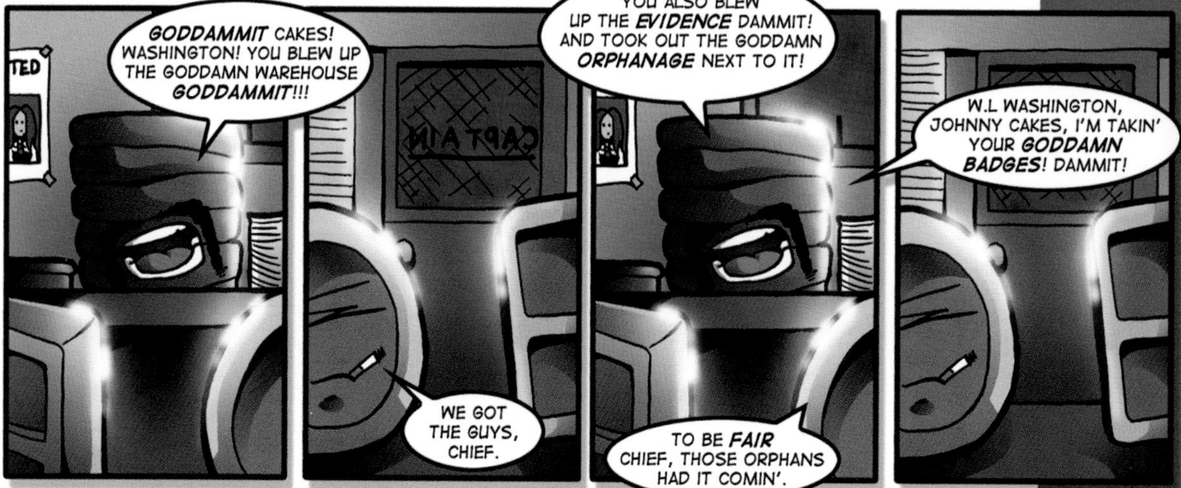
GODDAMMIT CAKES! WASHINGTON! YOU BLEW UP THE GODDAMN WAREHOUSE **GODDAMMIT**!!!
WE GOT THE GUYS, CHIEF.
YOU ALSO BLEW UP THE **EVIDENCE** DAMMIT! AND TOOK OUT THE GODDAMN **ORPHANAGE** NEXT TO IT!
TO BE **FAIR** CHIEF, THOSE ORPHANS HAD IT COMIN'.
W.L WASHINGTON, JOHNNY CAKES, I'M TAKIN' YOUR **GODDAMN BADGES**! DAMMIT!

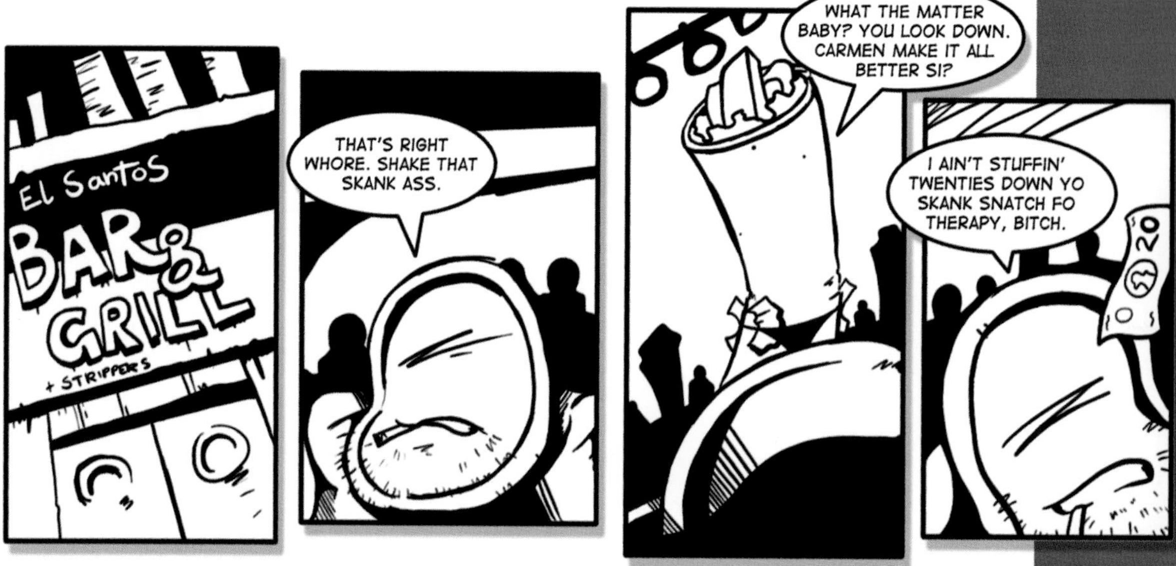
El Santos
BAR & GRILL
+ STRIPPERS
THAT'S RIGHT WHORE. SHAKE THAT SKANK ASS.
WHAT THE MATTER BABY? YOU LOOK DOWN. CARMEN MAKE IT ALL BETTER SI?
I AIN'T STUFFIN' TWENTIES DOWN YO SKANK SNATCH FO THERAPY, BITCH.
20

#122

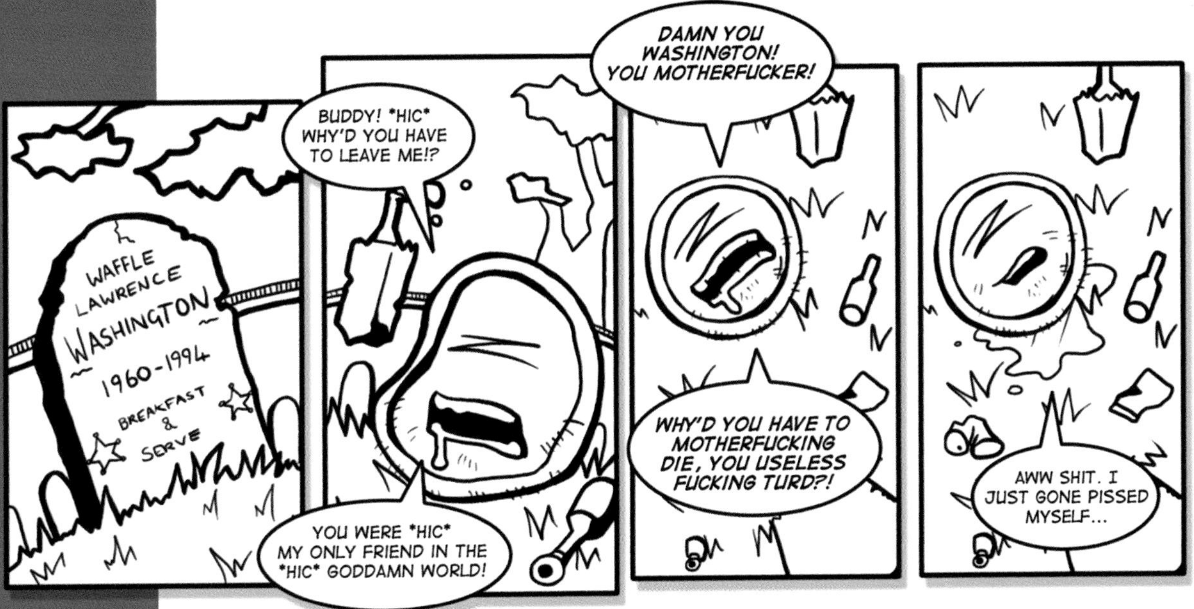
WAFFLE LAWRENCE WASHINGTON
1960-1994
BREAKFAST & SERVE
BUDDY! *HIC* WHY'D YOU HAVE TO LEAVE ME!?
YOU WERE *HIC* MY ONLY FRIEND IN THE *HIC* GODDAMN WORLD!
DAMN YOU WASHINGTON! YOU MOTHERFUCKER!
WHY'D YOU HAVE TO MOTHERFUCKING DIE, YOU USELESS FUCKING TURD?!
AWW SHIT. I JUST GONE PISSED MYSELF...

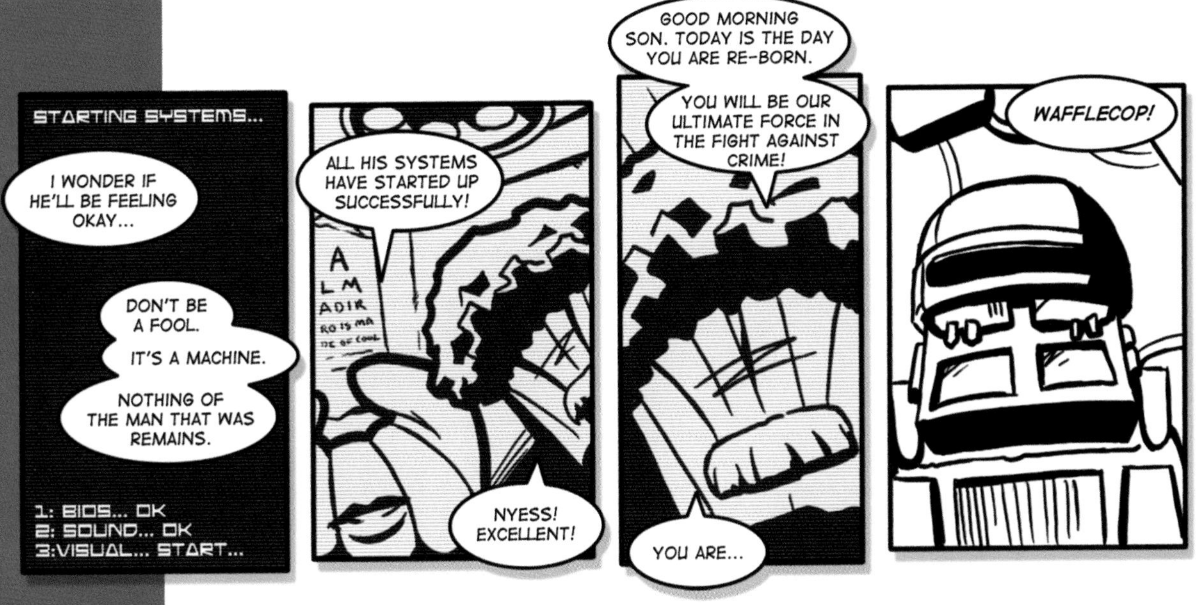
STARTING SYSTEMS...
I WONDER IF HE'LL BE FEELING OKAY...
DON'T BE A FOOL.
IT'S A MACHINE.
NOTHING OF THE MAN THAT WAS REMAINS.
1: BIOS... OK
2: SOUND... OK
3:VISUAL... START...
ALL HIS SYSTEMS HAVE STARTED UP SUCCESSFULLY!
NYESS! EXCELLENT!
GOOD MORNING SON. TODAY IS THE DAY YOU ARE RE-BORN.
YOU WILL BE OUR ULTIMATE FORCE IN THE FIGHT AGAINST CRIME!
YOU ARE...
WAFFLECOP!

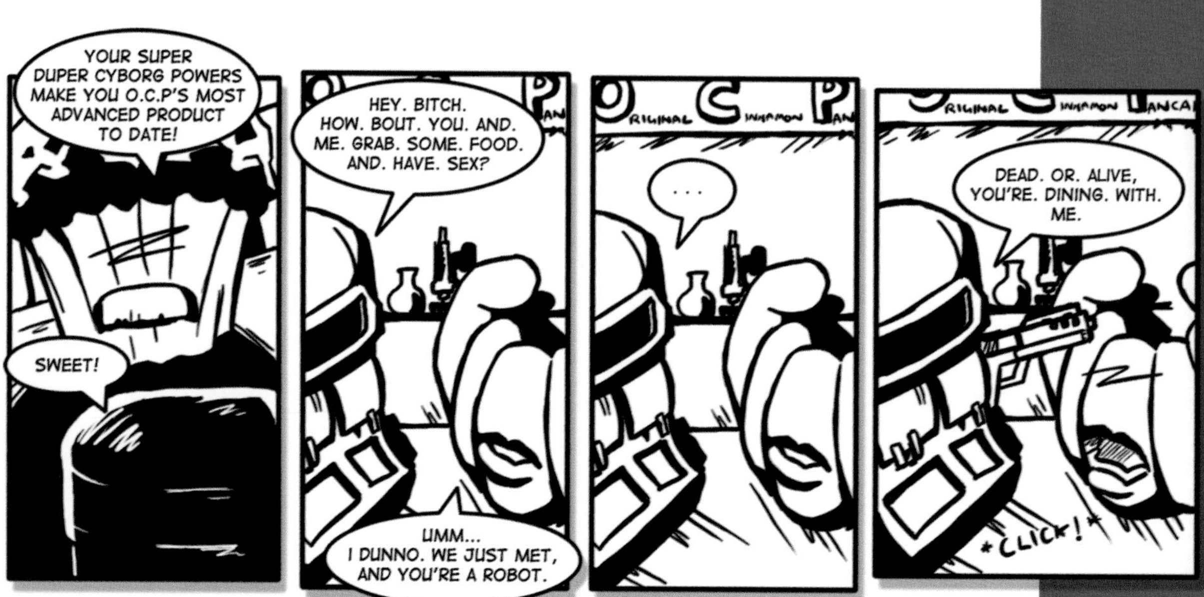
YOUR SUPER DUPER CYBORG POWERS MAKE YOU O.C.P'S MOST ADVANCED PRODUCT TO DATE!
SWEET!
HEY. BITCH. HOW. BOUT. YOU. AND. ME. GRAB. SOME. FOOD. AND. HAVE. SEX?
UMM... I DUNNO. WE JUST MET, AND YOU'RE A ROBOT.
. . .
DEAD. OR. ALIVE, YOU'RE. DINING. WITH. ME.
CLICK!

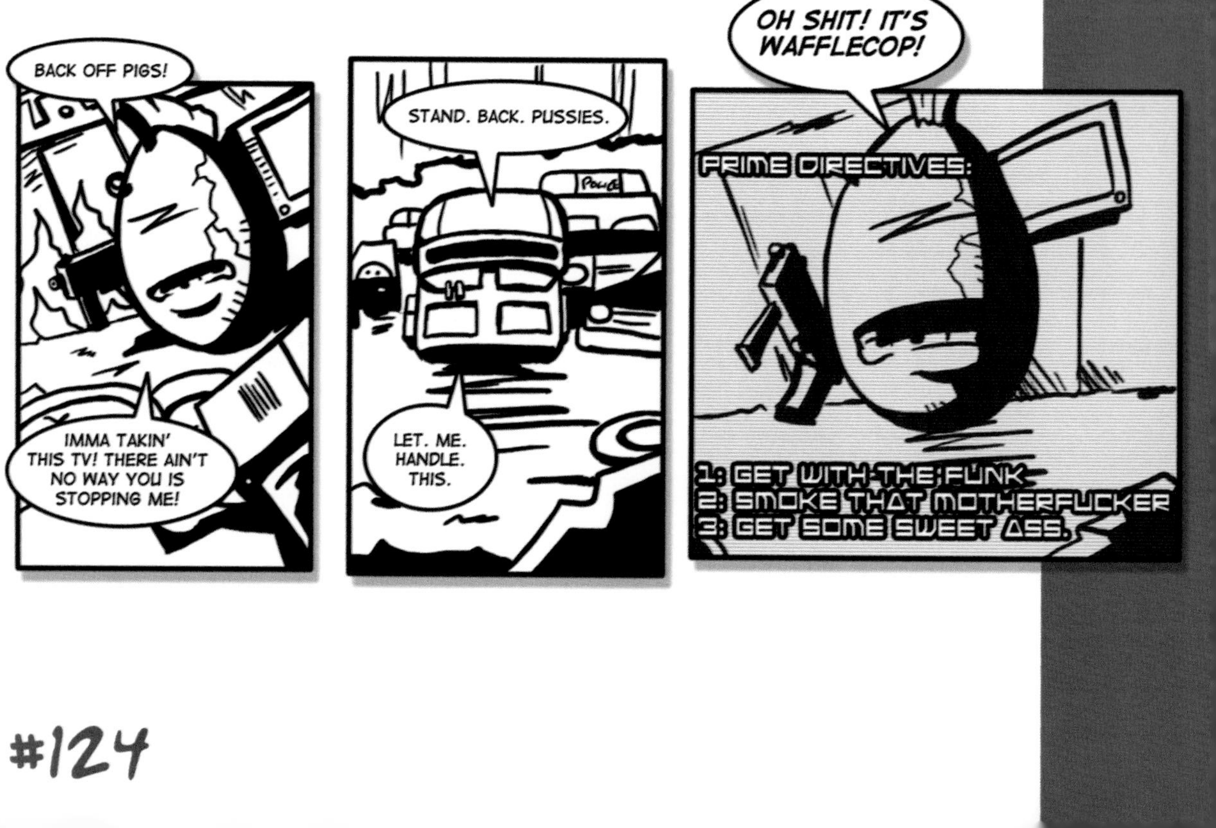
BACK OFF PIGS!
IMMA TAKIN' THIS TV! THERE AIN'T NO WAY YOU IS STOPPING ME!
STAND. BACK. PUSSIES.
LET. ME. HANDLE. THIS.
OH SHIT! IT'S WAFFLECOP!
PRIME DIRECTIVES:
1: GET WITH THE FUNK
2: SMOKE THAT MOTHERFUCKER
3: GET SOME SWEET ASS.

#124

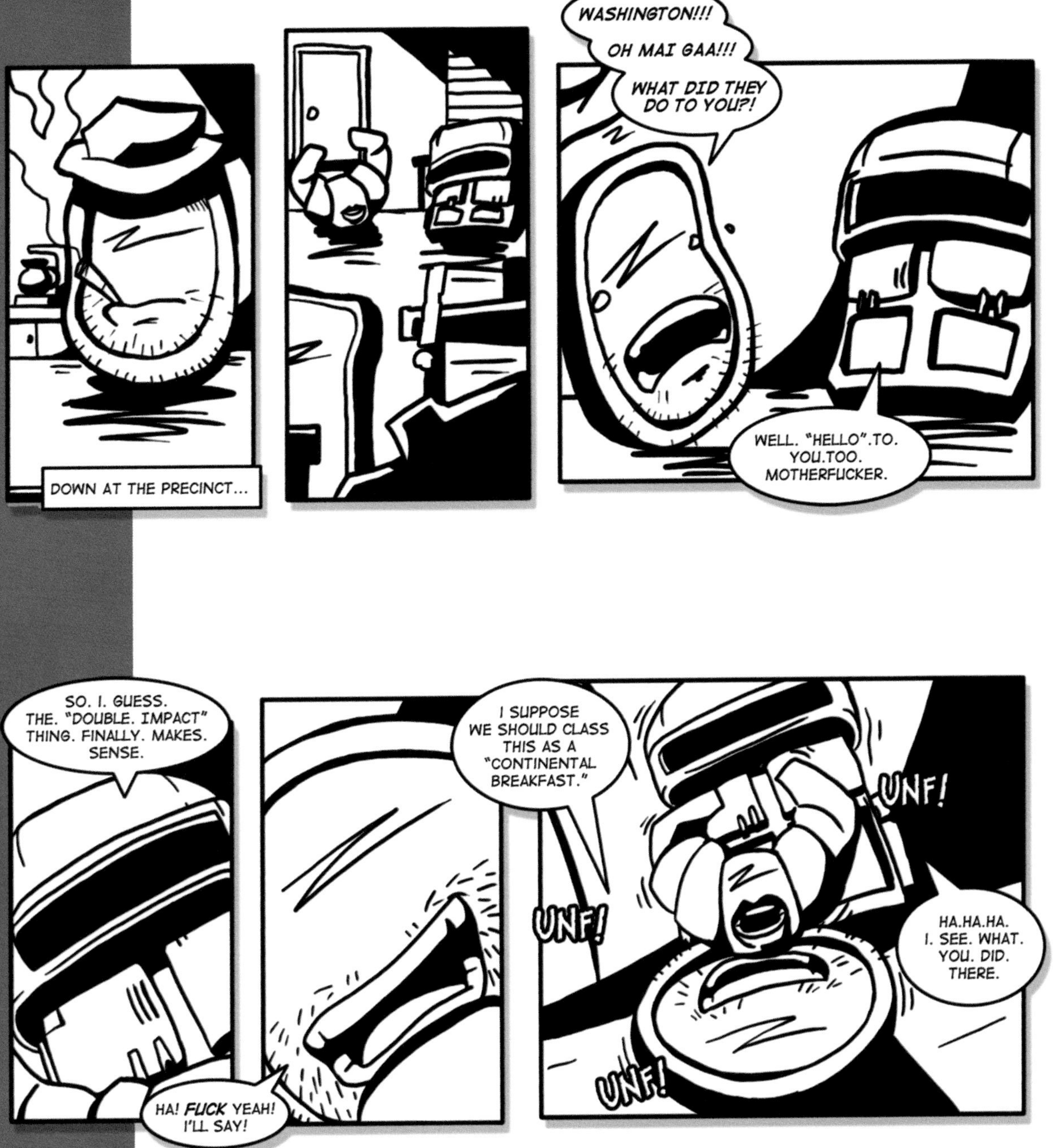
DOWN AT THE PRECINCT...
WASHINGTON!!!
OH MAI GAA!!!
WHAT DID THEY DO TO YOU?!
WELL. "HELLO".TO. YOU.TOO. MOTHERFUCKER.
SO. I. GUESS. THE. "DOUBLE. IMPACT" THING. FINALLY. MAKES. SENSE.
HA! **FUCK** YEAH! I'LL SAY!
I SUPPOSE WE SHOULD CLASS THIS AS A "CONTINENTAL BREAKFAST."
UNF!
UNF!
UNF!
HA.HA.HA. I. SEE. WHAT. YOU. DID. THERE.

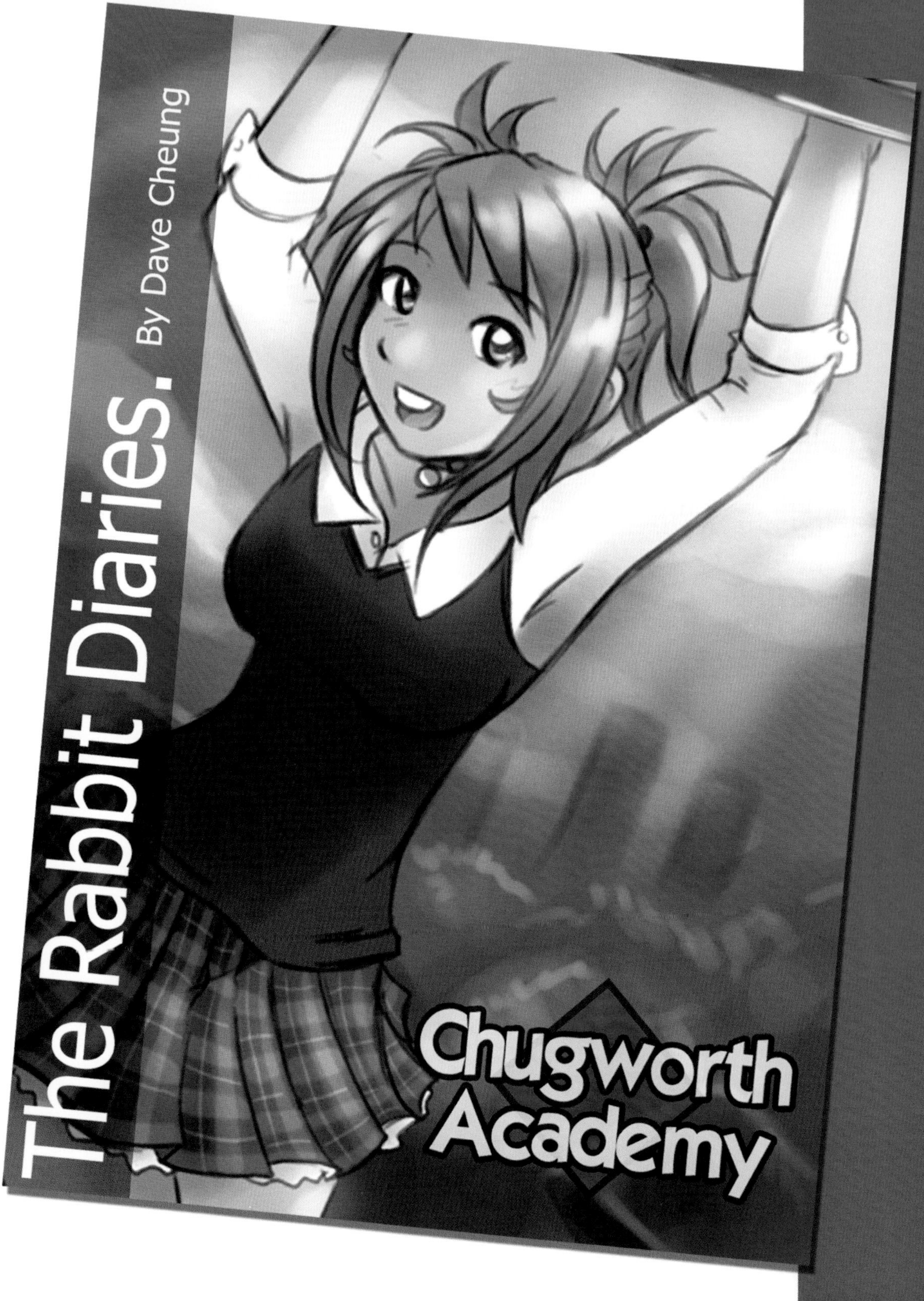
The Rabbit Diaries.
By Dave Cheung
Chugworth Academy

THE RABBIT DIARIES

IN THE SUMMER OF **2005**, FOR THE CONVENTION SEASON, A VERY SPECIAL DIARY WAS WRITTEN, COVERING THE EVENTS OF CHUGWORTH ACADEMY FROM THE PERSPECTIVE OF ONE BUNNIE MITTENS. THIS DIARY HAD A VERY LIMITED, SELF-PUBLISHED RUN, AND THUS, CAN NO LONGER BE AQUIRED.

BUT REJOICE! THE ENTIRE RABBIT DIARIES IS NOW HERE, FOR YOUR CONSUMPTION, OVER THE NEXT FEW PAGES IN THIS VERY TOME. OH JOYUS DAY INDEED. YOU'RE A LUCKY BASTARD AND YOU KNOW IT.

SO, REVEL IN YOUR GOOD FORTUNE, AND I HOPE YOU ENJOY THE SAGA OF IDIOCY THAT IS:

THE RABBIT DIARIES.

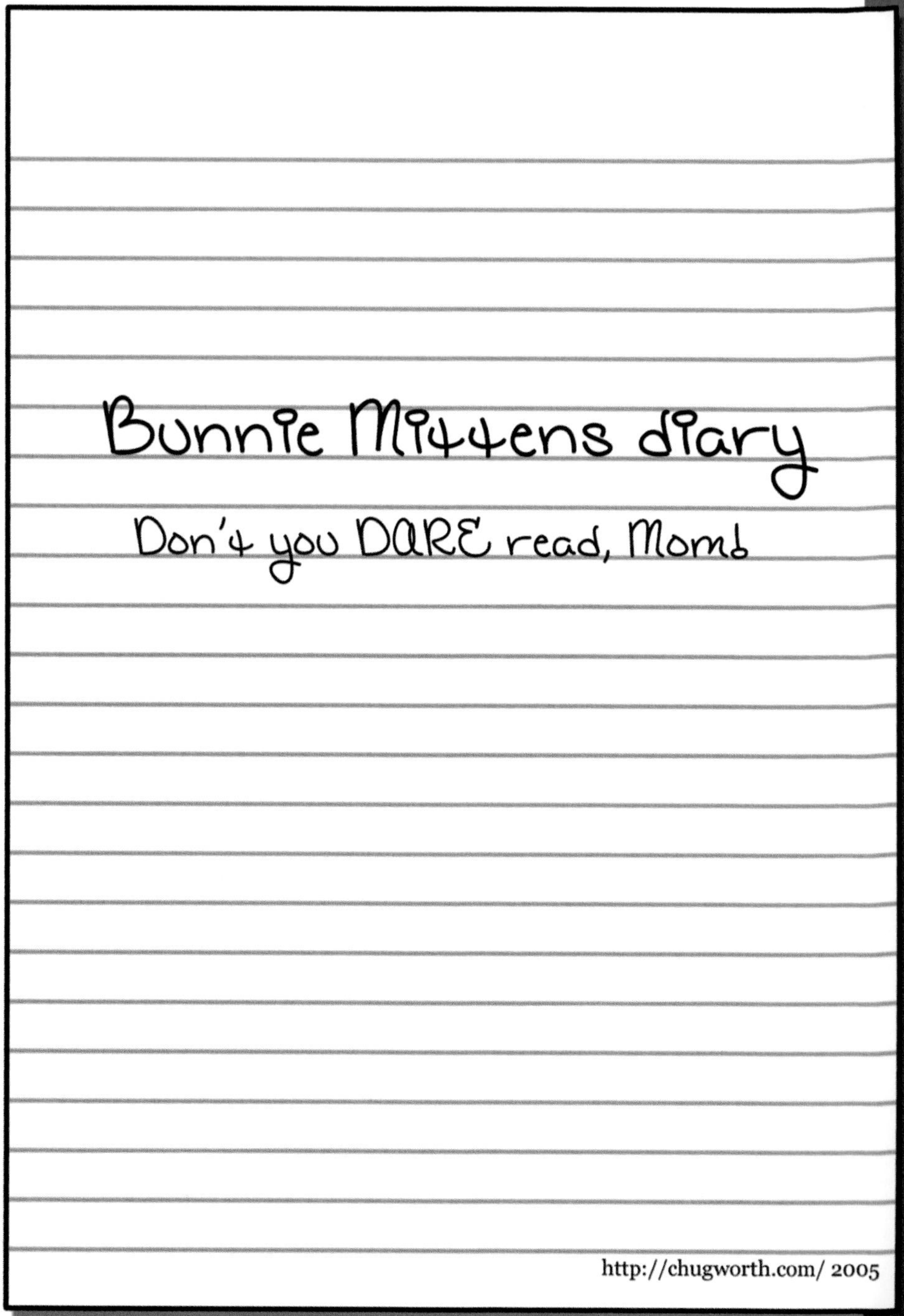
Bunnie Mittens diary
Don't you DARE read, Mom!
http://chugworth.com/ 2005

#128

Oh my God! Oh my God! Oh my God!
Aren't we just the CUTEST couple ever?!
After we left the Library, we borrowed
a camera from Mr Flibblejob in the Art
Department! He's totally creepy, but
we needed a decent Camera!

So like, when we went back down to the
Gym hall, Demitri was still there, so
I got Aimee to take photo of us!
Isn't it awesome!? Demitri looks SO
happy here too! I've decided that I'm
gonna marry him! Tru Luv 4Ever!

#131

Goddammit Bunnie,
I love you!

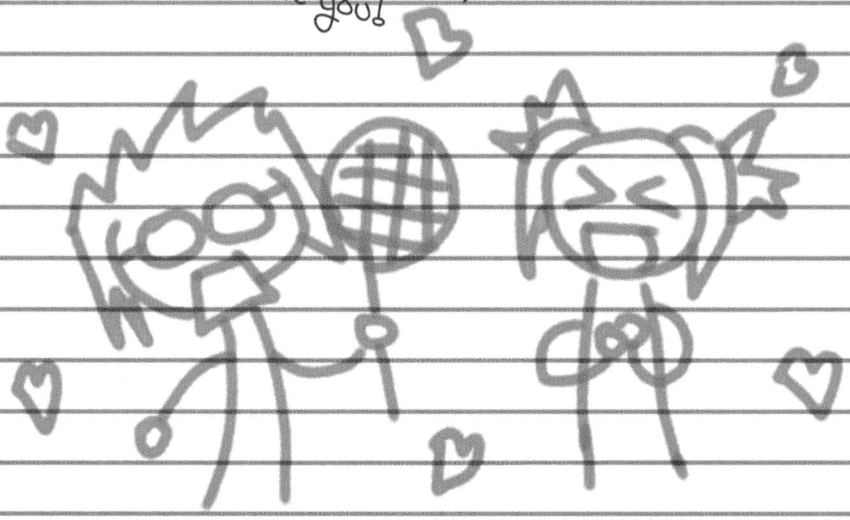

I've waited my entire life for this, so I'm gonna go for it! I've finally met my one true love and I think he loves me too! Isn't it SO exciting!?

Me and Aimee didn't really have time to take the camera back after Tennis practice, so we took it into classes with us and took loads and loads and loads and loads and loads of really really really really cute piccies!

#132

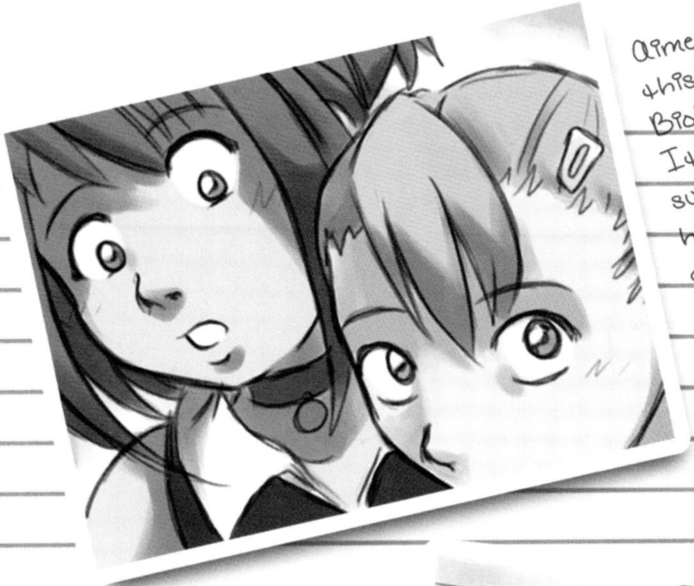

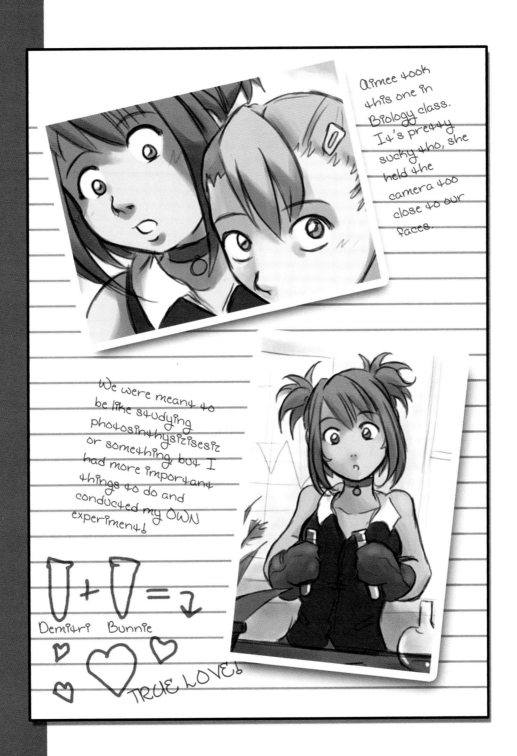

Aimee took this one in Biology class. It's pretty sucky tho, she held the camera too close to our faces.

We were meant to be like studying photosinthysizisesiz or something, but I had more important things to do and conducted my OWN experiment!

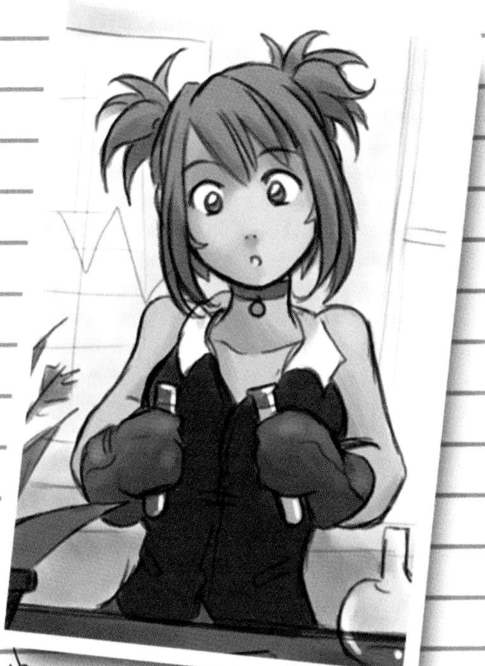

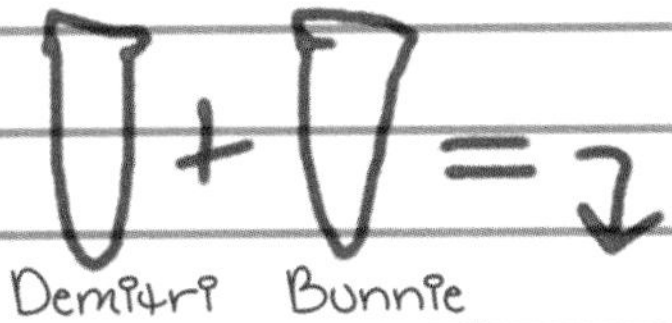

Demitri
Bunnie

TRUE LOVE!

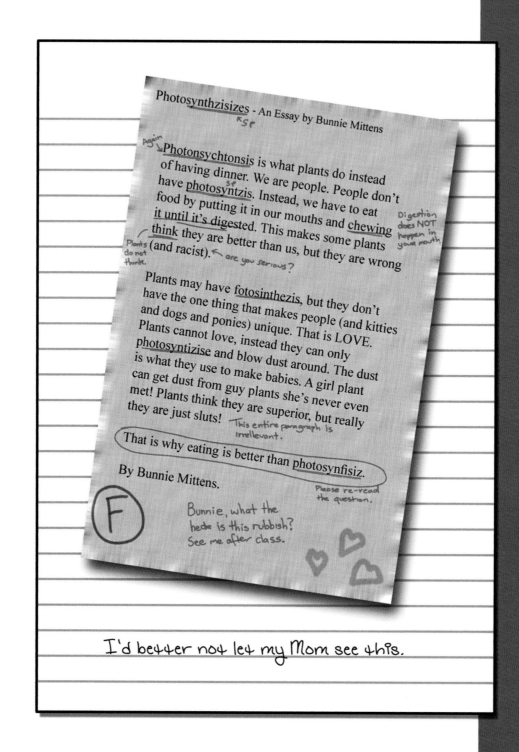

Photosynthzisizes - An Essay by Bunnie Mittens

s e

Again

Photonsychtonsis is what plants do instead of having dinner. We are people. People don't have photosyntzis. Instead, we have to eat food by putting it in our mouths and chewing it until it's digested. This makes some plants think they are better than us, but they are wrong (and racist).

se

Digestion does NOT happen in your mouth

Plants do not think.

← are you serious?

Plants may have fotosinthezis, but they don't have the one thing that makes people (and kitties and dogs and ponies) unique. That is LOVE. Plants cannot love, instead they can only photosyntizise and blow dust around. The dust is what they use to make babies. A girl plant can get dust from guy plants she's never even met! Plants think they are superior, but really they are just sluts!

This entire paragraph is irrellevant.

That is why eating is better than photosynfisiz.

By Bunnie Mittens.

Please re-read the question.

F

Bunnie, what the heck is this rubbish? See me after class.

I'd better not let my Mom see this.

#134

The rest of the school day was pretty boring, cos Mr Sundance confiscated the camera in 5th period! I can't believe him! What a big poopie head!

After school, me and Aimee saw Demitri again, but he was talking to Sally Richards. She was clearly trying to take my man, so I politely asked her to stop, at which point the bitch ATTACKED ME!

She's such a cow. Just cos she got the last hottest boy in school, she thinks she can steal mine? Yeah right! She has really small boobs too! I dunno what all those geeks see in her!

#135

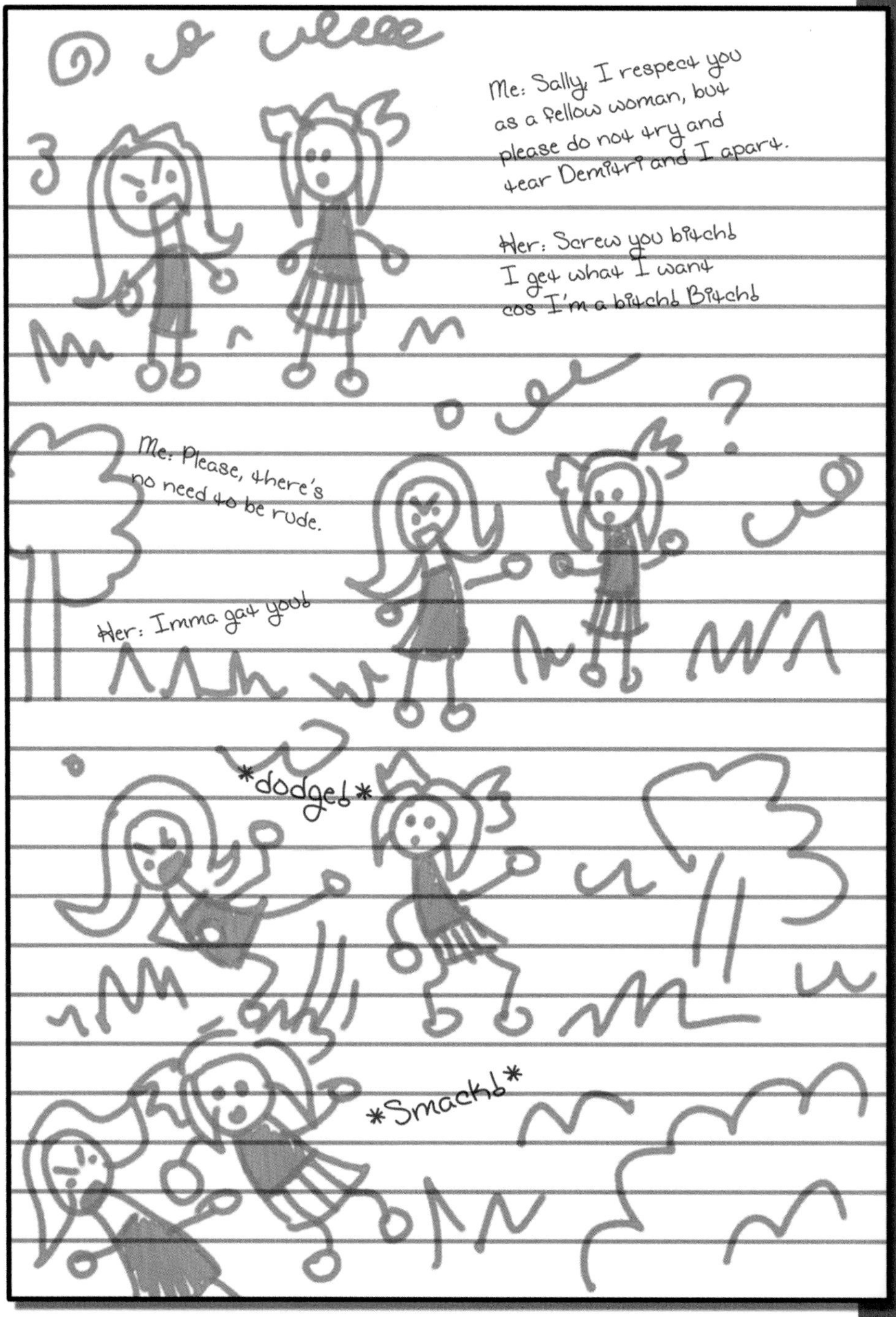
Me: Sally, I respect you as a fellow woman, but please do not try and tear Demitri and I apart.
Her: Screw you bitch! I get what I want cos I'm a bitch! Bitch!
Me: Please, there's no need to be rude.
Her: Imma get you!
dodge!
Smack!

#136

And that's how I won the day, and the hot guy! I got Aimee to take a piccy of me and Demitri afterward to celebrate my victory!

Ok, so you can't really see me very well here, but I got his phone number on the condition that I stop getting blood all over his shirt. Score!!!

#137

PANCAKE TOUGH GUYS!
WHAT YOU BURYING?
JUST MY MOTHER-IN-LAW.
SHE'S DEAD?
DON'T ASK SUCH STUPID QUESTIONS.
. . .
OF COURSE SHE ISN'T DEAD.

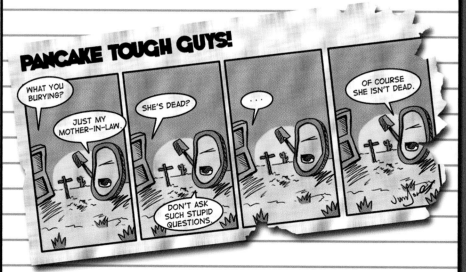

I cut this out of my Dad's newspaper. I don't really get it, but I LOVE pancakes!

I called Demitri and he said he'd go out on a date with me! I knew he loved me as much as I love him! I can't wait until tommorow! I need to be careful tho. I eat kind of a lot and my Mom says that boys will not like you if you eat too much on a date! I have to look delicate otherwise he might hate me!

Goodnight Diary. (hehehe Pancakes)

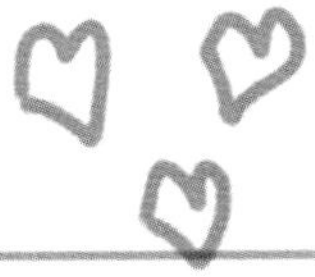

Friday

Oh my God! School was SO SO SO sucky today! I went in and the place was CLOSED! Apparently it's a Holiday Weekend but that was the first I'D heard of it! I called Aimee and asked why she didn't tell me, but she said she did and I just wasn't listening! That is SO totally a lie, but I'll let it slide since she bought me a Chocolate Sundae to say sorry.

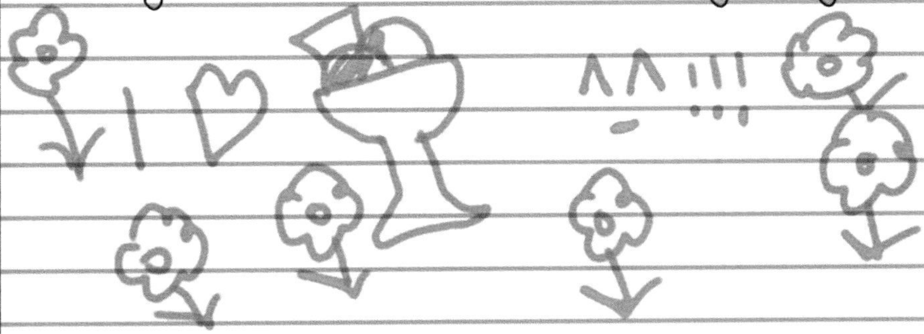

I
^^!!!

I got another essay from biology to do too, but this one is from like WEEKS ago. My teacher says I gotta do it again cos the first time it was nonsense, but I dunno what I'm going to change. It looks OK to me. I'll just hide the old one in here and not bother doing it...

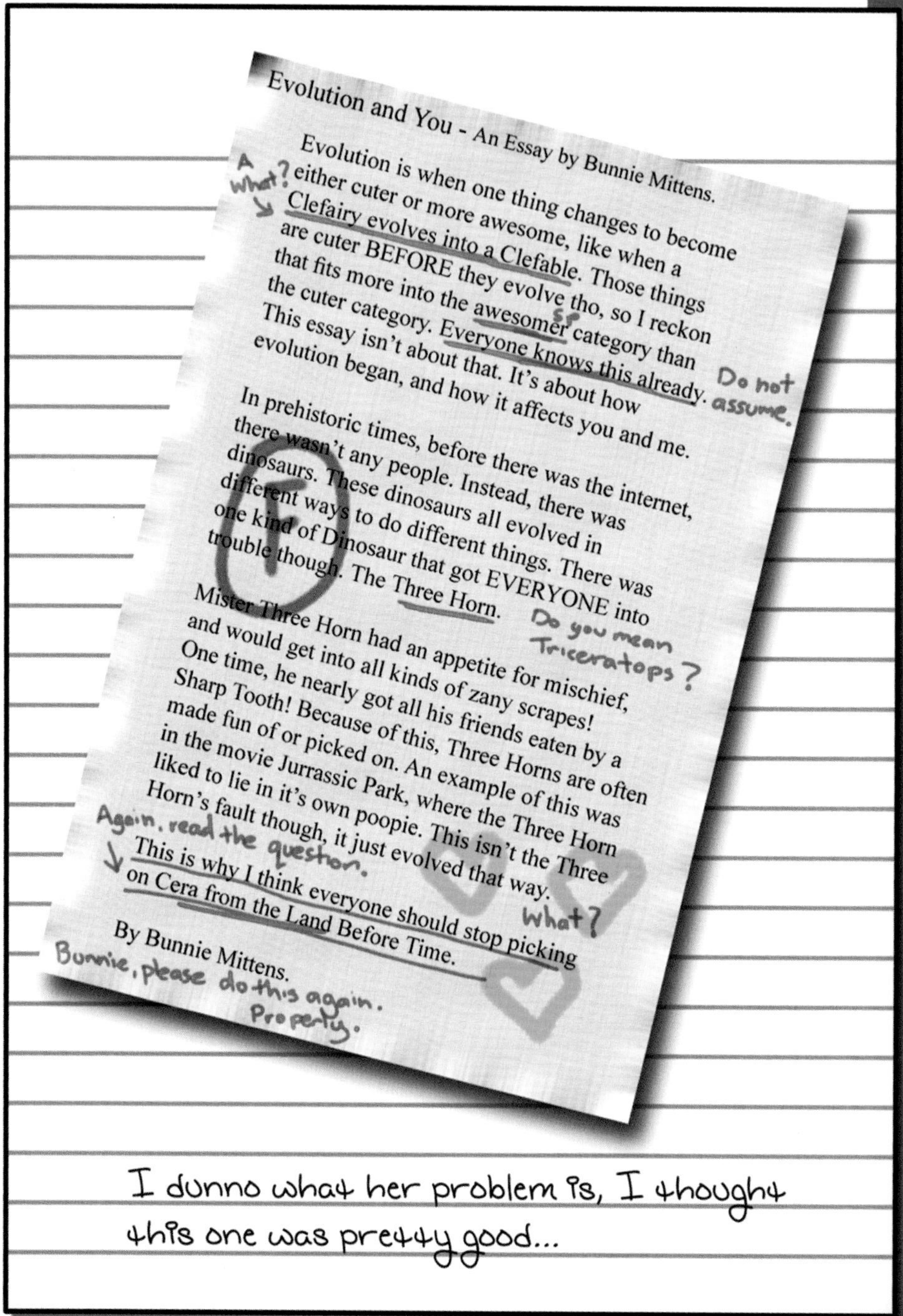
Evolution and You - An Essay by Bunnie Mittens.
Evolution is when one thing changes to become either cuter or more awesome, like when a Clefairy evolves into a Clefable. Those things are cuter BEFORE they evolve tho, so I reckon that fits more into the awesomer category than the cuter category. Everyone knows this already. This essay isn't about that. It's about how evolution began, and how it affects you and me.
In prehistoric times, before there was the internet, there wasn't any people. Instead, there was dinosaurs. These dinosaurs all evolved in different ways to do different things. There was one kind of Dinosaur that got EVERYONE into trouble though. The Three Horn.
Mister Three Horn had an appetite for mischief, and would get into all kinds of zany scrapes! One time, he nearly got all his friends eaten by a Sharp Tooth! Because of this, Three Horns are often made fun of or picked on. An example of this was in the movie Jurrassic Park, where the Three Horn liked to lie in it's own poopie. This isn't the Three Horn's fault though, it just evolved that way.
This is why I think everyone should stop picking on Cera from the Land Before Time.
By Bunnie Mittens.
A what?
sp
Do not assume.
F
Do you mean Triceratops?
Again, read the question.
What?
Bunnie, please do this again. Properly.
I dunno what her problem is, I thought this one was pretty good...

Aimee showed me this funny list called "You know you spend too much time on the internets when". It was funny LOL. (that was one of them I think.)
Don't worry diary, I don't REALLY write LOL, that would make me stupid!

Anyway, we decided I should go shopping for new clothes for my HOT date with Demitri, so after the whole school thing (which sucked) and after the sundaes (which were awesome) we went to the Mall for some SHOPPING!!!!!!!!!!

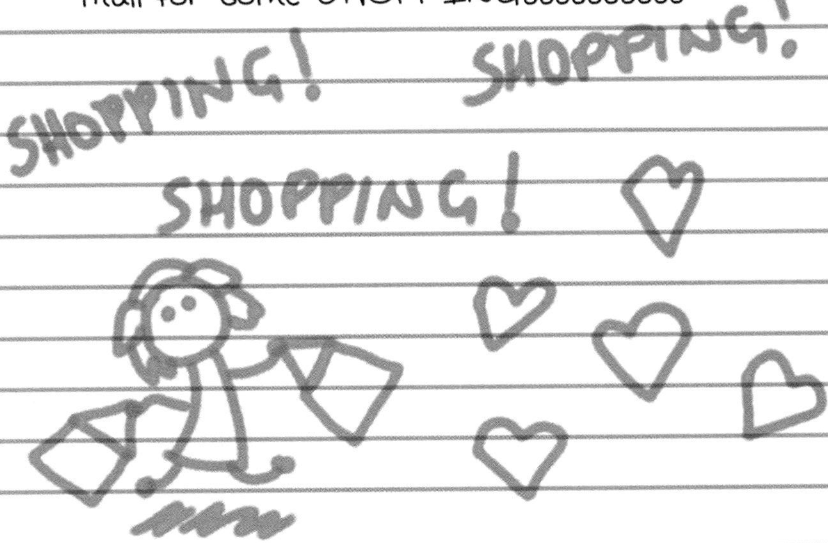
SHOPPING!
SHOPPING!
SHOPPING!

It was a REAL tough day! I had to try on all sorts of stuff!!!

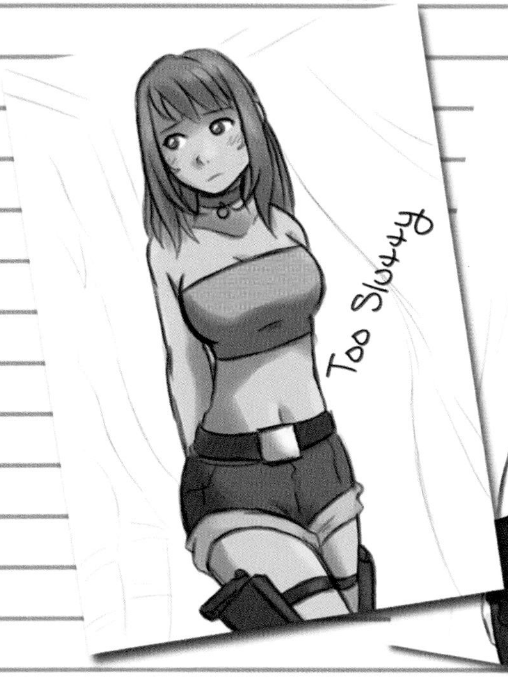
Too Slutty

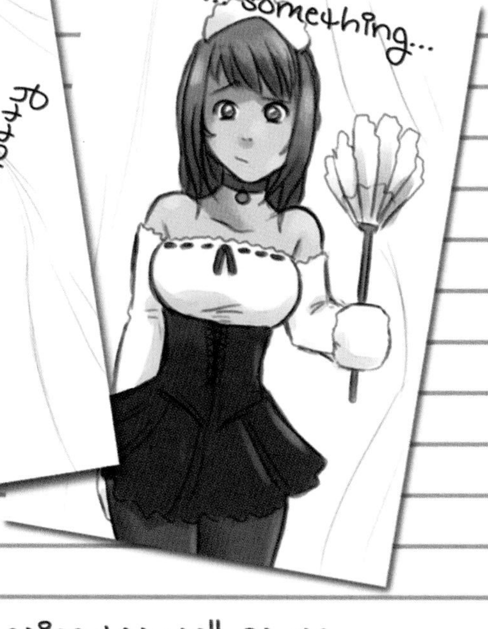
Too... something...

It really wasn't going too well, so we had to ask the lady in the store to help us out. She was really good actually, but for some reason she kept talking about my boobs. I think she might have been a lesbian!

#142

Lesbian or not, she had really really good taste in clothes! This is what we ended up with! I wanna see Demitri just TRY and resist popping my cherry when I look THIS cute!

#143

So that was our crazy Mall adventure! Well, apart from that homeless guy touching my leg... EEEWWWWWWWW!!! Aimee kicked him in the nuts and we ran away to tell an adult!

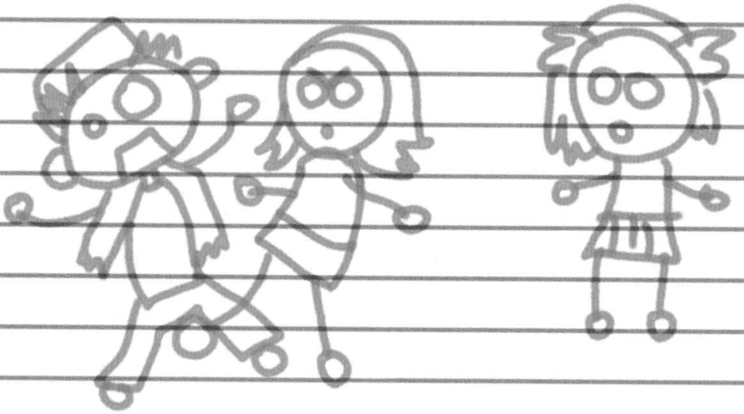

We told this security guy about the whole affair! He was really nice about it, and said that he'd shoot the homeless guy for us! Yay! What a cool person!

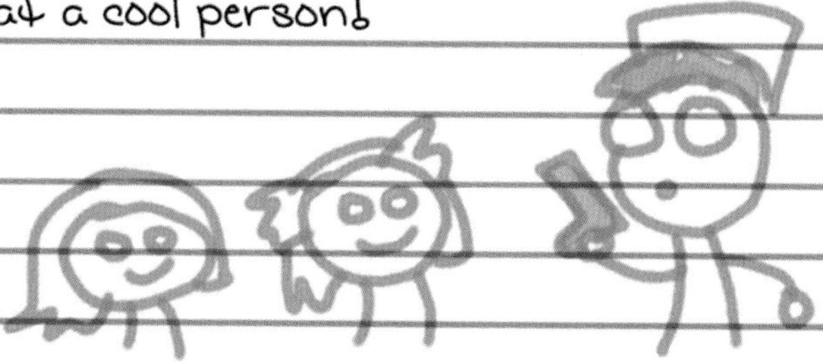

Since I'm here anyway, I think I'll try and write some romantic poetry that I can recite to Demitri during our date! Let's see...

You are my Greek Salad.
Like salad, you are both cool and crispy.
Your lucious muscles glimmer like the
dew on the greenest of lettuce.
You are the healthy option.
I am the not so healthy side.
I am your sweet dessert. Sweet and creamy.
With a cherry on top, just for you.
My Greek Salad.

Hey now! That's pretty good if I do say so myself! Maybe I should do more of these after Dinner! I wonder what Mom is making. I hope it involves Snackums...

#145

Ok Diary, I'm back! Guess what Mom made for dinner? That's right. GREEK SALAD! she must be psychic or something! She said it was a good idea cos I was going out on my first date tonight. I don't wanna look fat or anything.

My dad wasn't too happy about me going out alone with Demitri tonight, so he says he wants to meet him when he picks me up before we're allowed to go ANYWHERE! Stupid dad.

Local man murdered by Mall guard.

A local homeless man was today found shot dead by Mall Security supervisor Erik Schoenek.

Schoenek, 21, was discovered by Police standing over the body of the victim, laughing uncontrollably. When asked what he had done, he replied, "He touched the fairies! They told me to make him pay! The fairies told me to make him pay!"

Schoenek was arrested and will stand trial for murder in the coming months. Police Chief Arthur Johnston described the crime as, "Brutal and apparently motiveless."

I found another crazy story in my dad's paper! Seriously! Some people are just sick! What did that hobo guy ever do to him!?

Well, sounds like Demitri is here now! I'm
so excited! This will be the best date EVER!
Bye bye diary. I'll tell you all about it when
I get back!

10 Facts About Me!

1. I have too much love to give.
2. I like pancakes.
3. I'm good at tennis.
4. I think world peace would be good.
5. I want to be president.
6. I like ice-cream.
7. I love Demitri.
8. I am very mature for my age.
9. I like pancakes.
10. I am very clever.

#147

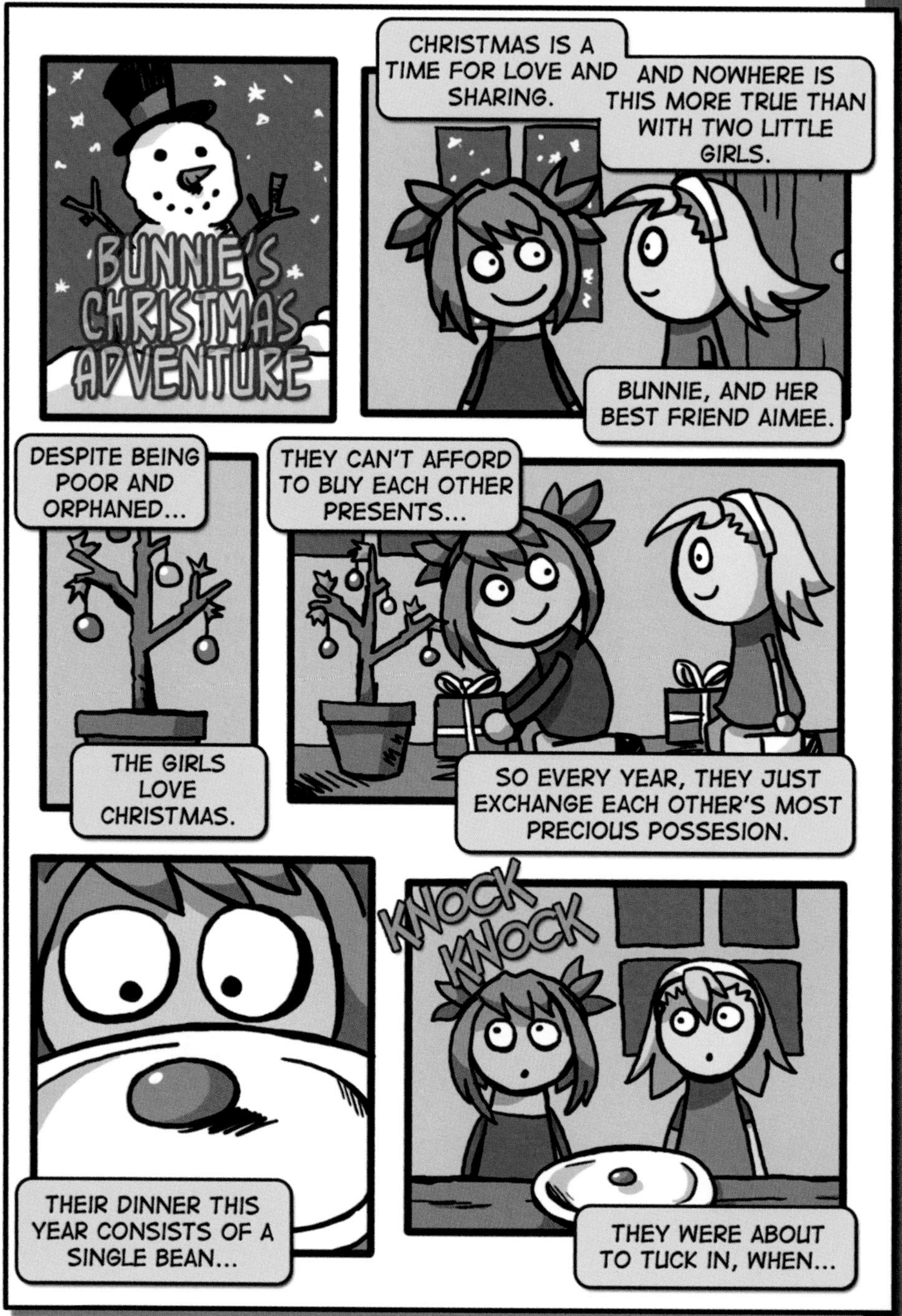
BUNNIE'S CHRISTMAS ADVENTURE
CHRISTMAS IS A TIME FOR LOVE AND SHARING.
AND NOWHERE IS THIS MORE TRUE THAN WITH TWO LITTLE GIRLS.
BUNNIE, AND HER BEST FRIEND AIMEE.
DESPITE BEING POOR AND ORPHANED...
THE GIRLS LOVE CHRISTMAS.
THEY CAN'T AFFORD TO BUY EACH OTHER PRESENTS...
SO EVERY YEAR, THEY JUST EXCHANGE EACH OTHER'S MOST PRECIOUS POSSESION.
THEIR DINNER THIS YEAR CONSISTS OF A SINGLE BEAN...
KNOCK KNOCK
THEY WERE ABOUT TO TUCK IN, WHEN...

#148

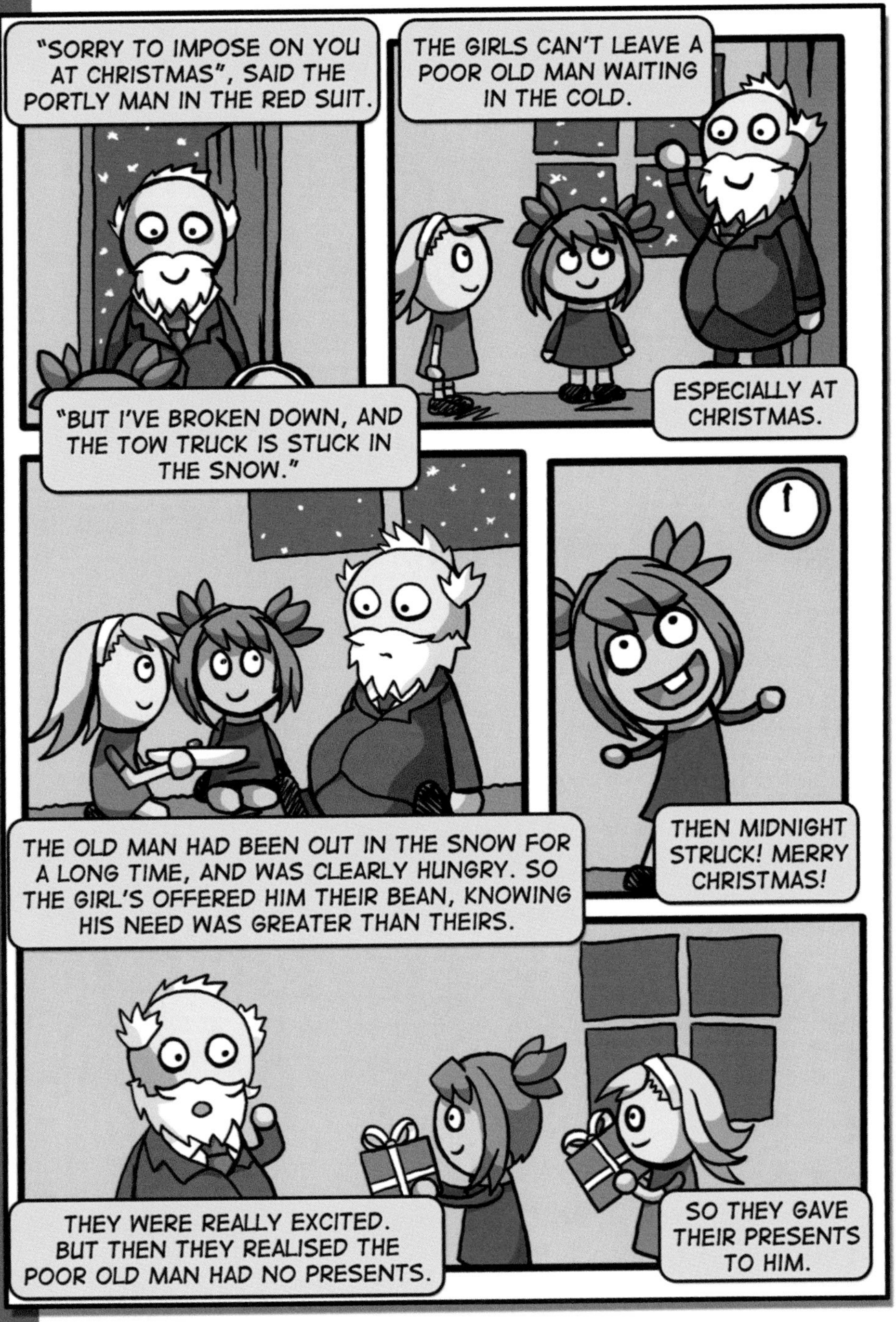
"SORRY TO IMPOSE ON YOU AT CHRISTMAS", SAID THE PORTLY MAN IN THE RED SUIT.
"BUT I'VE BROKEN DOWN, AND THE TOW TRUCK IS STUCK IN THE SNOW."
THE GIRLS CAN'T LEAVE A POOR OLD MAN WAITING IN THE COLD.
ESPECIALLY AT CHRISTMAS.
THE OLD MAN HAD BEEN OUT IN THE SNOW FOR A LONG TIME, AND WAS CLEARLY HUNGRY. SO THE GIRL'S OFFERED HIM THEIR BEAN, KNOWING HIS NEED WAS GREATER THAN THEIRS.
THEN MIDNIGHT STRUCK! MERRY CHRISTMAS!
THEY WERE REALLY EXCITED. BUT THEN THEY REALISED THE POOR OLD MAN HAD NO PRESENTS.
SO THEY GAVE THEIR PRESENTS TO HIM.

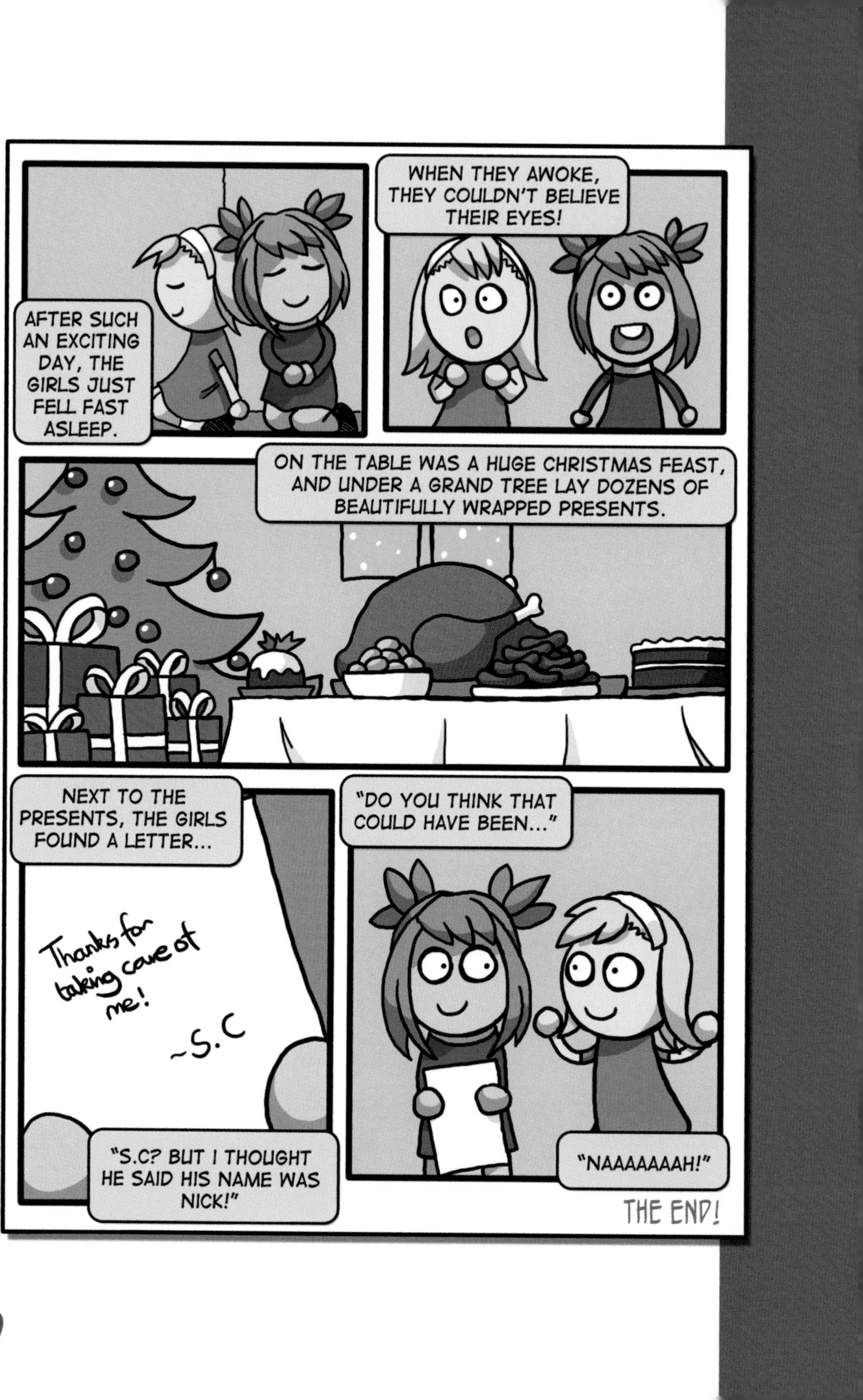
AFTER SUCH AN EXCITING DAY, THE GIRLS JUST FELL FAST ASLEEP.
WHEN THEY AWOKE, THEY COULDN'T BELIEVE THEIR EYES!
ON THE TABLE WAS A HUGE CHRISTMAS FEAST, AND UNDER A GRAND TREE LAY DOZENS OF BEAUTIFULLY WRAPPED PRESENTS.
NEXT TO THE PRESENTS, THE GIRLS FOUND A LETTER...
Thanks for taking care of me!
~S.C
"S.C? BUT I THOUGHT HE SAID HIS NAME WAS NICK!"
"DO YOU THINK THAT COULD HAVE BEEN..."
"NAAAAAAAH!"
THE END!

#150

Heeeey Diary!!! I'm back! Oh. My. God! Tonight was SO awesome! After I told my Dad that Demitri's dad was a billionaire, he totally had NO problem with us going out!

I thought we would go see a movie or something, but Demitri thought I was SO hot that we went STRAIGHT to his place! It wasn't just sex though, we had a REALLY deep and meaningful discussion beforehand!

We talked about music, and culture and about lots of other stuff like Elton James and it was really really romantic and everything! Then we ********** (Haha! I can't write this in here in case my Mom sees and thinks I'm a slut!)

So awesome! I can't wait to tell Aimee about it all tommorow! Goodnight Diary!

#151

The Rabbit Diaries

2005 http://chugworth.com/
Art and Writing by Dave Cheung.
"Bunnie's Christmas Adventure"
inspired by Peter Nguyen.

"Catholic Schoolgirl" Font from
http://blambot.com/

#152

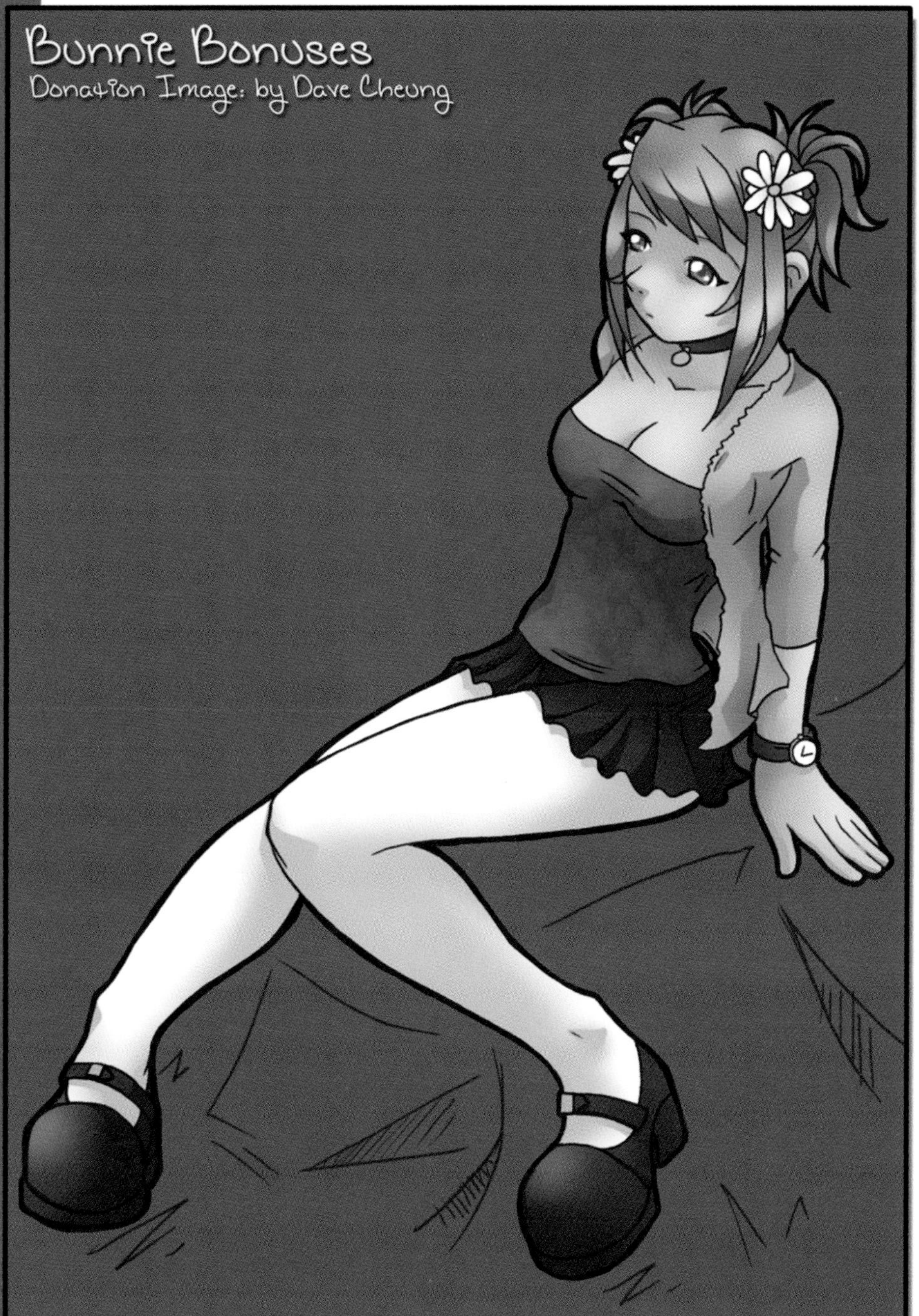
Bunnie Bonuses
Donation Image: by Dave Cheung

Cast of Characters

Chugworth Academy
Student Campus, Registration and Library Card.

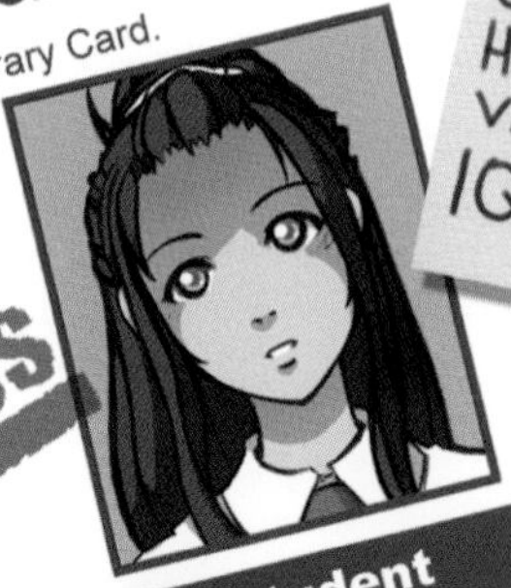

Name:
Sally Richards
Campus:
Off Campus
D.O.B:
02-14-1987 (16)
Academic Level:
High School

Prefect Privileges

Student
2003 - 2004

SALLY RICHARDS
AGE - 16
HEIGHT - 5'4"
WEIGHT - 118 lbs
OCCUPATION - SCHOOLGIRL
HOBBIES - TENNIS, VIDEOGAMES, RPGS.
IQ - 162

KIYOSHI MASAMUNE
AGE - 19
HEIGHT - 5'11"
WEIGHT - 145 lbs
OCCUPATION - MODEL/ ACTOR
HOBBIES - EATING, HAVING ADVENTURES
IQ - 97

American Guild of Wealthy Actors

Registry Number:
1367-6849-5193-00

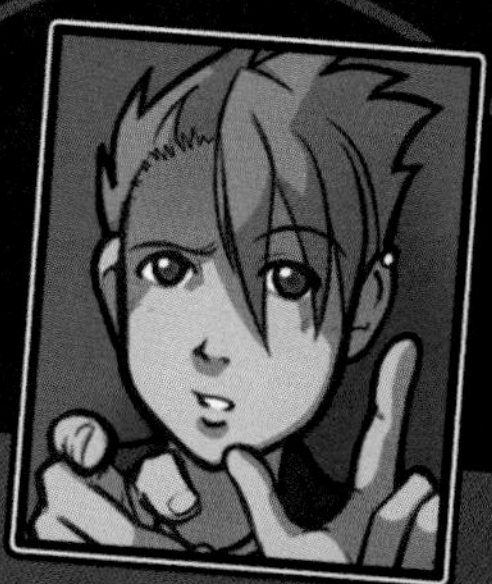

MEMBER

Name:
Kiyoshi Masamune
D.O.B:
12-16-1984

Chugworth Academy
Student Campus, Registration and Library Card.

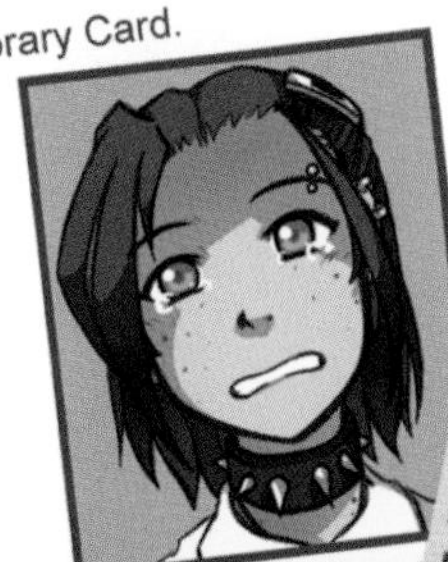

Name:
Chloe Winsdale
Campus:
Off Campus
D.O.B:
08-27-1986 (17)
Academic Level:
High School

Student
2003 - 2004

CHLOE WINSDALE
AGE - 17
HEIGHT - 5'3"
WEIGHT - 120 lbs
OCCUPATION - SCHOOLGIRL
HOBBIES - GYMNASTICS, PLAYING GUITAR (BADLY), RAWKING OUT!
IQ - 132

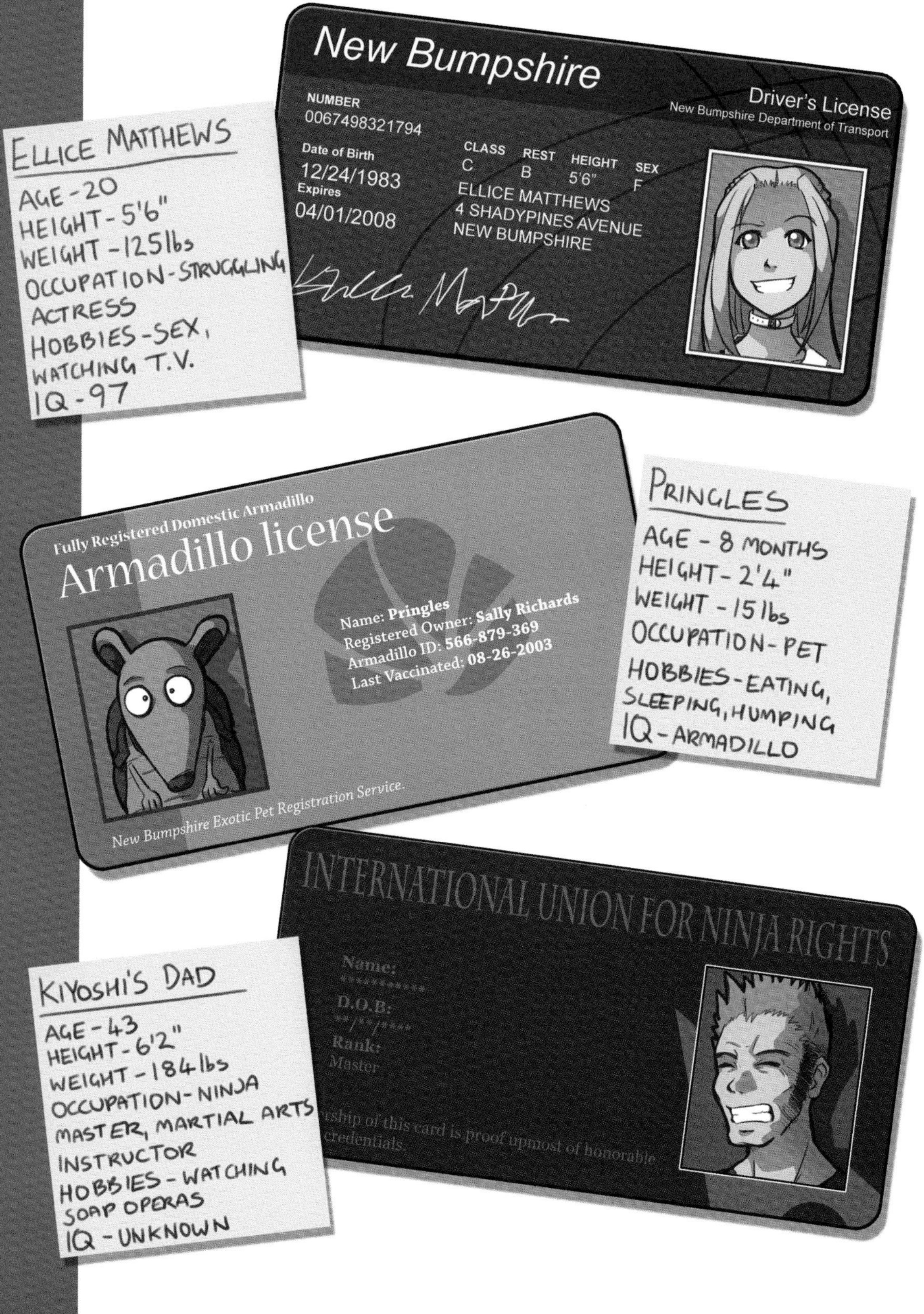

ELLICE MATTHEWS
AGE - 20
HEIGHT - 5'6"
WEIGHT - 125lbs
OCCUPATION - STRUGGLING ACTRESS
HOBBIES - SEX, WATCHING T.V.
IQ - 97
New Bumpshire
Driver's License
New Bumpshire Department of Transport
NUMBER
0067498321794
Date of Birth
12/24/1983
Expires
04/01/2008
CLASS C
REST B
HEIGHT 5'6"
SEX F
ELLICE MATTHEWS
4 SHADYPINES AVENUE
NEW BUMPSHIRE
Fully Registered Domestic Armadillo
Armadillo license
Name: Pringles
Registered Owner: Sally Richards
Armadillo ID: 566-879-369
Last Vaccinated: 08-26-2003
New Bumpshire Exotic Pet Registration Service.
PRINGLES
AGE - 8 MONTHS
HEIGHT - 2'4"
WEIGHT - 15lbs
OCCUPATION - PET
HOBBIES - EATING, SLEEPING, HUMPING
IQ - ARMADILLO
INTERNATIONAL UNION FOR NINJA RIGHTS
Name:
****
D.O.B:
//****
Rank:
Master
rship of this card is proof upmost of honorable
credentials.
KIYOSHI'S DAD
AGE - 43
HEIGHT - 6'2"
WEIGHT - 184lbs
OCCUPATION - NINJA MASTER, MARTIAL ARTS INSTRUCTOR
HOBBIES - WATCHING SOAP OPERAS
IQ - UNKNOWN

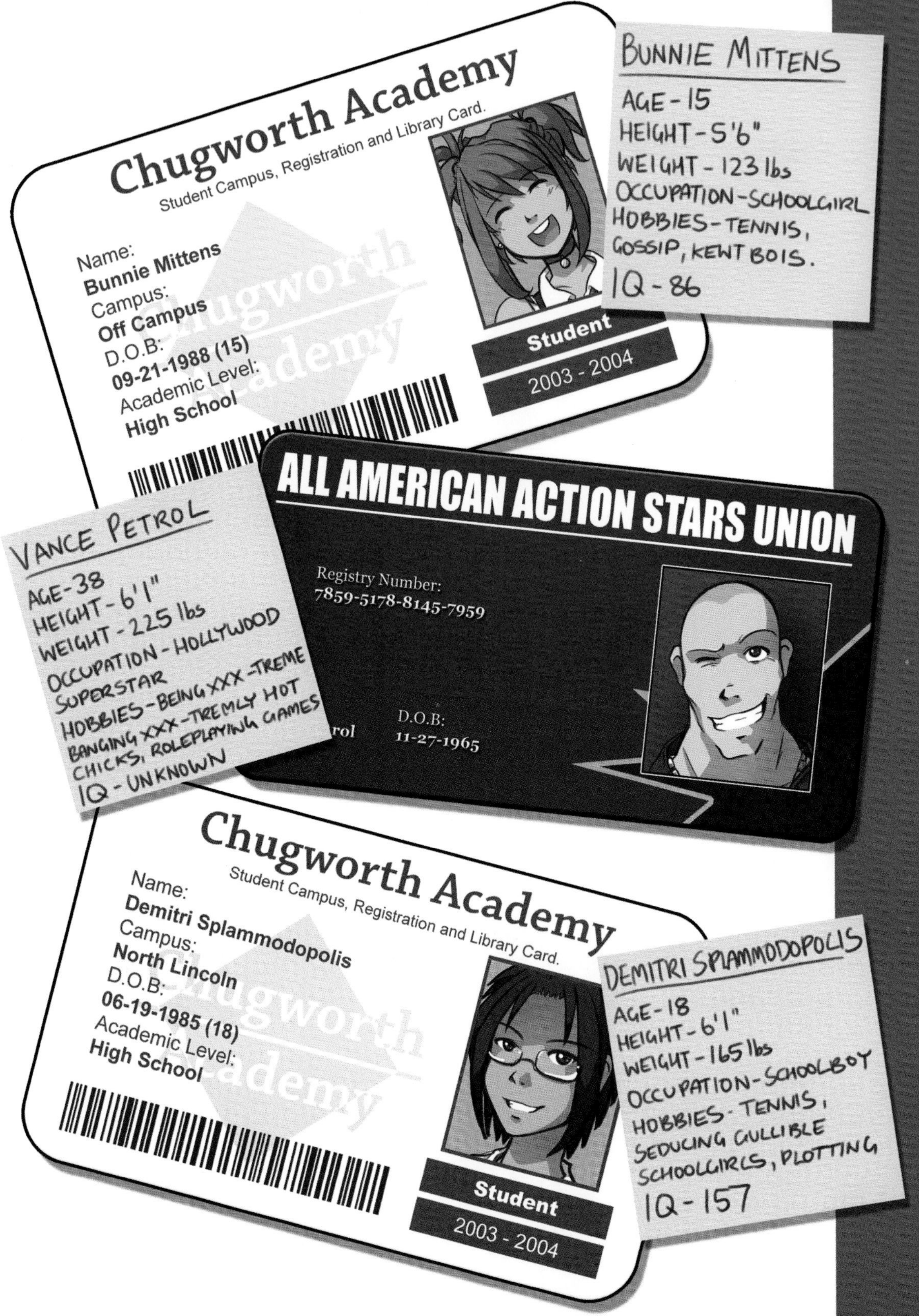
Chugworth Academy
Student Campus, Registration and Library Card.
Name:
Bunnie Mittens
Campus:
Off Campus
D.O.B:
09-21-1988 (15)
Academic Level:
High School
Student
2003 - 2004
BUNNIE MITTENS
AGE - 15
HEIGHT - 5'6"
WEIGHT - 123 lbs
OCCUPATION - SCHOOLGIRL
HOBBIES - TENNIS, GOSSIP, KEWT BOIS.
IQ - 86
VANCE PETROL
AGE - 38
HEIGHT - 6'1"
WEIGHT - 225 lbs
OCCUPATION - HOLLYWOOD SUPERSTAR
HOBBIES - BEING XXX-TREME BANGING XXX-TREMLY HOT CHICKS, ROLEPLAYING GAMES
IQ - UNKNOWN
ALL AMERICAN ACTION STARS UNION
Registry Number:
7859-5178-8145-7959
rol
D.O.B:
11-27-1965
Chugworth Academy
Student Campus, Registration and Library Card.
Name:
Demitri Splammodopolis
Campus:
North Lincoln
D.O.B:
06-19-1985 (18)
Academic Level:
High School
Student
2003 - 2004
DEMITRI SPLAMMODOPOLIS
AGE - 18
HEIGHT - 6'1"
WEIGHT - 165 lbs
OCCUPATION - SCHOOLBOY
HOBBIES - TENNIS, SEDUCING GULLIBLE SCHOOLGIRLS, PLOTTING
IQ - 157

Bonus Artwork
And Comics

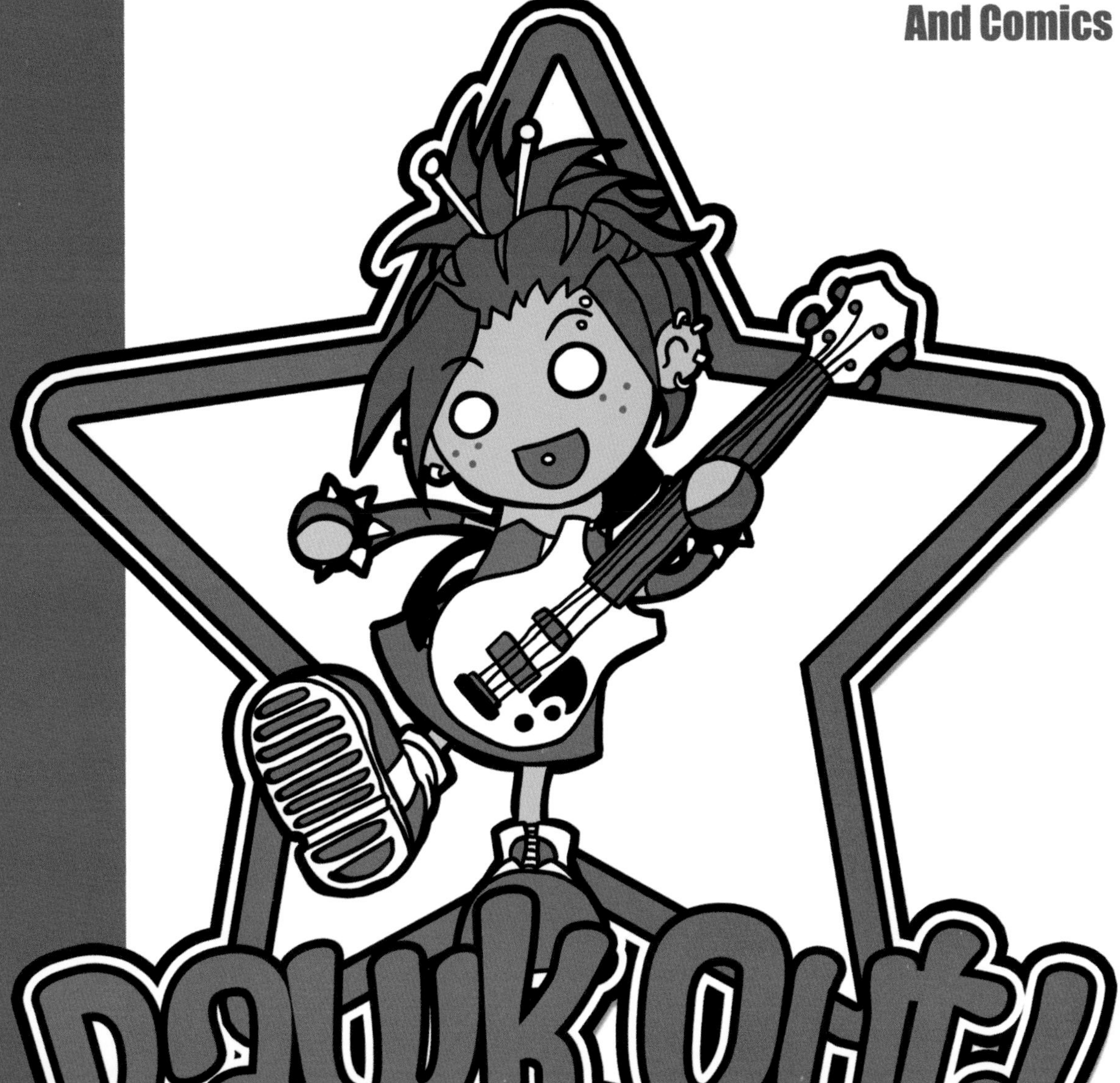
RAWK OUT!

JUST BECAUSE I LOVE YOU, I'VE FLESHED THE END OF THE BOOK OUT WITH A FINE SELECTION OF HIGH-RESOLUTION, CHUGWORTH RELATED ARTWORKS. HOORAY? I BELIEVE SO! WHATSMORE YOU'LL ALSO FIND FOUR VERY SPECIAL EXTRA COMICS MADE SOLEY FOR THIS BOOK!

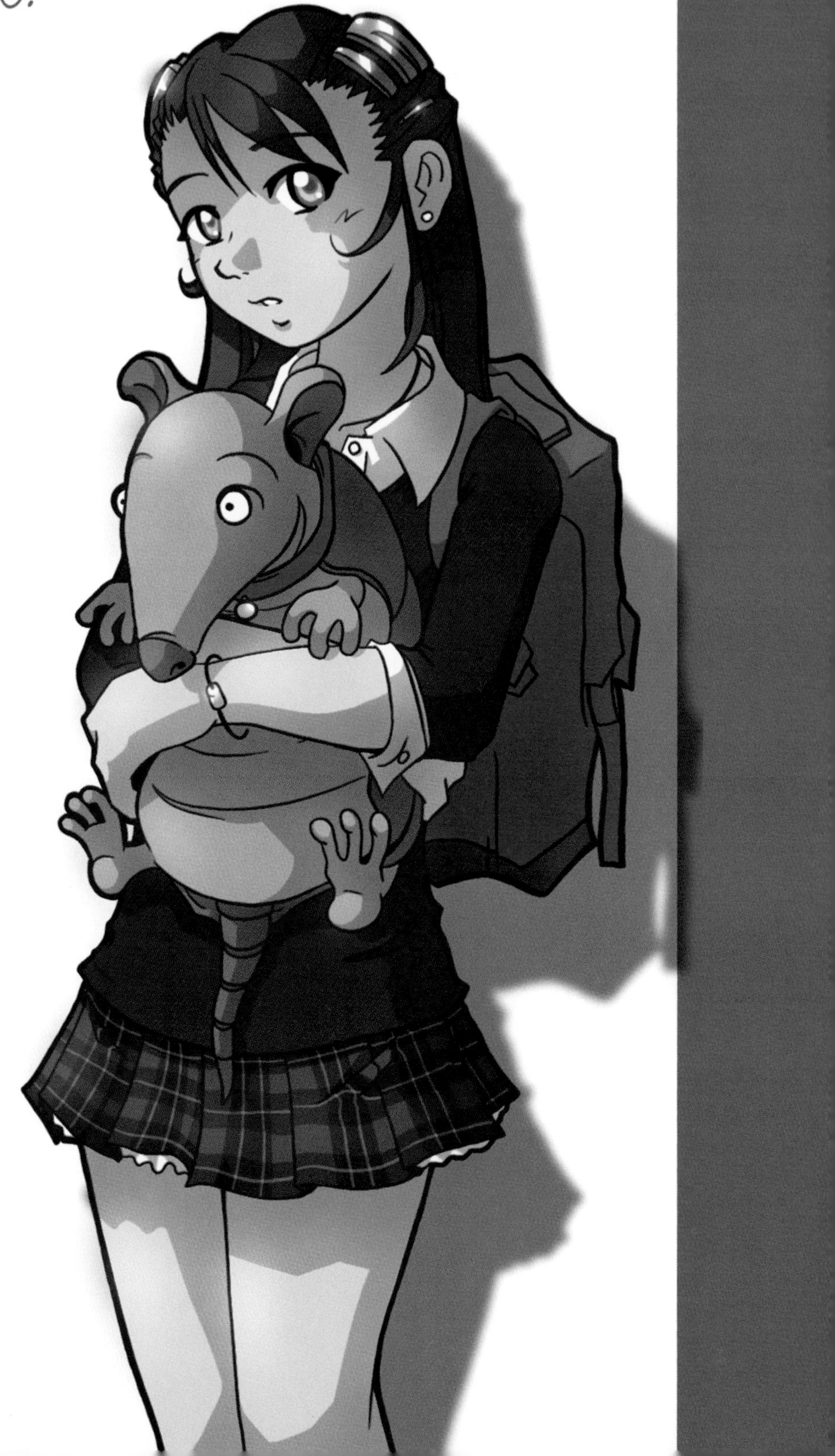

SALLY AND PRINGLES
THE ARMADILLO.

SALLY "WAKE UP, KIYOSHI!"

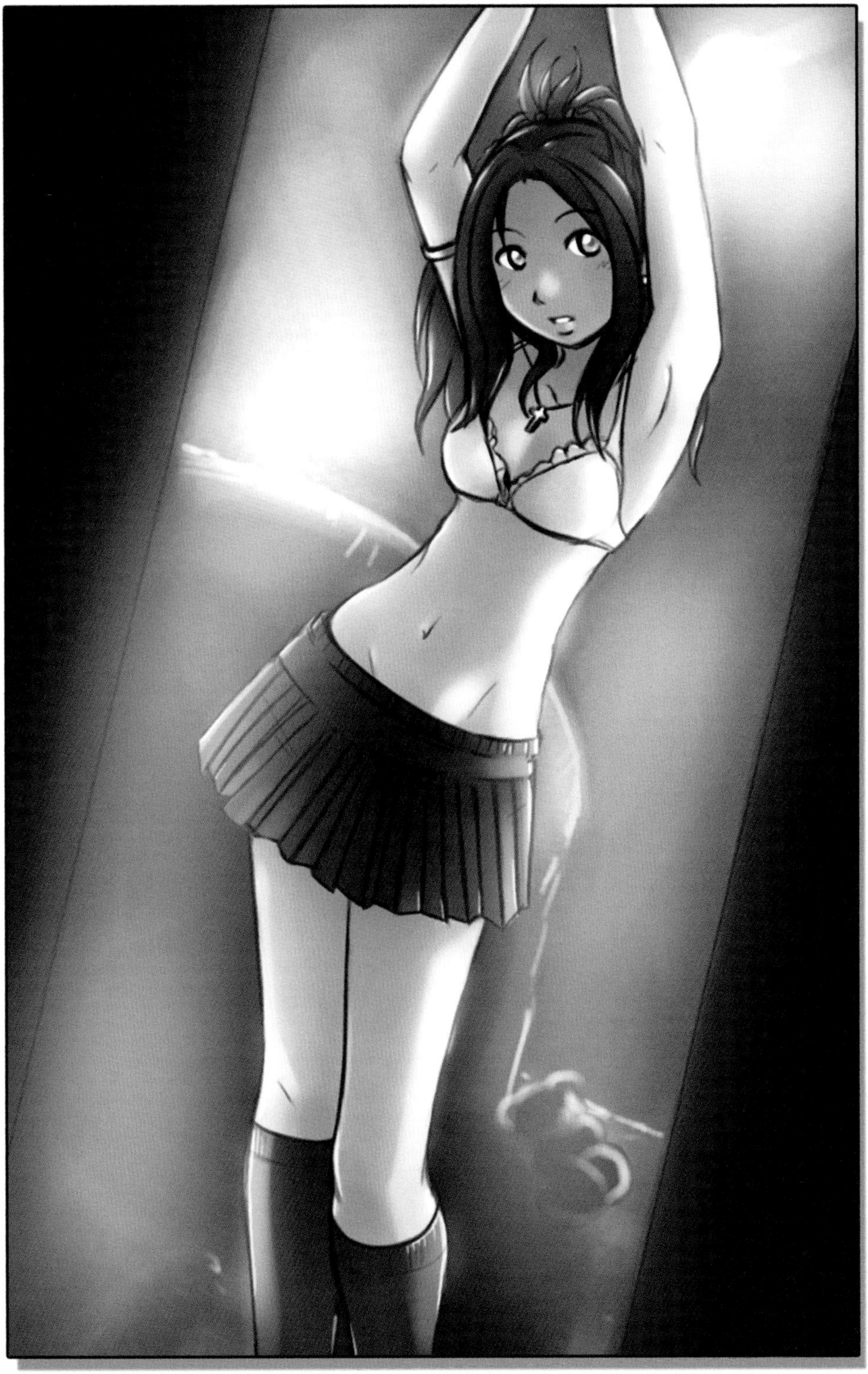

SALLY: SCUBA

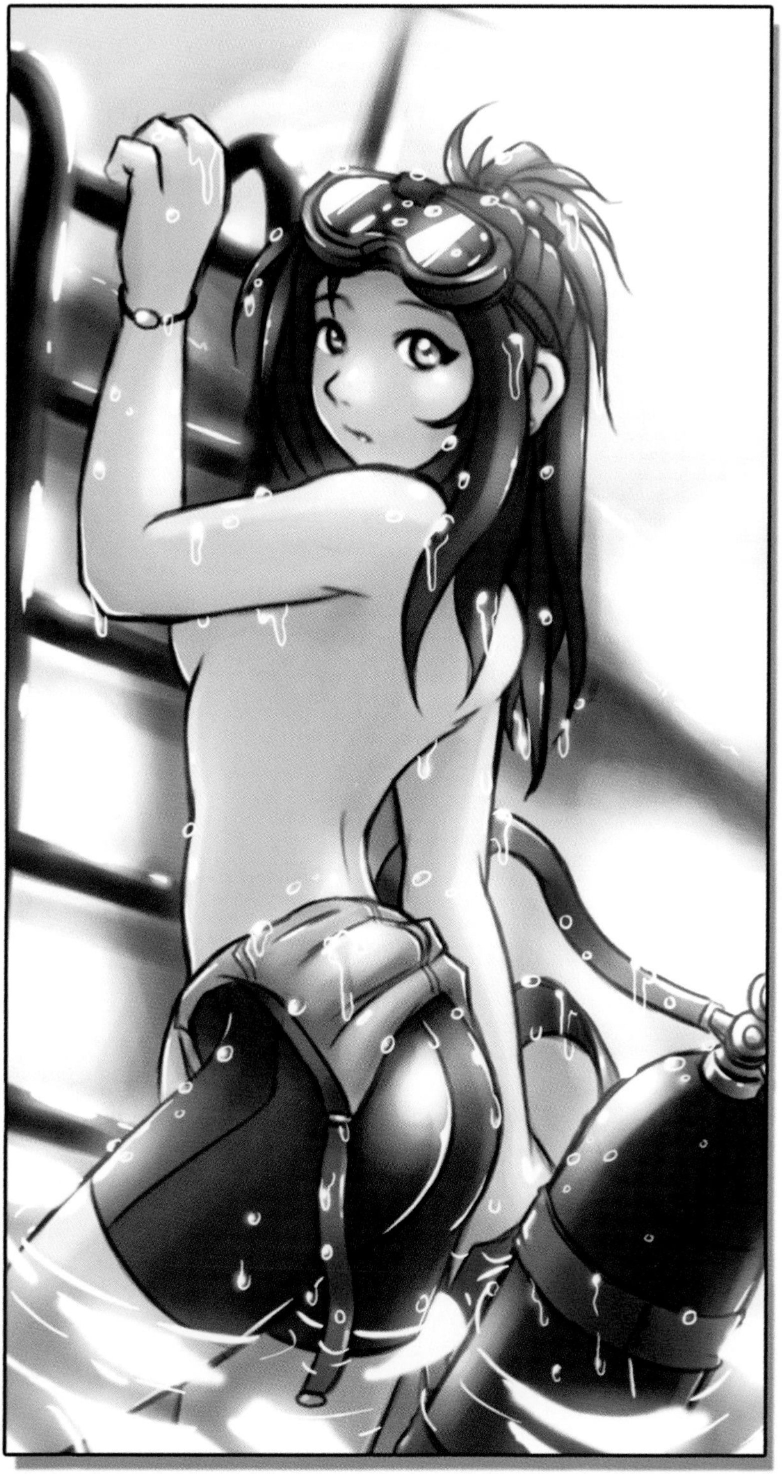

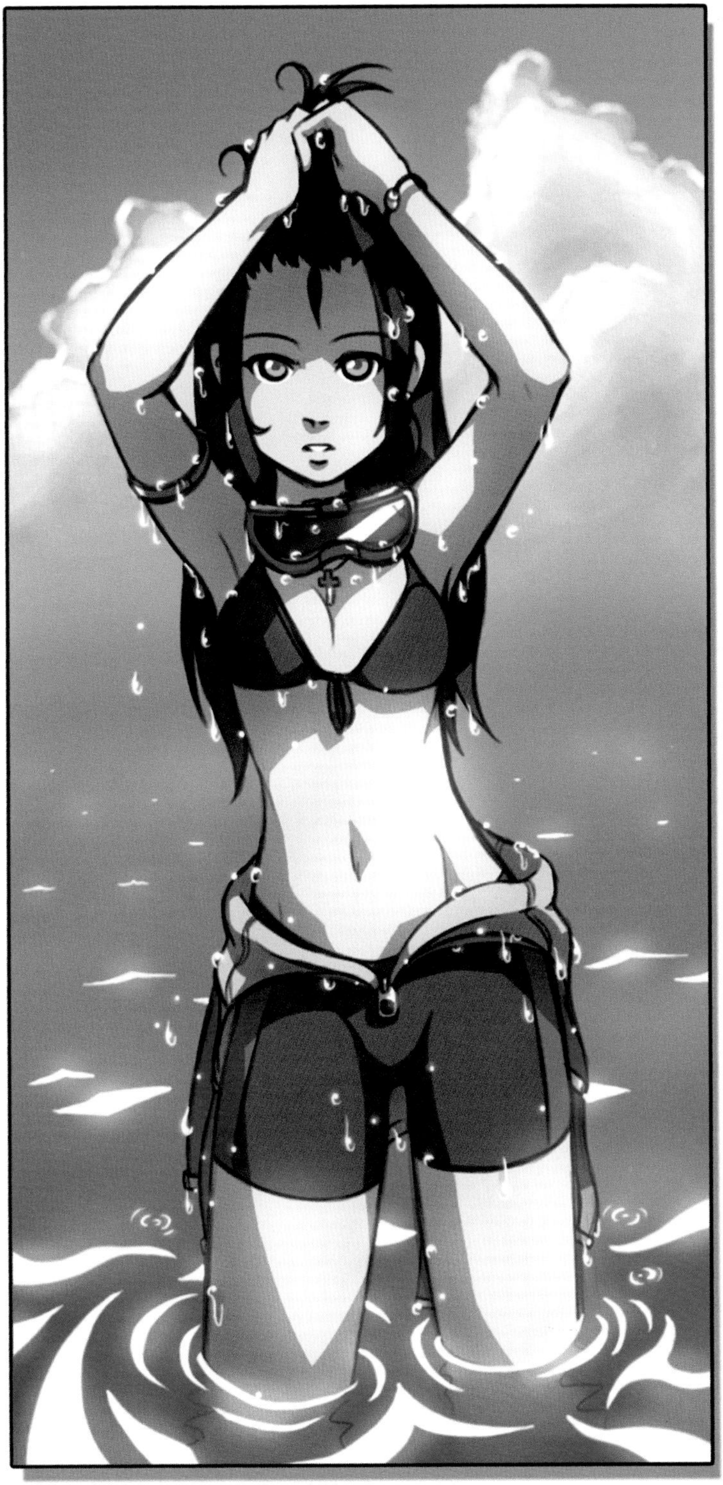

CHLOE: UPSIDE DOWN

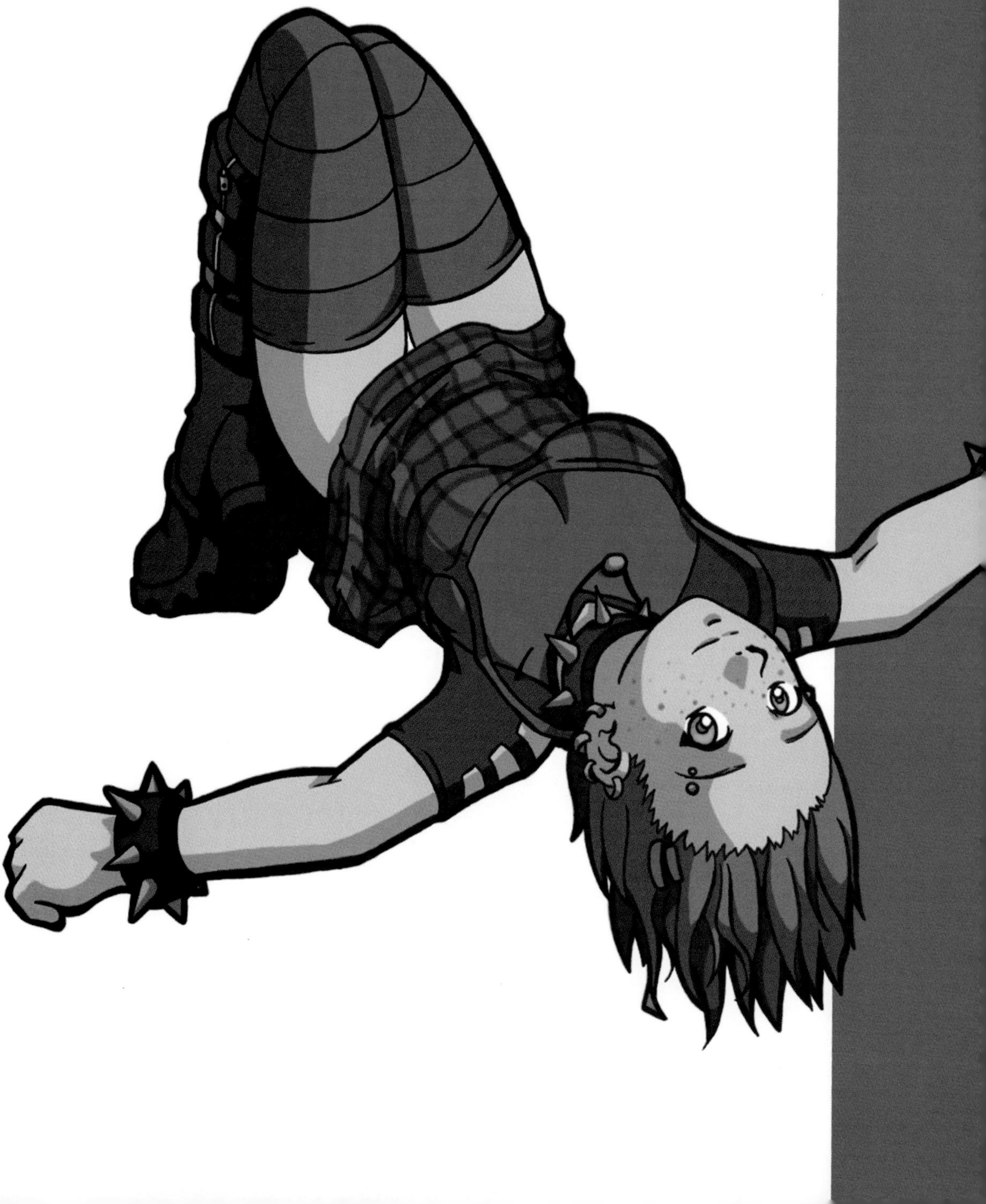

CHLOE PAINTY

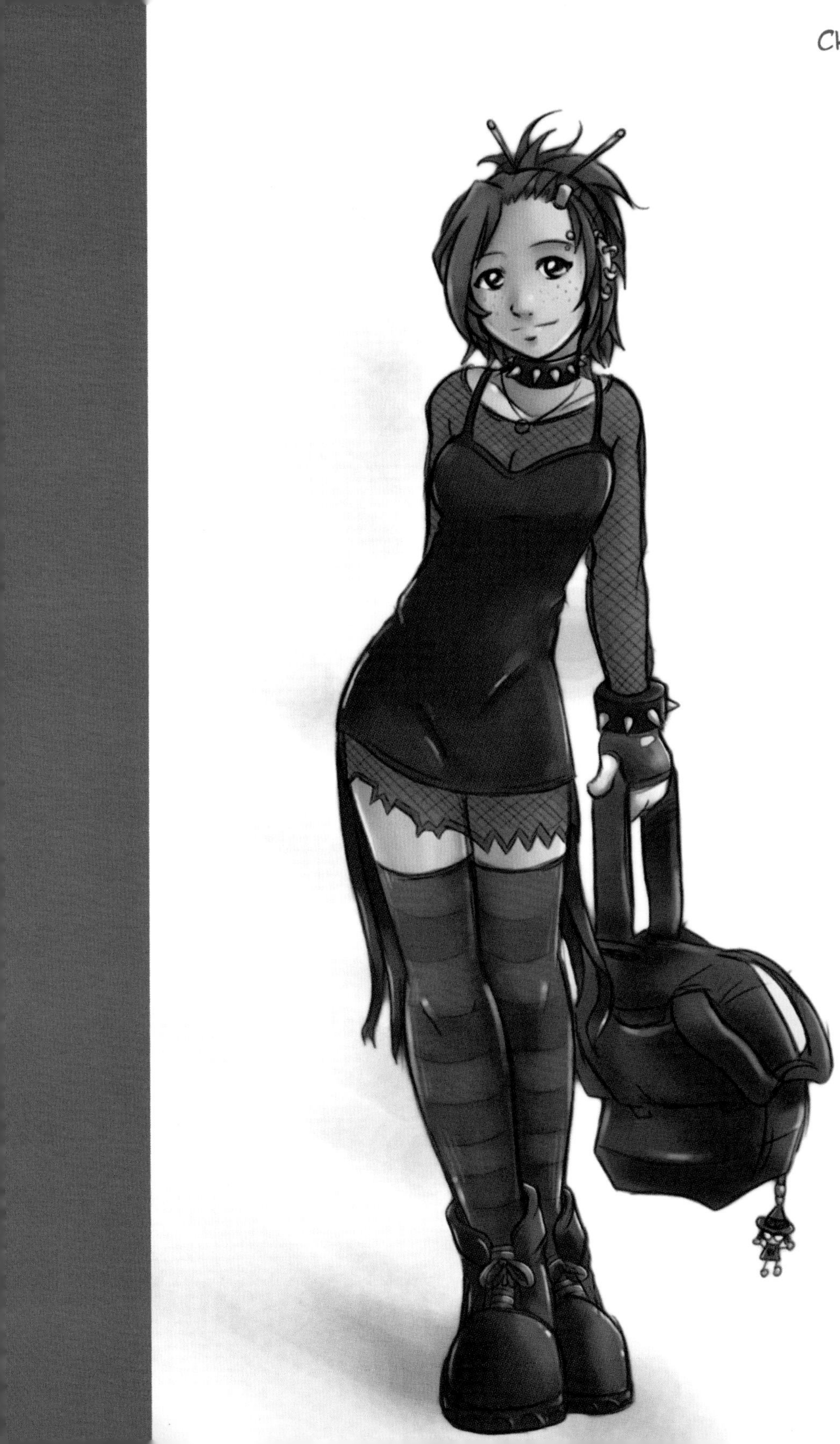

SALLY TENNIS

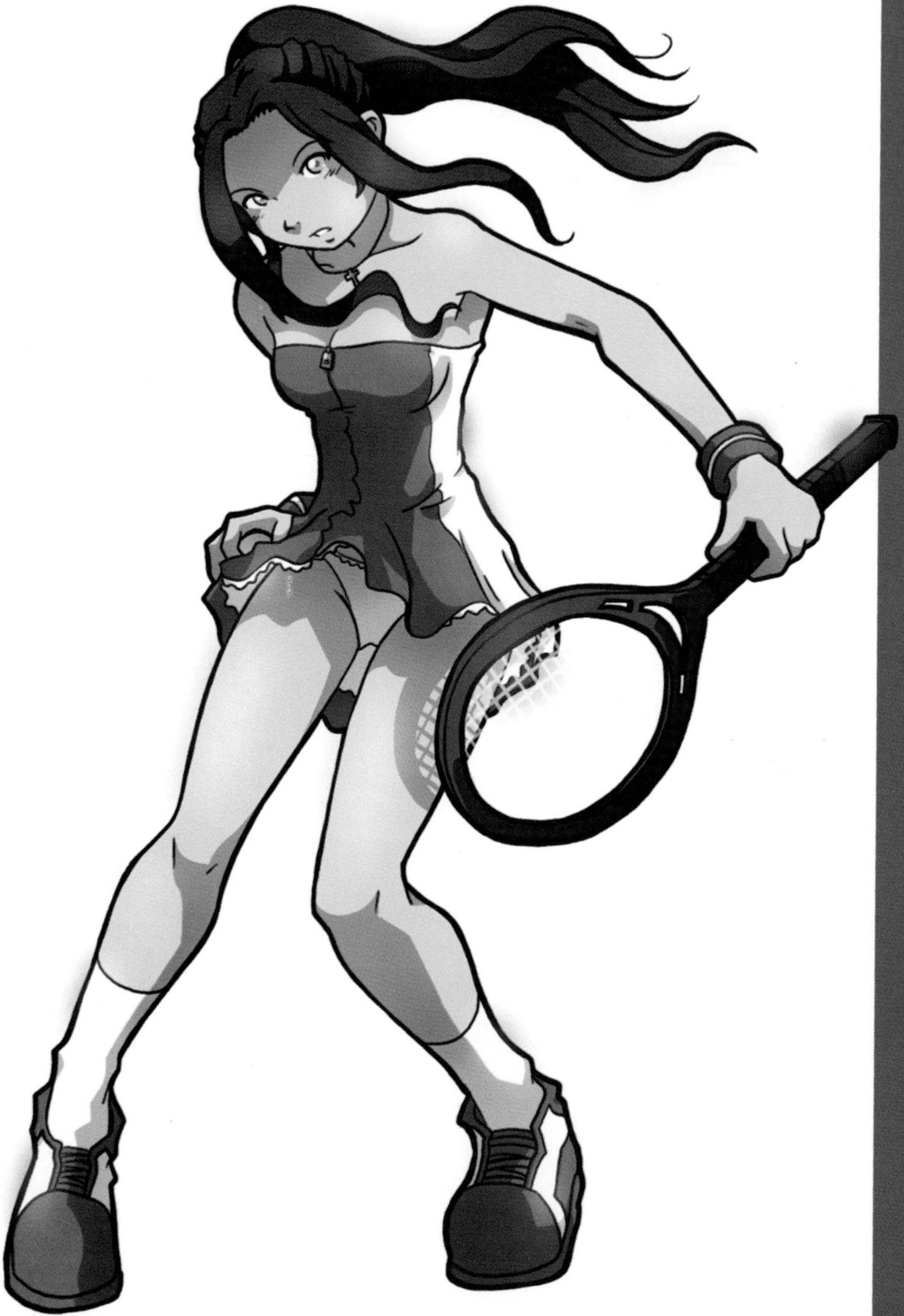

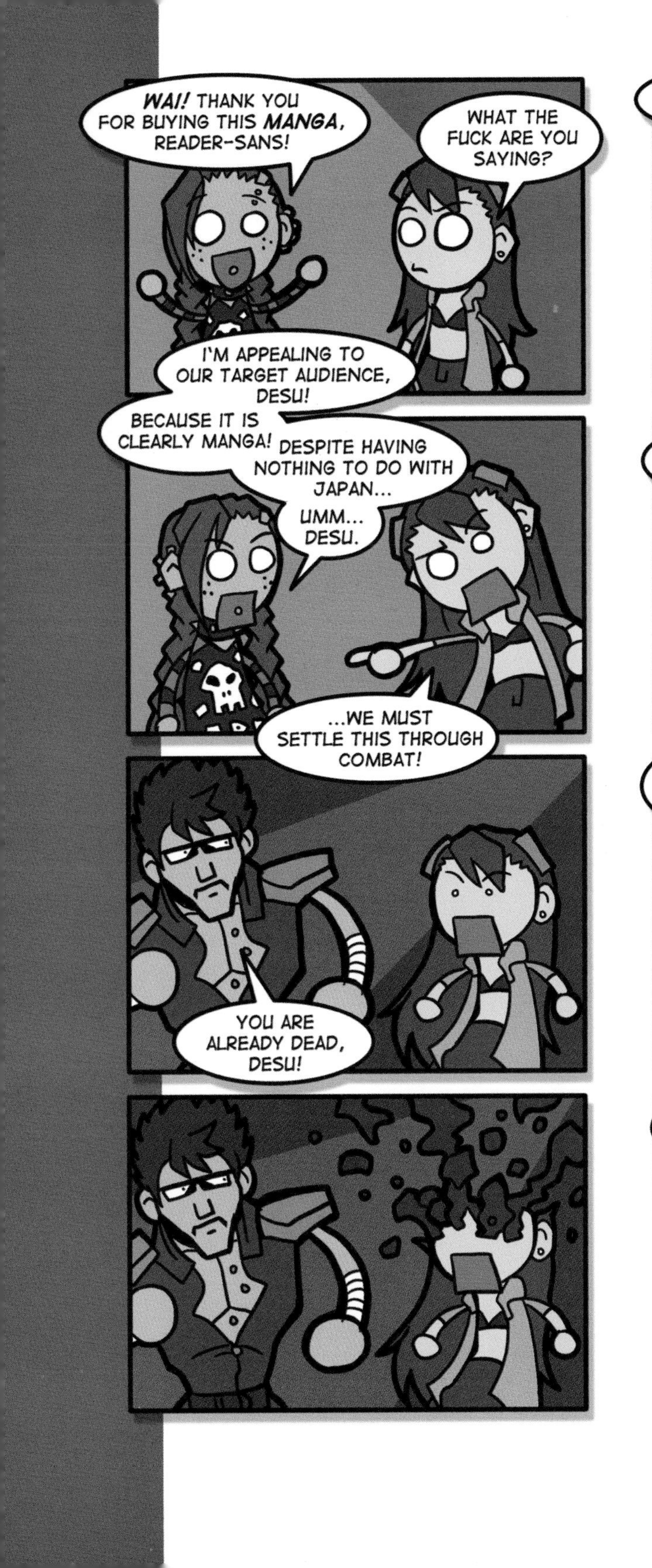
WAI! THANK YOU FOR BUYING THIS *MANGA*, READER-SANS!
WHAT THE FUCK ARE YOU SAYING?
I'M APPEALING TO OUR TARGET AUDIENCE, DESU!
BECAUSE IT IS CLEARLY MANGA!
DESPITE HAVING NOTHING TO DO WITH JAPAN...
UMM... DESU.
...WE MUST SETTLE THIS THROUGH COMBAT!
YOU ARE ALREADY DEAD, DESU!

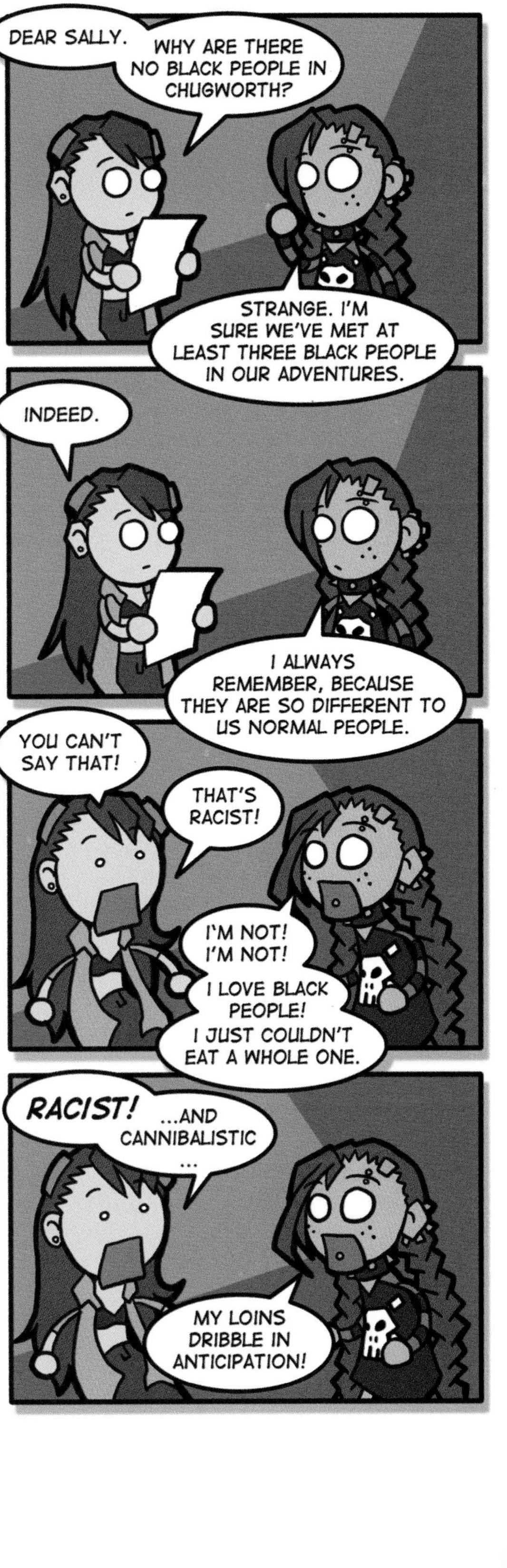
DEAR SALLY.
WHY ARE THERE NO BLACK PEOPLE IN CHUGWORTH?
STRANGE. I'M SURE WE'VE MET AT LEAST THREE BLACK PEOPLE IN OUR ADVENTURES.
INDEED.
I ALWAYS REMEMBER, BECAUSE THEY ARE SO DIFFERENT TO US NORMAL PEOPLE.
YOU CAN'T SAY THAT!
THAT'S RACIST!
I'M NOT! I'M NOT!
I LOVE BLACK PEOPLE!
I JUST COULDN'T EAT A WHOLE ONE.
RACIST!
...AND CANNIBALISTIC ...
MY LOINS DRIBBLE IN ANTICIPATION!

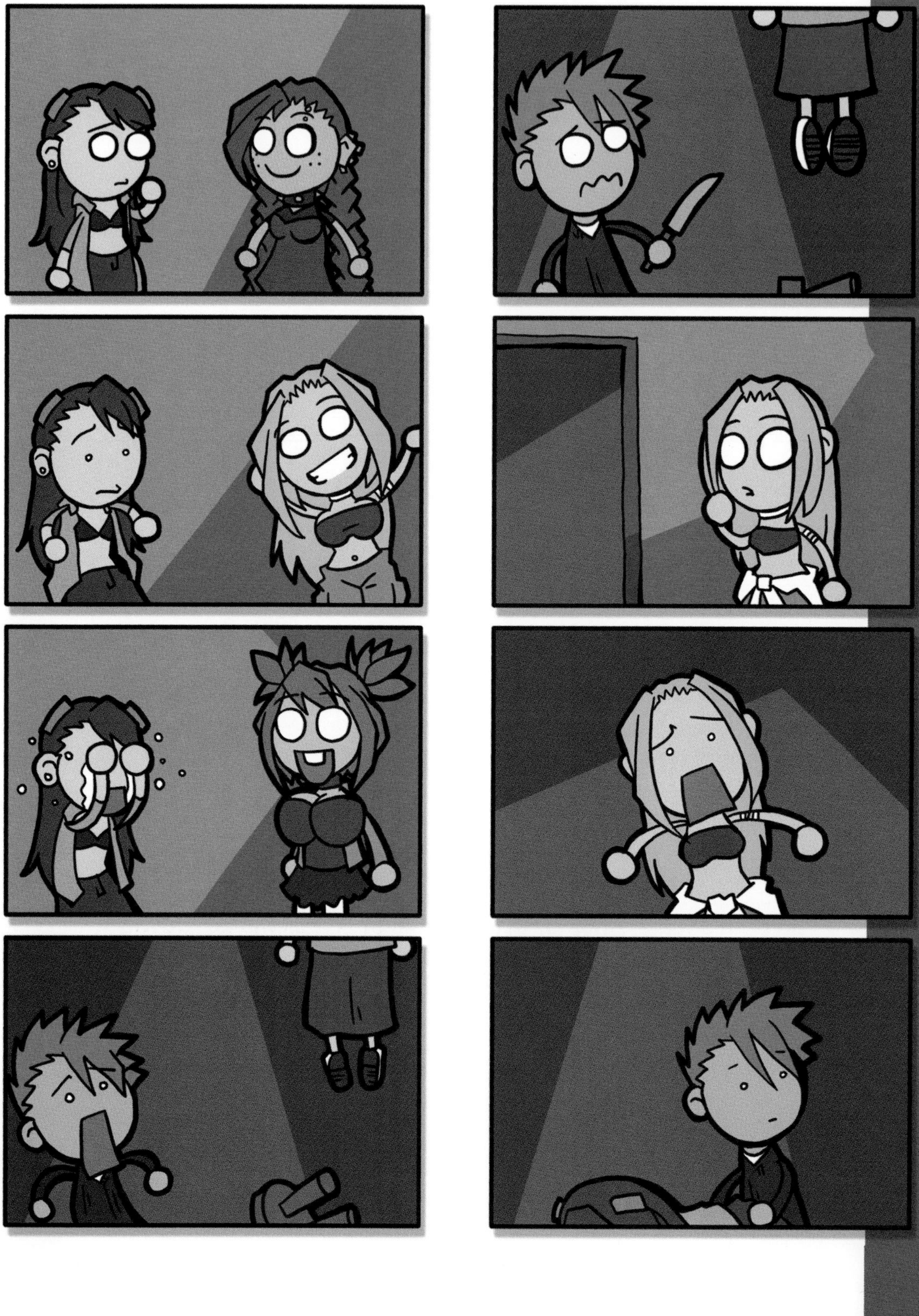

A WORD FROM THE AUTHORS

Writing a webcomic is a dream come true for anyone. Of course my biggest dream before that was being a mechanic, or maybe a truck driver. Like me, the characters get into all sorts of emotional and pop culture train wrecks. For example the other day I went to the store for some milk. That was a lot like being kidnapped by communist rebels. I like to think the lead character of the comic reflects many aspects of my personality, and what defines me as a man... wait, Sally's a girl? My thoughts on Chugworth?
What the hell is Chugworth?

The truth is, writing for the characters of Sally, Chloe, Kiyoshi, Ellice and all their whacky cohorts has been terrific fun. Webcomics, like filmmaking (my other "real" occupation), allow us to live through our characters and to laugh, cry, scream and be embarrassed with them. Tears and sweat... a lot of sweat, sweat like you wouldn't believe, has gone into these past few years. This would be cool if no one read the comics, but it's even cooler to know thousands of people are along the ride with us. Cheers to Dave, the people who've supported us over the years, and most of all you the reader!

Forever yours, or as long as my sanity holds.
- Jay (Writer, Chugworth Academy)

A lot of people ask me, "Dave, how does one go about making a comic?" Or probably more like, "LOL I WANNA MAEK A GUDE COMIX KAN U TAECH ME PLZ?!" To which I reply, "Just follow your dreams, and be true to your heart!" This is, of course, a lie on both counts. Another thing people often ask me is, "Dave, I have a particularly stubborn, burnt in stain on my kitchen hob and/or work surface. How do I get rid of it?" This is a much easier question to answer than the other. A little known secret to removing those tough, burnt in cooking stains is Bicarbonite of Soda. Mix up some of this stuff with water, and leave it bubbling on the stain for ten minutes or so. When you return, you can just wipe your worries away. This is what one learns growing up on the mean streets of Scotland!

I am helpful.
-Dave (Creator, Writer and Artist, Chugworth Academy)